REAPING SOMETHING NEW

REAPING
SOMETHING NEW

---

*African American Transformations
of Victorian Literature*

DANIEL HACK

PRINCETON UNIVERSITY PRESS
PRINCETON AND OXFORD

Published by Princeton University Press,
41 William Street, Princeton, New Jersey 08540
In the United Kingdom: Princeton University Press,
6 Oxford Street, Woodstock, Oxfordshire OX20 1TR

press.princeton.edu

Cover art: (clockwise) 1. Frederick Douglass. 2. Frances Harper.
3. W.E.B. Du Bois. 4. Background: torn typescript page from
"Rena" manuscript by Charles Chesnutt, Fisk University,
John Hope and Aurelia E. Franklin Library, Special Collections

Cover design by Amanda Weiss

First paperback printing, 2019
Paperback ISBN 978-0-691-19693-0
Cloth ISBN 978-0-691-16945-3

Library of Congress Control Number: 2016935599

British Library Cataloging-in-Publication Data is available

This book has been composed in Sabon Next LT Pro

FOR NANCY, MATTY, AND BENJAMIN

CONTENTS

ILLUSTRATIONS

ACKNOWLEDGMENTS

The character John Jarndyce, we learn early in Charles Dickens's *Bleak House*, "could never bear acknowledgments for any kindness he performed"; "sooner than receive any, he would resort to the most singular expedients and evasions, or would even run away." On one occasion, when Jarndyce saw a woman approaching his house to thank him for "an act of uncommon generosity," he "immediately escaped by the back gate, and was not heard of for three months."

As I come to the end of a project that began with the uncanny sense that *Bleak House* was, like that novel's famous fog, "everywhere," I cannot help but worry about setting in motion some version of the scenario Dickens describes here. Even so, I feel compelled to express my thanks for the many acts of uncommon generosity that have helped make *Reaping the New* possible. In fact, I am delighted to do so. I only hope that any recipients of this gratitude who share John Jarndyce's discomfort will resist the urge to take flight, at least until other reasons emerge for their wanting to distance themselves from this book.

My indispensable colleagues Adela Pinch and Gregg Crane served as sounding boards and first readers, and helped me think through the stakes and shape of the book as a whole. I have received crucial feedback, advice, and encouragement over the years from Rachel Ablow, Amanda Anderson, Elaine Freedgood, Ivan Kreilkamp, Sharon Marcus, Richard Menke, and Rachel Teukolsky. Lara Cohen, Barbara Hochman, Sam Otter, Yopie Prins, Xiomara Santamarina, and Sarah Winter have also generously read drafts of individual chapters and been valuable interlocutors. The many individuals to whom I am indebted for having shared their own work, pointed me toward important texts and references, brokered introductions, and both raised and answered questions, also include Stephen Best, William Cohen, Brent Hayes Edwards, Ben Fagan, Brigitte Fielder, Eric Gardner,

Susan Gillman, Cristanne Miller, Daniel Novak, Carla Peterson, Leah Price, Karen Sánchez-Eppler, and Herbert Tucker.

I am extremely grateful for the opportunities I have had to share work in progress from this project with audiences in the U.S., Canada, and the U.K. I am not exaggerating when I say that virtually every page of this book bears the impress of the feedback received and relationships forged on these occasions. In addition to several individuals I have already named, I am very happy to thank Kate Gaudet, Audrey Jaffe, Talia Schaffer, Jonathan Senchyne, and Jordan Stein for their invitations and hospitality. I thank as well the organizers of the conferences where I first tried out many of my ideas; the regular meetings of the North American Victorian Studies Association and C19: The Society of Nineteenth-Century Americanists in particular have been sites and sources of sustaining community.

I began this book at the University at Buffalo and wrote the bulk of it at the University of Michigan. I have benefited beyond measure from the intellectual generosity, camaraderie, and wisdom of many colleagues at both institutions, including (besides those already mentioned) Sara Blair, Jonathan Freedman, Sandra Gunning, Lucy Hartley, Stacy Hubbard, Marjorie Levinson, Tina Lupton, Ruth Mack, Carine Mardorossian, Mike Schoenfeldt, Doug Trevor, and the late Patsy Yaeger. I am grateful as well to my fellow Fellows at the University of Michigan's Institute for the Humanities in 2011–12, including Kathryn Babayan, Marlyse Baptista, Matt Lassiter, Artemis Leontis, David Porter, Sean Silver, and Xiaobing Tang, as well as institute director Daniel Herwitz.

I have been lucky enough to work through much of the material in this book in the classroom, and my students' insights and enthusiasm, not to mention their skepticism, have been invaluable. A series of students also provided helpful research assistance: Christie Allen, Kayla Grant, Tim Green, Ruth McAdams, and Gabrielle Sarpy. This research assistance was made possible by funding from the University of Michigan English Department and is only one example of the generous institutional support that has enabled me to write this book. In addition to the Institute for the Humanities Faculty Fellowship, the University of Michigan has also provided me with a Michigan Humanities Award and an award from the Associate Professor Support Fund as well as sabbatical support. U-M's amazing library and its amazing librarians, especially Sigrid Cordell and Aaron McCullough, have been indispensable resources.

It has been a great pleasure to work with Princeton University Press. Anne Savarese has been a model editor: supportive, responsive, tough-minded, and sure-handed. I am also appreciative for the skill and professionalism of Ellen Foos, Bob Bettendorf, Juliana Fidler, Tom Broughton-Willett, and Daniel Simon as well as the other staffers and freelancers who have helped turn my manuscript into a book.

I am profoundly grateful for the unstinting support of Ray and Elayne Hack, the late Phil Davis, Liz Hack and Rich Larach, and Tracy, Tim, Katie, and James O'Connell. Without Nancy Davis and Matty and Benjamin Hack, the writing of this book would have been unimaginable—along with much else besides. I know no way to adequately thank them. I can say, though, that one of the countless things for which I am grateful is that they will not mind being thanked alongside the feline members of our family, past and present: Emma, Piper, and Callisto. On the contrary, they would insist on it.

Earlier versions of chapter 1 were published as "Close Reading at a Distance: The African-Americanization of *Bleak House*," *Critical Inquiry* 34:4, © 2008 by the University of Chicago, and "Close Reading at a Distance: *Bleak House*," *Novel: A Forum on Fiction* 42:3, © 2009 Novel, Inc. Parts of chapter 2 appeared in "Wild Charges: The Afro-Haitian 'Charge of the Light Brigade,'" *Victorian Studies* 54:2, © 2012 by the Trustees of Indiana University, and "The Canon in Front of Them: African American Deployments of 'The Charge of the Light Brigade,'" in *Early African American Print Culture*, ed. Lara Cohen and Jordan Stein, © 2012 by the University of Pennsylvania Press. Some material in chapter 3 was published in "Transatlantic Eliot: African American Connections," in *A Companion to George Eliot*, ed. Amanda Anderson and Harry E. Shaw, © 2013 by John Wiley & Sons, Ltd. Part of chapter 5, along with a few paragraphs from the introduction and chapter 4, were published in "Contending with Tennyson: Pauline Hopkins and the Victorian Presence in African American Literature," *American Literary History* 28:3, © 2016 by Daniel Hack. I am grateful to the editors and manuscript reviewers for their encouragement and feedback, and to the publishers for permission to reprint.

REAPING SOMETHING NEW

THE AFRICAN AMERICANIZATION
OF VICTORIAN LITERATURE

One muffled strain in the Silent South, a jarring chord and a vague
and uncomprehended cadenza has been and still is the Negro. And
of that muffled chord, the one mute and voiceless note has been the
sadly expectant Black Woman,
    An infant crying in the night,
    An infant crying for the light;
    And with *no language—but a cry.*
    —ANNA JULIA COOPER, *A VOICE FROM THE SOUTH*

Reprinting Charles Dickens's *Bleak House* in an antislavery newspaper.
Reimagining David Copperfield as a mixed-race youth in the antebellum
South. Arguing that Alfred, Lord Tennyson plagiarized "The Charge of the
Light Brigade" from an African war chant. Using George Eliot's poetry to
promote African American solidarity. Reading a poem by Dante Gabriel
Rossetti as an allegory of African American literary history.

 These are some of the many unlikely and intriguing things African American writers and editors did to and with Victorian works of literature in the
second half of the nineteenth and early decades of the twentieth centuries.
No marginal phenomenon or fringe practice, these transnational, cross-
racial transpositions and repurposings were often the handiwork of major
figures in the African American literary and intellectual tradition, including
Frederick Douglass, Frances Ellen Watkins Harper, Charles Chesnutt, Pauline Hopkins, and W.E.B. Du Bois. Yet almost all these deployments of and
responses to Victorian literature remain little known; indeed, some of the
most sustained and provocative instances have gone entirely unrecognized.

1

Reaping Something New sets out to recover, make sense of, and learn from this remarkable yet neglected history.

As this book will show, nineteenth-century British literature was woven deeply into the fabric of nineteenth- and early-twentieth-century African American literature and print culture. Not only were African American writers and editors immersed in the transatlantic literary culture of the day, and not only were they working with and against prevailing generic norms and conventions: in addition, they regularly cited and reworked and repurposed specific features of selected Victorian poems and novels at the levels of diction, phrasing, dialogue, description, characterization, and plot. Typically, the texts chosen for such treatment evince little or no interest in the historical situation, political concerns, or everyday lives of African Americans. Yet through acts of what I will call *African Americanization*, these texts were viewed through the lens of and made to speak to these matters and used to produce new texts in which they are central.

"Whenever we encounter repetition in cultural forms," James A. Snead argues in a seminal essay on black culture, "we are indeed not viewing 'the same thing' but its transformation,"[1] and the practices explored in this book prove both inherently and intentionally transformative—even when they take the form of verbatim borrowing. In other words, through their engagement with Victorian literature, the figures studied here were "reaping something new." I borrow this phrase from Tennyson's "Locksley Hall"—as we shall see, a poem with a blatantly racist speaker that is nonetheless, or therefore, made use of by both Charles Chesnutt and Pauline Hopkins. In these instances as throughout *Reaping Something New*, we will find that close engagement with Victorian literature represented no mere capitulation to existing constraints, but instead constituted a deliberate political strategy and means of artistic expression. We will also find that this practice did not impede or undercut the development of a distinctive African American literary culture and tradition, but on the contrary contributed directly to its development. It did so through the very repetition of African Americanizing engagements, repetition that grew increasingly self-conscious and self-referential, as writers and editors built on, responded to, and positioned themselves in relation to prior instances.

Victorian literature's role as an important archive for the production of African American literature and print culture, I will also argue, makes African American literature and print culture an important archive for the study of Victorian literature. Recovering the African American uses of Victorian literature not only increases our knowledge of its dissemination, mobility, and adaptability but also, and thereby, contributes to our understanding of that literature itself. The responses Victorian works garnered and uses to which they were put—how they were read, recontextualized, retooled, and reimagined—powerfully defamiliarize these works and force a rethinking of their ideological investments, political import, and cultural significance.

While African American engagements with Victorian literature thus shed light on various aspects of that literature, they tend especially to provide new perspectives on its treatment of race. This may seem unsurprising, but it should not be taken for granted: as noted above, race is not obviously central to many of the Victorian works taken up by African American writers and editors, and depictions of African Americans in these works are virtually nonexistent. Yet rather than simply calling attention to this absence or marginal presence, African Americanizations make newly salient the specific ways and ends to which Victorian novels and poems do or do not represent individuals of African descent (and members of nonwhite races more generally). Conversely, if paradoxically, African Americanization can also call into question the importance of race in texts in which it has always seemed central, as we shall see especially when we come to George Eliot.

This apparent counterexample in fact exemplifies the unpredictability of the insights afforded by the history of engagement I explore. To capture this history in action and gain access to its insights, I practice a method I call *close reading at a distance*. Close reading at a distance combines detailed, granular textual analysis with consideration of a work's geographical dispersal and uptake, especially by readerships not envisioned or addressed by the work itself. Breaking from the (new-) historicist tendency to grant interpretive priority to a text's narrowly construed, originating historical context, close reading at a distance treats the meanings texts accrue as they move through space and time and the uses to which they are put not only as equally legitimate objects of inquiry in their own right but also as valuable resources for understanding the work itself. Unlike some versions of book history and reception studies, then, close reading at a distance does not bracket—or abandon the very notion of—"the work itself." Instead of dissolving the work into its reception or afterlives, close reading at a distance seeks to understand the relationship of these afterlives to the source text—to understand, that is, precisely what the afterlives do to and with their sources, as a way of better understanding both the sources and the afterlives.[2]

With the phrase "close reading at a distance" I also allude to Franco Moretti's coinage "distant reading." I share Moretti's interest in the ways literary works travel across space, but I do not therefore turn to analytical methods that, as he says, largely dispense with reading altogether. If, for Moretti, "distance [from reading itself] *is a condition of knowledge*," I am interested in the ways "distance" of various sorts between implied and actual readers serves as a source of critical understanding.[3]

Yet if "close reading at a distance" is this book's method, it is also in a very real sense the book's subject: that is, not only what I do but what the writers and editors I examine are doing. The felt "distance" these cultural producers are interested in probing and exploiting is geographical, national, racial, and eventually temporal as well. By calling the texts these individuals produced evidence or examples of "close reading," I do not mean to suggest that they conform to the protocols of academic literary criticism that developed in the twentieth century; rather, I mean to highlight the scale—which is to say, the granularity—of these engagements with Victorian literature. This granularity is worth highlighting both because it has gone largely unrecognized and because my own, similarly granular approach may require some defense in the current critical climate. Close attention to the formal structure and rhetorical particularities of literary texts is easily dismissed as decontextualizing, apolitical, or indeed narrowly "academic"; as we shall see throughout this book, however, from the perspective of African Americanizing close readers at a distance of Victorian literature, the stakes could not have been higher.

We can begin to recover and explore the African Americanization of Victorian literature with the help of the epigraph to this introduction. This passage occurs in the first paragraph of Anna Julia Cooper's 1892 collection of essays, *A Voice from the South*, a book now recognized as a milestone in African American literary and intellectual history. In this opening salvo of her "Raison d'Etre" (as she titles her preface), Cooper identifies the gap she intends her book to fill: "In the clash and clatter of our American Conflict," she writes, the one voice that has not been heard from is that of the "Black Woman of America."[4] She evokes this lack by quoting, without attribution, three lines from Tennyson's *In Memoriam A.H.H.* (first published in 1850).

How are we to understand Cooper's turn to Tennyson? In a certain respect, his appearance is unremarkable: at the time Cooper was writing, Tennyson was probably the best-known, most celebrated living poet in the English-speaking world. Moreover, his concluding phrase, "with *no language—but a cry*," neatly captures the paradoxical sense of Cooper's "mute and voiceless note." So far, so routine an act of citation. And yet the turn to Tennyson to make the point Cooper makes is itself paradoxical, if not self-contradictory: announcing her intention to give voice to black American women, Cooper quotes the poet laureate of Great Britain—who, needless to say, was not a black American woman.

As the preface continues, the tension between Cooper's argument and her use of Tennyson to advance that argument only grows more pronounced. Advocating an identitarian epistemology and model of representation, Cooper declares, "I feel it essential . . . that truth from *each* standpoint be presented at the bar." Efforts by individuals who do not occupy a particular "standpoint" to represent its "truth," she insists, will inevitably fall short: "as our Caucasian barristers are not to blame if they cannot *quite* put themselves in the dark man's place, neither should the dark man be wholly expected fully and adequately to reproduce the exact Voice of the Black Woman."[5] A self-identified "Black Woman of the South," Cooper raises her own voice accordingly in the hope that it can "help to a clearer vision and a truer pulse-beat in studying our Nation's Problem."[6] Insofar as she cedes her voice to Tennyson's right at the outset, then, Cooper seems to undercut her own argument and reaffirm the very hierarchy she intends to challenge.

Can we find a gain to match the loss Cooper risks with this seemingly self-defeating rhetorical maneuver? Apparently not, according to the literary historian who has given Cooper's prefatory words their widest circulation and indeed elevated them to emblematic status: the epigraph to General Editor Henry Louis Gates Jr.'s foreword to the Schomburg Library of Nineteenth-Century Black Women Writers—a foreword that appears in each of the two-dozen-plus volumes in that groundbreaking series—begins in the same spot as the epigraph to the present introduction. However, Gates omits Cooper's citation of Tennyson, replacing the poet's words with an ellipsis: "And of that muffled chord, the one mute and voiceless note has been the sadly expectant Black Woman. . . ." Skipping ahead a couple of paragraphs, Gates's epigraph resumes with Cooper's declaration that "The 'other side' has not been represented by one who 'lives there.'"[7]

Several factors presumably motivate this omission by Gates: even if Cooper's use of Tennyson did not seem like a blunder for the reasons noted above, the poet's presence in the opening lines of the Schomburg Library foreword—which is titled "In Her Own Write"—would clearly be a distraction. Even worse, Cooper's citation of Tennyson in her "Raison d'Etre" seems to violate the spirit of the Schomburg Library's own raison d'être as Gates presents it. "Literary works configure into a tradition," he argues, "because writers read other writers and *ground* their representations of experience in models of language provided largely by other writers to whom they feel akin. It is through this mode of literary revision . . . that a 'tradition' emerges and defines itself." Thanks to "the collective publication of these works by black women now, for the first time," he continues, "scholars and critics" will be able "to *demonstrate* that black women writers read, and revised, other black women writers."[8] Intertextuality, then, is central to Gates's version of literary history, and the source of the Schomburg Library's value as a "library"; that is, its value resides in the relationships among texts it makes more readily visible, rather than, say, in the interest or merit of individual titles. It seems fair to surmise, then, that the most prominent intertextual gesture in Cooper's introduction gets suppressed from a foreword that stresses the importance of intertextuality because Cooper chose the "wrong" intertext.

The model Cooper violates reflects Gates's influential theorization of the African American literary tradition as a whole. As he and his fellow editor put it in the introduction to the *Norton Anthology of African American Literature*, "writers in the black tradition have repeated and revised figures, tropes, and themes in prior works, leading to formal links in a chain of tradition," and in fact "the African American literary tradition exists as a formal entity because of the historical practice of repetition and revision."[9] Both in this introduction and in his monograph *The Signifying Monkey*, where he develops his theory at greatest length, Gates acknowledges that writers in the black tradition also repeat and revise texts from "the Western tradition," adding that "they often seek to do so 'authentically,' with a black difference, a compelling sense of difference based on the black vernacular."[10] Gates's own hugely important critical and editorial work, however, focuses almost exclusively on the ways African American writers "revise tropes from substantive antecedent texts in the African American tradition."[11]

It is no surprise that efforts to establish the legitimacy and value of a particular body of writing—to establishing its status as literature, and as *a* literature—would shy away from apparent evidence of indebtedness. As Gates among others has shown, moreover, "the concern to be original" is an enduring theme in black letters; he quotes—as an exemplar of "nearly two centuries' brooding on lack of originality in the black tradition"—W.E.B. Du Bois's statement that "we must turn from negation to affirmation, from the ever-lasting 'No' to the ever-lasting 'Yes.' Instead of drowning our originality in imitation of mediocre white folks . . . [we] have a right to affirm that the Negro race is one of the great human races, inferior to none in its accomplishments and in its ability."[12] As is well known, the twentieth century in particular saw repeated attempts to identify and celebrate expressive forms and practices deemed "authentically" black, whether the product of the unique experience of African Americans or New World permutations of an African cultural inheritance, or both.

By contrast, this book will follow Cooper's lead by risking attention to the attention that she, along with many other African American writers and editors in the nineteenth and early twentieth centuries, paid to Victorian authors and texts. To be sure, there now exists substantial encouragement to take such a risk: the lingering hegemony of the Gatesian model of literary tradition notwithstanding, over the past couple of decades a number of influential scholars have pioneered an alternative view of African American literature as productively engaged with other literatures. These scholars include feminist critics such as Frances Smith Foster, Carla Peterson, and Ann duCille, who identified and broke with a critical tendency to take African American women writers' ostensible debts to British literature as warrants to dismiss their work as overly genteel or bourgeois or elitist;[13] scholars of the "Black Atlantic," led by Paul Gilroy, who focus on the role of cross-cultural exchange and substitute hybridity for authenticity as norm and value;[14] relatedly, advocates of cosmopolitanism, such as Ross Posnock, who have tracked and defended black writers' embrace of what Posnock calls an "anti-proprietary view of culture as unraced," as exemplified for Posnock by Du Bois's famous statement, "I sit with Shakespeare and he winces not";[15] and scholars such as William W. Cook, James Tatum, and Dennis Looney, who have explored African American engagements with earlier European authors and traditions.[16] *Reaping Something New* is especially indebted to and aligned with work on the nineteenth century's transatlantic, interracial traffic in tropes and texts, work including Laura Doyle's history of the novel's "race-liberty plot," Elisa Tamarkin's analysis of "black anglophilia," and Elizabeth Young's study of "black Frankenstein."[17]

Building on these bodies of work, I seek to reconstruct a specific tradition of engagement with Victorian literature—a tradition that remains poorly understood and indeed largely invisible.[18] This tradition, I find, does not for the most part consist in efforts to bracket or transcend racial identity. Nor does it constitute prima facie counterevidence against the existence of a coherent, distinctive African American literary tradition. On the contrary, I show that major African American writers and intellectuals in the nineteenth and early twentieth centuries often leveraged nineteenth-century British literature in their very efforts to cultivate racial solidarity, to claim a distinctive voice, and to establish a distinct tradition or literature.[19] We can already see this strategy in play not only in Cooper's writing but even in the statement by Du Bois that Gates cites: with his talk of the "everlasting No" and "everlasting Yes," Du Bois paradoxically phrases his affirmation of "Negro" originality in terms provided by Thomas Carlyle, eminent Victorian sage and notorious apologist for slavery.[20]

My analysis also seeks to nuance and move beyond two common ways of describing, and implicitly justifying, a Victorian—or, more broadly, British or European or white—presence in African American literature. One of these approaches is to argue that African American writers' relationship to canonical literature is not one of indebtedness or imitation but rather subversive appropriation. For example, Ann duCille argues that, "making unconventional use of conventional literary forms, early black writers appropriated for their own emancipatory purposes both the genre of the novel and the structure of the marriage plot."[21] The other common approach is to read these writers' engagements with white literature as politically symbolic acts of cultural positioning. As Kenneth Warren puts it, "to insist on a manifold literary inheritance could count . . . as both a demonstration of the irrationality of segregation and a refutation of charges that black cultural expression was inferior to works produced by whites."[22]

There is clearly a good deal of truth to both these arguments. Returning to Anna Julia Cooper, we can see that her citational practices do the work Warren describes (and indeed, Warren mentions Cooper earlier in the same paragraph). Throughout *A Voice from the South*, Cooper protests the severe restriction of educational opportunities for both blacks and women and argues for the general social benefits that an expansion of such opportunities would yield. In making her case, she references a range of authors from the Western tradition, and the very act of making such references implicitly makes her case: by displaying her own cultural literacy and rhetorical sophistication, Cooper demonstrates that black women are capable of such literacy and such sophistication—capabilities that were by no means taken for granted in 1892.[23]

Yet the arguments I have identified with duCille and Warren only carry us so far: as we shall see repeatedly, these arguments tend to exaggerate the uniformity and conventionality of the white-authored literature taken up by African Americans, on the one hand, and to shortchange the constitutive nature and complexity of particular intertextual relationships, on the other. For example, insofar as African American authors *were* engaged in cultural positioning, this positioning necessarily depended on the current standing of the authors referenced. Yet the reputations of Victorian authors were by no means settled at this time. Rather than members of a timeless pantheon, even the most prestigious Victorians were, and signified as, contemporaries or recent predecessors; if the writers and editors I examine were "reaping something new" in the sense of creating something new, then, they were also "reaping"—working with—poems and novels that were themselves "new." This contemporaneity will be important to my argument, as will the shift that occurs over the time covered in this book. Frederick Douglass reprinted "The Charge of the Light Brigade" in 1855 immediately upon its publication; Anna Julia Cooper quotes *In Memoriam* just weeks before Tennyson's death in 1892; W.E.B. Du Bois juxtaposes decades-old poetry by Tennyson with newly published British poetry at the turn of the century. A quarter-century later, after the period I focus on—that is, well after the end of the Victorian era—Nella Larsen will have her character Helga Crane recall a line from *In Memoriam* in the 1928 novella *Quicksand*. What Tennyson signifies in each instance changes, in part because of the passage of time as such but also because of the changes in reputation and mode of access that accompany it. The fact that Helga Crane does not think of Tennyson by name but rather "recalled a line that had impressed her in her lonely school-days" speaks to the latter factor, even as that line itself speaks to the former (the passage of time): the line she recalls, from the first section of *In Memoriam*, is "The far-off interest of tears."[24]

I also insist, however, that there is often much more than cultural positioning to these intertextual engagements. African American writers and editors do not always just sit with, say, Eliot or Tennyson to show that these esteemed figures wince not. Nor are they necessarily intent on pulling the chair out from under these figures. Instead, African American cultural producers have a history—I will argue that they establish a self-reflexive tradition—of working with nineteenth-century British literature in generative and multivalent ways. These engagements shape texts, create meaning, reveal affinities, and establish affiliations. While it would be going too far to locate the marrow of the African American tradition in nineteenth-century Britain, we may take it as telling that the phrase "the marrow of tradition," made famous by Charles Chesnutt, is borrowed from a poem by nineteenth-century English writer Charles Lamb.[25]

What the tradition of engagement I describe does not do, however, is dissolve the boundaries between Victorian and African American literature. There are two reasons for this: first, the Britishness of the former frequently plays a key role in its meaning and significance for the African Americans who engage with it. Second, far from demonstrating the "Victorianness" of the African Americans who made use of Victorian literature, these engagements typically reveal racially and nationally inflected differences in perspectives and priorities as well as convergences. In the terms of Joseph Rezek's taxonomy of transatlantic work, then, this book does not belong to the group of "comparative or integrated studies of British and North American writing" that aim to show "that Anglo-American literature coheres through shared aesthetic qualities, common ideological investments, and transatlantic reading practices"; rather, it belongs to the body of work that "insists that even the distinctiveness of the cultures of Great Britain and North America can only be understood by attending to the transatlantic currents running through them."[26]

Even as I argue that African American engagements with Victorian literature help constitute and even form a distinctive tradition—that is, a self-aware, internally dialogic pattern over time—however, I would emphasize the heterogeneity and particularity of these engagements. The workings and implications of individual instances can only be determined on a case-by-case basis. And these cases often require—and reward—much finer-grained attention than has typically been paid by attempts to read African American literature in relation to British literature: attention not only to the borrowing or reworking or critique of generic forms and conventions, such as the marriage plot, but also to the specific language, tropes, and narrative structures of individual texts. It is at this level of granularity that many African Americanizations of Victorian literature take place and become legible.

Returning again to Anna Julia Cooper, then, I propose that instead of suppressing the lines from Tennyson she quotes, or resting content with viewing them as a demonstration of cultural literacy, we look at them more closely. Tennyson conjures the image of the crying infant at the end of section LIV of his elegy for his beloved friend Arthur Hallam, one of many sections in which the poet grapples with his religious doubts. The first four of the section's five stanzas elaborate on the speaker's opening declaration, "Oh yet we trust that somehow good / Will be the final goal of ill."[27] Yet the final stanza characterizes this faith as "my dream" and asks plaintively, "but what am I?"[28] Cooper quotes the despairing answer to this question.

The concerns prompting this passage in *In Memoriam* are distant from those of Cooper's "Raison d'Etre." But if this distance suggests that the original context does not matter to *A Voice from the South*, the distance itself does: as suggested above, the gap between original and new contexts serves as a measure of creative agency. Consider, by way of contrast, an earlier citation of the same *In Memoriam* passage that appeared in the African American press. The writer of an 1861 article entitled "Modern Literature," reprinted in the African Methodist Episcopal Church's *Christian Recorder*, laments that "We have no great literary writers save, perhaps, Mrs. Stowe, who are wreathing with their genius the cross of Christ." He or she then declares that "Tennyson's painful confession leaps unwittingly from all their lips" and quotes the lines Cooper quotes (along with the preceding question to which they provide an answer).[29] Thus, this writer uses lines originally expressing religious doubt to express religious doubt, whereas Cooper uses them to describe the virtual absence of black American women's voices from the national discourse.

Citation is by definition an act of recontextualization, but not all recontextualizations are alike. The contrast between these two citations of the same passage makes plain that Cooper's is not self-effacing after all, but instead self-asserting. Moreover, her citation is less a demonstration of the cultural literacy that enables one to cite a well-known poem than of the cultural mastery that allows one to make free with it for one's own purposes. Cooper's failure to name poet or poem reinforces the appropriative dimension of her quotation: she undoubtedly expects her readers to recognize the passage—indeed, her display of mastery depends on it—but at the same time her choice not to cite Tennyson by name underscores the extent to which she makes these lines her own.[30]

Significant as this recontextualization is, the work Cooper does on and with Tennyson's lines goes further. Unlike any other citation of these lines I have come across, Cooper manipulates the passage at the level of punctuation and typography: *In Memoriam* reads "And with no language but a cry," whereas *A Voice from the South*, as we have seen, adds a dash between "language" and "but" and italicizes the last five words, giving us "And with *no language—but a cry.*" This visual play registers and signals her conceptual and referential play: Cooper quotes all of Tennyson's words but quotes them slant.

More specifically, by accenting and setting off the final words as she does, Cooper indicates to the reader what is most important about these lines for her purposes. Focusing attention on these particular words and suggesting that they are especially freighted with meaning, she also makes it more likely that the reader will read them allusively. And in fact the word *cry* figures prominently in one of the best-known poems by one of the best-known African American women to precede Cooper in entering the public sphere. Frances E. W. Harper's early poem "Ethiopia" (1854) begins,

> Yes! Ethiopia yet shall stretch
>   Her bleeding hands abroad;
> Her *cry* of agony shall reach
>   The burning throne of God.[31]

Here indeed we find "the sadly expectant Black Woman . . . with *no language—but a cry.*"

Cooper's recontextualization of Tennyson's lines thus makes them into an allusion to Harper's. Cooper reinforces this allusion later in *A Voice from the South* by including these very lines from Harper's poem: discussing "the work and influence of the colored women of America," Cooper quotes this passage to illustrate her claim that "Frances Watkins Harper could sing with prophetic exaltation in the darkest days."[32] Through her use of Tennyson, then, Cooper subtly positions herself within African American history as the successor to Harper and the generation of "pioneers" she represents.[33]

Read thus, Cooper's citation of Tennyson paradoxically conforms to an understanding of African American literary tradition as constituted primarily by intertextual relations among African American texts. This will often prove true in the following pages: as we shall see, one way African American writers used nineteenth-century British literature was to establish or negotiate relationships with other African American writers. When African American writers turn to nineteenth-century British literature, in other words, they are not necessarily turning away from African American literature. On the contrary, often they are either revealing or creating links between the two, as in the Cooper / Tennyson / Harper example,[34] and sometimes they are self-consciously participating in and even referencing an African American tradition of citation and appropriation.

Indeed, if African American writers and editors treat nineteenth-century British literature as an archive, they might also be said to create their own nineteenth-century British canon, through repeated recourse to certain authors, texts, and passages. This is especially true with regard to Tennyson, whose presence looms larger than that of any other British author in the period covered by this book. That is, while Tennyson's outsized presence derives in part from his stature in the culture at large as well as from the particularities of specific poems, it is also the case that this presence is self-perpetuating and self-reflexive.

My brief reading of Cooper's citation of Tennyson begins to suggest the rewards of closer attention to moments of intertextual engagement between

African American and Victorian literature for those interested in African American literature. At the same time, however, this reading could conceivably call into question the value of such attention for anyone intent instead on better understanding Victorian literature itself: the more fully Cooper makes Tennyson's lines do her own bidding, the less relevant her citation may seem to an understanding of those lines themselves, the poem from which they are drawn, or the poet who composed them.

Yet sometimes the less true a citation is to a passage's original context, the more revealing it proves, precisely by virtue of this defamiliarizing recontextualization. In this instance, for example, I noted above that Tennyson, *needless to say*, was not himself a black American woman. The use to which Cooper puts Tennyson's lines made it necessary to say this, and the sheer oddness of this necessity might startle us into asking a host of questions: Is there anything in Tennyson's self-presentation that invites the implicit identification Cooper enacts through her borrowing of his words? Does Tennyson share the identitarian epistemology with regard to race, nationality, and gender that Cooper is articulating when she quotes him? How is Tennyson's status as not a black American woman inscribed or reflected in his poetry? Does Tennyson himself ever write in the voice of a black American woman—or of a black, or an American, or a woman tout court? Does he ever allude to or borrow from writers assignable to these categories? Does he ever engage in Cooper-like acts of radical recontextualization or transpositioning with any source? If we were to follow Cooper's lead and reread section LIV of *In Memoriam* as if it were in the voice of a black American woman, would the poem read differently? How does it compare with the most famous Victorian poem actually written in such a voice, Elizabeth Barrett Browning's "The Runaway Slave at Pilgrim's Point"?

Some of these lines of inquiry would no doubt prove more productive than others. Pursuing for a moment the last one, we might note that Tennyson's and Barrett Browning's speakers figure, in similar terms, similar doubts about the meaningfulness of existence: in the stanzas preceding the one Cooper quotes, the former strives to believe "That nothing walks with aimless feet; / That not one life shall be destroyed, / Or cast as rubbish to the void / . . . / That not a worm is cloven in vain,"[35] while the latter surmises (in lines that intermittently employ *In Memoriam*'s iambic tetrameter) that if God made her "He must have cast his work away / Under the feet of his white creatures, / With a look of scorn—that the dusky features / Might be trodden again to clay."[36] Cooper's use of Tennyson thus puts his poem in dialogue with another Victorian poem as well as an African American one.

For the purposes of this introduction, I am more interested in identifying the kinds of questions an African Americanization such as Cooper's raises than in attempting to answer them, but these questions are by no means rhetorical. (I return to Tennyson himself in chapters 2, 4, 5, and 6, with chapter 2 in particular teasing out the implications of a reframing more explicit and more radical than Cooper's.) Both implicitly and explicitly, African Americanizations of Victorian literature pose provocative questions and make provocative claims that it will be the work of this book to tease out and address. As we shall see, sometimes these provocations are a byproduct of an appropriation or citation made primarily for an author's or editor's own purposes, whereas at other times they motivate the textual encounter.

The insights afforded by African Americanizations of Victorian literature vary widely in scale, from the most local of textual moments to our understanding of the cultural work of literature. These African Americanizations revise our understanding of the formal features of particular works; of the shape of a particular author's oeuvre, including newly visible preoccupations, patterns, and interrelations among texts; and of the political significance of major works. Most consistently, these practices make us see differently Victorian literature's treatment of race, and reveal how intimately the treatment of race is bound up with other, ostensibly unrelated aspects of an author's work. At the same time, though, even as African Americanizations of Victorian texts highlight and clarify the role race plays in particular texts, they also make clear that a text's treatment of race does not negate or exhaust its interest and value from an African American perspective. By the same token, the insights these African Americanizations afford into Victorian literature extend beyond its treatment of race.

The Victorian literature in question here—that is, the Victorian literature that mattered most to African American authors and editors in this period—is paradoxically both familiar and surprising. Familiar, because many of the texts seized upon for reprinting, rewriting, commentary, quotation, or allusion were well known in their day and are now canonical; the texts themselves, and even more so their authors, were and continue to be viewed as central to mainstream—white, middle-class—nineteenth-century Anglo-American culture. Thus, while a number of Victorian authors will appear in the following pages, in addition to Tennyson the ones who appear most frequently are Charles Dickens and George Eliot. But the African American archive of Victorian literature is surprising nonetheless because, as I have emphasized, the Victorian texts with the richest African American afterlives do not themselves depict African American characters.

This archive is also surprising for its inclusion of works that are not canonical or even well known today. Remaining with the example at hand, for instance, we might note that Anna Julia Cooper's epigraph to part 1 of *A Voice from the South* reads:

> For they the Royal-hearted Women are
> Who nobly love the noblest, yet have grace
> For needy, suffering lives in lowliest place;
> Carrying a choicer sunlight in their smile,
> The heavenliest ray that pitieth the vile.
>
> . . . .
>
> Though I were happy, throned beside the king,
> I should be tender to each little thing
> With hurt warm breast, that had no speech to tell
> Its inward pangs; and I would soothe it well
> With tender touch and with a low, soft moan
> For company.
>   —GEORGE ELIOT[37]

At least as striking as any use Cooper makes of these lines from Eliot's 1869 poem "How Lisa Loved the King" is the fact that she cites this particular poem: even within the corpus of Eliot's poetry, which in general receives little scholarly attention, "How Lisa Loved the King" is an obscurity.[38]

Citations such as this revise our knowledge of which Victorian texts even have afterlives—knowledge that may play a larger role in determining our sense of a canon, or more simply of which works merit critical attention, than we tend to acknowledge. As we shall see, the most dramatic shift in perspective encouraged by the history of engagement traced in *Reaping Something New* will in fact relate to George Eliot, albeit not thanks to this citation of "How Lisa Loved the King"—its further citation by Mrs. Booker T. Washington notwithstanding.[39]

This book covers what I argue is the heyday of the African Americanization of Victorian literature, from the editorial practices of Frederick Douglass in the mid-nineteenth century to the citational practices of W.E.B. Du Bois in the early twentieth century. The book's organization is basically chronological, although a focus on afterlives means that there are multiple chronologies in play: that of the publication of the works being taken up, and those of their taking up. The governing chronology here is more the latter, although the chronologies often coincide, since the African American responses I look at often occur (or begin) at the time of initial publication.

Each of the first three chapters of the book explores the multiple uses to which one particular Victorian author—and indeed one primary work—was put by African Americans. Each of the last three chapters takes the opposite tack and considers the uses an individual African American author made of works by multiple Victorian authors. Each approach offers certain analytical advantages, and both involve tradeoffs in coverage and emphasis. The use of both speaks to my sense of how best to capture the complexities of individual encounters and to narrate the development of these practices over time. In addition, though, this organization also reflects my desire to grant primacy to neither the African American nor the Victorian dimension of my argument. Even as this book seeks to reveal the unacknowledged links between African American and Victorian literature, it also, by the same token, seeks to heighten the fluidity of movement between African Americanist and Victorianist orientations or approaches. While it remains quite possible that African Americanists and Victorianists will find different aspects of the following analyses of greater interest, I hope to show that the history I am excavating renders "African Americanist" or "Victorianist" analyses fully entangled with one another, and at times indistinguishable.

Chapter 1 explores the reprinting of *Bleak House* in *Frederick Douglass' Paper* and its rewriting in or as Hannah Crafts's *The Bondwoman's Narrative*. Breaking from the critical history of determining the ideological effects of Dickens's novel on the basis of its intrinsic formal features, I look at actual uses to which the novel was put. At the same time, I argue that a proper understanding of the work Douglass and Crafts do on and with the novel cannot replace but, on the contrary, requires close attention to the text itself. Focusing in particular on a cultural function that has come to be seen as one of the novel-form's most important—the cultivation of national identity—I tease out the paradox whereby *Bleak House*'s attempt to consolidate the community it imagines through the exclusion of slaves and people of color becomes most conspicuous when members of those very groups make Dickens's novel a resource for their own efforts to build communities and transform the nation.

Chapter 2 takes as its focus another now-iconic Victorian text reprinted and discussed in *Frederick Douglass' Paper* immediately after its initial publication: Alfred Tennyson's poem about a disastrous yet heroic battle in the

Crimean War, "The Charge of the Light Brigade." I do not quite use this deployment of the poem to consider the relationship of African Americans to the dominant cultural tradition, nor to explore the nature and politics of interracial cultural appropriation—instead, I show that Douglass and his contributors deployed the poem to raise and address these very issues. This is most dramatically the case in James McCune Smith's stunning argument that "The Light Brigade" was plagiarized from an African war chant used to call the slaves to rebel in Haiti. In addition to unpacking the logic and performative force of this seemingly outlandish claim, I also take it seriously as a source of insight into Tennyson's poem. McCune Smith's racializing recontextualization of "The Light Brigade," I argue, repositions it within Tennyson's oeuvre and helps make visible Tennyson's own strategy of de-racializing recontextualization. Introducing a temporal dimension to my analysis, I also trace the persistent use of this seemingly topical poem to address African American experience over the second half of the nineteenth century.

While these two chapters focus on reprintings, readings, and rewritings that switch the racial context or referent of Victorian texts, the next three chapters explore the uses of texts that are themselves about the switching of races, whether through the discovery of ancestry or a decision to pass (or both). In chapter 3, I show that Eliot's epic poem *The Spanish Gypsy*, which most critics in its own day and ever since have dismissed as a failure, was embraced by Frances Ellen Watkins Harper and other late-nineteenth- and early-twentieth-century African American writers as a politically salutary effort to break the narrative link between discovered minority ancestry and victimization, and to imagine such a discovery instead as the occasion for affirmative identification and heroic (if often sacrificial) action. Verbally echoing the poem and borrowing its plot of unwitting passing and voluntary racial affiliation, these writers turn *The Spanish Gypsy* into a response to the tragic mulatto/a plot—or rather, they pick up on and highlight the ways it already was one. Both what these writers take from Eliot and what they choose to leave behind—including her emigrationist conclusion—cast Eliot's poem and central aspects of her career more broadly in a different light and even suggest a new explanation of her choice of the pseudonym "George Eliot."

Narratives of passing and racial re-identification remain important in chapters 4 and 5, which consider the presence of Victorian literature in the work of the two most widely studied African American novelists of the turn of the twentieth century: Charles Chesnutt and Pauline Hopkins, respectively. Chapter 4 traces the career-long engagement with Victorian literature of Chesnutt, the author who provided what is quite possibly the first fictional depiction of an African American reader of that literature: Mr. Ryder, the Tennyson-loving protagonist of the short story "The Wife of His Youth." While Mr. Ryder aspires to *not* be African American, I argue that Chesnutt himself never treats Victorian literature merely as a symbol of whiteness. Instead, he draws on that literature to help construct his own narrative investigations of racial identity and identification even as he probes the limitations of its treatment of race. In particular, Chesnutt repeatedly references and reworks Victorian depictions and invocations of mixed-race identity. This pattern receives its fullest articulation in *The House Behind the Cedars*, which explores what it would mean if the protagonists of two classic Victorian bildungsromans who are both fleetingly figured as mulattoes—David Copperfield and Maggie Tulliver—really were mixed race. Turning his attention to characters who actually are mixed race (rather than merely figured as such) in his last, posthumously published novel *The Quarry*, Chesnutt conducts a final reckoning with Victorian literature, one that addresses head-on the charge of derivativeness his close reworking of Victorian texts knowingly courted.

Chapter 5 traces Pauline Hopkins's complex engagement with Victorian literature from the numerous yet little-noted citations of Tennyson in her first novel, *Contending Forces*, to her unacknowledged verbatim borrowings from Edward Bulwer Lytton in her last one, *Of One Blood*. Hopkins's engagement with Victorian literature, I argue, is crucially mediated and motivated by that literature's existing presence within African American literature, in particular in the work of her exact contemporary Chesnutt. Like Chesnutt and in dialogue with him, she uses Victorian literature to explore the ways cultural transmission can both supplement and circumscribe biological genealogy. Unlike Chesnutt, Hopkins also uses mainstream, ostensibly conservative Victorian literature in ways that systematically amplify the transgressive currents of her work with regard to gender and sexuality as well as race.

Chapter 6 revisits the best-known citations of nineteenth-century British literature in the African American literary tradition: the chapter epigraphs in W.E.B. Du Bois's *The Souls of Black Folk*, many of which pair lines of music from Negro spirituals with passages of nineteenth-century British poetry. I show that just as Hopkins used Victorian literature to respond to Chesnutt, so too do Du Bois's citations of nineteenth-century British literature self-consciously intervene in the larger history of African American engagement with that literature. Even as he uses this literature to evoke a realm free from racial prejudice and strife, as many critics emphasize, he also locates these poems within and brings them to bear on black history and experience, deploying them as weapons in the ongoing struggle for racial equality.

In addition to re-citing poets and poems with a history of African American citation, Du Bois also expands his archive from earlier nineteenth-century poets to include more recent works. This is not a break from previous practice but rather an extension: Du Bois maintains the spirit of engagement with contemporary literature that played such an important role for virtually all his predecessors in the African Americanization of Victorian literature. But in doing so he also signals the beginning of the end of this phenomenon, at least in its major phase—his own late, bravura reading of Dante Gabriel Rossetti's "The Blessed Damozel" as an allegory of African American literary history notwithstanding. As I show in my afterword, however, two twenty-first century novels suggest that Victorian literature still has a distinctive role to play in literature written by African Americans, both through and despite efforts to consign it to the past.

While the scope of *Reaping Something New* should be clear by now, questions may remain regarding the rationale for this scope as well as my terminology. I will attempt to anticipate and address the most important ones:

Why Victorian *literature?* In other words, if one is interested in African American engagements with non–African American literature, why focus on Victorian literature in particular? As I show, Victorian literature has a distinct status and appeal for literary African Americans during the period covered in this book. This is partly a function of this literature's Britishness: as Elisa Tamarkin in particular has shown, British culture was widely viewed as superior to American culture in the nineteenth-century United States, and African Americans had heightened "anglophiliac" tendencies due to Britain's history of support for abolition and the freedom from racism or even racial identity it putatively offered to African American travelers and refugees.

In addition, the literary encounters I describe are structured as much by the contemporaneity or near-contemporaneity of the British literature in question as by this Britishness itself. My point is not that authors or editors ignored older literature but rather that contemporary or recent literature signified differently—namely, as contemporary or recent. As we shall see, such factors as topicality, form or site of encounter, cultural capital, and positioning in the literary field come into play and play out differently depending on a text's relative recentness or historical remoteness. For example, whereas citing earlier literature stakes one's claim to a culture's heritage, engaging with contemporary literature establishes one's status as a full participant in an ongoing cultural conversation or literary movement. Often an act of self-positioning among or in relation to prominent contemporaries, such engagements can also serve to position those contemporaries themselves, whether as allies, interlocutors, or objects of critique.[40]

Victorian or nineteenth century? While most of the British literature I discuss will be Victorian in the strict sense—that is, composed and published during the reign of Queen Victoria, 1837–1901—I will at times also discuss British literature from earlier in the nineteenth century. For my analysis—as, I argue, for the authors and editors themselves—the distinction between Romantic and Victorian does not carry great weight, and of course writers at midcentury are as close in time to, say, a second-generation Romantic such as Byron as those at the end of the century are to a high Victorian writer such as Eliot. As William St. Clair and other scholars have shown, moreover, the distribution and availability of much Romantic-era literature was undiminished or even enhanced in the second half of the nineteenth century, in the U.S. as well as Britain.[41]

Why African American *literature and print culture?* In other words, if one is interested in the afterlives of Victorian literature, why look to African American afterlives in particular? Work on the dissemination of, and responses to, Victorian literature has tended to focus its sights on the nations that made up the British Empire, for good and obvious reasons. Yet even work specifically on the literary relations between the U.S. and Britain has, until recently, tended to ignore African American literary culture. The historical situation and subject-position of African Americans is distinct from that of the British Empire's colonial (and postcolonial) subjects as well as that of other Americans, and distinct in ways that crucially inflect attitudes toward Britain and its literature.

In a compelling discussion of what he calls "colonial Victorianism," Simon Gikandi argues that "Victorianism was not a discourse or ideology that was simply imposed on the colonized; it was also a set of ideas and ideals that were deployed by colonial subjects as a means to a different end—their freedom."[42] I argue, similarly, that African Americans deployed Victorian literature for their own purposes; however, the relationship of that literature to the forces of domination in the U.S. was much more equivocal than in the colonial context. African American engagements with Victorian literature thus merit separate attention, and the elaborate and unpredictable forms these engagements took ensure that they reward it. The sustained, manifold African American engagement with Victorian literature generates a version and vision of that literature unavailable elsewhere.

Why "engagements," "afterlives," "uses," "deployments," "transpositions," "recontextualizations," "repurposing," "citations," "translations," etc.? Why, that is, the proliferation of terms to name the relationship(s) in question, and why these terms in particular, most of which are as vague as they are clunky? Perhaps the broadest term we have to denote relationships between texts is "intertextuality." I have used this term sparingly, however, for two reasons: first, because it often carries a narrower meaning, associated with poststructuralist theorists such as Julia Kristeva and Roland Barthes, that is not dominant here; and second, because even when "intertextuality" is taken in its broadest, most neutral sense, it still leaves out practices and forms of cultural presence or modes of response that are important to this book. Foremost among these are commentary or criticism—a relationship between texts that could conceivably be brought under the umbrella of "intertextuality" but rarely is—and the reprinting of Victorian texts in African American periodicals. (While my focus is on literature and print culture, I should also note that there are other forms of presence that I only touch on, such as inclusion in school curricula and public performance, as in the public recitation of poetry.)[43] In this book I bring together a wide range of seemingly disparate formal and material practices, precisely to argue that they form a continuum, a set of practices and relationships that can be better understood when viewed as just that: a set. However, this is not standard operating procedure in literary studies: while there has been rapid growth in periodical and print culture studies, the work of framing and reframing performed by a work's publication format or inclusion in a particular periodical is rarely considered alongside or in relation to the (what I would argue is comparable) work of framing and reframing performed by such literary devices as allusion, parody, or diegetic transposition.[44] For this reason, no one term exists that covers all the necessary bases. The closest is perhaps "engagement," which is capacious and introduces an element of agency without implying a specific power dynamic—unlike, say, terms such as "influence" or "debt" or even "reception" and "adaptation," on the one hand, and "writing back" or "critique" or "confrontation" or even "response," on the other.

I will often use the term "afterlives," which I find useful both for its generality and its implication of a spatial and even conceptual remove: African

Americans were not the intended or imagined audience for these works, and the uses they made of Victorian literature were entirely unanticipated, even when they were in keeping with the spirit of the work, and even when that work itself envisions its own dissemination and repurposing (as is especially the case with *Bleak House,* as we shall see in chapter 1).[45] On the other hand, this term can be misleading insofar as it suggests a temporal remove, whereas, as I have been arguing, contemporaneity and even immediacy play important roles in prompting engagements with particular texts and determining their significance. It matters that Frederick Douglass began reprinting *Bleak House* before Dickens finished writing it.[46]

What about the Victorian uses of African American literature? Radically disparate levels of political power or cultural capital between groups do not preclude the possibility of symmetrical cultural traffic between them, or even of a subaltern group's forms of cultural expression wielding a disproportionate influence on—or undergoing appropriation by—a dominant one. U.S. history makes this plain, with the role of African American music in the national culture Exhibit A. It is not unreasonable to ask, then, whether there is not a Victorian archive of African American literature to match the African American archive of Victorian literature this book explores. This is, in fact, a question I will ask of two of the Victorian authors I focus on, Dickens and Eliot; while with regard to the third, Tennyson, I will examine at length the posing in the period itself of a cognate question—not of African American but of African or Afro-Haitian influence. In none of these cases, however, will I find a level of presence or engagement comparable to those I find with regard to Victorian literature in African American literature and print culture (although writings *about* African Americans do prove especially significant for Eliot).[47] I do not consider this surprising, given the limited amount of writing published by African Americans before the end of the nineteenth century and the even more limited access Victorian writers had to this literature. But nor is it disheartening or discomfiting, given what I do find: to focus on the Victorian presence in African American literature and print culture may seem to risk resurrecting discredited beliefs in the latter's derivativeness or imitativeness, but the story I tell offers scant support for such views. Quite the opposite. Indeed, although my task and my tone are analytical rather than celebratory, I do not mind acknowledging that in writing this book I have repeatedly had my breath taken away by the inventiveness and sheer audacity that characterize the African Americanization of Victorian literature.

CHAPTER ONE

CLOSE READING *BLEAK HOUSE* AT A DISTANCE

On October 1, 1851, in Syracuse, New York, a man named Jerry was arrested by federal marshals acting under the authority of the Fugitive Slave Act. Within hours, Jerry was freed by a crowd and, several days later, surreptitiously transported to Canada and freedom. Two years after these events, the defendants in what became known as the Jerry Rescue case still had not been tried. Protesting what it saw as "the indirect punishment of persons obnoxious to the Government, whom it does not hope to convict," the abolitionist paper *The Liberator* exclaimed, "Had we an American Dickens, this might afford a text for a new Bleak House, quite as suggestive as the Court of Chancery itself. But, *le bon temps viendra!* Better times will come."[1] And so better times did come, indeed had already come, if better times mean new *Bleak Houses*, Americanized and even African Americanized *Bleak Houses*: antebellum African Americans and abolitionists seized upon *Bleak House* and put it to work in a surprising number of ways, from brief if suggestive references such as this one to reprintings of the novel in whole or in part, and from the literal reenactment of one of its events to an actual rewriting of the novel in something like the way *The Liberator* envisioned.

Attention to these antislavery afterlives of *Bleak House* alters our understanding of Dickens's novel. At the same time, though, a proper understanding of these afterlives themselves requires close attention to the text of *Bleak House*. As I argue in my introduction's discussion of "close reading at a distance," the methods of close reading and formal analysis, on the one hand, and of book history and reception studies, on the other, need to be combined if we are to grasp as fully as possible *either* a text's intrinsic features *or* its cultural impact, let alone the relationship between the two.[2] In the present instance, we will find that the African Americanization of *Bleak House* makes newly visible and meaningful certain aspects of the novel even as it calls into question the power of such features to determine the cultural work the novel—and, by extension, any text—performs.

This doubly estranging dynamic will be particularly clear with regard to a cultural task that has come to be seen as one of the novel-form's most important: the cultivation of national identity, or what Benedict Anderson famously called the "imagined community" of the nation-state.[3] As we shall see, *Bleak House* does not merely fail to imagine a community that includes Africans, African Americans, slaves, and people of color in general; rather, it consolidates the national community it does imagine by means of their exclusion. Paradoxically, however, this strategy becomes most conspicuous when it is least efficacious: engaging in their own forms of close reading at a distance, members of these groups and their advocates find in Dickens's novel a material and imaginative resource for their own efforts to tell the stories they want to tell and build the communities they seek to build.

FREDERICK DOUGLASS'S *BLEAK HOUSE*

"Devoted," in the words of its editor, proprietor, and namesake, "to the freedom of the slave, . . . the moral and mental elevation of the free colored people," and "the cause of Human Rights, generally, at home and abroad,"[4] *Frederick Douglass' Paper* began publication in 1851 as the successor to Douglass's earlier *North Star* and continued through the decade. *Douglass' Paper* typically devoted the first three of its four pages to political news, with the last page given over to literary matter—poems, sketches, stories, and book reviews—along with advertisements. Many decisions concerning this literary content undoubtedly involved one of Douglass's main collaborators, Julia Griffiths, an Englishwoman who served as secretary of the Rochester Ladies' Anti-Slavery Society and bore primary responsibility for the paper's Literary Notices column (which is often signed with her initials).[5] Adopting an integrationist policy with obvious political significance, *Douglass' Paper* published original material by African American authors, including the poets J. C. Holly and James Whitfield, and by white Americans associated with the antislavery cause, including Harriet Beecher Stowe, John Greenleaf Whittier, and Henry Wadsworth Longfellow; in addition, it reprinted pieces by and sketches about leading British writers not closely identified with the paper's political stance, such as John Ruskin, Robert Browning, and Alfred, Lord Tennyson. Occasionally the paper serialized fiction, such as Douglass's own "The Heroic Slave," but not often and nothing very long. Or rather, almost nothing: from April 1852 to December 1853, *Douglass' Paper* printed Dickens's mammoth *Bleak House* in its entirety.[6]

The anomalous decision to publish Dickens's novel is not well documented. However, we can be sure that it was made with very limited knowledge of the novel's contents, since only the first of *Bleak House*'s nineteen monthly parts had appeared in London and New York (where it was serialized in *Harper's New Monthly Magazine*) when *Douglass' Paper* began running it. The paper's brief notice announcing its intention to "treat our readers to this *celebrated Story*" offers little explanation, but it does note that it is "following in the wake of the *Boston Commonwealth*."[7] As this phrase suggests, quick as it was to reprint *Bleak House*, *Douglass' Paper* was not the first antislavery paper to do so. The free-soil *Commonwealth*, a four-page daily edited at the time by the well-known abolitionist Elizur Wright, began publication of *Bleak House* in March 1852, immediately after the first part's initial publication ("36 hours after the appearance of the Harper edition," according to a gloating notice).[8] Announcing somewhat defensively that "we think [our readers] will not only forgive us but thank us when they have read it," the *Commonwealth* dedicated its entire first page and most of its fourth to the first installment of the novel.[9]

The *Commonwealth*'s reasons for offering *Bleak House* are suggested by a piece from the *New York Times* it had reprinted the previous day, an article that summarizes the opening of *Bleak House* and states that the novel "will seek to turn the swelling tide of public contempt, ridicule, indignation, and hatred against that great engine of oppression, made sacred by ages of abuse, and venerable in the eyes of all who live to adore the past [i.e., the Court of Chancery]. It will be a most interesting and powerful book [with] a clear, practical purpose—the demolition of abuses and the reform of institutions which impede the progress and crush the energies of the race."[10] A biographical sketch also published in the *Commonwealth* and reprinted in *Douglass' Paper* the day it began running the novel similarly emphasizes Dickens's status as a reformer.[11] Surprisingly, no reference is made in either of these pieces to Dickens's criticism of slavery in his *American Notes*, published a decade earlier. Nonetheless, it is fair to assume that this notorious work contributed to the sense of ideological compatibility. Douglass himself was familiar with *American Notes*, referring to it in speeches at least as early as 1846.[12]

Beginning, however, with the last chapter of that first monthly number which Douglass and Griffiths may or may not have read before deciding to run *Bleak House*, there is good reason to question the fit of novel to journal.[13] This chapter introduces Mrs. Jellyby, an activist working to send white settlers to "Borrioboola-Gha, on the left bank of the Niger," where they are to cultivate the coffee and educate the natives.[14] So consumed is Mrs. Jellyby by her efforts on behalf of "the Brotherhood of Humanity" (*BH*, p. 41) that she scandalously neglects her duties as a wife and mother. This satire of what Dickens famously and damningly calls "telescopic philanthropy" (*BH*, p. 34) clashes directly with Douglass's advocacy of transatlantic political activism and his close collaboration with British and female abolitionists such as Griffiths.[15] As the novel proceeds, moreover, this initial criticism of Mrs. Jellyby and her "African project" (*BH*, p. 38) proves no isolated incident. On the contrary, such criticism recurs throughout *Bleak House* to support what emerges as the novel's implicitly British project of promoting a localism that begins with concern for those "immediately about [one]" and extends at best to the nation's borders; the governing image here is Esther Summerson's "gradually and naturally" expanding "circle of duty" (*BH*, p. 96).[16] This stance is directly opposed to what Douglass, in his famous speech on "The Meaning of July Fourth for the Negro," celebrates as "the obvious tendencies of the age":

> No nation can now shut itself up from the surrounding world and trot round in the same old path of its fathers without interference. . . . Oceans no longer divide, but link nations together. From Boston to London is now a holiday excursion. Space is comparatively annihilated.—Thoughts expressed on one side of the Atlantic are distinctly heard on the other.[17]

This speech appeared in *Douglass' Paper* only a few weeks after Esther's anti-Jellyby credo.[18]

The presence of Dickens's novel in the paper is all the more jarring because the novel's treatment of place is at the same time a treatment of race: *Bleak House* consistently opposes its ethics of proximity to an interest in what we would now call people of color. Thus, the rough handling of Mrs. Jellyby is complemented by the novel's moving depiction of the dispossessed London streetsweep Jo, whose neglect is used to indict those who concern themselves instead with "the spiritual destitution of a coral reef in the Pacific" (*BH*, p. 199). Most striking of all, in the context of *Douglass' Paper*, is the novel's one direct reference to American slavery, which again contrasts attention to darker-skinned people with the fulfillment of one's domestic (in both senses) responsibilities. Describing what he calls his "cosmopolitan . . . sympathy" with "enterprise and effort," the dilettante Harold Skimpole says, "Take an extreme case. Take the case of the Slaves on American plantations. I dare say they are worked hard, I dare say they don't altogether like it, I dare say theirs is an unpleasant experience on the whole; but they people the landscape for me, they give it a poetry for me, and perhaps that is one of the pleasanter objects of their existence. I am very sensible of it, if it be, and I shouldn't wonder if it were!" (*BH*, p. 227). Skimpole is of course meant to be seen as a moral monster. However, the essence of this monstrousness is captured by Esther's response, which makes clear the racial exclusion upon which the novel's moral order rests: "I always wondered on these occasions whether he ever thought of Mrs. Skimpole and the children, and in what point of view they presented themselves to his cosmopolitan mind. So far as I could understand, they rarely presented themselves at all" (*BH*, p. 227). In other words, Skimpole's moral deficiency consists not in the point of view in which American slaves present themselves to his mind, as one might imagine, but rather in the very fact that he thinks about them. Through moments such as this, *Bleak House* emerges as a remarkably incongruous choice for the former slave Douglass to people his own landscape with, and give it a poetry.

I will argue below that Douglass and Griffiths takes various steps to downplay this incongruousness. In this particular instance, though, editorial decisions have the opposite effect: the weekly installment containing Skimpole's troubling musings and Esther's equally troubling response breaks off midchapter, right after this very passage (ending with ". . . rarely presented themselves at all"), thereby heightening its prominence. Moreover, the installment is immediately—and mischievously?—followed, in the same column, by an item titled "Why Slaves Escape."[19]

Additional aspects of *Bleak House* also threaten to become more salient and more troubling when framed by *Douglass' Paper*. In particular, there is John Jarndyce's ostensibly benevolent trafficking in women: when Jarndyce hires Charley Neckett to be Esther's maid, Charley announces this to Esther by saying, in what are clearly Jarndyce's words, "If you please, miss, I'm a present to you, with Mr. Jarndyce's love" (*BH*, p. 299); and at the end of the novel, Jarndyce releases Esther from her promise to marry him and hands her over to Allan Woodcourt, saying, "take from me, a willing gift" (*BH*, p. 753). The language of gift-exchange here registers, even as it seeks to prettify, profound disparities in agency and power. Present in the text but muted, this discordant note resonates more loudly and to different effect when sounded in a newspaper dedicated to ending the treatment of persons as possessions.

In making these claims about the framing effect of *Douglass' Paper*, I recognize that we must take care not to assume that what seems clear now would have seemed clear in the past. Readers must be tuned to the right frequency to hear these notes. It is likely that Dickens's earlier antislavery stance and continued reputation as a reformer did prevent some antislavery activists from registering *Bleak House*'s problematic politics; the reference in the *Liberator* article I opened with suggests as much. Similarly, after publishing the first monthly part of *Bleak House*, the *Commonwealth* went so far as to defend itself against criticism for underselling *Harper's* (which it reports as having paid $2,000 for advance sheets of the novel) by joking, "If we make one hundredth part as much money on it as the Harpers have made on pirated English literature, we will give a hundred dollars for the education of Mrs. Jellyby's daughter, or some other charitable object."[20] Nonetheless, we know that it does not require hindsight to see the trouble with *Bleak House*, and we know it the only way we can with any certainty: through the recorded reactions of contemporary readers. Before the novel had finished publication, even finished being written, a prominent British abolitionist publicly denounced Dickens's depiction of Mrs. Jellyby as implicitly proslavery: in a series of articles quickly reprinted as a pamphlet, Lord Denman charged Dickens with "do[ing] his best to replunge the world into the most barbarous abuse that ever afflicted it." "We do not say that he actually defends slavery or the slave trade," Denman explains, "but he takes pains to discourage, by ridicule, the effort now making to put them down."[21] The ridicule of Mrs. Jellyby prompts him to demand, "*Who but the slave traders can gain by this course of argument?*"[22]

In a letter to Denman's daughter responding to this attack, Dickens claimed that "No kind of reference to Slavery is made or intended" in his depiction of Mrs. Jellyby.[23] Whether or not Lord Denman's daughter was convinced by this claim, Mrs. Jellyby's daughter clearly is not: "Talk of Africa! I couldn't be worse off if I was a what-'s-his-name—man and a brother!" (*BH*, p. 166), says Caddy, invoking the famous abolitionist slogan. And in fact Denman's concern over the use to which Dickens's satire could be put was well founded: two weeks before Dickens wrote his letter, a letter to the *Times* of London criticized an antislavery petition signed by thousands of British women by saying that efforts should not be made to "regenerate Borrioboola Gha" when there is so much work to be done "within a stone's throw of our own dwellings."[24] Dickens may resist this application of his novel, but the novel itself does not.[25]

I have found one contemporary reading of *Bleak House* as explicitly antislavery, but even this counterexample ends up reinforcing the sense that the novel's treatment of place and race makes it out of place in *Douglass' Paper*. In *The Planter; or, Thirteen Years in the South, by a Northern Man* (1853), David Brown quotes the beginning of the speech by Harold Skimpole discussed above, through "I dare say theirs is an unpleasant experience on the whole" and takes umbrage at this unchallenged characterization of slavery as "unpleasant": "I dare say, Mr. Skimpole Dickens, you know very little about it. I dare say, that English writers who meddle with our affairs in this way, would often appear less ridiculous and damage their own country less, if they would try honestly to know more and write less about what they are shamefully and it seems blissfully ignorant."[26] Isolating one moment, Brown manages to miss the isolationism advanced by the passage as a whole. Ironically, however, Brown does capture the spirit of the novel in his criticism of Dickens's wife, Catherine, for having signed the antislavery petition just mentioned: "I wonder if Mrs. Charles Dickens has read Oliver Twist and the Bleak House? They might point her to other work to be done, nearer home, than our Southern States; where there is no poor Oliver '*to want more*' nor poor homeless Joe [*sic*], who could not have had less."[27] Brown's call to tend to those "nearer home" is Dickens's own, and the fact that Brown himself seems not quite to realize this only reminds us that such arguments against outside meddlers were already a staple of anti-antislavery discourse.

Given the obvious friction between the ideological agendas of *Bleak House* and *Frederick Douglass' Paper*, perhaps we should conclude that the decision to reprint *Bleak House* in the antislavery paper was simply uninformed and, in retrospect, a mistake. Yet while the initial decision to publish the novel was necessarily made with limited knowledge, we should not overlook the fact that this decision was repeatedly renewed, over a period of twenty months. By contrast, the *Commonwealth* stopped publication of *Bleak House* without comment after publishing about a quarter of it.[28] I would argue that Douglass's persistence stems not from inertia or inattention but rather a determination to enlist "the universal favorite of the people" in the cause, if necessary despite himself.[29] To achieve this, Douglass did not rely solely on the introductory linking of novel and author to reform, nor even on the implicit argument of the novel's very presence; instead, he and Julia Griffiths continued working to frame their readers' understanding of *Bleak House* and the presence of *Bleak House* in the paper.

The most telling of Douglass and Griffiths's tactics emerges in the Literary Notices column early in the novel's run, in a statement that tacitly recognizes the need to overcome some unspecified readerly resistance: "We make no apology to our readers for devoting our fourth page to 'Bleak House.' To those among them who have read 'UNCLE TOM'S CABIN,' (and who has not read it ere this?) we commend this attractive story of the most popular of English writers."[30] This notice appeared just a month after Stowe's novel appeared in book-form and completed its serialized run in *The National Era*, and it establishes a pattern, as *Douglass' Paper* consistently aligns the two novels, on both aesthetic and ideological grounds.[31] To choose one typical example, an excerpt from the *London Examiner* reprinted in October 1852 states that "Mrs. Stowe['s] . . . success in America . . . corresponds to that which Mr. Dickens, finds in England, because, like Mr. Dickens, whose influence we trace in many pages of her book, she has spent great wealth of genius in the service of humanity."[32] (I should add that it may well have been the *National Era*'s success in serializing a long social protest novel that inspired Douglass to publish *Bleak House* in the first place.) *Douglass' Paper* was hardly alone in aligning Stowe and Dickens, but it was fully committed to promoting this alignment—an alignment that did not go uncontested, most prominently by Lord Denman, who in the articles discussed above explicitly contrasts Dickens's faults with Stowe's virtues.[33] *Douglass' Paper* noticed Denman's articles but did not mention their criticism of *Bleak House*.

In fact, no expressions of hostility to *Bleak House* on ideological grounds appear in *Douglass' Paper*. Some complaints do crop up: "We prize your paper, and generally read all you publish, except advertisements and *Bleak House*," writes one subscriber; "In renewing my subscription for your paper, excuse me if I find a little fault with it. Could not the space occupied by Dickens' 'Bleak House' be better occupied?" asks another.[34] These readers' lack of sympathy for the novel may reflect its lack of sympathy for them, its failure to include them in its imagined community. However, nothing more pointedly critical appears in *Douglass' Paper*, and the objections are outnumbered by friendly allusions, as the novel becomes incorporated into the discourse of the paper. Picking up on the name John Jarndyce uses for the study to which he retreats when in a bad mood, for example, one correspondent announces, "I have just dedicated a new 'Growlery' and the enclosed, is the first issue of thoughts therefrom."[35] Another writer simply borrows Mr. Snagsby's catchphrase "not to put too fine a point on it."[36] Through moments such as these, *Douglass' Paper* works to create a community bound together not only by a common set of political commitments but also by a common vocabulary and range of cultural references. In doing so it not only creates a community but also asserts membership in, and thus creates anew, the larger community of Dickens readers.

As part of this effort, *Douglass' Paper* even tackles one of *Bleak House*'s most recalcitrantly national moments. James Buzard singles out the famous scene where the streetsweep Jo dies as the quintessential episode in which Dickens cultivates an Andersonian sense of national identity, of Britain as a *"specific* moral community."[37] This scene prompts the most sustained discussion the novel was to receive in the "Literary Notices" column of *Douglass' Paper*, as Julia Griffiths recognizes but attempts to overcome its national localism. Griffiths asserts that Dickens's "delineations are true, to the life; and his being able to give them evinces his being intimately acquainted with the dense ignorance, squallid [*sic*] misery, and pressing wants of *'the London poor.'*"[38] For American readers, or readers in America, it seems, Jos are not "dying thus around us every day." Griffiths's point is not, however, that American readers will not or should not be moved by the scene; on the contrary, they should be doubly moved—that is, moved imaginatively to the geographical locale where they can be moved emotionally: "He who can stand by the death-bed of the poor idiot 'Jo,' without having the kindly sympathies of his nature called forth, must be callous to the wants and miseries of his kind." The appeal of scene and novel is universal, even though their address is not. Or at least the appeal ought to be, but Griffiths finally acknowledges indirectly that she is fighting an uphill battle with a scene that, as Buzard puts it, so "effectively consolidates the national 'us'": "We wish we could induce every one to read *'Bleak House,'*" she concludes. "'Tis true that 'the story is long;' but time spent upon its perusal is *not ill bestowed.*" [39]

Bolder efforts to insert *Douglass's* readership into the novel, or the novel into their world, occur after its serialization ended. The more elaborate of these exercises is an anonymous, eighty-line poem titled "Borroboola Gha: A Poem for the Times," published in 1855.[40] This poem begins by describing a preacher's appeal for charity to minister to "some heathens, / Thousand of miles afar, / Who live in a land of darkness, / 'Borroboola Gha.'" After hearing this sermon, the speaker of the poem happens upon a starving child and its dying mother who live nearby. This encounter leads the speaker to exclaim: "Alas for the cold and hungry / That met me every day, / While all my tears were given / To the suffering far away!" The poem concludes with its own appeal to the reader:

O! Christian, God has promised
Whoe'er to thee has given
A cup of pure cold water

Shall find reward in Heaven.
Would you secure the blessing
You need not seek it far;
Go find in yonder hovel
A "Borroboola Gha."[41]

The writer here alludes to *Bleak House* and adopts the novel's antitelescopic stance while simply ignoring its racial specificity.

An 1854 item alludes more briefly to *Bleak House* but goes even further in repurposing the novel. This article expresses outrage that the imprisonment of a Protestant missionary in Florence has prompted public indignation in the U.S., whereas the imprisonment of a woman in Virginia for teaching slaves to read "is taken quite calmly." The writer complains, "Like 'Jellyby,' our sympathies run warmly for 'Borrioboola Gha' Missions, but oppression and imprisonment nearer home are things 'not in our line.'"[42] Here, then, to be like Mrs. Jellyby is to be indifferent to the plight of slaves and their supporters. The form of Dickens's criticism is maintained, but its content is virtually reversed. Today, we might be apt to argue that race serves as a Derridean supplement to place in *Bleak House*, buttressing the novel's appeal to proximity but thereby revealing the inadequacy of proximity as a source of solidarity or even proximity's status as an alibi for race. Opting instead for a kind of strategic anti-essentialism, Douglass rejects the notion that racism is intrinsic to localism or *Bleak House*, treating that racism instead as merely a surface phenomenon, skin deep.

Ironically, this strategic anti-essentialism—or more broadly, Douglass's strategy of transformative reproduction and creative appropriation—is itself in the spirit of *Bleak House*, which, as Buzard has shown, offers numerous examples of what he calls the "ambivalent refunctioning of the cultural past," "keeping-but-changing or changing-but-keeping."[43] Moreover, the novel's interest in processes of material, textual, and symbolic circulation, appropriation, and reproduction extends to its own afterlife: an early dialogue points to what we might call the novel's refunctionability—"'Jarndyce of Bleak House, my Lord,' said Mr. Kenge. 'A dreary name,' said the Lord Chancellor. 'But not a dreary place at present, my Lord,' said Mr. Kenge" (*BH*, p. 31)—and the novel ends with an allegory of its own dissemination, as Esther moves from Bleak House to a second Bleak House, outfitted to resemble the original.

Again, though, to enter into the logic of the novel as he does, Douglass must ignore his exclusion from it since *Bleak House* in no way envisions the active participation in these processes of reproduction and appropriation of those who have been abjected from the text. The closest Dickens comes is when he has Jo repurpose "the door-step of the Society for the Propagation of the Gospel in Foreign Parts" (*BH*, p. 198) as a place to sit and eat breakfast. Yet the illiterate Jo is only unwittingly the agent of the irony here, and however similar his predicament may be to that of dark and distant others, he cannot stand for them because he is made to stand against them, and never more so than at this moment.

It is tempting to say that *Bleak House* renders the notion that those dark others might grow up to participate in this process unimaginable, except that it manifestly did not. Instead, *Douglass' Paper* so fully appropriates *Bleak House*'s logic of reproduction and appropriation that it uncannily anticipates its final expression in the novel: in the last installment of the novel, published fifteen months after one of Douglass's correspondents "dedicated a new 'Growlery,'" as we have seen, Esther reports that "With the first money we saved at home, we added to our pretty house by throwing out a little Growlery expressly for my guardian" (*BH*, p. 768). Twenty-five years later, in a crowning extension and disruption—that is, disruptive extension—of this pattern, Frederick Douglass himself followed suit: jumping national, racial, and even ontological divides, he erected a small one-room structure behind his home in Washington, D.C., and dubbed it "The Growlery."[44]

HANNAH CRAFTS'S *BLEAK HOUSE*

The treatment of *Bleak House* in *Frederick Douglass' Paper* helps inaugurate a decades-long tradition of African Americanizing deployments of Victorian literature. As we have already begun to see, such deployments vary widely in the forms they take and purposes they serve. However, among the hallmarks of this tradition—indeed, what helps make it a tradition—are the repeated recourse to specific authors and texts, and the frequent self-consciousness of this repetition, as writers and editors build on and respond to prior African Americanizations. From this perspective, the outsized presence of *Bleak House* in *Douglass' Paper* makes it fitting that the most sustained and elaborate African Americanizing rewriting of any Victorian text is a rewriting of this very novel. In some respects, though, the rewriting in question proves an outlier: while almost definitely written within a decade of the publication of Dickens's novel, this work was not published until the twenty-first century; the identity—including the race—of the author has not been definitively established; and we do not know if the author was in fact aware of the novel's enlistment by Douglass. As we shall see, however, this work not only proves fascinating in its own right and for its intriguing resonance with the treatment of *Bleak House* in *Douglass' Paper*; in addition, it comes to seem like a missing prototype, uncannily anticipating and magnifying later African Americanizing practices.

The existence of this work first became public in November 2001, in a *New York Times* article announcing Henry Louis Gates Jr.'s discovery of a previously unknown antebellum manuscript, the title page of which read "The Bondwoman's Narrative, by Hannah Crafts, a Fugitive Slave Recently Escaped from North Carolina." Although the identity of the apparently pseudonymous Hannah Crafts was and (as of this writing) remains uncertain,[45] this seemingly autobiographical first-person narrative was widely hailed for its potential status as "the earliest known novel by a female African-American slave," "the earliest known novel by a black woman anywhere," and the sole "surviving handwritten manuscript of a book by an escaped slave."[46] As is well known, however, with the publication soon thereafter of an article by Gates containing excerpts from the novel, and even more so with the publication of the book itself later in 2002, it became clear that *The Bondwoman's Narrative* borrowed extensively from other works, especially *Bleak House*. Early attempts to gauge the impact of this discovery on the work's literary and historical significance were not as edifying as one might have hoped: some critics used the charge of plagiarism to belittle or dismiss the work, while others defended Crafts by downplaying the extent and significance of her apparent debts. Partly as a result of this immediate polemicization and polarization; partly because this issue is inherently fraught due to the long history of racist skepticism concerning claims of African American authorship; and partly because of the enduring disciplinary divide between the fields of American and British literature, the relationship of *The Bondwoman's Narrative* to *Bleak House* remains poorly understood—and so too therefore does *The Bondwoman's Narrative* itself.[47]

It is evident that Crafts was not simply familiar with *Bleak House* but in fact must have written her narrative with a copy of Dickens's novel open in front of her. Consider, for example, Crafts's scene-setting description of Washington, D.C.:

Washington, the Federal City. Christmas holidays recently over. The implacable winter weather. The great President of the Great Republic looks perhaps from the windows of his drawing room, and wonders at the mud and slush precisely as an ordinary mortal would. . . .

Gloom everywhere. Gloom up the Potomac; where it rolls among meadows no longer green, and by splendid country seats. Gloom down the Potomac where it washes the sides of huge war-ships. Gloom on the marshes, the fields, and heights. Gloom settling steadily down over the sumptuous habitations of the rich, and creeping through the cellars of the poor. Gloom arresting the steps of chance office-seekers, and bewildering the heads of grave and reverend Senators; for with fog, and drizzle, and a sleety driving mist the night has come at least two hours before its time.[48]

This is, of course, a rewriting of the opening paragraphs of *Bleak House:*

London. Michaelmas Term lately over, and the Lord Chancellor sitting in Lincoln's Inn Hall. Implacable November weather. As much mud in the streets. . . .

Fog everywhere. Fog up the river, where it flows among green aits and meadows; fog down the river, where it rolls defiled among the tiers of shipping, and the waterside pollutions of a great (and dirty) city. Fog on the Essex marshes, fog on the Kentish heights. . . . Most of the shops lighted two hours before their time. (*BH*, 5)

This sort of sustained rewriting occurs frequently in *The Bondwoman's Narrative,* and begins at the beginning of the novel—which does not, however, begin with the above passage, but instead with its version of the beginning of the strand of *Bleak House* written in the other of that novel's two narrative voices. Thus, just as Esther Summerson begins the part of *Bleak House* labeled "Esther's Narrative" by stating, "I have a great deal of difficulty in beginning to write my portion of these pages, for I know I am not clever" (*BH*, p. 17), Crafts's narrator, a light-skinned, escaped slave named Hannah, begins the first chapter of *The Bondwoman's Narrative* by stating, "It may be that I assume to[o] much responsibility in attempting to write these pages. . . . I am neither clever, nor learned, nor talented" (*BN*, p. 5); and just as Esther promises "to be industrious, contented, and kind-hearted, and to do some good to some one, and win some love to myself if I could" (*BH*, p. 20), Hannah resolves "to be industrious, cheerful, and true-hearted, to do some good though in an humble way, and to win some love if I could" (*BN*, p. 11).

The Bondwoman's Narrative as a whole does not track *Bleak House* with this level of precision, but throughout the novel Crafts variously reworks, adopts, and lifts verbatim plot elements, dialogue, and characters as well as scene-setting and descriptive passages. For example, after Hannah is injured in a carriage crash, her illness and recovery are described in language recalling Esther's epochal illness, and the mansion where she recovers closely resembles Bleak House as Esther first describes it. The novel features a blackmailer, Mr. Trappe, who is closely based on *Bleak House*'s Mr. Tulkinghorn, with some of his conversations with his victim, Hannah's mistress, drawn word for word from those of Tulkinghorn and Lady Dedlock.⁴⁹ Hannah's move to Washington, D.C., produces the long pastiche of the opening paragraphs of *Bleak House* excerpted above, and when she is taken to North Carolina, Dickens's description of the London slum Tom-All-Alone's is reproduced virtually verbatim as a description of the field slaves' quarters, while his evocation of the streetsweep Jo's subjectivity is adapted to represent that of the field slaves. The final chapter of *The Bondwoman's Narrative* echoes the final chapter of *Bleak House*, as Hannah brings her story up to the time of writing, when she is living as a free woman in New Jersey, happily married to a minister and running a school. (I return to these passages below.)

Crafts draws on other works as well—for example, a description of a prison comes from Walter Scott's *Rob Roy*, and, as we shall see, the last sentence of the novel reworks that of Charlotte Brontë's *Villette*—but none nearly as extensively or centrally as *Bleak House*.⁵⁰ These debts undeniably complicate or even transform what we can learn from Crafts's work, but they hardly drain it of interest. Just the opposite, and not only for Dickens scholars: read as the lightly fictionalized autobiography of an escaped slave, as Gates first proposed reading it, *The Bondwoman's Narrative* may not tell us much we did not already know about slavery. However, once its technique is recognized, the novel emerges as a wholly unexpected and deeply enigmatic literary exercise that challenges and deepens our understanding of nineteenth-century transatlantic print culture. As I hope to show, moreover, Crafts's bricolage, in particular her reworking of *Bleak House*, does not compromise but instead generates her novel's most subtle and compelling formal effects, effects that cast *Bleak House* itself in a new light.

Crafts's technique bears comparison to the first two published novels by African Americans, William Wells Brown's *Clotel*, from 1853, and Frank J. Webb's *The Garies and Their Friends*, from 1857 (both first published in Britain), since the former borrows heavily from other texts and the second also references *Bleak House*. In contrast to *The Bondwoman's Narrative*, however,

Clotel does not rely as heavily on any single work, borrows largely from American texts explicitly concerned with slavery and freedom, and acknowledges its indebtedness (at least some of it) in its final chapter.[51] The echoes of other works in *The Garies and Their Friends*, while a little unconventional, are less extensive and more allusive than those in either *The Bondwoman's Narrative* or *Clotel*. The novel features various Dickensian tropes, an illiterate shopkeeper clearly based on *Bleak House*'s Krook, and enough borrowed character names to induce cognitive dissonance in the reader of *Bleak House* with passages such as this:

> "Oh, here he comes, and Caddy with him. They have just turned the corner—open the door and let them in."
>
> Esther arose, and on opening the door was almost knocked down by Charlie's abrupt entrance into the apartment, he being rather forcibly shoved in by his sister Caroline, who appeared to be in a high state of indignation.[52]

Yet despite this suggestive context, the sheer extent of Crafts's reliance on one particular text does seem sui generis. Moreover, there remains a true weirdness to her use of Dickens, insofar as she neither advertises nor disguises this use. For example, just as a short temperance novel serialized in *Douglass' Paper* in 1852 calls itself *Uncle William's Pulpit, or Life among the Lofty*,[53] one might expect Crafts to broadcast her work's relationship to one of the most popular novels of the day, perhaps by calling it something like "Bleak House in America"; there was, in fact, an *Uncle Tom in England*. By the same token, it makes no sense for someone who really intends to pass off her work as fully original or as having an autobiographical basis to rely so transparently on a popular novel, including passages that were immediately famous; compare, again, *Uncle William's Pulpit*: "There [Uncle William] was in his great arm chair; he was surrounded by pyramids of books. Books, books, books, books, everywhere like the fog in Dickens' story of the Bleak House—and some of them full as foggy—as the fog, we mean."[54] In short, Crafts seems steeped in the literature of the day and yet largely indifferent to the protocols of print culture.[55] It is tempting to conclude that she did not publish her novel not because she was unable to but rather because she never intended to—because, in the words of another enigmatic Americanization of *Bleak House*, she preferred not to.

Whatever Crafts's intentions, a closer look at her text reveals that her response to Dickens goes much deeper than merely taking what she needs and leaving the rest. Whereas Lord Denman sought to raze *Bleak House* and Douglass to retrofit it, Crafts renovates the novel—in part, paradoxically, by deconstructing it. This transformative effect is most immediately visible with regard to the most disturbing and potentially disabling aspect of the novel from Crafts's and Douglass's perspective, its race-based localism. Through the very act of making her Esther-figure an African American slave, Crafts does not merely defy or hijack this localism but rather breaks down its defining opposition between attention to people of color and attention to family and friends. In *The Bondwoman's Narrative*, these objects of attention are no longer separable, let alone antithetical. Nor is the opposition between near and far reconstituted by the substitution of another distant other. This is not because *The Bondwoman's Narrative* is truly cosmopolitan or without its own prejudices but rather because Crafts is attacking institutions and attitudes—and institutions more than attitudes—that promote subordination and exploitation rather than disorder and neglect, as in *Bleak House*. That is, while Crafts may want to call attention to the suffering of slaves, she does not argue that this suffering is the direct result of inattention, the way it is for Dickens's lumpenproletariat. On the contrary, she makes it clear that the condition of the slaves she describes is a matter of policy on the part of their owner, who "didn't think it worth while to take much pains with such brutalised specimens of humanity," believing that "They could work just as well, and it might be even better to leave them alone in their degradation," since "he expected nothing of them but toil. He wanted nothing else" (*BN*, p. 207). Tellingly, Crafts imagines field slaves thinking Jo's thought that he has "no business here, there, or anywhere," but immediately adds the phrase "except just to work—work—work" (*BN*, p. 206). Dickens's rhetoric of misdirected attention drops away.

This shift in focus creates a further, striking change in emphasis in Crafts's recasting of Jo's thought processes as those of the field slaves. "It must be a strange state to be like Jo!" writes Dickens, and that strangeness has two key, related components: first, Jo's illiteracy, as he "shuffle[s] through the streets, unfamiliar with the shapes, and in utter darkness as to the meaning, of those mysterious symbols, so abundant over the shops, and at the corners of streets, and on the doors, and in the windows" (*BH*, p. 198); and second, Jo's sense of exclusion: "To be hustled, and jostled, and moved on; and really to feel that it would appear to be perfectly true that I have no business, here, or there, or anywhere; and yet to be perplexed by the consideration that I *am* here somehow, too, and everybody overlooked me until I became the creature that I am!" (*BH*, p. 198). Crafts's version of this passage pays less attention to literacy, noting that the Constitution and the Bible are "sealed book[s]" to the field slaves but transforming the initial description of Jo's illiteracy into one of the slaves' ignorance of nature: "Isn't it a strange state to be like them," she writes. "To shuffle up and down the lanes unfamiliar with the flowers, and in utter darkness as to the meaning of Nature's various hieroglyphical symbols, so abundant on the trees, the skies, in the leaves of grass, and everywhere" (*BN*, p. 206). This is a surprising revision in light of slave narratives' typical emphasis on the importance of literacy. In part this shift results from Crafts's relocation of the scene from an urban to a rural setting, but it also reflects the change in emphasis from the neglect that Jo's illiteracy epitomizes to the active exploitation and brutalization to which the slaves are subjected, and which are better captured in other ways: thus, Crafts also adds the sentence, "It must be a strange state to be prized just according to the firmness of your joints, the strength of your sinews, and your capabilities of endurence [*sic*]" (*BN*, p. 206).

The preference for the proximate that we have seen on display in *Bleak House* works in tandem with its frequent retreat from institutions to individuals, the social to the domestic, and politics to ethics.[56] Crafts's abandonment of the rhetoric of abandonment signals her refusal of this retreat, and even of these dichotomies, which both structure and trouble Dickens's novel. Despite the attention to forced labor we have just seen, the key move here is the treatment of sexual exploitation and the destruction of families as defining features of American slavery.[57] Consider, for example, Crafts's reworking of the expression of outrage and readerly implication that concludes Jo's last scene, discussed above. Crafts's version of this passage comes not when she is describing the Jo-like field slaves but instead when Hannah's fellow slave Lizzy tells the story of her master's "haram [*sic*]" of slaves and "their lovely children" (*BN*, pp. 177, 182): rather than allow her child to be sold, one of these women kills her infant and herself. With an improbability that only confirms the stakes here for Crafts, Lizzy concludes her story with these words: "A slight spasm, a convulsive shudder and she was dead. Dead, your Excellency, the President of this Republic. Dead, grave senators who grow eloquent over pensions and army wrongs. Dead ministers of religion, who prate because poor men without a moment[']s leisure on other days presume to read the newspapers on Sunday, yet who wink at, or approve of laws that occasion such scenes as this" (*BN*, p. 183). As in her rewriting of *Bleak House*'s opening, Crafts Americanizes a passage virtually word by word, only here she replaces Dickens's powerfully expansive yet nonetheless geographically and analytically circumscribed concluding sentence ("And dying thus around us every day") with an emphatic reminder of institutional contexts and causes: "laws that occasion such scenes as this."

Crafts's use of the rhetoric attending Jo's death to address the control of women's sexuality and the forced separation of mother and child is even more striking because these matters are also central to the plot of *Bleak House*, only there they are separated from the novel's main political and social agendas. Esther is removed at birth from her mother, Lady Dedlock, because she is illegitimate, and Lady Dedlock is subject to blackmail because she has borne a child out of wedlock. *Bleak House* is critical of the stigma attached to illegitimacy, but it does not defend sex outside marriage. Moreover, as important as these scenarios are to the novel, neither is directly linked to what it presents as its more public concerns, such as Chancery and poverty—or at least, as Hilary Schor has argued, the links are largely occluded, with Esther doing the occluding.[58] By contrast, Crafts broadcasts the equivalent connections in her novel, so that when she retells *Bleak House*'s stories of blackmail and mother-daughter separation, she tells them as stories about slavery. Thus, whereas Lady Dedlock's secret is her scandalous liaison with Esther's father, the secret of the woman similarly blackmailed in *The Bondwoman's Narrative*, Hannah's mistress, is her race: as her blackmailer has discovered, she was removed from her slave mother as a baby to take the place of her owner's dead child.[59] The Tulkinghornian blackmailer, Mr. Trappe, uses his knowledge to extort money from Hannah's mistress, and when she is no longer able to pay he threatens to expose her real parentage, at which point, like Lady Dedlock, she takes flight and dies.

Although Hannah's mistress relives the experience of Lady Dedlock, then, she more closely resembles Esther Summerson—that is, not the unmarried mother but the illegitimate daughter separated from her mother at birth, not a sexual transgressor but instead an innocent victim of an unjust society—and in Hannah's mistress's case, though not Esther's, a victim of what her novel presents as her society's defining injustice.[60] Similarly, Hannah's own resemblance to Esther goes beyond the personality traits and experiences noted earlier to include early separation from her mother (of whom she has no memory and no knowledge except for the racial identity that is inferable from her own enslavement, and which explains the separation itself). At the end of her narrative, however, Hannah's story breaks dramatically from Esther's when she is reunited with her mother in New Jersey. As blatant wish-fulfillment that hardly bothers to deny its status as such—Crafts writes, "We met accidentally, where or how it matters not" (*BN*, p. 245)—this ending threatens to go beyond escape to escapism. This threat seems to be confirmed by the novel's lack of a final call for political action, a typical gesture in slave narratives and abolitionist fiction. However, because Crafts has represented the separation of mothers and children as one of slavery's greatest evils, the wish being fulfilled here should be understood as political, and as much a syllogism completed as a wish fulfilled: if slavery is identified with mother-child separation, then freedom must mean mother-child reunification.

Esther too meets her mother, but whereas Hannah and her mother see their reunion and the close bond they form as "the greatest blessing of [their] lives" (*BN*, p. 245), Esther has only one meaningful encounter with Lady Dedlock, whose self-described "earthly punishment" (*BH*, p. 450) is that she cannot acknowledge her daughter publicly without disgracing her husband's family. Indeed, while Hannah finds herself "nearly crazy with delight" to be "then resting for the first time on [her] mother's bosom" (*BN*, p. 245), Esther can only thank God that the scars from her illness have left her so changed that she "could never disgrace her [mother] by any trace of likeness" (*BH*, p. 449). *Bleak House* presents this separation of mother and daughter as a personal tragedy, divorced from the social ones it describes. In terms of both the events narrated and the meaning they carry, then, the gap between the two texts is at its widest here.[61]

Strikingly, however, even here, where Crafts departs radically from *Bleak House*, she continues to rewrite it virtually line by line. As with the relocation of Borrioboola Gha to Europe in *Douglass' Paper*, the effect is truly startling; for example, the weeping Lady Dedlock's anguished "O my child, my child, I am your wicked and unhappy mother! O try to forgive me!" (*BH*, p. 449) becomes Hannah's mother's "child, I am your mother," words now "sobbed out in rapturous joy" (*BN*, p. 245). The very image that encapsulates the fulfillment granted to Hannah but denied to Esther, and that thus epitomizes Crafts's departure from Dickens—"then resting for the first time on my mother's bosom" (*BN*, p. 245)—is itself lifted verbatim from *Bleak House* (*BH*, p. 449). With a similar violence, Crafts rewrites the opening sentence of the omniscient narrator's last chapter in *Bleak House* to form the first sentence of her own final chapter, transforming a sentence describing the sense of defeat and shame in Lady Dedlock's household after her death into a description of Hannah's enduring contentment: "There is a hush upon Chesney Wold in these altered days, as there is upon a portion of the family history" (*BH*, p. 763) morphs into "There is a hush on my spirit in these days, a deep repose a blest and holy quietude" (*BN*, p. 244). It is only in the novel's last sentence that Dickens is truly left behind: whereas *Bleak House* ends in midsentence with Esther's "they can very well do without much beauty in me—even supposing——" (*BH*, p. 770), *The Bondwoman's Narrative* ends with syntactic as well as narrative closure, as Hannah assures the reader that she cannot adequately describe her happiness and writes, "I will let the reader picture it all to his imagination and say farewell" (*BN*, p. 246). However, while this final sentence owes nothing to Dickens, it recalls—and, as with the last borrowings from *Bleak House*, not only recalls but, in its very sunniness, also perverts—the famously perverse ending of Charlotte Brontë's *Villette*, where narrator Lucy Snowe "leave[s] sunny imaginations hope" that her fiancé has not died and lets them "picture union and a happy succeeding life" before ending with the same word as Hannah, "Farewell."[62] Continuing to the last to rely on British novelists, even as it makes free with their work, *The Bondwoman's Narrative* thus enacts on the level of form the complex play of autonomy and dependence missing from its utopian ending.[63]

CODA: CHARLES DICKENS'S *FREDERICK DOUGLASS*

A focus on the reception and reworkings of a particular literary work runs the risk of insinuating a categorical if not ontological distinction between that work and those reworkings: even if the latter are viewed as creative or imaginative or transformative or critical, as opposed to merely derivative, their very treatment as reactions or responses to a prior text can lend that text an aura of originality, singularity, and primacy which they themselves lack. The preceding discussion and this book as a whole seek to show that this is a risk worth running for the insights it generates into both Victorian literature and African American literature and print culture. However, the pitfalls this risk entails are also worth guarding against, in several ways: by recalling and taking seriously the intertextual nature of all literary works; relatedly, by calling into question the very hierarchy that grants ontological or aesthetic priority to the chronologically prior; by considering the "source" text's own sources; by being alert to the possibility of reciprocal influence or presence; and, finally, by attending to the ways African American writers themselves addressed this issue.

With regard to *Bleak House*, I will conclude by noting that the rich intertextual stew out of which *Bleak House* emerges includes, importantly, American ingredients. It is not exactly a secret that *Bleak House* is indebted to *The House of the Seven Gables* and *The Scarlet Letter*, although this is also not something scholars have thought through in light of recent decades' work on national identity, realism and romance, the gothic, print culture, and the like. Ironically, *The Bondwoman's Narrative* makes Dickens's relationship to Hawthorne newly pertinent, as some aspects of Crafts's novel that have been traced back to the latter's work are more accurately described as re-workings of Dickens's reworkings.[64]

More of a secret—that is, a question that has not really been asked—is the extent to which *Bleak House* may be in dialogue with and positioned in the literary field in relation to African American writings. For example, we have seen how Hannah Crafts wrenches Esther's narrative out of context, but perhaps we should also view the very word *narrative* in the recurring chapter title "Esther's Narrative" in the context of the widespread circulation of slave narratives, including preeminently *The Narrative of the Life of Frederick Douglass*. Recall that Esther's most obvious precursor, Jane Eyre, writes an "autobiography," not a "narrative." Like Esther's telltale resemblance to her mother, then, the word *narrative* may suggest a kinship the novel is otherwise eager to disavow.

I would not push this argument too far: it is obviously not the case that Douglass's *Narrative* is to *Bleak House* as *Bleak House* is to *The Bondwoman's Narrative*. However, if we turn in closing to a passage in one of Dickens's letters, we see that Dickens did in fact take a page from Douglass's *Narrative*. As shocking as it is enigmatic, this gesture manages to capture quite neatly what Douglass and, even more so, Crafts do to Dickens: "Here is Frederick Douglass," Dickens wrote to a friend in 1848, sending him a copy of the *Narrative*. "There was such a hideous and abominable portrait of him in the book, that I have torn it out, fearing it might set you, by anticipation, against the narrative."[65] Just as Dickens here reframes Douglass's *Narrative*, so too does Douglass reframe Dickens's; and just as Dickens combines admiration and aggression in a violent sundering of text from author, so too does Crafts, who similarly defaces Dickens's text in the very act of transmitting it.

Bleak House is undoubtedly the longest Victorian text reprinted in the African American press, and *The Bondwoman's Narrative* the most sustained and intensive African Americanizing reworking of a Victorian text. Yet while the African Americanization of *Bleak House* is therefore not typical, it does prove exemplary, as over the course of the following half-century virtually all the forms its African Americanization takes recur in the treatment of other Victorian works. What the treatment of *Bleak House* itself does not anticipate, however, is the way that the fraught questions of originality and derivativeness and the politics of appropriation raised *by* the practices of African Americanization will also be raised and addressed *through* such practices. As we shall see in the next chapter, however, this self-reflexive turn occurs very soon after the reprinting of *Bleak House* in *Frederick Douglass' Paper*, and in the pages of *Douglass' Paper* itself.

CHAPTER TWO

(RE-)RACIALIZING "THE CHARGE OF THE LIGHT BRIGADE"

In a 1990 episode of the television sitcom *The Fresh Prince of Bel-Air* wittily titled "Def Poets' Society," Will Smith joins the school poetry club. Commending this newfound interest in poetry (which of course is really an interest in girls), Geoffrey, the family's excruciatingly proper Afro-British butler, informs Will that he too loves poetry, and in fact received first prize at the All-Devonshire Poetry Recital of 1963. Reliving his triumph, he begins to recite:

> Cannon to the right of them,
> Cannon to the left of them,
> Cannon in front of them
> Volleyed and thundered.

The choice of "The Charge of the Light Brigade" by the makers of *The Fresh Prince* accurately reflects its status as an enduring favorite for the study of elocution.[1] What I want to call attention to is the role the poem takes on here as a marker, even (given its presumptive recognizability) an icon, of squareness—which is to say, of whiteness. This identification is reinforced later in the episode, when, for reasons that need not concern us, Geoffrey gets disguised in Afro and dashiki as "street poet" Raphael de la Ghetto. After reciting a poem that begins "Listen to the street beat" and ends "Listen, or I'll kill ya!" he responds to the cries of "Encore!" by launching into "The Charge of the Light Brigade," thereby blowing his cover and quickly losing the formerly rapt audience. The episode ends soon thereafter with

Will's aunt reciting a poem by Amiri Baraka. Canon to the right of them, canon to the left of them, indeed.

"The Charge of the Light Brigade" is a good choice to play the role it plays in *The Fresh Prince* because its subject matter—a disastrous advance by British cavalry in the Crimean War—and perhaps, more subtly, its cadence (which contrasts with that of Will Smith's rapping, with which the episode opens) make the poem seem ludicrously removed from the experiences, interests, and expressive traditions of African Americans. What makes "The Light Brigade" an inspired choice, however, is not the self-evidence of this contrast but its history and historicity: there exists, in other words, a history of placing Tennyson's poem in relation to African American culture, and this history is one in which this relationship has been variously construed and vigorously contested. As I will show, from the moment it was published, "The Charge of the Light Brigade" was mobilized, especially though not exclusively by African Americans, as a site or tool to address the kinds of issues adumbrated by *The Fresh Prince*: the relationship of African Americans to the dominant cultural tradition; the nature and politics of interracial cultural rivalry, mimicry, and appropriation; and the role of poetry and the arts—and violence ("I'll kill ya!")—in the fight for racial empowerment and equality.

The unlikeliness of "The Charge of the Light Brigade" filling this role reflects not only the poem's subject matter but also its subsequent reputation as, in Jerome McGann's words, "Tennyson at his most 'official' and most 'Victorian'—a period piece."[2] While the historicist turn in literary criticism that McGann's 1982 treatment of "The Light Brigade" advocated and exemplifies transformed the poem's marked historical embeddedness into a source of value and interest (rather than contempt), this shift nevertheless has left intact an understanding of Tennyson's poem as inextricably linked to the time and place of its composition and initial publication; thus, much recent scholarship on the poem focuses on specifying how the poem derives from and participates in the discourse attending the Crimean War.[3] Yet the poem's history is one of unusually widespread circulation and promiscuous susceptibility to adaptation and appropriation. (Paradoxically, even the poem's felt obsolescence has contributed to its enduring cultural presence: think of the aging Victorian patriarch Mr. Ramsay in *To the Lighthouse*, with his self-dramatizing, self-pitying habit of reciting the poem to himself—not to mention *The Fresh Prince*.) Despite the insights they generate, then, efforts to locate Tennyson's poem in its original historical context run the risk of construing that context too narrowly and freezing in one particular time and place a poem remarkable precisely for its broad appeal, longevity, and adaptability. This is a danger, I would suggest, to which the dominant recent modes of historicist work are especially prone, precisely because of their commitment to reconstructing the discursive context out of which a particular text emerges.

Consider the criticism McGann himself makes of Henry David Thoreau in his groundbreaking "Light Brigade" essay: quoting Thoreau's comment that the charge of the Light Brigade proves "what a perfect machine the soldier is," McGann says that "Thoreau's view of the poem and its recorded events is based upon a gross misreading not only of the objective facts of the situation, but of the British response to those events," a misreading Mc-Gann links to Thoreau's "alien American vantage."[4] As we shall see, the nature and extent of this vantage's alienness is and was debatable; indeed, Paul Giles has shown how Thoreau works to establish the distinctiveness and autonomy of American identity in the very text McGann cites.[5] With regard to "The Light Brigade" in particular, McGann's curious decontextu-alization of Thoreau's remarks (curious because it comes in the midst of an argument for historical contextualization) misrepresents Thoreau's inten-tion and neglects or even, in its dismissiveness, obscures the real interest of his statement. Here is the complete sentence from Thoreau's text, an 1859 speech titled "A Plea for Captain John Brown":

> The momentary charge at Balaclava, in obedience to a blundering command, proving what a perfect machine the soldier is, has, prop-erly enough, been celebrated by a poet laureate; but the steady, and for the most part successful, charge of this man [John Brown], for some years, against the legions of Slavery, in obedience to an infinitely higher command, is as much more memorable than that, as an intel-ligent and conscientious man is superior to a machine.[6]

McGann's criticism seems misguided insofar as Thoreau is clearly not trying to explicate the poem but rather to put it to use, rhetorically. Such a use is worth exploring on its own terms. This is especially so in this case because, as I will show, Thoreau is participating in a tradition that begins before and extends after him: that is, a tradition of deploying "The Charge of the Light Brigade" to think about antislavery violence. The recovery of this tradition promises to produce a more capacious understanding of the cultural work Tennyson's warhorse of a poem has been called upon to perform.

Attention to this tradition can also alter our view of the poem itself. The example of Thoreau is again to the point: Thoreau's ostensible "misreading" of the poem, if it is a misreading at all, is not "gross" but strong: after all, one meaning of "machine" is "a person who acts mechanically or unthinkingly, as from habit or obedience" ("Machine," *OED*, def. 8b.), and the nobility of Tennyson's soldiers lies precisely, notoriously, in their willingness to obey an order without "reason[ing] why." Conversely, Thoreau's belittling description of the Light Brigade's charge as "momentary," in contrast to John Brown's "steady" effort, blatantly disregards the work the poem does to impart just such a sense of steadiness and prolongation to the Light Brigade's action (especially through the use of repetition, as in the opening lines "Half a league, half a league, / Half a league onward"); yet by the same token, Thoreau's drawing of this contrast calls attention to this aspect of the poem and suggests its stakes.[7] Thus, insofar as Thoreau's "vantage" differs from that of Tennyson's English readers, this difference works to our advantage as well as his, as it produces insight into the nature and limitations of what Tennyson values about the charge of the Light Brigade. We will remain alert to the opportunity to garner similar insights from other contributions to the tradition at hand—a tradition, as we shall see, that itself quickly engages the very question of the value of such insights in the cause or in the face of matters of great political urgency.

RELOCATING TENNYSON

"The Charge of the Light Brigade" was first published in the London *Examiner* on December 9, 1854, five weeks after the event it describes. Among the many publications that quickly reprinted the poem was *Frederick Douglass' Paper*, which ran the poem on January 12, 1855. As we saw in chapter 1, *Douglass' Paper*—the most prominent antebellum publication owned and edited by an African American—routinely reprinted new British literature, running it alongside cultural reporting and original work by African American and white American authors as well as miscellaneous items from Dickens's *Household Words* and other British periodicals. We have also seen that, while the American poetry and prose tended to be explicitly political or reformist, and often came from authors closely associated with the antislavery movement, the selections from British writers were more eclectic, with authors' prominence rather than their declared or perceived political commitments often decisive.

The reprinting of a widely circulated poem by Britain's poet laureate—prestigious, popular, and not known as a political activist—would seem to fit this model, but in fact this is not simply a case of the anglophile Douglass and his English literary editor, Julia Griffiths, showing their fealty to the canon in front of them. The Tennyson that emerges over the years in *Frederick Douglass' Paper* has—or is ascribed—a politics, and a congenial one at that. The paper first published his work in 1851, soon after it began publication, reprinting the "Ring out, wild bells" section of the previous year's *In Memoriam*. This selection's call to "Ring in redress to all mankind" holds clear appeal for a reform-minded newspaper—and indeed, the reprinting of the poem in the context provided by *Douglass' Paper* has the effect of giving specific content to the poem's vague utopianism. Two years later, this implicit enlistment of Tennyson in the paper's cause received confirmation of a sort when it was reported that Tennyson's wife was among the thousands of signatories of an abolitionist petition from "the ladies of England"; a brief item in the paper wonders whether this will lead some supporters of slavery to refuse to read the poet's work.[8]

Viewed, then, in the context of these other appearances by Tennyson and *Douglass' Paper*'s literary offerings more generally, the appearance of "The Charge of the Light Brigade" is nothing out of the ordinary. Framed differently, however, "The Light Brigade" does stand out, not as an enigma but just the opposite, as one of the most transparently motivated British works to appear in *Frederick Douglass' Paper*. For "The Charge of the Light Brigade at Balaklava"—to give the poem its full title as printed in *Douglass' Paper*—was one item among many the paper published about the Crimean War. This coverage treats the war as a world-historical event and, more specifically, one front among several (including of course the antislavery movement itself) in the international battle for human rights and democracy. For example, one article celebrates the fall of Sebastopol to British and French troops as a victory over "the great Autocrat of Europe" and declares that "the hypocritical sympathies of American Republicanism in [Russia's] behalf, will do her no good whatever."[9] Another piece published the same day goes even further in forging this connection: calling for a "convention of ideas," the paper's New York correspondent writes, "Old Thomas Aquinas held such a meeting when he discovered that 'all men are born equal.' ... I rather think the general or public meeting which Aquinas inaugurated, and at which Jefferson reported his celebrated 'Declaration,' is not yet adjourned: committees are out, which are yet to report, some at Sebastopol, some in Kansas."[10] If "The Charge of the Light Brigade" is relevant to an antislavery readership, then, it is not because the poem transcends its occasion, but rather because its occasion, properly understood, transcends the particular time and place of its setting. This relevance was sufficiently evident that another leading abolitionist journal, the New York–based *National Anti-Slavery Standard*, also reprinted the poem, one day after *Douglass' Paper*.

While the appearance of "The Charge of the Light Brigade" in *Frederick Douglass' Paper* may have been unremarkable, the poem itself did not go unremarked. In contrast to most of the poems and stories published in *Douglass' Paper*, which inspired no further comment,[11] "The Light Brigade" immediately became part of the discourse of the paper, serving as a resource in the ongoing dialogue among its African American contributors. The first, most sustained, and most provocative of these rhetorical mobilizations of "The Light Brigade" appeared in the same issue as the poem itself. In fact, it appeared on the page *preceding* that on which "The Light Brigade" was printed, the recto to the poem's verso. As we shall see, this upsetting of priorities proves entirely apt.

This piece, headlined "From Our New York Correspondent" and bearing the specification "For Frederick Douglass' Paper," is by James McCune Smith, the same writer who later aligns Sebastopol with Kansas. A regular contributor to *Douglass' Paper* under the pseudonym "Communipaw," Smith was the first African American to earn a medical degree (from the University of Glasgow) and has been called "the foremost black intellectual in nineteenth-century America."[12] His column's treatment of the "Light Brigade" takes the form of a dialogue with "Fylbel," a version of Smith's friend Philip A. Bell, himself a leading African American editor and activist and regular contributor to *Douglass' Paper*. Fylbel begins by asking Communipaw his opinion of the first two lines of Tennyson's new poem, which he quotes approvingly. Communipaw responds with an appreciative formal analysis that takes the Western literary tradition as its frame of reference: Tennyson's opening, he declares, "beats Virgil's *'quatit ungula campum;'* for we have not only the sound of the horses' feet, as they begin with a canter, but the rush into the gallop. . . ."[13] However, when Fylbel next quotes the same four lines we saw Geoffrey the butler recite in *The Fresh Prince* ("Cannon to the right of them," etc.), Communipaw abruptly withdraws his approval of the poem with the startling accusation, "Flat burglary! . . . Tennyson has stolen the sweep's blanket." He then goes on to advance an understanding of the poem diametrically opposed to that evoked by *The Fresh Prince*, where, as we saw, the poem's metrical form, historical referent, Englishness, and history as a recitation piece combined to signify whiteness. Here, by contrast, Smith declares that these lines are "a translation from the Congo, feebler than the original."

Elaborating on this surprising claim, Smith juxtaposes Tennyson's lines with a Congo chant "as old as—Africa": "Canga bafio te, / Canga moune de le, / Canga do ki la, / Canga li." Communipaw does not know the meaning of the chant's words; what he is arguing, rather, is that Tennyson has "stolen" the chant as a formal construct—the anaphora, the stressed first syllable "can," the short line-length, and, roughly, the meter. This form itself, moreover, seems to have a content, and one that the chant more or less shares with Tennyson's poem as, before learning anything else about it, Fylbel responds "Hurrah for our mother-land! 'Canga li!' Glorious war cry; it beats 'Volleyed and thundered,' out of sight." Fylbel's identification of the poem's function proves correct, as Communipaw goes on to explain that the chant was used to call slaves to rebel in Saint Domingo. Having first been transported beyond the site of its origination by enslaved Africans brought to the New World, the chant achieved wider dissemination via the circuits of cosmopolitan print culture, making it possible for Tennyson to have learned about it the same way Smith did: by reading about it in a French periodical. Smith even provides the citation ("Look in the *Revue des Deux Mondes*, Vol. 4ᵗʰ, page 1040").[14]

The relative "feeble[ness]" of Tennyson's poem, it turns out, is implicitly performative as well as aesthetic. Quoting (and translating) his source, Smith explains that the chant helped transform "indifferent and heedless slaves into furious masses, and hurled them into those incredible combats in which stupid courage balked all tactics, and naked flesh struggled against steel." Thus, whereas Tennyson's poem commemorates an advance against superior forces, the chant inspires such an advance—which, unlike the Light Brigade's, is ultimately successful. Thrilled by what he learns from Communipaw—and as if intent on matching or exceeding the outrageousness of Communipaw's accusation against Tennyson—Fylbel envisions using the Congo chant to reproduce the Haitian Revolution in the United States. Suggesting that "'Canga li' must yet ring in the interior of Africa," he proposes renewing the African slave-trade to import a million Africans a year for six years: "then, in six years," he reasons, "away down in the sunny South, these six millions of 'children of the sun,' restless under the lash, and uncontaminated, unenfeebled by American Christianity, may hear in their midst 'Canga li,' and the affrighted slave owners . . . will rush away North faster than they did from St Domingo."[15]

In Smith's column, then, Tennyson's account of the heroic but doomed actions of British soldiers both derives from and gives rise to visions of equally heroic—but not always doomed—slave rebellions. While this account of the origins of Tennyson's poem is unique to Smith, the rest of the pattern he establishes proves remarkably enduring. We will track it over the course of the century, but to see it a second time one need only turn the page of *Douglass' Paper:* there, "The Charge of the Light Brigade" itself appears, followed immediately by another poem, "Loguen's Position," by E. P. Rogers. In this dramatic monologue, written by one African American minister and activist in the voice of another, the speaker describes himself as a fugitive who will not allow himself to be "drag[ged] back / To servitude again":

> I would not turn upon my heel,
> To flee my master's power;
> But if he come within my grasp,
> He *falls* the self same hour.

The speaker acknowledges that he "may be wrong" to reject "godlike" forgiveness, but he rejects it nonetheless—"But, were your soul in my soul's stead, / You'd doubtless, feel as strong"—even as he ends with an appeal for God's help:

> Hasten, oh God! The joyful day,
> When Slavery shall not be
> When millions, now confined in chains,
> Shall sound a jubilee.

The layout of this column of *Douglass' Paper* thus recapitulates the discursive movement of Smith's article from Tennyson's poem to an embrace of violent resistance to slavery and anticipation of slavery's end. It is as if the speaker of Rogers's poem, like the reader of *Douglass's Paper,* has just read "The Charge of the Light Brigade," and done so through the lens Smith provides.

At the same time, the fact that the closing prayer in "Loguen's Position" finesses the link between the speaker's violence and the desired jubilee underscores how radical, if fantastic, Fylbel's vision is. Communipaw himself retreats from Fylbel's revolutionary plan, telling him not to raise his voice and changing the subject (even as Smith, of course, puts the plan in print). However, Communipaw (and Smith) are not done with Tennyson's poem. Having viewed the poem through the lens of the antislavery struggle, Smith nimbly reverses course and uses the poem itself as a lens through which to view that struggle: claiming that Oliver Johnson, editor of the rival *National*

Anti-Slavery Standard (which, as noted above, also published "The Charge of the Light Brigade"), "said 'some one [i.e., Communipaw] had blundered,'" Smith responds by offering what may be the first in the long history of "Light Brigade" parodies and pastiches, one that capitalizes on the serendipitously trochaic names of his putative opponents within the abolitionist movement: "Wilson to right of them, / Chapman to left of them, / Johnson in front of them, / Volleyed and thundered."[16] Communipaw and Fylbel spin out this allegorical reworking ("You don't mean to say Johnson cussed in volleys, do you?"), and the conversation ends with Fylbel asking "what, connected with your light Brigade, fits in with 'all the world wondered,'" to which Communipaw replies, "Why, all the world wondered to see in the columns of the *National Anti-Slavery Standard* a light brigade of readable matter, not scissored from the New York Tribune, nor transcribed from Mother Goose's melodies, nor Sinbad the Sailor." In this final rhetorical maneuver, Smith's extravagantly arbitrary metaphorization of "light brigade" repeats in miniature his radical recontextualization of "The Light Brigade" as a whole. These creative appropriations contrast sharply with the mechanical practices of "scissor[ing] and "transcrib[ing]"—practices that recall in turn the thievery of the poet laureate himself, who has "stolen the sweep's blanket."

Faced with this rhetorically slippery, tonally ambiguous treatment of "The Charge of the Light Brigade," one is tempted to paraphrase General Bosquet's famous remark about the charge itself: *c'est magnifique, mais ce n'est pas le poème.* James McCune Smith might easily concede this point, while denying its significance: like Thoreau a few years later, he clearly seeks to make use of "The Charge of the Light Brigade" for his own purposes. I will argue below that Smith's treatment of "The Light Brigade" does in fact reveal more about the poem than simply its ready availability for appropriation. First, though, we should ask: if Smith is using "The Light Brigade" for his own purposes, what are those purposes? What does he hope to accomplish through his deployment of "The Charge of the Light Brigade"?

Accusations of plagiarism were common in mid-nineteenth-century American print culture.[17] Then as now, such claims served as sources of rhetorical and cultural authority. Indeed, Smith returns to the matter of plagiarism after he leaves "The Light Brigade" behind, this time claiming that a recent column in *Douglass' Paper*, by the regular contributor William Wilson (who published under the name "Ethiop"), contained two stolen passages: "the description of the Irish is vivid, only needing quotation marks and a reference to Frederick Douglass' Address at Western Reserve College, from which it is copied with considerable accuracy"; "I don't know that he has read Miss Brontë's *Villete* [*sic*], else I would say that Dr. John [from that novel] and Mr. Meagher [from Wilson's piece] had been drawn at the same sitting." Smith does not bother to flesh out these accusations (there are no quotations, from either Wilson or his supposed sources), as if to underscore the authority that accrues from the very act of making them, or the role of his own authoritativeness in giving the charges weight.[18]

Smith's claims themselves may seem strained or hyperbolic, but they are not outrageous by the standards of the day, for example in comparison to the best-known such charge, Poe's attacks on Longfellow.[19] As Pierre Bourdieu might put it, Smith is playing the game of literary and cultural criticism according to its prevailing rules. And playing it gleefully, as is made plain by yet another accusation of plagiarism by Smith in an earlier column; describing his discovery of the historian George Bancroft's supposed borrowings from William Whewell's *The Plurality of Worlds*, Smith writes, "Before I had finished the fourth paragraph, I clapped my hands and shouted, as Byron did, when he detected in Ivanhoe fourteen gems culled from Shakespeare within a few pages."[20]

Like Poe, though, Smith displays his true mastery by not only playing the game but playing with the game, pushing its rules to their limits. In particular, he pushes the question of relative originality and derivativeness to the extremes of an originality so absolute as to seem originless ("old as Africa"), on the one hand, and an indebtedness that is sheer repetition ("flat burglary"), on the other.[21] At the same time (to slide from one Bourdieuian metaphor to another), Smith expands the boundaries of the playing field, in two ways: first, by virtue of his own participation as an African American, and second, in his treatment of plagiarism as not only what we might call white-on-white (Bancroft/Whewell) and black-on-white (Wilson/Brontë), but also black-on-black (Wilson/Douglass) and, crucially, white-on-black (Tennyson/Congo). Given prevailing beliefs in the fundamental imitativeness of members of the African race and the absence of cultural or aesthetic value in their artifacts and activities, the notion of influence and indebtedness running in this direction is almost unthinkable at the time.

Such a notion is perhaps rendered less unthinkable by the contemporary popularity of blackface minstrelsy, a genre of performance Eric Lott has identified as "the first formal public acknowledgment by whites of black culture."[22] Yet it is one thing to ask "Why may not the banjoism of a Congo, an Ethiopian or a George Christy [a famous blackface performer], aspire to an equality with the musical and poetical delineators of all nationalities?," as a writer in another antislavery journal asks a few months after Smith's column, and another to argue that such equality or even superiority has been achieved; one thing to accuse "the filthy scum of white society" of "hav[ing] stolen from us a complexion denied to them by nature, in which to make money, and pander to the corrupt taste of their white fellow citizens," as Frederick Douglass wrote of blackface performers in his newspaper in 1848, and another to lodge an accusation of theft against the most prestigious living practitioner of what was arguably the society's most prestigious cultural form.[23] Smith's claim of African influence on high Western culture is quite possibly unprecedented, and even if his specific accusation proves unpersuasive, it introduces the profoundly subversive possibility of such influence. What matters most about the scenario Smith describes, then, is less its truth-content than its very expression, its being put into discourse. For Smith, no less than Tennyson, a (seemingly) wild charge can fail on one level and still succeed on another.

Similar considerations underwrite Smith's deployment of "The Light Brigade" in his quarrel with the *National Anti-Slavery Standard*. As we saw, Smith claims that the editor of that paper had used the phrase "some one had blundered" in reference to Smith. In fact, the *Standard* had not quoted Tennyson's poem, but it had called Smith "a mendacious blunderer."[24] The timing of this name-calling, only two weeks after the London publication of the poem and three weeks before its reprinting in both *Douglass' Paper* and the *National Anti-Slavery Standard*, makes it unlikely that an allusion to Tennyson was intended. However, by retroactively turning the line into an allusion Smith again conjures a vision of an interracial, cosmopolitan discursive field, just as he did when tracing Tennyson's poem back to Africa via Haitian revolutionaries and French reporting. Moreover, this swerve in the deployment of Tennyson's poem from violent revolution to literary rivalry is not as great as it seems, for the column in question had claimed that the *Anti-Slavery Standard* did not adequately support the antislavery efforts of African Americans. As with Tennyson's plagiarism and the Haitian Revolution, then, at issue here is the proper crediting of Africans and African Americans, and the crediting of them in particular with agency in fighting for their own freedom and equality. This emancipation and equality are intellectual as well as political and are what Smith's bravura performance is designed to demonstrate as well as what it demands.

Smith's agenda becomes more explicit in a companion piece published two months later. This essay, centering on a performance by the African American singer Elizabeth Greenfield, the so-called "Black Swan," argues for the crucial role of the artistic achievements of "negros" in cultivating racial pride and combating discrimination. Gazing at Greenfield's integrated audience, Smith asserts that "True Art is a leveler."[25] Crucially, however (and I will return to this point), this interracial leveling works not by leaving race behind but rather through its affirmation: thus, Smith particularly admires Greenfield for refusing to bend "to the requirements of American Prejudice" by "shrinking . . . under the cover of an Indian or a Moorish descent," but instead "stand[ing] forth simple and pure a black woman." "There is one thing our people must learn, and the victory is won," Smith declares. "We must learn to love, respect and glory in our negro nature!"[26]

This column does not mention Tennyson explicitly, but the reader schooled in Smith's own hermeneutic techniques has no trouble detecting his reworking of elements from "The Light Brigade": while Tennyson enjoins us to "Honor the Light Brigade, / Noble six hundred!" Smith describes a company of the same size, similarly surrounded and outnumbered, witnessing if not performing a spectacular display of nobility: Greenfield's concert, he reports, was attended by "upwards of two thousand persons . . . of whom at least six hundred were colored!" including fellow *Douglass' Paper* correspondents Cosmopolite, Ethiop, and Observer, each of whom "had the luck to sit like thorns between blushing roses" while the Black Swan demonstrated "the nobleness of her nature."[27] Again, then, "The Light Brigade" is radically reimagined in such a way as to address race relations and celebrate black achievements.

No one ever seems to have taken up Smith's accusation of Tennyson. The poet himself, I will argue below, was uniquely well positioned to recognize its uncanny power, but he was presumably unaware of Smith's column.[28] However, other aspects of Smith's treatment of "The Light Brigade" did not go unnoticed—or unchallenged—in the pages of *Frederick Douglass' Paper* itself. The use of Tennyson's poem to envision an antislavery insurrection prompted one forceful response, as did its use to theorize the relationship between race and culture. Both of these responses, printed back-to-back in the April 20, 1855, issue of *Douglass' Paper*, rejected the positions Smith used "The Light Brigade" to advance, and used the poem instead to envision a postracist and indeed postracial world.

In the first piece, a letter, the antislavery activist Uriah Boston advocates a policy of "lessen[ing] the distinction between the whites and colored citizens of the United States" by having "colored people" renounce their identity as Africans to claim full and sole American citizenship. He distinguishes his position from one he attributes to Smith and William Wilson (Ethiop), who, he says, "would not have the colored people imitate nor mix with the whites" but instead "would have . . . three millions of Africans contending with 24 millions of Americans . . . for the rights of American citizens." Such a contest, writes Boston, "would be more fatal to the colored race than the brave and daring charge of the British Light Brigade at Balaklava. Nay," he continues, "the foolish daring of the British Light Brigade would be justly considered an act of wisdom, compared with the conduct of 3 millions Africans charging 24 millions Americans on the ground selected by the Americans themselves. One such charge would result in the annihilation of the African Brigade, with no prospect of recruits." Boston thus rejects both Smith's oft-articulated stance of racial exceptionalism and the specific, "Light Brigade"–inspired (or ur–"Light Brigade"–inspired) advocacy of insurrection voiced by "Fylbel," finding these positions less subversive than suicidal.[29]

"Fylbel" himself—Philip Bell—gets his say in a column immediately following Boston's letter. Writing under his regular pseudonym, "Cosmopolite," Bell leaves aside talk of violence to focus more squarely on Tennyson's poem, which he compares favorably to "Balaklava," another Crimean War poem reprinted in *Douglass' Paper*. Bell praises Tennyson's "thrilling lyric" for its vividness: "we can almost hear the stern command, 'Forward the Light Brigade!' and the tramping of the steeds, as 'Into the valley of Death / Rode the Six Hundred!'"[30] The "short, terse, and epigrammatic repetition" of "Half a league, / Half a league, / Half a league onward," he asserts, is "unsurpassed in the language, and only equaled by Coleridge's 'Alone! Alone! All, all alone! / Alone on the wide, wide sea!'"

Bell thus returns here to the kind of apolitical, appreciative formal analysis we saw Smith engage in before his ostensible discovery of plagiarism. Yet Bell's column as a whole makes it clear that this lack of engagement with race is pointed—and pointed directly at Smith. Bell begins by taking issue with Smith's comments on the "Black Swan": "True Art," he declares, "is an elevator, not a leveler, as an old low Dutch writer once remarked." The distinction between leveling and elevating may seem a fine one, but it indicates very different political visions. For Bell as for Smith, art defeats prejudice, but for the former the equality it establishes is less one of mutual respect between races, as for Smith, than one where race is transcended altogether: according to Bell, art "elevates the mind above the petty prejudices of caste and color." Bell develops this position by recounting his visit to an art gallery, where he sees a wealthy, refined white woman turn to the

African American woman next to her and say of the painting before them, "How beautiful!" Bell interprets this moment as showing that for this white woman, "the ennobling influence of Art elevates the hitherto despised being at her side to her own standing." Elaborating, he asserts that "in the presence of that inimitable and inspired work of art, no prejudice can enter. Caste is forgotten, and colorphobia is rebuked into silence." He then goes on to analyze Tennyson's poem. Thus, although Bell does not make explicit the relationship between his column's parts, his discussion of "The Charge of the Light Brigade" serves to enact this ideal silence and forgetting.[31]

Yet Bell's deracialization of art turns out to be just as willful as was Smith's racialization. For the painting with which Bell chooses to make his case is almost perfectly unsuited to the task: while Ary Scheffer's *Temptation of Christ* contrasts "the sublime features and angelic countenance of Christ" with "the fiendish expression of the Tempter," as Bell says, it does so by invoking the very codes he sees art negating: Christ's skin tone is much lighter than Satan's, and Christ is standing on a mountaintop slightly higher than Satan.[32] (See figure 2.1)

The painting thus depicts and celebrates the scenario Bell describes it as repairing: a light-toned figure elevated above one of "darker hue" at its side. One might view this irony as testimony to the utopian potential of aesthetic experience, whereby even racist art can have an antiracist impact—that is, whereby even art that encodes racist beliefs can produce an aesthetic experience that does not reinforce but instead transcends those beliefs. However, Bell's failure to spell out this argument himself raises the possibility that his devotion to Western art has blinded him to its racism.

Bell's problematic appreciation of Scheffer's painting casts a shadow over his subsequent appreciation of "The Light Brigade." If, in attempting to demonstrate the silencing of "colorphobia" Bell instead overlooks the presence and persistence of that colorphobia, then the forgetting of race enacted by his discussion of "The Light Brigade" risks seeming naïve, ineffectual, or even inadvertently complicit with the racism it seeks to combat. Recognition of the painting's racialized visual vocabulary also raises the question of whether a similarly racialized rhetoric is at work in Tennyson's poem. For example, does the poem pun on "light," so as to suggest "not-dark" as well as its original meaning of "not-heavy"? Is Tennyson's light brigade the light brigade not only because it is not the heavy brigade but also because it is not, in Uriah Boston's phrase, "the African brigade"?

Philip Bell's commitment to a color-blind, race-transcending cultural sphere keeps him from asking such questions, and the exchange

2.1. Ary Scheffer, *The Temptation of Christ*, 1854. Oil on canvas,
136″ × 95″. Musée du Louvre, Paris. Photo: Hervé Lewandowski.
© RMN–Grand Palais / Art Resource, NY.

in *Douglass' Paper* concerning "The Charge of the Light Brigade" ends
with his column. However, that exchange—and James McCune Smith's
column in particular—not only invites us to address such questions ourselves but also points the way toward answers. Rather than tacitly employ-
ing racialized imagery, I will argue, "The Charge of the Light Brigade"
constitutes an active withdrawal or disengagement on Tennyson's part
from the racial rhetoric he employs elsewhere. The very topicality of this
most topical of poems can be fruitfully understood as a deracializing
recontextualization—can be fruitfully understood, that is, along lines
first proposed by James McCune Smith.

TENNYSON RELOCATING

James McCune Smith's initial insights into "The Charge of the Light Brigade"— his identification of Virgil as Tennyson's key precursor and his reading of the rhythm and repetition of "The Light Brigade" as mimetically
representing the cavalry's advance—are now widely accepted. Indeed, even
Smith's version of the poem's genesis bears a striking resemblance to the
well-known version later related by Tennyson's son Hallam, who similarly
claimed that "the origin of the metre of [the] poem" came from a passage
in a periodical—specifically, from the phrase "some one had blundered" in
the *Times*.[33] Only when Smith transforms the Crimea into a palimpsest of

Haiti and Africa, then, does his acumen as a reader of Tennyson come into question—or start to seem beside the point.

In leaving behind emerging Tennysonian commonplaces, however, Smith does not leave behind common Tennysonian places. Instead, his revisionary framing of "The Light Brigade" takes the English poet to places his poetry had already visited and would return to again: earlier in his career Tennyson wrote a number of poems set in the tropics, including both Africa and Haiti, and he would write about Haiti again toward the end of his life (in "Columbus"). Of particular interest here is "Anacaona," which Tennyson wrote sometime between 1828 and 1830 but refused to publish during his lifetime: drawing from the transatlantic circulation of accounts of transatlantic circulation to bring together Haiti, song, and the violent replacement of one racial regime by another, this poem bears an uncanny resemblance to "The Light Brigade"—according-to-Smith.

Basing his account on an American text—Washington Irving's *Life of Columbus*[34]—Tennyson begins the poem by describing the edenic life of "The Indian queen, Anacaona" (28) in her "cedar-wooded paradise" (20):

A dark Indian maiden,
    Warbling in the bloomed liana,
Stepping lightly flower-laden,
    By the crimson-eyed anana,
Wantoning in orange groves
    Naked, and dark-limbed, and gay,
Bathing in the slumbrous coves,
In the cocoa-shadowed coves,
    Of sunbright Xaraguay,
Who was so happy as Anacaona,
    The Beauty of Espagnola,
    The golden flower of Hayti? (1–12)[35]

The arrival of "The white man's white sail" (49) interrupts this idyll, although at first Anacaona, in her innocence, welcomes the "fair-faced and tall" Spaniards:

Naked, without fear, moving
    To her Areyto's mellow ditty,
Waving a palm branch, wondering, loving
    Carolling "Happy, happy Hayti!"

She gave the white men welcome all,
  With her damsels by the bay. (61–66)

As Irving recounts, despite this welcome the Spanish execute Anacaona
and massacre her people. This fate is rendered elliptically in the poem,
which ends:

But never more upon the shore
  Dancing at the break of day,
In the deep wood no more,—
By the deep sea no more,—
  No more in Xaraguay
Wandered happy Anacaona,
  The beauty of Espagnola,
  The golden flower of Hayti! (77–84)

In "Anacaona," as in Smith's ur-version of "The Light Brigade," then, the
dark-skinned people of Haiti use song as they attempt to negotiate their
relationship to Europeans. The earlier poem depicts natives as victims,
rather than slaves of African descent as revolutionaries, yet even so we
are not as far off from Smith's version as it might seem: as Marcus Wood
points out, "Anacaona" not only draws from Irving but also "develops out
of the tropes of abolition poetry dealing with the natives of Hispaniola"[36];
Wood goes so far as to include the poem in an anthology entitled *The
Poetry of Slavery*. In Samuel Whitchurch's 1804 poem *Hispaniola*, in particular, the voice of the murdered Anacaona (there spelled "Anacoana")
curses future generations of European conquerors and prophesies the
Haitian Revolution itself:

"Then mourn not much-loved summer isle,
Again on thee shall freedom smile,
Though on thee prey the vultures of the north:
Brave sable nations shall arise,
And rout thy future enemies,
Though Europe send her hostile legions forth."[37]

Here we come close to the past Communipaw describes and the future Fylbel envisions. Smith's column thus rewrites "The Light Brigade" as "Anacaona" as "Hispaniola."

The series of transformations here may seem dizzying, but the ironies are multiple and pointed. By reading Tennyson in the context of the Haitian Revolution, Smith undoes the work of "Anacaona" itself, for the Haitian Revolution is not simply absent from "Anacaona" but rather is absented from it, abjected. That is, "Anacaona" does not simply fail to invite thoughts of the Haitian Revolution but instead actively combats them—or more precisely, it invites readers to combat the very thoughts it invites. Tennyson gives his poem an actual historical setting (as opposed to his frequent preference, especially early in his career, for literary and mythical locales), and one with a well-known recent past that other poems have linked to the more distant past he evokes. The ghost of the Haitian Revolution thus threatens to haunt "Anacaona" just as the ghost of Whitchurch's Anacoana haunts the Haitian Revolution. However, the ending of the poem attempts to lay this ghost by emphatically sealing off the represented historical moment: quoth the poet, "never more . . . no more . . . no more,— / No more." The repetition here is as anxious as it is paradoxical, as if the poet does not so much lament the irrevocable silence of Haiti's colored inhabitants as fear that it is not irrevocable, that these inhabitants may one day assert themselves violently and successfully. From this perspective, Smith's claim that Tennyson has plagiarized a poem that does not merely represent but in fact incited the Haitian Revolution constitutes the return of the repressed with a vengeance, as the return of repressed vengeance.

One might object that Tennyson's insistence on the irrevocable nature of Anacaona's silencing can be attributed not to a fear of black agency but to a commitment to historical truth: after all, the natives of Haiti were in fact wiped out and are not interchangeable with the slaves of African descent who later populated the island. Yet anxiety over the agency of people of color is plainly visible, and this agency plainly rendered invisible, in the (non)publication history of the poem itself. As noted earlier, Tennyson refused to publish "Anacaona" during his lifetime. According to his son, the primary reason he gave for this refusal was the poem's scientific inaccuracies: "My father liked this poem but did not publish it, because the natural history and the rhymes did not satisfy him. He evidently chose words which sounded well, and gave a tropical air to the whole, and he did not then care, as in his later poems, for absolute accuracy."[38] In the words of Edward FitzGerald's similar report, Tennyson worried that the poem "would be confuted by some Midshipman who had been in Hayti latitudes and knew better about Tropical Vegetable and Animal."[39] Leaving aside for a moment the persuasiveness of this explanation, we can note that, on this account, the possibility of being confuted by someone who actually inhabits, rather than visits, "Hayti lati-tudes" does not seem to occur to Tennyson (or FitzGerald): again, here, the agency of people of color is absent. Yet the letter in which Tennyson in fact refuses to allow publication of the poem conjures a disturbing image of just such agency: referring to "that black b— Anacaona and her cocoa-shadowed *coves* of niggers," the poet says, "I cannot have her strolling about the land in this way—it is neither good for her reputation nor mine."[40] Tennyson not only grants people of color dangerous agency here, but also does so in language that collapses any distinction between the island's extinct original inhabitants and its present-day, recently self-empowered inhabitants. This letter thus affirms the transhistorical, interracial link Whitchurch elaborates and, I have argued, "Anacaona" forcibly forgets.

Viewed through the lens provided by James McCune Smith, then, Ten-nyson's most widely circulated poem morphs into a version of a poem Ten-nyson refused to publish, albeit a version that highlights the very agency, and the very historical event, that the latter poem itself represses. Although Smith himself could not have been aware of this irony, it is very much in keeping with the spirit and tactics of his column, which ends by turning another poem by a prominent white poet into a celebration of black agency. Asserting the necessity of black solidarity to defeat slavery, Smith writes:

dark hands must be knit to dark hands, and the souls of blacks must be bent into one soul, to make the strong pull which shall

"shake the pillar of our common weal"

free from the Mammoth Evil.

Smith here cites Henry Wadsworth Longfellow to make vivid his own argu-ment that the unified efforts of African Americans will bring an end to slav-ery. As its title indicates, however, Longfellow's poem is a "Warning": rather than calling on blacks to "shake the pillars of this Commonweal," as Smith does, Longfellow warns that slavery must be abolished in order to prevent slaves from committing this Samson-like act, which he believes would leave "the vast Temple of our liberties / A shapeless mass of wreck and rubbish." Smith's rhetorical sleight of hand transforms this representation of black action as a threat to be avoided into a call for just such action.

Smith's commentary on "The Light Brigade" also reinscribes another as-pect of "Anacaona" that that poem's suppression seems intended to suppress.

Even as the earlier poem obscures the Haitians' latter-day political agency, it highlights Anacaona's artistic creativity as the composer and performer of "areytos," which Washington Irving glosses as "the legendary ballads of her nation."[41] As A. Dwight Culler was perhaps the first to note, Anacaona thus serves "as a symbol of the poet"[42]; going further, James Eli Adams suggests that Tennyson's disavowed identification with this Indian queen contributes to his "uneasy relation" to the poem and decision not to publish it.[43] In Smith's article, however, the kinship between Tennyson and a dark-skinned composer of legendary national ballads returns in nightmarishly exaggerated form: identification collapses into identity, as one of Tennyson's own areyto-like compositions is "revealed" as a pilfered (Afro-)Haitian chant.[44]

Beyond these ramifying ironies, Smith's reframing of "The Charge of the Light Brigade" sheds new light on the poem's place in Tennyson's oeuvre. If, as I have argued, Smith's argument regarding the origins of "The Charge of the Light Brigade" unearths a buried dynamic in the buried "Anacaona," in so doing it does not simply leave behind the original "Light Brigade"—that is, Tennyson's—but instead invites us to read it in the company of "Anacaona" and those poems with which "Anacaona" is invariably grouped: Tennyson's poems set in or fantasizing about exotic locales at or beyond the margins of the West, such as "Timbuctoo," "The Hesperides," "Locksley Hall," and especially "The Lotos-Eaters," which also draws from Irving's *Life of Columbus*.[45] Critics have read these poems as exhibiting, and to varying degrees policing, an eroticized resistance to the demands of Victorian masculine self-discipline and the perceived marginalization of the imagination in increasingly utilitarian England.[46] By contrast, "The Charge of the Light Brigade" is typically read as a jingoistic celebration of just such self-discipline.[47] When brought into contact with these other poems, however, suggestive similarities emerge, and the Crimea becomes visible as another such seductively exotic locale, Lotosland—or Haiti—by another name. Thanks to their self-discipline, for example, the soldiers in the Light Brigade achieve the death that Ulysses' weary men, "stretched out beneath the pine" (144), so obviously crave in "The Lotos-Eaters," even as Tennyson himself seeks to improve on the performance of the "minstrel" who sings of their "great deeds, as half-forgotten things" (123); indeed, this pairing brings out the anxiety lurking beneath the boastfulness of the seemingly rhetorical question posed in the final stanza of "The Light Brigade": "When can their glory fade?" (50).

The pairing of "The Light Brigade" with "Anacaona" is perhaps even more suggestive. For all their differences, both poems commemorate the victims of massacres resulting from international contact, and both end with an exclamatory reference to the massacred. The image of the royal Anacaona leading the Spaniards "down the pleasant places" contrasts with the noble Light Brigade's ride "Into the valley of death," but the descents prove equally tragic. One key difference is that the soldiers, unlike Anacaona, know what to expect. "The Light Brigade" thus stands as the song of experience to the earlier song of innocence. Or perhaps vice versa, insofar as "Anacaona" mourns the tragic encounter of innocence with experience, while "The Light Brigade" celebrates the heroic achievement of willed innocence ("Their's not to reason why").

This convergence of the two poems is captured by one key word that links the Indian queen and the British cavalry: *wild*. Anacaona sings "her wild carol" (73) while the Light Brigade, of course, makes its "wild charge." This echo calls attention to the curiousness of Tennyson's word choice in the later poem: as critics have noted, there was nothing wild about the charge as described in the press accounts Tennyson would have seen (recall Thoreau's word, "machine").[48] Indeed, to describe the Light Brigade's actions with a word that carries among its primary meanings "not under, or not submitting to, control or restraint" and "rebellious"[49] directly contradicts the burden of the poem. It does, however, suggest a point where the pure wildness of Anacaona's song (its uncultured naturalness, its freedom from restraint) meets the wild (reckless, imprudent) purity of the Light Brigade's discipline.[50]

These similarities between "Anacaona" and "The Charge of the Light Brigade" render one difference between the two poems particularly striking. Anacaona and her wild carol are repeatedly, insistently situated in and identified with a particular place, but the Light Brigade and its wild charge are not: almost every stanza of "Anacaona" mentions Xaraguay and every stanza ends by describing Anacaona as "The beauty of Espagnola, / The golden flower of Hayti," whereas "The Charge of the Light Brigade" mentions neither a place name nor the nationality or race of the Light Brigade itself. One might argue that the circumstances of the latter poem's production and initial publication rendered such specifications superfluous—one would hardly expect Tennyson to write of "the British Light Brigade," as we saw Uriah Boston do—but the additional contrast between the earlier poem's detailed attention to Haiti's flora and fauna (however erroneous) and the later poem's terse evocations of a diagrammatic, allegorized landscape ("right of them," "left of them," "in front of them," "behind them"; "the valley of Death," "the mouth of Hell") underscores the centrality of this referential reticence to Tennyson's aesthetic strategy.[51] If, as I have argued,

"The Light Brigade" constitutes a resituating on Tennyson's part of interests and desires he had explored previously in poems set in the tropics, then it also constitutes a retreat from situatedness itself.

In a final irony, however, the race-neutralizing abstraction and allegory of "The Charge of the Light Brigade" heightens the poem's availability for adaptation or particularization; in other words, Tennyson's decontextualization paradoxically facilitates the poem's recontextualization. It is ironic but not necessarily surprising, then, that even though James McCune Smith's dialectical negation of the poem's negations may be uncannily precise and revealing, his African Americanization of "The Light Brigade" is also only the first in a decades-long series that extends well beyond the initial responses he inspired in the pages of *Frederick Douglass' Paper*. Despite and because of Tennyson's best efforts, "The Charge of the Light Brigade" will be repeatedly deployed in contexts where race is explicitly at issue.

BLACK BRIGADES: THE CIVIL WAR "LIGHT BRIGADE"

This initial engagement with "The Charge of the Light Brigade" ends with Bell's column. However, Tennyson's poem will maintain a presence in the lives and writings of nineteenth-century African Americans. In the following decade and beyond, this presence will continue to raise questions—and "The Charge of the Light Brigade" will continue to be used to address questions—about the role of culture in reproducing and challenging racism, the costs and benefits of participation in the dominant culture, the universality and particularity of literature, and, in Uriah Boston's stark terms, African American assimilation and annihilation.

One form taken by the African American engagement with Tennyson's poem in the nineteenth century is the form it takes in *The Fresh Prince:* recitation, both in schools and public performances.[52] Such recitation of "The Light Brigade" provides a means to lay claim to participation or membership in the dominant culture, like the performance by James McCune Smith's Black Swan. Yet absent anything like Smith's claim for an African role in the making of this poem, or this culture, on the one hand, and given what we have just seen of Philip Bell's vexed color blindness, on the other, we might ask whether we should understand the teaching and performance of Tennyson's poem as promoting an empowering cultural literacy, on the one hand, or a deracinating cultural mimicry, on the other—or, indeed, some combination of the two, with deracination the price of empowerment? For young African Americans in the 1860s, what is the Crimea to them, or they to the Crimea, that they should read and recite about it?

Eventually, the teaching of Tennyson's poem will be criticized along these lines. In a 1922 essay advocating, as its title indicates, "Negro Literature for Negro Pupils," "The Charge of the Light Brigade" is one of the few works Alice Dunbar-Nelson targets by name for replacement in the curriculum. Arguing for the need to "instill race pride into our pupils" by giving them "the poems and stories and folk lore and songs of their own people," Dunbar-Nelson proposes substituting George Henry Boker's 1863 poem "The Second Louisiana" (also known as "The Black Regiment").[53] While also by a white author, "The Second Louisiana" celebrates the pivotal role of an African American regiment in the Battle of Port Hudson, Louisiana. As in *The Fresh Prince of Bel-Air*, "The Charge of the Light Brigade" comes to represent that which must be cleared away to make room for black history, experience, and expression. In a similar spirit, at around the same time, when the pan-Africanist Marcus Garvey attempted to purchase a ship named the *Tennyson* for the Universal Negro Improvement Association's Black Star Line, he announced his plan to rechristen it the *Phyllis Wheatley*.[54]

No hint of such criticism or such a binary opposition is present in the 1860s reports in the African American press on the recitation of Tennyson's poem. What one finds in their place is not necessarily an indifference to the question of fit between text and student, nor an attempt to relocate both poem and reader to a realm of universality; instead, there are indications that Tennyson's poem has been selected with an eye toward its timeliness and felt relevance for these students, as a poem about war.[55] Thus, "The Light Brigade" is reported being read at one high school exam along with a poem called "Restoration of the Flag to Fort Sumter."[56] In direct contrast to Dunbar-Nelson, another article reporting on a reading by graduates of the Institute for Colored Youth does not oppose Tennyson and Boker but instead aligns them: the evening's main performer, we learn, first came to prominence "as an orator . . . on the occasion of the organization of the Pennsylvania State Equal Rights League" two months earlier, "when he recited 'Boker's Black Regiment,' in such an able and masterly style."[57]

It is not surprising that Boker's poem in particular gets paired with Tennyson's, since this pairing begins in Boker's poem itself: in celebrating the sacrifices of African American troops in the Civil War, "The Second Louisiana" takes "The Light Brigade" as its model. This African Americanization of Tennyson's poem indicates both the poem's continued resonance and its limitations. On the one hand, that is, the turn from "The Light Brigade" to "The Black Regiment" does not leave Tennyson's poem behind but instead maintains and affirms its presence, as resource or influence. On the other hand, the existence of a "black" version of "The Light Brigade" turns "The Light Brigade" into a "white" version of itself—that is, into the racially marked poem Dunbar-Nelson will see, rather than the race-transcending one praised by Philip Bell.

Boker's formal debt to Tennyson is evident, as his poem commemorates the martyrdom of a regiment in the distinctive dactylic dimeter of "The Light Brigade":

> Trampling with bloody heel
> Over the crashing steel,
> All their eyes forward bent,
> Rushed the Black Regiment.[58]

Boker also borrows Tennyson's use of anaphora:

> "Freedom!" their battle-cry—
> "Freedom! or leave to die!"
>
> . . . .
>
> Glad to strike one free blow,
> Whether for weal or woe;
> Glad to breathe one free breath,
> Though on the lips of death.

Boker's ending reworks Tennyson's, replacing the imperative to "Honor the charge they made, / Honor the Light Brigade, / Noble six hundred" with a demand focusing on the survivors:

> Oh, to the living few,
> Soldiers, be just and true!
> Hail them as comrades tried;
> Fight with them side by side;
> Never, in field or tent,
> Scorn the Black Regiment.

Rather than the recitation of "The Charge of the Light Brigade" serving to demonstrate the humanity, equality, or artistry of African Americans, then, the poem gets adapted to describe—and increase—their own agency in securing that equality. Whereas Uriah Boston feared a suicidal charge resulting in "the annihilation of the African Brigade, with no prospect of recruits," Boker celebrates a small-scale annihilation, and does so precisely to generate more recruits: "The Second Louisiana" was published by Philadelphia's Supervisory Committee for Recruiting Colored Regiments.

When Dunbar-Nelson proposes that "Negro pupils" read "The Second Louisiana" instead of "The Light Brigade," she suspends her essay's emphasis on black authorship (even as she is careful to omit Boker's name, in contrast to her practice of identifying the African American authors of the works she recommends).[59] Yet "The Light Brigade" also gets deployed in poems *by* as well as *about* African Americans—on the very same subject as Boker's.[60] The first such poem is likely James Madison Bell's monumental, 750-line "The Day and the War" (1864). Unlike Boker, Bell abandons the metrical form of "The Light Brigade" in favor of a more conventional iambic tetrameter, usually in rhymed couplets; also unlike Boker, however, Bell openly thematizes his relationship to Tennyson, acknowledging the English poet's precedent while claiming an originality of his own:

> Though Tennyson, the poet king,
> Has sung of Balaklava's charge,
> Until his thund'ring cannons ring
> From England's center to her marge,
> The pleasing duty still remains
> To sing a people from their chains—
> To sing what none have yet assay'd,
> The wonders of the Black Brigade.[61]

Bell's characterization of Tennyson as "the poet king" is less unequivocal as praise than it might seem, for earlier in the poem he criticizes Britain for supporting the South in the Civil War and states that "kindred spirits there are none, / Twixt a Republic and a throne." This stance may have contributed to Bell's decision to present himself and the African American soldiers at the battle of Milliken's Bend as competing with Tennyson and the Light Brigade, rather than emulating them:

> Let Balaklava's cannons roar
> And Tennyson his hosts parade,
> But ne'er was seen and never more
> The equals of the Black Brigade![62]

Like James McCune Smith, Bell uses Tennyson's poem as a foil to assert the primacy of black freedom fighters. Superiority over the Light Brigade takes the form of a more complete martyrdom:

> out of one full corps of men,
> But one remained unwounded, when
> The dreadful fray had fully past—
> *All* killed or wounded but the last![63]

As opposed to "The Charge of the Light Brigade," moreover, this martyrdom portends the eventual triumph of the cause: "The Day and the War" was written to celebrate the first anniversary of the Emancipation Proclamation.

Although Bell's insistence on the unequaled valor of the Black Brigade comes at the expense of the Light Brigade, he does not devalue the actions of the Light Brigade, or the poetry of Tennyson, as aggressively as we saw Thoreau do when celebrating John Brown and his men. Like Thoreau's speech, however, "The Day and the War" also positions Brown and his men in relation to the Light Brigade. James Madison Bell was Brown's friend and supporter, and "The Day and the War" is dedicated to "the hero, saint and martyr of Harper's Ferry . . . by one who loved him in life, and in death would honor his memory."[64] In Bell's poem, I would suggest, the Light Brigade ironically comes to serve as a kind of stand-in for or displaced version of Brown and his men. The Black Brigade's comrades in arms, they are also their rivals in valor, an inspiring but humbling example of heroic resistance to slavery. The combination of the poem's opening dedication to Brown and its closing near-apotheosis of Abraham Lincoln—the last two lines are "And tribes and people yet unborn, / Shall hail and bless his natal morn"[65]—underscores the burden the Black Brigade carries in the middle of the poem as its specifically African American (counter)example of heroic agency.

With their treatment of "The Light Brigade" as a resource with which to conjure images of African American freedom fighters, James Madison Bell and George Henry Boker take a stance closer to James McCune Smith's revolutionary "Fylbel" than Philip Bell's proto-Arnoldian "Cosmopolite." By the time of the publication of "The Day and the War," however, such images have migrated from the realm of militant prophecy to that of current events. This historical development helps explain an increased openness to such racializations of the poem on the part of Philip Bell himself: Bell contributed a summarizing "Introductory Note" to "The Day and the War."[66]

Nonetheless, the war hardly settled the question of transracial elevation vs. interracial leveling, and Bell seems never to have abandoned his belief in the former: in an article a year later, even as he describes "The Light Brigade" being read at a fundraiser for San Francisco's African Methodist Episcopal Zion Church, Bell retains his earlier practice of strategic color blindness or silence, never identifying the performer by race. This article appears in a newspaper Bell himself had recently founded: the *Elevator.*[67]

FADED GLORY: THE WANING "LIGHT BRIGADE"

The end of the Civil War did not end the use of "The Light Brigade" pioneered by "The Black Regiment" and "The Day and the War." However, the passage of time did change the poem's resonance. We see this in Paul Laurence Dunbar's 1895 poem "The Colored Soldiers," which again makes use of "The Charge of the Light Brigade" to celebrate the role of African American troops in the Civil War.[68] Dunbar's soldiers, like Tennyson's, valiantly storm "the very mouth of hell" (32), and the final stanza of "The Colored Soldiers" tracks that of "The Light Brigade":

> When can their glory fade?
> O the wild charge they made!
>   All the world wondered.
> Honour the charge they made!
> Honour the Light Brigade,
>   Noble six hundred!
>
> And their deeds shall find a record
>   In the registry of Fame;
> For their blood has cleansed completely
>   Every blot of Slavery's shame.
> So all honor and all glory
>   To those noble sons of Ham—
> The gallant colored soldiers
>   Who fought for Uncle Sam! (73–80)

The unmistakable echo of the "Light Brigade" here derives not simply from the shared vocabulary—"honor," "glory," "noble"—and assertions of immortality, which are arguably generic, but from these features in combination with the similar syntax of the poems' final sentences, as Dunbar's concluding exclamation bestows the honor Tennyson's demands.

Crucially, however, unlike Tennyson's poem—and Boker's and Bell's—Dunbar's poem does not inhabit the moment it describes. Instead, "The Colored Soldiers" looks back three decades, and the poem takes as its topic the difference this temporal gap makes. As Jennifer Terry has noted, Dunbar is writing "against a backdrop of rising anti-black violence and the widespread collapse and reversal of political and legal gains made by African Americans during the post-war period."[69] He calls on an earlier heroic moment and poetic model to counteract this backsliding, which is directly addressed in the poem: "They were comrades then and brothers, / Are they more or less to-day?" (57–58), "And the traits that made them worthy,— / Ah! those virtues are not dead" (63–64). Tennyson's poem not only models a call for permanence but, forty years after its publication, models that permanence itself.

Yet there are poignant ironies in Dunbar's turn to "The Light Brigade," deriving from both the specific content of Tennyson's poem and its subsequent reputation. When Boker and James Madison Bell deploy Tennyson's poem, they pick up the theme of martyrdom but leave behind the poem's crucial attention to the fact that the charge it describes was also a mistake and a failure: a blunder. Dunbar similarly argues that the sacrifices he describes contributed to victory:

> Yes, the Blacks enjoy their freedom,
>   And they won it dearly, too;
> For the life blood of their thousands
>   Did the southern fields bedew.
> In the darkness of their bondage,
>   In the depths of slavery's night,
> Their muskets flashed the dawning,
>   And they fought their way to light. (49–57)

The problem, however, is that Dunbar's goal is precisely to counteract the possibility that this mission failed—that these flashing muskets are no less glorious but also no more successful than the Light Brigade's flashing sabers. The turn to Tennyson thus implies exactly what "The Colored Soldiers" is intended to refute: that the colored soldiers "fought their way to light[-brigade status]" *as opposed to* the "light" of freedom. Instead of underwriting freedom, that is, glory and honor become consolation prizes in its absence. Even as "The Colored Soldiers" seeks to reclaim the "Light Brigade"'s triumphalism, then, it is haunted by the poem's negativity.

Another irony in Dunbar's use of "The Charge of the Light Brigade" to figure permanence is that the poem's currency had gotten debased over time. Thanks to its enduring place in the curriculum, "The Light Brigade" remained familiar throughout the second half of the nineteenth century; at the same time, though, it became increasingly subject to promiscuous, casual, and irreverent citation and appropriation. This is as true in the African American press as in the white press. The poem's decline is uneven, but we can get a sense of it from an 1882 article in the African Methodist Episcopal Church's widely read *Christian Recorder*. Mocking the supposed Negro love of titles, a reporter complains that a recent convention "to discuss the moral, social and political condition of the negro" devolved into a display of what he calls "titular twaddle": "Professors to right of us, professors to left of us, professors in front of us volleyed and thundered."[70] Thus does glory fade, not into oblivion but bathos.

This decline notwithstanding, "The Charge of the Light Brigade" also appears in the most influential work produced in this period by an African American writer, W.E.B. Du Bois's *The Souls of Black Folk* (1903).[71] Like Dunbar, Du Bois turns to "The Light Brigade" when grappling with the failed promise of Reconstruction.[72] True to Du Bois's more negative vision, however, it is precisely the poem's negativity that he calls upon. Whereas Dunbar asserts that "the Blacks enjoy their freedom," Du Bois counters that "despite compromise, war, and struggle, the Negro is not free." Discussing the Freedmen's Bureau, established at the end of the Civil War to promote the rights and welfare of freed slaves, Du Bois defines its "legacy" as "the work it did not do because it could not."[73] Defending nonetheless the efforts of the Freedmen's Bureau and its first commissioner, Oliver Howard, he writes:

> nothing is more convenient than to heap on the Freedmen's Bureau all the evils of that evil day, and damn it utterly for every mistake and blunder that was made.
>
> All this is easy, but it is neither sensible nor just. *Some one had blundered*, but that was long before Oliver Howard was born; there was criminal aggression and heedless neglect, but without some system of control there would have been far more than there was.[74]

As expansive as it is brief, this allusion transforms Tennyson's blunt characterization of a miscommunicated order into a tragicomic euphemism for one of the most momentous events in world history, the establishment of slavery in the New World. The victims of *this* "blunder" number in the millions, not the hundreds. Such a shift in scale has the effect of parochializing the concerns of "The Charge of the Light Brigade," even as the very act of alluding to the poem reflects its lingering cultural presence.

Du Bois's unmarked allusion to "The Charge of the Light Brigade" is in many respects quite different from James McCune Smith's sustained engagement with the poem a half-century earlier. In an uncanny turn of events, however, the afterlife of the very passage containing Du Bois's citation ends up repeating the dynamic of cross-racial plagiarism McCune Smith described. As Du Bois gleefully documents in a 1912 editorial in *The Crisis*, the winning entry in a contest sponsored by the United Daughters of the Confederacy for the best essay on the Freedman's Bureau by a University of South Carolina student included long passages lifted verbatim from Du Bois's chapter (or the *Atlantic* article where it first appeared). "There is nothing to mar the fulness of the tribute here involved," Du Bois exclaims, "not even quotation marks!"[75] McCune Smith's scenario of a white writer stealing from Africans to create "The Charge of the Light Brigade" thus returns in the form of a (presumptively) white writer stealing an African American's text citing the same poem.

In this chapter and the preceding one we have seen Victorian novels and poems serving variously as topics for discussion, topoi, and shared points of reference within African American discourse and print culture. In this chapter, we have also seen that the African American engagement with a particular Victorian text could extend over time and, further, take a shape or form a pattern that begins to look less like a series of isolated actions than a self-conscious tradition. The remaining chapters of this book will continue and expand the diachronic dimension of the story I am telling. We shall see that Victorian literature—and a small subset of Victorian authors and texts in particular—was called upon repeatedly and revealingly by African American authors and editors through the turn of the twentieth century (and therefore the end of the Victorian era itself) and into the period of the Harlem Renaissance. Those writers with the most sustained, generative, and complex relationships to Victorian literature are now recognized as major figures in the development of the African American literary tradition, albeit largely despite, not because of, these relationships: Frances Ellen Watkins Harper, Charles Chesnutt, and Pauline Hopkins as well as Du Bois. And while these writers' attention to Victorian literature has been largely denigrated and neglected, we will see that they themselves often inscribed this attention in ways that suggest an awareness of similar attention on the part of earlier and contemporary African American writers.

Tennyson himself, it turns out, is by far the most ubiquitous Victorian author in this African American tradition. While the presence of "The Charge of the Light Brigade" wanes somewhat, a number of other poems take its place—chief among them, perhaps, the one we saw (in the introduction) Anna Julia Cooper quote so prominently in *A Voice from the South: In Memoriam*.[76] In general, though, these later engagements with Tennyson lack the singleness of focus we have seen on display in this chapter: typically, more than one poem by Tennyson will be in play, as will more than one Victorian author. For that reason, rather than isolate this strand for chapter-length treatment, I will weave it into the broader discussion in the second half of the book.

First, though, I will turn to the third Victorian author who, along with Tennyson and Dickens, plays the most significant, reciprocally revealing role in the African American literary tradition: George Eliot. As we have seen, *Bleak House* directs attention away from Africans and African Americans, and "The Charge of the Light Brigade" stages a retreat from race; by contrast, the most frequently and elaborately African Americanized text by Eliot makes race (although not African Americans) a central concern. While an elective affinity with Eliot may thus seem unsurprising, it has gone almost entirely unexplored. As we shall see, the forms taken by the African American engagement with Eliot shed new light on her own career-long exploration of racial affinities and affiliations—elective, surprising, and otherwise—as well as those of her African American repurposers.

CHAPTER THREE

AFFILIATING WITH GEORGE ELIOT

Traveling through Europe as a young woman in 1890, Mary Church Terrell's final destination was Florence. There, as the Oberlin graduate and daughter of former slaves recounted decades later in her autobiography, *A Colored Woman in a White World*, she purchased "an edition de luxe of George Eliot's *Romola* in two volumes bound in white and trimmed in red" with "photographs of the places and pictures mentioned by the author . . . pasted in the book opposite the pages in which they were described."[1] "It was a delightful experience," she recalls, "to take this book, visit the places, and look at the pictures to which Eliot referred."[2]

That is all Terrell says about *Romola* or its author, and the diary she kept at the time only adds some specifics about the places visited and pictures looked at.[3] Eliot's historical novel, set in Renaissance Florence, thus seems to have been used by Terrell as a classy guidebook, with the deluxe edition she carried about serving as well as a conspicuous marker of cosmopolitan sophistication. "Bound in white," the book seems, if not bound up with whiteness, of a piece with the exhilarating freedom from the burdens of racialized identity Terrell experiences in Europe: "But now the time had come for me to return to my native land, and my heart ached when I thought about it. Life had been so pleasant and profitable abroad, where I could take advantage of any opportunity I desired without wondering whether a colored girl would be allowed to enjoy it or not."[4] In fact, however, the aspect of Terrell's experience, as she recounts it, that most recalls *Romola* is the quintessentially Eliotic tension she feels between her desire for self-fulfillment and her sense of duty and loyalty, combined with the quintessentially Eliotic choice she makes: "I knew I would be much happier trying to promote the welfare of my race in my native land, working under certain hard conditions, than I would be living in a foreign land where I could enjoy freedom from prejudice, but where I would make no effort to do the work which I then believed it was my duty to do. I doubted that I could respect myself if I shirked my responsibility and was recreant to my trust. . . . So I was glad when the steamer began to plough the sea to bring me home."[5] Terrell's account suggests that she has taken to heart the words of Eliot's Savonarola, whose "arresting voice" stops Romola on her flight from Florence: "If your own people are wearing a yoke, will you slip from under it, instead of struggling with them to lighten it?"[6] Like the protagonist of the novel she is reading, Terrell chooses to return to her "own people."

The year after Terrell's visit to Florence, Eliot's novel made a more extended appearance in William Dean Howells's novella *An Imperative Duty*, which tells the story of a young woman facing a dilemma very similar to Terrell's. Like Mary Church Terrell, Rhoda Aldgate is light-skinned enough to live as white, and like Terrell, she can and must decide whether or not to commit to an African American identity and vocation: "I'm going to find my mother's people," she declares. "Oughtn't I to go down there [from Boston to New Orleans] and help them; try to educate them, and elevate them; give my life to them? Isn't it base and cowardly to desert them, and live happily apart from them . . . ?"[7] Unlike Terrell, however, Rhoda has been raised in ignorance of her African American ancestry. She learns of this ancestry from her aunt, Mrs. Meredith, who acts out of a sense of duty cultivated by her reading of George Eliot. We first meet Mrs. Meredith engaged in "a long and serious analysis of *Romola*" that bespeaks her "conscience of prodigious magnifying force, cultivated to the last degree by a constant training upon the ethical problems of fiction."[8] "Do you believe that any one can rightfully live a lie?" she demands of her interlocutor, Dr. Olney (Rhoda's eventual love interest); "Do you believe that [Romola's husband] Tito was ever really at rest when he thought of what he was concealing?"[9]

Olney concludes that Mrs. Meredith is "hopelessly muddled as to her plain, every-day obligations by a morbid sympathy with the duty-ridden creatures of the novelist's brain,"[10] and the novella as a whole would seem to agree with him, as no good comes from her revelation of Rhoda's ancestry. Rhoda's one attempt to interact with African Americans is a disaster, and while she ultimately decides to marry Olney and continue living as white, she remains haunted by a sense of "guilty deceit."[11] This guilt does not suggest that she should have followed through on her sense of duty, but rather that she would have been better off never having known about the African American strand of her lineage in the first place. A final, ironic echo underscores the un-, indeed anti-, Eliotic stance of the novella: like *Romola*, Rhoda and Olney return to Florence (where they first met), only for Rhoda this move enacts not a commitment to her ancestral "people" but just the opposite.

While *A Colored Woman in a White World* and *An Imperative Duty* thus represent and advocate (explicitly in the former case, implicitly in the latter) opposed positions toward the acknowledgment and embrace of African American identity, both works implicitly align George Eliot on the same, affirmative side of this question. In neither text is a strong link articulated between Eliot and this position; nonetheless, especially in combination, these references to Eliot suggest her felt relevance to this issue. They also adumbrate a larger pattern. When nineteenth- and early-twentieth-century African American writers reference or rework Eliot, they tend to do so not because they view her work as inhabiting a cultural realm that transcends race, nor because they seek to locate themselves or their own work in such a realm. Instead, like Mary Church Terrell, they typically call on George Eliot in the course of, or in support of, their affirmations of specifically racial affiliation and solidarity.

As this chapter will show, Eliot's presence in African American literature and print culture begins in the 1860s, when she was in the middle of her career and at the height of popularity and prestige. The African American engagement with her work crests in the late nineteenth and early twentieth centuries, when Eliot's reputation is usually thought of as being in decline.[12] This virtually unknown afterlife takes a range of forms, from brief quotations to extended allusions and borrowed plot devices. We saw in the introduction, for example, that Anna Julia Cooper takes the epigraph for the first half of her essay collection *A Voice from the South* from Eliot's little-read poem "How Lisa Loved the King." Cooper also takes one of the epigraphs to the second half of her book from Eliot's novel *Felix Holt*. (Given this affinity for Eliot, it is no surprise that one of the essays in the book contains a devastating attack on *An Imperative Duty*.) As we shall see in the next chapter, Charles Chesnutt's novel *The House Behind the Cedars* is in dialogue with *The Mill on the Floss*, as are later novels by W.E.B. Du Bois and Jessie Redmon Fauset.[13] In this chapter, however, I will focus on the one work by Eliot that seems to have been of greatest interest to African American writers and editors at the time. While not quite as obscure as "How Lisa Loved the King," this work stands, in one critic's words, as "one of the most conspicuously neglected major works left behind by any Victorian writer of the first rank."[14] In African American literary culture in the late nineteenth and early twentieth centuries—as perhaps nowhere else—George Eliot is first and foremost the author of *The Spanish Gypsy*.

A book-length dramatic poem set in fifteenth-century Spain, *The Spanish Gypsy* was published simultaneously by Blackwood and Sons in the UK and Ticknor and Fields in the US in 1868. Starting soon after its publication, the poem was repeatedly put to use in efforts to promote African American solidarity and establish a race-affirmative body of literature. Although this African Americanizing afterlife has much in common with those discussed in the previous chapters, it differs from them in one crucial respect: deploying *The Spanish Gypsy* in positive depictions or discussions of African Americans does not directly flout the poem's own protocols with regard to race. Whereas *Bleak House* criticized attention to Africans and people of color in general, and "The Charge of the Light Brigade" enacted what I have called a deracializing decontextualization, *The Spanish Gypsy* treats a racial minority with respect while foregrounding the role of race in determining individual and group identity. The very act of bringing the poem to bear on the experience of African Americans, then, is not inherently ironic or subversive, and does not brush against the poem's grain. On the contrary, I will argue that the use the writers considered here make of *The Spanish Gypsy* shows that they had a greater understanding of and appreciation for the spirit of the poem than did many Victorian critics—and many more recent ones as well.

AFRICAN AMERICANIZING *THE SPANISH GYPSY*

The Spanish Gypsy tells the story of a young woman, Fedalma, who learns that she is not Spanish, as she has believed her whole life, but rather a Zincala, or gypsy. She learns this when by chance she meets her father, Zarca, the king of the gypsies, from whom she was separated as a baby. Zarca demands that Fedalma embrace her ancestral identity and help him lead their people to a new homeland. After much soul-searching, Fedalma accepts her newfound Zincala identity and vocation. Tragic complications ensue, including the murder of Zarca by Fedalma's Spanish fiancé, Don Silva, who had tried to gain membership in the Zincali himself to preserve his relationship with Fedalma. The poem ends with the gypsies sailing off, led by Fedalma.

I offer this brief plot summary not only because of the poem's relative obscurity but also to direct attention to the plot itself, which figures centrally in the poem's African American afterlife. Before turning to this afterlife, however, we should note this plot's recurrence in Eliot's own oeuvre:

in many respects, the poem's plot is the same as that of her much better-known work, *Daniel Deronda*—her final novel, published eight years after *The Spanish Gypsy*. In both works, the protagonists grow up as members of their society's dominant race or nationality (Spanish or English, respectively) but learn as young adults that by virtue of their ancestry they belong to a despised minority (gypsy or Jew). Despite this revelation, the characters are in a position to continue living with the identity they grew up with. Instead, though, they choose to affiliate themselves with their ancestral people and dedicate their lives to bettering its lot.

As striking as the fact that Eliot saw fit to tell this story of what I will call unwitting passing and voluntary racial affiliation twice is the fact that virtually no other major British writer ever told it at all.[15] By contrast, a number of nineteenth- and early-twentieth-century American writers—most of them African American—constructed this same scenario, almost invariably in stories about African American identity; the best-known example is Frances Ellen Watkins Harper's novel *Iola Leroy, or Shadows Uplifted* (1892).[16] Within American literary history, such stories are legible as refutations of what has come to be known as the tragic mulatto/a plot. In stories with this plot, the discovery that a character who has believed him- or herself to be white has some African ancestry is cataclysmic, leading directly to enslavement, sexual violation, madness, and/or death. As many scholars have discussed, this plot was invented before the Civil War to inspire abolitionist sentiment by bringing home to white readers the horrors of slavery, if not the irrationality of the "one-drop rule" of racial categorization. However, to some writers the plot's equation of African ancestry with tragedy, suffering, and death came to seem limited and offensive—yet instead of rejecting the plot outright, they reworked it to envision less dire consequences to the discovery of African American ancestry.[17] *An Imperative Duty* is one such narrative, but those written by African Americans tend to transform the tragic mulatto/a plot into the story of solidarity and uplift that Howells's Rhoda considers but rejects. *Iola Leroy*, published a year after *An Imperative Duty*, is often read as a direct response to that work.

Due perhaps to the neglect of *The Spanish Gypsy* as well as the divide between African American and Victorian literary studies this book seeks to bridge, the similarities between these American narratives of unwitting passing and Eliot's have gone unremarked by scholars. Yet this kinship was no secret to the authors of these narratives themselves, nor something they sought to hide. On the contrary, African American writers immediately saw the relevance of Eliot's work to the stories they wanted to tell and causes they wanted to promote, and they made use of her work accordingly. The recovery of this interracial textual affiliation thus revises the genealogy of this plot of genealogical affiliation. In doing so, it refines our understanding of an important strand of the African American literary tradition and reframes *The Spanish Gypsy* in ways that force a rethinking of the poem's ideological project as well as its cultural impact. This affiliation also sheds new light on the development of George Eliot's sense of vocation as an imaginative writer and even, I will suggest, points to a new explanation for her choice of the name "George Eliot" itself.

The African American afterlife of *The Spanish Gypsy* extends to little-visited precincts of print culture, but it was instigated and shaped by one of the leading African American authors and public intellectuals of the second half of the nineteenth century: Frances Ellen Watkins Harper. Returning repeatedly to the poem over the span of a quarter-century, Harper made *The Spanish Gypsy* her own, and in doing so established its place in the African American literary and intellectual tradition.

Two of Harper's four novels feature the *Spanish Gypsy* plot of unwitting passing and voluntary racial affiliation: not only her best-known work, *Iola Leroy*, as noted earlier, but also her first novel, *Minnie's Sacrifice*. One of three serialized novels by Harper rediscovered in the 1990s by Frances Smith Foster, *Minnie's Sacrifice* tells the story of two mixed-race individuals, Minnie and Louis, both of whom are raised believing they are white. Minnie learns of her African American ancestry from her mother and Louis from his grandmother, both of whom are black. Both protagonists eventually embrace this lineage and identity, with their feelings of personal loyalty supplemented in both cases by gratitude for specific acts of rescue—Minnie is nursed to health by her mother, and Louis is helped on his flight to the North by several African Americans. After Minnie and Louis marry, they commit themselves to working for the good of "the colored race,"[18] a goal to which Louis reaffirms his commitment at novel's end, after Minnie is murdered by white supremacists.

Minnie's Sacrifice was published serially in the African Methodist Episcopal Church's *Christian Recorder* in 1869—the year after the publication of *The Spanish Gypsy*. Notwithstanding this suggestive timing, it is of course possible that Harper arrived at her version of the plot of unwitting passing and voluntary racial affiliation independently. Lydia Maria Child, an originator of the tragic mulatto/a plot, had already begun to rethink that plot in her 1867 novel *The Romance of the Republic*, and it is certainly the case, as Frances Smith Foster points out, that *Minnie's Sacrifice* is "a deliberate retelling of the Old Testament Moses story," to which Harper openly alludes.[19] Indeed, Moses's story is the ur-version of the plot of unwitting passing and voluntary racial re-identification; Eliot too will explicitly reference it in *Daniel Deronda*, when Mordecai discusses the advantages of having "an accomplished Egyptian"—that is, someone raised as a privileged member of the dominant culture—as a leader and spokesman for a minority group.[20] In *Minnie's Sacrifice*, the biblical story serves as a model and catalyst within the narrative itself, as Louis is raised as white at the insistence of his owner's daughter, Camilla, who is inspired by her reading of the Book of Exodus: "It was a fine story; and I read it till I cried. Now I mean to do something like that good princess. I am going to ask Pa, to let me take him to the house, and have a nurse for him, and bring him up like a white child, and never let him know that he is colored."[21] Ironically, of course, this "fine story" proves a closer match than Camilla anticipates, as Louis, like Moses, learns of his lineage and avows the identity it confers.

Yet if *Minnie's Sacrifice* begins with the Bible, it ends with *The Spanish Gypsy:* the final sentence of the novel borrows its phrasing from Eliot's poem. This verbal echo shows that Harper was not simply aware of the parallels between her novel and Eliot's poem, but in fact was working closely with her geographically removed precursor text—was engaged, in other words, in close reading at a distance. In addition to confirming the direct connection between Eliot's version of the Mosaic plot and Harper's own, this echo pinpoints a moment in *The Spanish Gypsy* of enduring importance to Harper and later African American writers.

Reinforcing her novel's message of racial loyalty, Harper's postscript announces that "The lesson of Minnie's sacrifice is this, that it is braver to suffer with one's own branch of the human race,—to feel, that the weaker and the more despised they are, the closer we will cling to them, for the sake of helping them, than to attempt to creep out of all identity with them in their feebleness, for the sake of mere personal advantages. . . ."[22] The argument and wording here recall the pivotal scene in *The Spanish Gypsy* in which the Gypsy chieftain Zarca reveals to Fedalma that he is her father and calls upon her to join her ancestral people. Stunned, Fedalma grapples with the notion that she belongs to what she sees as

> a race
> More outcast and despised than Moor or Jew. . . .
> A race that lives on prey, as foxes do

With stealthy, petty rapine; so despised,
It is not persecuted, only spurned,
Crushed under foot, warred on by chance, like rats,
Or swarming flies, or reptiles of the sea
Dragged in the net unsought, and flung far off
To perish as they may.[23]

Surprisingly, Zarca responds to this extravagantly harsh characterization by declaring, "You paint us well." But then he continues,

So abject are the men whose blood we share;
Untutored, unbefriended, unendowed;
No favorites of heaven or of men,
Therefore I cling to them! (I.2754–58)

The echo of these lines in *Minnie's Sacrifice* is unmistakable: "the weaker and the more despised they are, the closer we will cling to them."

This Eliotic formulation became something of a talisman for Harper. It appears again two decades later in the last of the three novels Harper published serially in *The Christian Recorder*, *Trial and Triumph* (1888–89), and both plot and phrase recur yet again in *Iola Leroy*. In *Trial and Triumph*, one character seeks to dissuade another from "pass[ing] as a white man" by arguing: "I do not think it possible that however rich or strong or influential you may be as a white man, that you can be as noble and as true a man as you will be if you stand in your lot without compromise or concealment, and feel that the feebler your mother's race is the closer you will cling to it."[24] In *Iola Leroy*, Harper reworks *Minnie's Sacrifice*, again telling the story of two individuals (Iola Leroy and her brother Harry) who are raised as white, learn of their African American ancestry as young adults, and refuse opportunities to return to life as a white person. As in *Minnie's Sacrifice*, these refusals are motivated first by love of family and later by a desire to help uplift the race.

Like George Eliot, Harper gives her second narrative of unwitting passing and voluntary racial affiliation a happier ending than her first one, as Iola and Harry both marry (Iola to a Dr. Latimer—no relation, it seems, to the Latimer who narrates Eliot's novella "The Lifted Veil") and settle into productive lives working on behalf of the "people" with whom they have "cast . . . [their] lot."[25] Like Deronda and unlike Fedalma, they are not placed in a position "with inclination impelling one way and duty compelling another";[26] unlike Fedalma and Minnie, they are not called upon to make a tragic sacrifice. In a possible nod to *Daniel Deronda*, Harper makes the rare move of ending her novel by quoting several lines of unattributed poetry, as had Eliot—although, in a self-assertive twist, whereas Eliot quotes Milton, Harper quotes herself.[27] When Harper does echo Eliot more closely, she does not turn to *Daniel Deronda* but rather reworks her earlier reworking of *The Spanish Gypsy:* praising Latimer's refusal to pass, which she calls "the grandest hour of his life," Iola declares that "when others are trying to slip out from the race and pass into the white basis, I cannot help admiring one who acts as if he felt that *the weaker the race is the closer he would cling to it.*"[28]

This formulation appears in Harper's nonfiction as well. For example, in one of her most widely circulated lectures, "The Great Problem to Be Solved" (1875), she declares, "Oh, it is better to feel that the weaker and feebler our race the closer we will cling to them than it is to isolate ourselves from them in selfish, or careless unconcern."[29] Yet even as she made Eliot's words her own, Harper seems never to have lost sight of their origin: in her 1885 essay "A Factor in Human Progress," published sixteen years after *Minnie's Sacrifice,* she shifts from equivocally allusive paraphrase to direct quotation. Harper cites some fifty lines from *The Spanish Gypsy,* culminating in Zarca's "Therefore I cling to them" speech, in support of her argument that an individual's "education is unfinished" unless "he prefer[s] integrity to gold, principle to ease, true manhood to self-indulgence."[30] Celebrating the effects of "the recital, or the example of deeds of high and holy worth" on a "people," no matter how "low down [they] may be in the scale of character and condition," Harper demands: "Where in the wide realms of poet[r]y and song, will we find nobler sentiments expressed with more tenderness, strength and beauty?"[31] As her practice over a quarter-century indicates, for Harper this is indeed a rhetorical question.

For Frances Harper as for Eliot's Zarca, then, the fact that one's people is despised and dispossessed motivates solidarity and dedication to their betterment. Harper found in *The Spanish Gypsy* a phrase to encapsulate this view and a plot to dramatize it. Quite possibly following Harper's lead, several turn-of-the-century African American writers also approvingly quote passages from Eliot's poem that call for the uplifting of a downtrodden race and also script versions of the *Spanish Gypsy* plot. Like Harper, that is, and local variations aside, these writers consistently embrace and mobilize the logic, narrative, and rhetoric of group affiliation and affirmation Eliot's poem models.

For all these writers, I would stress, as essential as one's ancestral link to the group in question is that group's status as "outcast, scorned, and wandering" (I.1468). Far from irrelevant or an impediment to identification and solidarity, this stigmatization and immiseration demand and justify them: "So abject are the men whose blood we share / . . . / *Therefore* I cling to them!" (emphasis added). This solidarity in turn gives purpose and meaning—"a much grander significance," as Iola Leroy puts it[32]—to an individual life.

This dynamic is akin to one that Kwame Anthony Appiah describes in his influential work on contemporary identity categories. Following Ronald Dworkin, Appiah argues that "some of our circumstances . . . act as *parameters* . . . defining what it is for us to have lived a successful life," whereas "others are *limits* [or *limitations*]—obstacles that get in the way of our making the ideal life that the parameters help define."[33] Armed with this distinction, he observes that "so many of the identity categories that are politically salient are precisely ones that have functioned as limits, the result of the attitudes and acts of hostile or contemptuous others." Crucially, though, "categories designed for subordination can also be used to mobilize and empower people as members of a self-affirmative identity"; "as a parameter, identities provide a context for choosing, for defining the shape of our lives, but they also provide a basis for community, for positive forms of solidarity."[34] This process whereby stigmatized identities are transformed from limitations into parameters—and, I would emphasize, become parameters not despite but rather by virtue of their current status as limitations—is the story Harper and other African American writers after her extract from and associate with *The Spanish Gypsy*.

For example, Emmett J. Scott, the executive secretary of the Tuskegee Institute, cites Eliot's poem in the first chapter of *Tuskegee and Its People: Their Ideals and Achievements* (1905). Arguing that "the school teaches no more important lesson than that of cultivating a sense of pride and respect for colored men and women who deserve it because of their character, education, and achievements," Scott "borrow[s] a line from George Eliot" to drive home the importance of "pride of race"; indeed, he borrows ten lines—five from Zarca's "Therefore I cling to them" speech followed without a break, as if part of the same sentence, by lines the gypsy leader speaks later in the same scene:

Because our race has no great memories,
I will so live, it shall remember me
For deeds of such divine beneficence

As rivers have, that teach men what is good
By blessing them—
And make their name, now but a badge of scorn,
A glorious banner floating in their midst,
Stirring the air they breathe with impulses
Of generous pride, exalting fellowship
Until it soars to magnanimity.[35]

For Scott, the appeal of Eliot's lines stems from their eloquent and authoritative affirmation of the crucial role "race pride" plays in "race development" for a stigmatized race—but also, more specifically, for a race that cannot turn to its past to cultivate that pride or counter that stigma. Two recent *Spanish Gypsy* critics, Herbert Tucker and David Kurnick, both note that, in contrast to *Daniel Deronda*'s Jews, *The Spanish Gypsy*'s gypsies are represented as lacking any "proud cultural tradition" or cherished "grounding myth of origin" on which to base their collective identity.[36] Tucker calls this a "unique ethnic handicap," but for some African American writers it became instead a source of identification—and one reason, we might infer, to turn to *The Spanish Gypsy* rather than *Daniel Deronda*.[37]

We see this aspect of the poem's appeal even more clearly in "Club Movement among Negro Women," a 1902 essay by Fannie Barrier Williams, a leader of that movement. Despite appearing in a volume expansively titled *Progress of a Race; or, The Remarkable Advancement of the American Negro from the Bondage of Slavery, Ignorance and Poverty to the Freedom of Citizenship, Intelligence, Affluence, Honor and Trust*, Williams's essay emphasizes the barrenness of a past still to be overcome: "In America," she declares, "the Negro has no history, no traditions, no race ideals, no inherited resources, either mental, social or ethical, and no established race character."[38] According to Williams, the task of "colored women" is therefore to help "make history for a race that has no history," to furnish "material for the first chapter which shall some day recite the discouragements endured, the oppositions conquered, and the triumph of their faith in themselves."[39] This ambition, Williams declares, resembles that of "old Zarca in George Eliot's 'Spanish Gypsy,'" and she too quotes the passage about transforming "a badge of scorn" into "a glorious banner." "No race can long remain mean and cheap," she comments, "with aspirations such as these."[40]

Like Harper, Fannie Barrier Williams not only cites *The Spanish Gypsy* but also adapts its plot—in Williams's case, in one of her only forays into fiction. Published the same year as "Club Movement among Negro

Women," Williams's short story "After Many Days" again tells the story of a privileged young woman, raised as white, who learns that her mother was an enslaved African American (the story is set in the 1880s). "No one need ever know, no one ever can or shall know," her maternal grandmother tells Gladys Winne, yet Gladys refuses to keep this aspect of her identity secret.[41] Learning of the disparate attitudes of her white and black relatives—"Only think of it, through all the years of my life, and though I have many near relatives, I have been cherished in memory and yearned for by only one of them, and that an old and despised colored woman"—Gladys overcomes her initial horror at her grandmother's revelation, declares that "the almost infinitesimal drop of [the grandmother's] blood in my veins is really the only drop that I can consistently be proud of," and tells her white fiancé of her parentage.[42] In a departure from both *The Spanish Gypsy* and Harper's novels, the story ends on a note of interracial harmony—literally so, as Gladys Winne and her fiancé come together while the voice of a white singer "mingl[es] in singular harmony with the plaintive melody as sung by a group of dusky singers."[43] Strikingly, though, the story says nothing about the couple's future, a silence which reads less as a betrothal-plot convention than an implicit acknowledgment of the difficulty of imagining this future.[44]

Williams's "After Many Days" was one of several short stories featuring the plot of unwitting passing to appear in the first decade of the twentieth century in the *Colored American Magazine*, published in Boston.[45] Marie Louise Burgess-Ware's "Bernice, the Octoroon," which ran nine months after Williams's story, adds further twists in its version of the story. Like Eliot's Fedalma, when Burgess-Ware's Bernice learns of her ancestry she refuses to continue living as a member of the dominant race, proclaiming that "if one drop of that despised blood flows in my veins, loyal to that race I will be."[46] Also like Fedalma, Bernice takes this step even though she believes it will separate her from her beloved, who is white; although he does not reject her, Bernice herself sees the barrier as insurmountable. However, Burgess-Ware's dénouement revises Eliot's: in the poem Fedalma's fiancé, Silva, tries and fails to renounce his Spanish identity and become a gypsy so that he can still be with Fedalma, whereas in the story, Bernice's fiancé eventually learns that he too is a mulatto. Eliot's Silva kills Fedalma's father and at the end of the poem watches Fedalma depart before embarking on his effort to restore his good name as a Spaniard; in Burgess-Ware's story, by contrast, Bernice and Garrett end up happily married and active on behalf of "the race with which they are identified."[47]

By the time of Burgess-Ware's story, enough stories of unwitting pass-ing and voluntary racial affiliation had been published that the connection to Eliot's poem may seem attenuated at best. Some of the ways in which Bernice resembles Fedalma are also ways in which she resembles her im-mediate precursor Gladys as well as Harper's earlier unwitting passers, and in some ways Bernice's story differs greatly from Fedalma's. Burgess-Ware's careful formulation, "the race with which they are identified," suggests she may have had *Iola Leroy* in mind as her model, as there we see Iola looking ahead to "a brighter future for the race with which she was identified."[48] Yet Burgess-Ware explicitly links "Bernice, the Octoroon" to *The Spanish Gypsy* by giving Bernice the same last name as Fedalma's beloved: Silva. The use of this name adumbrates the story's departure from the poem, as the assign-ment of the last name of the fiancé from the earlier text to the heroine of the later one allusively foreshadows her eventual marriage, a marriage denied Fedalma and her Silva. This revision moves "Bernice, the Octoroon" closer to *Daniel Deronda* while maintaining the commitment to racial exclusivity shared by both of Eliot's works.

THE *SPANISH GYPSY*'S STIGMA

The *Spanish Gypsy* that emerges through its African American afterlife is especially remarkable because it differs dramatically from the poem as it was understood and evaluated by contemporary white British and Amer-ican reviewers and critics as well as by recent scholars. While the poem's critical reception was mixed, critics tended to single out for harsh treatment the very plot point that African American writers saw fit to celebrate and reproduce: Fedalma's decision to affiliate with the Zincali. Objections were made on both psychological and moral grounds, often inflected by racial considerations. Henry James was the rare critic to note and grudgingly ad-mire the logic and rhetoric of solidarity so important to African American writers: "The reader will admit that it is a vision of no small beauty, the conception of a stalwart chieftain who distils the cold exaltation of his pur-pose from the utter loneliness and obloquy of his race."[49] Yet even James argues that Eliot "committed herself to a signal error, in a psychological sense,—that of making a Gypsy girl with a conscience." He explains: "Either Fedalma was a perfect Zincala in temper and instinct,—in which case her adhesion to her father and her race was a blind, passionate, sensuous move-ment, which is almost expressly contradicted,—or else she was a pure and intelligent Catholic, in which case nothing in the nature of the struggle can be predicated."[50]

Pitching his criticism of the poem's psychology differently, while rejecting its morality as well, John Morley declares that "The single point in which the structure [of the poem] appears to us less nicely conformable to the rigours of fact and the often tragic demands of duty, is the nature of the circumstances that draw Fedalma away from her love." He develops this criticism at length:

> Is it compatible with what experience teaches us of the known probabilities of character, that the suddenly awakened sense of kinship should instantly suffice to overthrow the long and solidly reared fabric of training and the common life; that the apparition of Zarca should in a moment steal all their colour and force from the traditions of young and of riper days, and immediately choke up the streams of thought and affection that had their beginnings from the earliest conscious hours? . . . The question arises whether it is true or ethically sound to assume that in the past of a maiden of twenty summers all that has befallen her from childhood may be taken to count for nothing in the sum of influence and duty. . . . It is surely, too, as ethically doubtful as it is ethologically unreal. . . .[51]

The objection to the morality of Fedalma's choice is perhaps voiced most strongly by Leslie Stephen, in his 1902 book on Eliot. "Her doctrine, stated in cold blood," he writes, "seems to be that our principles are to be determined by the physical fact of ancestry," and he makes clear his view of this doctrine, in particular as it plays out in the poem: "to throw overboard all other ties on the simple ground of descent, and adopt the most preposterous schemes of the vagabonds to whom you are related, seems to be very bad morality whatever may be its affinity to positivism."[52] Stephen thus blames Eliot's failure on her philosophical commitments, seeing Fedalma's choice as a version of the altruism that was Comtean positivism's highest value. His phrasing suggests, however, that it is not simply the value attached to ancestry that he finds objectionable, but more specifically or especially the value attached to ancestors who are members of a dispossessed, despised people: "vagabonds."

Aiming his contempt elsewhere, William Dean Howells, while finding it "poetic, if not probable," that Fedalma might yield briefly "to the wild motions of her ancestral blood," caps his criticism of "[her] renunciation, at her father's bidding, of Don Silva, Spain, and Christianity" by proposing, "That [Fedalma] should act as she did was woman's weakness, perhaps,— the weakness of Miss Evans."[53] This swerve from racism to sexism not- withstanding, it is no surprise that the future author of *An Imperative Duty* would bridle at the poem's evident endorsement of an individual respond- ing to the discovery of her descent from an oppressed race by choosing to affiliate herself with that race—Howell's Rhoda Aldgate decides against just such a choice. Indeed, the novella's divergence from the poem in this regard suggests that *The Spanish Gypsy* may be Howells's true Eliotic target in *An Imperative Duty*, despite its references to *Romola*.

Alternately, Howells may have never noticed the similarity between the scenarios he and Eliot conjure up. This seems quite possible, because Howells saw *The Spanish Gypsy* as "representing a conflict between national religions and prejudices and personal passions and aspirations."[54] It was left to African American writers to notice the way Eliot's poem resonated with narratives concerned specifically with revelations of African Ameri- can ancestry, and the aftermath of such revelations. As we have seen, their perspective helps them locate the poem in a different literary-historical con- text than the ones its white British and American reviewers highlighted, and to see it as engaging in a different project. Rather than exemplifying a moral philosophy, exploring "the conflict of love and duty,"[55] or dramatiz- ing "those aspirations for independent national existence, which now more than ever before are stirring,"[56] these writers saw *The Spanish Gypsy* as a politically salutary effort to break the narrative link between discovered minority ancestry and victimization, and to imagine such a discovery in- stead as the occasion for affirmative identification and heroic (if potentially sacrificial) action.

Although critics no longer point to Eliot's sex or Fedalma's race to explain *The Spanish Gypsy*'s failings, they still rarely view the Zincali's debased status as central to the poem's aspirations, let alone its place in literary history. The same oversight is true of *Daniel Deronda* criticism, although the Jews share with the gypsies this status as dispossessed and stigmatized.[57] For example, Anthony Appiah turns to *Daniel Deronda* not to demonstrate the transfor- mation of limitations into parameters, as one might expect, but instead to support his own advocacy of a "partial cosmopolitanism" that balances or combines "the partialities of kinfolk and community" with a sense of mem- bership in "a broader human community." For Appiah, Deronda's embrace of his Jewishness is exemplary because "in claiming a Jewish loyalty . . . [he]

is not rejecting a human one."[58] Strikingly, while Appiah here is talking about identities and loyalties in general—the passage comes in the introduction to his *Cosmopolitanism: Ethics in a World of Strangers*—this brief discussion of *Daniel Deronda* appears virtually verbatim in a lecture he published several years earlier, where he uses it to capture the stance of W.E.B. Du Bois: "The challenge of cosmopolitanism is to combine this recognition of the need for partiality and the value of difference with the recognition of the value of encounter across identities. Du Bois, I believe, almost always got this balance right."[59] Yet even here, the shared status of African Americans and Jews as stigmatized minorities does not underwrite the comparison of Du Bois to Deronda; instead it drops out, despite the massive role this status plays in structuring the "encounter[s] across identities" of both historical individual and fictional character, and in determining each one's vocation.

Viewed as a belated contributor to the African American tradition of enlisting George Eliot to promote a particular relationship to one's genealogical identity, the Ghanaian-American Appiah stands out for his use of Eliot to model the proper balance between that identity and a more global perspective, rather than allegiance to that identity. Within recent Eliot criticism, the question of whether Eliot does successfully model a "partial cosmopolitanism" of the sort Appiah describes, or if she even seeks to, has been vigorously debated.[60] Like Appiah in his brief remarks, however, even the best Eliot critics in their sustained treatments of her work typically treat the stigmatized status of gypsies and Jews as incidental to her consideration of ethnic, racial, and national identity as such.[61] Why Eliot focuses on dispossessed minorities in particular, and how this status influences the characters' sense of identity and vocation, are questions that rarely arise.[62]

Eliot's critics tend to obscure the importance of stigma and differentials in power and status in her texts by highlighting parallels between minority and majority groups—Gypsy and Spanish in *The Spanish Gypsy*, Jewish and English in *Daniel Deronda*. The protagonists' mode of membership or participation in their dispossessed, stigmatized group becomes, on this reading, a model for that of members of the dominant group, most immediately for the potential love-interests from whom the protagonists are separated by their differences in group identity: the Spanish Silva from the Gypsy Fedalma, the English/Christian Gwendolen Harleth from the Jewish Deronda. For example, James Buzard argues that "Gwendolen's consciousness of Daniel's different national consciousness, her incorporation of his positive and irreducibly alien aspirations into her own mentality, decenters her (English) nationalism but also provides the impetus for more valuably recentering it."[63] According to Buzard, "the category of race" determines "for Daniel and for Gwendolen alike which culture and which nation are properly *theirs*," and therefore "would seem to be preparing the way for a 're-patriation' of both."[64] "Only the stubborn persistence of the intermarried, admirable Klesmers [she an English heiress, he an ambiguously Jewish musician] in England," he continues, "stands in the way of a recommendation for the wholesale ethnic cleansing of each nation and the clean partitioning of the civilized world into airtight container-nations for the occupation of single races."[65]

Herbert Tucker's similarly bracing reading of *The Spanish Gypsy* argues that the poem constitutes "a set of variations on one theme: Heredity Equals Destiny," as "Gypsy and Jew and Christian and Moor alike find their identities and acts biologically foredoomed—and culturally policed, for good measure."[66] Comparing Fedalma's discovery of her identity with Don Silva's "parallel plot of identity-confirmation," Tucker does acknowledge differences between their situations, but he glosses these as a difference between "majestic simplicity" and "comparative complexity": while for Fedalma "to adopt a Zincala identity and lead her people to their appointed North African home is simply to become what she always was," Silva, "as a man, and one moreover to the manor born . . . moves in a richer web of allegiances and antagonisms than Fedalma has known."[67] Tucker also addresses the Zincali's distinctive lack of a storied past, but on his account this is not a deficit to be remedied, as it is in the African American citations of the poem we have looked at, but instead portends the failure of their national project.[68] He concludes by grouping Fedalma with Daniel Deronda and *Middlemarch*'s Dorothea Brooke as three characters through whom Eliot "grappled with the question what the freedom of the cosmopolitan liberal—if freedom is what it was—might prove good for."[69]

Viewed through the lens of Eliot's African American reworkings and citations, readings such as these seem too quick to collapse (when they acknowledge at all) the difference between stigmatized and unstigmatized identities. *Pace* Buzard, for example, *Daniel Deronda* offers no suggestion that Gwendolen's sense of English identity as such is renewed or newly motivating at the end of the novel: any hope of a meaningful existence resides in her sex, not her Englishness, and the last we hear of her, in her passive-aggressive note to Daniel on his wedding day, does not inspire confidence: "*I have remembered your words—that I may live to be one of the best of women, who make others glad that they were born. I do not yet see how that can be, but you know better than I.*"[70] Similarly, rather than demonstrating the equation

Heredity=Destiny, as Tucker argues, *The Spanish Gypsy* dramatizes the process by which Inherited Stigma is embraced as the site where one's Destiny gets worked out. Tucker does not ask why the alternative Eliot repeatedly offers to illusory cosmopolitan liberalism is affiliation with a dispossessed and stigmatized race or nationality; by contrast, the African American writers considered here make visible a *Spanish Gypsy* dedicated to exploring the burdens and opportunities afforded by just such affiliation.

This emphasis on power- and status-differentials also explains a seeming inconsistency in Eliot's treatment of inherited identity itself. "What makes *The Spanish Gypsy* particularly intriguing," notes Sylvia Kasey Marks, "is that all the novels up to and including *Felix Holt* portray a character who opts for the past of his experience, or his adopted past. In *The Spanish Gypsy*, and in *Daniel Deronda* which follows it, the character determines in favor of his hereditary or racial past."[71] The most prominent Eliot characters who choose their "adopted past" over their "hereditary . . . past" are Eppie in *Silas Marner* and Esther Lyons in *Felix Holt.* In both these cases, though, the adopted past to which the character remains loyal is working class, while the hereditary one she eschews is upper class: as in *The Spanish Gypsy* (and *Daniel Deronda*), then, characters choose—and, Eliot makes clear, rightly choose—to affiliate with the lower status group.[72]

As we have seen, the ways in which African American writers took up *The Spanish Gypsy* illuminate and potentially recuperate aspects of Eliot's work many critics have found troubling. But if this more positive view depends in large part on what African American writers chose to highlight, it also depends on what they chose to change or omit. The African American engagement with *The Spanish Gypsy* is highly selective and involves fundamental changes in form and genre as well as referent and setting. But two departures from this chosen intertext are especially revealing—one because it involves the wholesale rejection or discarding of the aspect of the poem that would seem to clinch the connection between African Americans and Zincali, and the other because it involves a subtle reworking of the very aspect of the poem these writers embrace most fully. In addition to mitigating some of the most off-putting dimensions of Eliot's "unpleasing poem,"[73] such pointed departures underscore these writers' own key commitments.

The more obvious of these departures from *The Spanish Gypsy* pertains to its vision of the future. The lifework in which Zarca enlists Fedalma is the establishment of a homeland for their people. In the very next sentence of the speech Fannie Barrier Williams and Emmett J. Scott both quote about transforming the Zincali's name from "a badge of scorn" to "A glorious banner," Zarca announces his plan to "guide [their] brethren forth to their new land" (I.2823–28). The depth of Eliot's commitment to this nationalist model of group identity is reinforced by *Daniel Deronda*, where the lifework to which Deronda commits himself is the founding of a Jewish national state, and both poem and novel end with the title character's departure from the land in which she or he was raised to embark on this mission. As best I can determine, however, African American texts that adapt Eliot's plot uniformly jettison this nationalist/emigrationist project, and with one exception (to which I will return) African American citers of *The Spanish Gypsy* never mention this aspect of the poem.

This omission is particularly striking because Eliot's Zincali originate in Africa, and it is to Africa they plan to return to establish a homeland. Yet this common geography plays no apparent role in the African American engagement with the poem. This is so even though there did exist at the time an active back-to-Africa movement. Indeed, one leader of this movement, Edward Blyden (who was born in Saint Thomas and spent most of his life in Liberia), does cite Eliot—albeit a different work—in an 1883 speech (reprinted as a pamphlet) on "The Origin and Purpose of African Colonization." Explaining that "We do not ask that all the colored people should leave the United States and go to Africa," since "For the work to be accomplished much less than one-tenth of the six millions would be necessary," Blyden quotes a passage from Eliot's little-read last book, *Impressions of Theophrastus Such* (1879), which states that "Plenty of prosperous Jews remained in Babylon when Ezra marshalled his band of forty thousand," but "in a return from exile, in the restoration of a race . . . the question is not whether certain rich men choose to remain behind, but whether there will be found worthy men who will choose to lead the return."[74] However, neither *The Spanish Gypsy* nor *Daniel Deronda* seems to have been cited in support of the back-to-Africa movement.

Frances Harper openly addresses the question of emigration in *Iola Leroy*, and the scene in which she does so virtually stages this break from Eliot. Like chapter 42 of *Daniel Deronda*, chapter 30 of *Iola Leroy*, "Friends in Council," presents a set-piece political and philosophical discussion that brings together main characters with a number of characters who, while assigned names and given basic identifying features (such as appearance or occupation), appear only in this one chapter to serve as mouthpieces for various positions. The main topic of debate at the working-class Philosopher's Club meeting to which Deronda accompanies the proto-Zionist prophet Mordecai is whether the Jewish "race" should have a nation of its own, while the "select company of earnest men and women deeply interested in the welfare of the race" who gather in Harper's novel begin their evening with a discussion of "a paper on 'Negro Emigration'" prepared by a "Bishop Tunster"—a thinly veiled stand-in for a leading American advocate of emigration, Bishop Henry McNeal Turner.[75] Just as Mordecai's interlocutors—with the signal exception of Deronda himself—reject his position, so too do Tunster's reject his, with the final word going to Iola Leroy, who states, "We did not . . . place the bounds of our habitation. And I believe we are to be fixtures in this country."[76] Iola's next sentence, "But beyond the shadows I see the coruscation of a brighter day," stands as a particularly authoritative pronouncement, as it echoes the novel's subtitle and is echoed in turn in the final lines of the poem by Harper that ends the novel: "Yet the shadows bear the promise / Of a brighter coming day."[77] This echo of Iola's statement reinforces the novel's locating of this better future in the United States—which is to say, the echo reinforces the novel's rejection of Eliot's emigrationist solution.

The Spanish Gypsy itself was brought to bear on the emigration debate on at least one occasion, and with reference to Bishop Turner in particular. However, in this rule-proving exception, the poem was deployed to help make the case *against* emigration to Africa. Thus, a 1902 editorial in the Indianapolis-based *Freeman* aligns Turner with Zarca, but only to reject their shared position. Titled "Bishop Turner," the editorial takes as its epigraph a long extract (two dozen lines) of dialogue between Zarca and Fedalma from the end of book I, where Zarca wins over the hesitant Fedalma by daring her to

> Let go the rescuing rope, hurl all the tribes,
> Children and countless beings yet to come,
> Down from the upward path of light and joy,
> Back to the dark and marshy wilderness
> Where life is nought but blind tenacity
> Of that which is. (I.3108–13)[78]

The editorial does not spell out the passage's relevance, but the reader is implicitly invited to see Zarca as a figure for the subject of the editorial it heads. Yet rather than aligning itself with Eliot, the editorial rejects the Zarca/Turner position, treating it as a last resort whose time has not come: Turner's "chimera must not become our dream," the editors argue, "until the age grows so palsied with social and political infirmities that the future stands an endless blight." Moreover, the very alignment of Turner with Zarca serves not to aggrandize Turner but rather to diminish him by highlighting their shared rhetorical violence: Turner is described as using "terrific language—cloud compelling—jovian" to heap "censure and abuse" on "Negroes" who continue to hope for a future in America. The proper reaction to this onslaught is not acquiescence or even a response in kind, but rather, devastatingly, a condescending admiration: "Everybody loves [Bishop Turner]," the editorial explains, "because he seems so sincere, so picturesque."[79] Implicitly, the same is true of Zarca as well, in a rare questioning of his—and Eliot's—authority.

Clearly, then, African American writers ignored the advocacy of a separate homeland showcased in Eliot's work not because they found it irrelevant to their concerns but rather because they rejected it as a goal, even as they were drawn to other aspects of Eliot's rhetoric and narrative strategy.[80] The disarticulation of Eliot's racial-affiliation plot from its emigrationist, homeland-founding conclusion is particularly striking because both *The Spanish Gypsy* and *Daniel Deronda* seem to conflate the protagonists' affiliation with their discovered ancestry with their adoption of a nationalist project, as if the former entailed the latter. Yet for Harper and those who follow her lead, the establishment of a homeland does not constitute the inevitable telos and ultimate truth of the kind of story Eliot tells. In *Iola Leroy* in particular, however, traces of this model remain: as Hazel Carby observes, "the overall structure" of Harper's novel progresses "increasingly toward a complete separation of the black community from the white world."[81] From this perspective, the didactic explicitness with which the novel confronts and rejects "Negro Emigration" reflects both the felt necessity of placing a limit on this separatist trajectory and the strain involved in doing so—a strain generated, I am suggesting, not only by the historical existence of the "Negro Emigration" movement but also by the Eliotic narrative Harper is adapting.[82]

Just as African American writers who make use of *The Spanish Gypsy* reject its nation-based model of racial collectivity, so too do they depart from its understanding of racial identity itself. This is the case even though, as we have seen, these writers reproduce versions of its plot whereby individuals choose to affirm—that is, to own and make central to their sense of identity—their newly discovered, genealogically determined membership in a dispossessed, stigmatized people; and these writers regularly cite or borrow rhetoric from the poem in support of this choice. Despite these textual affiliations, these writers do not fully share Eliot's understanding of the nature of and motivation for the choice that gets made.

The characters who choose to affirm their identity as African American in *Minnie's Sacrifice, Iola Leroy,* "After Many Days," and "Bernice, the Octoroon" do so for two primary reasons: out of a sense of loyalty and gratitude toward specific African Americans who have welcomed, aided, and loved them (coupled with resentment of or disgust at the hostile reaction their revealed ancestry garners from whites); and out of a belief in the nobility of, and prospects for doing good through, publicly owning one's membership in an oppressed people. *The Spanish Gypsy* features versions of both these reasons, albeit in a much darker key. Thus, it is not her father's love but rather his sense of loss that affects Fedalma: "when you looked at me my joy was stabbed— / Stabbed with your pain. I wondered . . . now I know . . . / It was my father's pain" (I.2710–12, ellipses in original). And while Zarca voices the rhetoric of uplift African American writers will seize upon, Fedalma herself dwells less on what is right and hopeful about identifying with her suffering ancestral people than on the guilt she would feel at refusing to do so: "Father, I choose! I will not take a heaven / Haunted by shrieks of far-off misery" (I.3115–16).

But there is another factor in Fedalma's choice absent from the African American texts that recall *The Spanish Gypsy:* her "fully text-endorsed conviction," as Herbert Tucker puts it, that she is being restored "to her true identity."[83] The first hint of a tension between Fedalma's social identity and her essential self comes early in the poem, when she scandalously breaks into dance in the public square, "sole swayed by impulse passionate" (I.1315). Comparable, Eliot writes, to the "dance religious" of "Miriam, / When on the Red Sea shore she raised her voice / And led the chorus of her people's joy" (I.1318–20), this dancing expresses Fedalma's unassimilated and unassimilable difference even as it foreshadows her Mosaic destiny. While Eliot does not explicitly attribute Fedalma's impulse to her gypsy ancestry, Fedalma's avowal to Silva suggests that she herself comes to understand such moments in these terms. "'Twas my people's life that throbbed in me," she explains to Silva: "An unknown need stirred darkly in my soul, / And made me restless even in my bliss" (III.1060–62).

Writing about late-nineteenth- and early-twentieth-century American passing narratives, Walter Benn Michaels argues that these texts increasingly represent the choice of one's race less as "a question of personal honesty" than of "personal identity," with race increasingly treated as "an object of affect," and with "racial pride . . . supplemented . . . by what is understood

to be racially appropriate behavior."[84] Michaels sees this development as reflecting the ascendance of what he calls "nativism" or, more provocatively,
"pluralist or nativist racism."[85] Yet African American writers who adapt
and invoke *The Spanish Gypsy* eschew this nativist rhetoric and ideology; in
fact, *Iola Leroy* serves as Michaels's main example of the "personal honesty"
model: in *Iola Leroy*, he observes, the choice not to pass "is made for reasons
that are not themselves racial—Harper's characters feel they can do more
good work among poor Negroes as a Negro, or they scorn to conceal from
the white world the 'one drop' of Negro blood in their veins."[86] Michaels
claims that Harper's approach is not characteristic of fictions about passing
and implies that it reflects an increasingly outmoded concept of race; in
M. Giulia Fabi's similar, more explicit formulation, *Iola Leroy* represents "a
nineteenth-century concern with race loyalty" as opposed to "a twentieth-
century preoccupation with defining a distinctive African American identity."[87] As we have seen, however, both models are in play in *The Spanish
Gypsy*, and therefore both were readily available to Harper. The absence of
the "identity" model in her work, despite its presence in her chosen precursor text, makes it clear that this absence did not simply reflect her historical
moment but instead was a deliberate choice on her part.

   This choice may be where Harper in particular comes closest to brushing
The Spanish Gypsy against the grain: that is, by representing the affiliation of
her unwitting passers with the African American portion of their ancestry
as itself a fully deliberate choice—a simultaneously rational and sentimental
affiliation that requires a biological link but does not constitute a capitulation to or expression of one's authentic self or racial essence. Ironically, then,
when Harper uses *The Spanish Gypsy* to tell stories about African Americans and advocate a commitment to the betterment of their condition, she is
not racializing or reracializing Eliot's work, as we have seen writers do with
Dickens and Tennyson, but instead in this sense rendering it *less* racial. By the
same token, while Harper and her protagonists have been accused at times
of being too "Victorian," a fuller commitment to the very idea of "racially
appropriate behavior"[88] would have brought her even closer ideologically
to her Victorian predecessor—that is, would have made her *more* Victorian.

BECOMING GEORGE ELIOT

The African American engagement with *The Spanish Gypsy* is significant for
its role in African American literary history and George Eliot's reception
history—and for marking the intersection of these histories. Yet given the

selectivity of the African American engagement with *The Spanish Gypsy*, and its softening if not abandonment of the poem's ethnic nationalism and racial essentialism in particular, we may begin to wonder if this engagement does not so much illuminate the poem as falsify it—creating, as it were, a kinder, gentler *Spanish Gypsy* by smoothing over its most disturbing elements and downplaying its negativity. It remains the case, however, that while the poem is undoubtedly more conflicted and even rebarbative than its African American afterlife indicates, this afterlife makes newly visible and compelling Eliot's attention to stigmatized collective identities.

Moreover, beyond serving as a valuable corrective, African American deployments of the poem may paradoxically be truer to the poem's origins than is the poem itself. That is, rather than transport Eliot's work into an African American context, they may be bringing it *back* into this context. Going further, we might entertain the possibility that these writers do not so much turn *The Spanish Gypsy* into a response to the tragic mulatto/a plot as pick up on and highlight the ways it already was one. Ostensibly reframing the poem, they return it and its author to their roots.

Although there is no evidence that Eliot ever read anything written *by* an African American, several critics have detailed the importance of Harriet Beecher Stowe's novelistic depictions *of* African Americans for her work, especially *Daniel Deronda*.[89] But the alacrity with which African American writers beginning with Frances Harper brought Eliot's work to bear on their own concerns, and the affinities their efforts reveal, suggest that the literary treatment of African Americans may be even more germane to Eliot's project as an imaginative writer than we have realized. It may also have been germinal: after working for years as a translator, reviewer, essayist, and editor, Eliot turned to writing fiction a mere three days after appreciatively reviewing Stowe's *Dred*, which she praised for its focus on "that grand element—conflict of races."[90]

One can only speculate about why Eliot herself did not write about African Americans, but we might conjecture that she was ceding that territory to American writers such as Stowe. In writing about contemporary European Jews she extends rather than duplicates Stowe's project, while her focus on gypsies in fifteenth-century Spain suggests a desire to address her interests on a more general and less immediately topical level (she began work on the poem in 1864, in the midst of the American Civil War). Tellingly, though, one of the few instances in her writing when Eliot does refer to blacks comes in her own reflections on *The Spanish Gypsy*, in a posthumously published essay called "Notes on the Spanish Gypsy and Tragedy in General." Describing fit subjects for tragic presentation, Eliot conjures

"a woman, say, [who] finds herself on the earth with an inherited organi-
sation: she may be lame, she may inherit a disease, or what is tantamount
to a disease: she may be a negress, or have other marks of race repulsive in
the community where she is born, &c., &c."[91] Blackness serves here as the
quintessential inherited stigmatized identity.

Eliot's use of a stigmatized "negress" to exemplify "Tragedy in General"
paradoxically threatens to obscure the extent to which her own poem participates in and revises the specific tradition of the tragic mulatto/a plot. Yet
the very fact that Eliot makes this reference perhaps hints at an awareness on
her part of the special relevance of "negress[es]" to the story she is telling.[92]
In fact, Eliot's desire to revisit the tragic mulatto/a plot may even explain her
choice of the name "George Eliot" soon after she began publishing fiction—a
choice that has never been adequately explained.[93] This name—spelled
"George Elliot"—appears in what may be the first tragic mulatta story: "The
Quadroons," an 1842 story by Lydia Maria Child, a white American abolitionist author with whom Eliot corresponded (as she did with Stowe). An
Englishman in Georgia, George Elliot is the fiancé of a woman whose African ancestry is discovered. Attempting to save his beloved from the brutal
consequences of this discovery, Elliot is killed; she too dies. In what we might
see as a tribute to this heroic English character, Marian Evans takes his name
and succeeds where he failed—transforming the revelation of *her* unwitting
passers' minority ancestry from a source of unmitigated suffering into an
occasion for meaningful sacrifice, from a death sentence into a calling.

This theory is speculative, but by no means outlandish; we do not know
if it reflects Eliot's conscious motives, but Frances Harper and her successors
show why it would make sense. By African Americanizing her poem about
unwitting passing, they make visible the close kinship of "George Eliot" to
"George Elliot," whether Eliot was aware of it or not.

The preceding analysis ignores one profound difference between George
Eliot's version of the plot of unwitting passing and voluntary racial affiliation and the American versions with which, I argue, it is in dialogue.
All the protagonists of the latter versions are mixed race—"mulattoes" and
"mulattas"—whereas Fedalma, and Daniel Deronda as well, are not. This
means, among other things, that although both sets of characters are choosing between the identity with which they were raised and their ancestry, the
American characters are also choosing between different strands of their ancestry. This difference would seem to affect the fundamental nature of the
choice the characters make, and its omission sidelines a host of additional

issues typically addressed through the representation of mixed-race characters, such as sexual violence, the "one-drop" rule of racial identity, and the
possibility of racial amalgamation.

In overlooking this difference, however, I have simply followed the lead
of the writers I discuss. Eliot, for her part, may have chosen not to write
about mixed-race characters precisely in order to sideline the specific issues
raised by racial mixing and keep the focus where she wanted it: on the
drama of voluntary affiliation with a stigmatized, dispossessed people.[94]
The use of Eliot by Harper and the other African American writers discussed here reflects and reinforces the priority they themselves placed on
highlighting and promoting such affiliation—to the point where the very
mulattoness of the erstwhile tragic mulatto/a becomes secondary.

A very different situation pertains in the work of the author to whom we
turn next. As we shall see, Charles Chesnutt's career-long engagement with
Victorian literature is tightly bound up with his career-long exploration of
racial mixing, and he is preternaturally alert to even fleeting references to
"mulattoes" in that literature. Chesnutt will seize upon and reimagine such
moments in the work of all three Victorian authors we have seen as having
particularly intense African American afterlives: Dickens, Tennyson, and
Eliot—the latter's eschewal of mixed-race characters in *The Spanish Gypsy*
and *Daniel Deronda* notwithstanding.

Beginning with the chapter on Chesnutt, the second half of this book
flips the organizational structure of the first half: whereas each of the
first three chapters tracked African Americanizing engagements with the
work of a single Victorian author—for the most part, with a single work—
each of the second three will explore a single African American author's
engagement with fiction and poetry by multiple Victorians. For these
turn-of-the-century writers—Chesnutt, Pauline Hopkins, and W.E.B. Du
Bois—late-Victorian literature in particular continues to matter for its contemporaneity or near-contemporaneity. Increasingly, though, British literature from earlier in the nineteenth century loses this sense of immediacy
yet retains a particular historical position: that is, the works writers engage
with have not quite passed into the timeless realm of the classic or canonical, but instead remain identified with the recent past. In addition, though,
and more unexpectedly, certain authors and texts will remain worth engaging for these writers precisely because of their prior African American
afterlives. Ultimately, as we shall see, the very citation of Victorian literature
will become a form of meta-citation, a way of referencing and engaging in
dialogue with prior African American citations of that literature.

CHAPTER FOUR

RACIAL MIXING AND TEXTUAL
REMIXING: CHARLES CHESNUTT

"I have just finished Thackeray's 'Vanity Fair,' his first great novel" reports the twenty-two-year-old Charles Chesnutt, writing in the journal he kept as a teenager and young adult. "Every time I read a good novel, I want to write one," he continues. "It is the dream of my life—to be an author!" Chesnutt follows this declaration with a frank analysis of his "mixture of motives," which include "fame," "money," and the desire "to raise my children in a different rank of life from that I sprang from." Looking ahead to his summer vacation, the recently installed principal of the State Colored Normal School in Fayetteville, North Carolina, vows to "strike for an entering wedge in the literary world."[1]

This passage is perhaps the best known in Chesnutt's journals, with the phrase "to be an author" even borrowed to serve as the title of a collection of his letters. Little attention has been paid, however, to the remainder of the entry, a short sketch entitled "Tom McDonald's Lesson." Tom is a young man who shows up at a wedding to which he was not invited. At first the host's seemingly cordial greeting puts Tom at ease—"come in Tom come in; you ain't invited here, but God knows you're just as welcome as if you was"—but the constant repetition of this formula eventually leads him to flee the party in humiliation. "Must go, eh? Well I'm sorry," announces the host. "You wasn't invited here, but we've enjoyed your company just as much as if you had been." The sketch ends as the roar of laughter accompanying Tom's departure leads him to swear "a deep and solemn vow never to go again where he was not invited."[2]

What is the relationship between the two halves of this journal entry? The sketch seems less an attempt to "be an author" like Thackeray than a commentary on the plausibility—or rather, the implausibility—of such a prospect. In other words, the sketch reads as an allegory of attempted authorship, and specifically of the fear of rejection and failure that the first half of the entry strives to keep at bay: "'Where there's a will etc,' and there is certainly a will in this case" are the final words preceding the sketch,[3] but the sketch itself calls into question the validity of the invoked truism—especially when the world into which one is trying to "strike . . . an entering wedge" is not merely competitive, as Thackeray emphasizes in his own depictions of the literary marketplace, but also fundamentally hostile to one's presence.

"Tom McDonald's Lesson" never explains why Tom was not invited to the wedding in the first place. However, it does point to a likely reason for Chesnutt's figuring of "the literary world" as a party to which not everyone is invited and at which not everyone is welcome: "[T]here's plenty to eat," the host assures Tom. "You wasn't invited here, but you're just as welcome as if you was. Don't be bashful; there's plenty for all; and there'll be some left for the niggers."[4] Chesnutt says nothing about race when discussing his ambition in his journal entry, and "Tom McDonald's Lesson" does not portray explicitly African American characters. With this line, though, the sketch not only registers the status of African Americans in the society depicted but also aligns its protagonist with African Americans—or rather more pointedly, with "niggers"—as people excluded from full participation in society's bounty.

The lesson of "Tom McDonald's Lesson" notwithstanding, Chesnutt did of course become an author, and in fact this sketch, as the editor of his journals notes, "forms the germ of one of Chesnutt's first published stories, 'Tom's Warm Welcome,'" which appeared five years later.[5] More importantly, the journal entry as a whole forms the germ of one of Chesnutt's most famous stories, "The Wife of His Youth." In "The Wife of His Youth" as in the journal entry, the reading of Victorian literature and dreams of a better future are followed by the story of a party crasher. In fact, similar plots figure prominently in the first novel Chesnutt published, *The House Behind the Cedars*, and the last one he wrote, *The Quarry*. Repeatedly, that is, Chesnutt makes the reading of nineteenth-century British literature a feature and indeed engine of plot—in particular, a plot of aspiration, upward mobility, and conflicted racial identity.

Yet while Chesnutt's interest in Victorian literature is sustained, it does not remain static. Instead, and in contrast to Frances Harper's loyalty to the racial-loyalty rhetoric and plot of George Eliot's *The Spanish Gypsy* (as we saw in the previous chapter), Chesnutt's engagement with Victorian literature forms a plot of its own, developing over time and ultimately bringing to the surface aspects of this engagement that remain submerged in his earlier work. Moreover, Chesnutt not only leverages Victorian literature to tell the stories he wants to tell but also, and again in contrast to Harper, takes a more critical stance toward his intertexts, probing and exposing shortcomings in their treatment of race. Borrowing the title of his last novel, then, we might say that Victorian literature is Chesnutt's quarry: both source and prey. As we shall see, the double-edged nature of this engagement manifests itself most fully and strikingly when Chesnutt seizes on Victorian references to an identity as marginal and marginalized in that literature as it is central to his own writings: that of the racially mixed individual, the mulatto.[6]

(DIS)CONTINUOUS LIFE: "THE WIFE OF HIS YOUTH"

In contrast to Tom McDonald, who showed up at a party to which he was not invited, the protagonist of "The Wife of His Youth," as that story's first sentence announces, "was going to give a ball."[7] Mr. Ryder is in a position to do so because he has succeeded in working his way up in the world, just as the young author of "Tom McDonald's Lesson" resolves to do: "by industry, by thrift, and by study" he has achieved economic advancement and social status (111). Mr. Ryder is not an author, although his job does involve the materials of writing: he is the stationery clerk in charge of distributing office supplies for a railroad company. However, he does have "decidedly literary tastes" (102) and a passion for Tennyson that matches his creator's enthusiasm for Thackeray. In its opening pages, then, "The Wife of His Youth" reads as a kind of happy sequel to the 1881 journal entry.

From the outset, though, this reimagining of the journal entry differs dramatically from its precursor in its treatment of race: largely a subtext in the journal entry, race is explicitly central to "The Wife of His Youth." Mr. Ryder is introduced as "the dean of the Blue Veins"—"a little society of colored persons organized in a certain Northern city shortly after the war" whose members "were, generally speaking, more white than black" (101)—and the first of the story's three sections details, mainly in a tone of bemused irony, the group's fitfully and unconvincingly disavowed obsession with skin color. Mr. Ryder himself, for example, claims to "have no race prejudice" but longs nonetheless for "absorption by the white race" of "people of mixed blood" such as himself, a fate he opposes to "extinction in the black" (104). Indeed, he is giving his ball in honor of the woman to whom he intends to propose marriage, and her "many attractive qualities" include not only her "refined manners and the vivacity of her wit" but also the fact that "she was whiter than he" (103).

The greatest desire, then, of the man who is perhaps the first African American fictional character ever portrayed as a reader of Victorian literature, is to *not* be African American. I will return to the question of whether we are to understand Mr. Ryder's love of "the great English poets" (102) and Tennyson in particular as a function of this desire, as it is often read; however, the second part of "The Wife of His Youth" certainly makes clear Mr. Ryder's eagerness to put the poetry he loves to work in the service of his intertwined racial, social, and romantic aspirations. The section opens with Mr. Ryder preparing "to respond to the toast 'The Ladies' at the supper" by "fortifying himself with apt quotations" drawn "from a volume of Tennyson—his favorite poet" (104). Chesnutt shows him considering passages from three poems, all of which are quoted in the text. First Mr. Ryder reads aloud lines from "A Dream of Fair Women": "At length I saw a lady within call, / Stiller than chisell'd marble, standing there; / A daughter of the gods, divinely tall, / And most divinely fair" (104). Evidently satisfied with this passage, he "marked the verse and turning the page read the stanza beginning,—'O sweet pale Margaret, / O rare pale Margaret,'" from the poem "Margaret" (104–5). Rejecting these lines because although "Mrs. Dixon was the palest lady he expected at the ball . . . she was of a rather ruddy complexion," Mr. Ryder "ran over the leaves until his eye rested on the description of Queen Guinevere" from "Sir Launcelot and Queen Guinevere" (105). Chesnutt quotes two passages from the poem, a five-line description of Guinevere's outfit and the last six lines of the poem, which concludes, "A man had given all other bliss, / And all his worldly worth for this, / To waste his whole heart in one kiss / Upon her perfect lips." Satisfied, Mr. Ryder murmurs the words "with an appreciative thrill" (105).

In the first part of the story, Mr. Ryder's literary taste was specifically exempted from the section's otherwise pervasive irony: "He could repeat whole pages of the great English poets; and if his pronunciation was sometimes faulty, his eye, his voice, his gestures, would respond to the changing sentiment with a precision that revealed a poetic soul and disarmed criticism" (102). Here in the second part, though, criticism is re-armed, in two ways. First, Tennyson's appeal for Mr. Ryder is shown to lie at least partly in the eloquence with which the poet celebrates the beauty of white skin.

Yet Mr. Ryder is forced to acknowledge the mismatch between the Tennysonian ideal and his own reality. Second, and more subtly, the two passages Mr. Ryder chooses seem far less appropriate for the intended occasion when one recalls the women being described: the passage from "A Dream of Fair Women" describes Helen of Troy, who turns on the speaker "The star-like sorrows of immortal eyes" and announces, "Where'er I came / I brought calamity,"[8] and the adulterous love of Launcelot and Guinevere has similarly destructive consequences.

The extraction of passages in disregard of their original context is of course a common practice, and the extent to which such extracts ask to be read or ought to be read in relation to the text from which they are drawn is a perennially open question. It is a question raised regularly, sometimes pointedly, by Tennyson's own practices of allusion and rewriting of scenes from myths and legends, including those cited here. In "The Wife of His Youth," Chesnutt's emphasis on both Mr. Ryder's familiarity with Tennyson and the physical activity of handling a specific volume of his poetry—marking verses, turning pages—encourages us to treat the quoted passages not as free-floating gems but rather as extracts from specific texts. Indeed, Chesnutt gives us enough clues to infer that Mr. Ryder owns a copy of the standard edition of *The Poetical Works of Alfred Tennyson* that was reprinted repeatedly in both Britain and the United States over the last three decades of the nineteenth century: in this edition, as in Mr. Ryder's volume of Tennyson, "A Dream of Fair Women" is immediately followed by "Margaret," with "Sir Launcelot and Queen Guinevere" some pages further on in the book. These contextualizing signals reinforce the irony of Mr. Ryder's choices.[9]

This ironic treatment of Mr. Ryder's taste for Tennyson—or at least, in a distinction I will continue to insist on, of the use he makes here of Tennyson—is ostensibly reinforced by the event that occurs just as he is feeling his "appreciative thrill" (105): a "very black" woman appears at his door—a woman "who looked like a bit of the old plantation life" (105), and whose appearance contrasts sharply with that of Tennyson's Helen, Margaret, and Guinevere. Although Mr. Ryder and this woman, 'Liza Jane, do not recognize each other, it will emerge that she is the wife of his antebellum youth as a free black in the South, when his name was Sam Taylor; separated before the Civil War, she has been searching for him for a quarter-century, while he, after a brief search, moved up north, up in the world, and on with his life. As 'Liza Jane tells her story, her voice quite literally replaces Tennyson's—"'My name's 'Liza,' she began, ''Liza Jane. W'en I wuz young

I us'ter b'long ter Marse Bob Smif, down in ol Missoura. I wuz bawn down dere" (106). The poet laureate is mentioned only one more time, at the end of the second section, when Mr. Ryder writes 'Liza Jane's address "on the fly-leaf of the volume of Tennyson" (109). In the final section of the story, Mr. Ryder responds to the toast "The Ladies" not with his planned quotations but instead by telling 'Liza Jane's story and acknowledging her as "the wife of my youth" (112). In accepting in the person of 'Liza Jane the black past and identity he has sought to escape, Mr. Ryder seems to be giving up Tennyson as much as his light-skinned fiancée.[10]

Yet Tennyson's role in "The Wife of His Youth" is more ambiguous than this reading suggests. In fact, Mr. Ryder's (and therefore Chesnutt's) choice of Tennyson has a logic and a resonance that go beyond the poet's celebration of beautiful women or the cultural capital he represents. To begin with, the turn from Tennyson's women to 'Liza Jane can be read in terms of continuity as well as disruption: Mr. Ryder's writing of 'Liza Jane's address in the volume of Tennyson can be read as overwriting Tennyson, or as a move from reading white stories to writing black ones, but alternatively it might suggest a desire on Mr. Ryder's part to include 'Liza Jane within Tennyson's volume, to see her story as itself Tennysonian. Similarly, while 'Liza Jane's arrival interrupts Mr. Ryder's reading, Chesnutt presents this appearance as a phenomenon analogous to if not continuous with his readerly experiences: "She looked like a bit of the old plantation life, summoned up from the past by the wave of a magician's wand, as the poet's fancy had called into being the gracious shapes of which Mr. Ryder had just been reading" (105).

Continuity or break? 'Liza Jane's appearance raises this question not only with regard to Mr. Ryder's activity reading Tennyson, but with regard to his life as a whole. More precisely, the ensuing revelations about Mr. Ryder's past show that the question of the relationship between his present, Tennyson-reading self and his prior, 'Liza Jane–marrying self has already been central to his life, and that he felt that he had answered it: "Suppose," he says to his guests, in recounting his own history as that of someone else, "that he made his way to the North, as some of us have done, and there, where he had larger opportunities, had improved them, and had in the course of all these years grown to be as different from the ignorant boy who ran away from fear of slavery as the day is from the night," and "Suppose, too, that as the years went by, this man's memory of the past grew more and more indistinct, until at last it was rarely, except in his dreams, that any image of this bygone period rose before his mind" (111). There is good reason that "The Wife of His Youth" is "usually read . . . as a ringing endorsement of racial solidarity and a repudiation of . . . color prejudice."[11] Here we see, though, that the issue for Mr. Ryder as he himself frames it is one of loyalty not to one's race but to one's own past. And this subject, in various manifestations—the fixity or fluidity of identity over time, the extent to which the passage of time does or does not loosen one's past attachments and commitments, the potential disappointments of reunions and homecomings—is one of Tennyson's great preoccupations. It is little wonder that Mr. Ryder favors a poet who famously asks whether "men" can or should "rise on stepping-stones / Of their dead selves to higher things."[12]

The passages we see Mr. Ryder reading do not foreground this aspect of Tennyson's poetry, but the story does allude subtly to one especially relevant poem in this vein. Tennyson's hugely popular "Enoch Arden" (also reprinted in the editions that model Mr. Ryder's) tells the story of a sailor who returns home ("home—what home? had he a home?") after over a decade's absence, "so brown, so bowed, / So broken" as to be unrecognizable.[13] Both the poem and story's common scenario and their divergent dénouements are underscored by their identically worded revelations of identity: "I am the man," says Enoch Arden; "this is the woman, and I am the man," says Mr. Ryder.[14] Yet Enoch Arden only announces himself to a third party: learning that his wife, believing him dead, is happily remarried, he keeps his identity secret from her until his death, so as "not to break in upon her peace."[15] "The Wife of His Youth" obviously plays out differently. Yet that difference, we might surmise, is why Mr. Ryder turns away from Tennyson: not away from his beloved English poets in general but away from a poet who repeatedly highlights the changes wrought by the irreversible passage of time—changes, we have seen, that have been central to Mr. Ryder's self-conception. Matched with an agèd wife who comes like a ghost to trouble joy and remind him of his ties to a savage race in this rewriting of Tennyson's rewritings of the *Odyssey*, Mr. Ryder . . . yields.[16]

When thus revising his view of himself and his concomitant attitude toward his past, Mr. Ryder turns to the preeminent figure in the literary tradition of which Tennyson is the preeminent living representative: "This above all: to thine own self be true, / And it must follow, as the night the day, / Thou canst not then be false to any man."[17] These are, as Mr. Ryder says, "words that we all know" (112)—and they are also, one critic argues, an expression of "Polonius's fatuous complacency" that begs the question of "to which self . . . the story's protagonist [should be] faithful: Sam Taylor or Mr. Ryder."[18] But in fact these lines revise Mr. Ryder's own earlier statement in a way that captures precisely his shift in thinking from viewing these two identities as discontinuous to affirming their continuity. Refusing to be blinded by these lines' familiarity, Chesnutt breathes new life into Polonius's facile simile: for the man who, as we have seen, had previously used the difference between night and day to figure opposition rather than continuity—the grown man, Mr. Ryder had said, is "as different from the ignorant boy . . . as the day is from the night" (111)—the fact that night follows day is no commonplace but instead a revelation.

In "The Wife of His Youth," then, neither Tennyson nor British literature writ large stands simply or solely for whiteness: Chesnutt's intertextuality is richer and subtler than that.[19] The story also shows, however, that such a refusal to treat that literature reductively need not mean overlooking or excusing its racial assumptions and investments: Tennyson's role and resonance in the story go beyond his status as a prestigious and quotable celebrant of fair skin, but that status remains central to his significance, not incidental. For Mr. Ryder, both this colorism and Tennyson's emphasis on the irrecoverability of the past become reasons to leave the poet behind; for Chesnutt, by contrast, this combination underwrites his interest in continued investigation and dialogue. Thus, in his first published novel, *The House Behind the Cedars* (1900), he expands dramatically on "The Wife of His Youth"'s exploration of racial identity, upward mobility, and the burdens and rewards of leading what the novel will call "a continuous life."[20] Putting added pressure on these questions by taking as his protagonists mixed-race characters who, unlike Mr. Ryder, are capable of passing for or living as white, Chesnutt accords British literature, especially nineteenth-century British literature, an even more prominent role in the articulation of these concerns.

As he moves from sketch to short story to novel, Chesnutt makes increasingly explicit the ways in which the reading of such literature bears on characters' aspirations, in particular as these aspirations involve acts of racial positioning. While the journal entry with which we began barely hints at the reckoning with race that Chesnutt's Thackerayan literary ambition will require, and "The Wife of His Youth" implicitly aligns Mr. Ryder's love of Tennyson with his desire to leave behind his black past, *The House Behind the Cedars* openly narrates the role such reading plays in the *Bildung* and self-presentation of mixed-race characters who decide to live as white.

As we shall also see, though, Chesnutt's engagement with Victorian literature goes well beyond these explicit references in both scope and complexity. Indeed, his very depiction of readerly *Bildung* draws on and reworks specific Victorian models, as does his plotting. In an especially striking pattern, Chesnutt repeatedly brings into play moments where Victorian literature itself puts in play the figure of the mulatto. The recovery of this extensive and constitutive intertextuality reveals—in the terms made available by "The Wife of His Youth"—that *The House Behind the Cedars* follows from Victorian literature as the night the day.

SUSTAINING IDEAS: *THE HOUSE BEHIND THE CEDARS*

The House Behind the Cedars tells the stories of siblings Rena and John Walden, the products of a longstanding if unacknowledged union between a free, light-skinned woman whom "Tradition gave . . . to the negro race" (370) and a prominent white man in antebellum North Carolina. Rejecting the notion that he is "black" (373), the light-skinned John leaves home as a young man and eventually establishes himself as a successful white lawyer in South Carolina. The main action of the novel is set in the late 1860s, when, after a decade without any contact with his mother and younger sister, the recently widowed John returns to his hometown and suggests that Rena come live with him—as a white woman—and help raise his son. Rena agrees reluctantly, and, after a year at a finishing school, joins her brother, and is quickly courted by his friend and client, George Tryon. By chance, however, George catches a glimpse of Rena when she returns home to see her sick mother; learning that she is "negro" (362), he breaks off the engagement. George does not "out" John, who returns to his life as a white man and disappears from the novel. By contrast, Rena decides to dedicate her life to helping the "darker people" whom she had been "taught to despise" but now views as "her inalienable race" (396), and becomes a teacher at a rural school. The final section of the book shows Rena fending off the advances of a violent, vulgar man who is prominent in the black community and rejecting the renewed overtures of George, who is ostensibly engaged to another woman but can neither forget Rena nor resolve firmly to marry her despite her race. Fleeing from both suitors, Rena gets lost in a swamp during a storm and is taken to her mother's house to die, acknowledging on her deathbed that she was "loved . . . best" by Frank Fowler, a loyal, working-class black man who has worshiped her her whole life (459).

Nineteenth-century British literature figures prominently in *The House Behind the Cedars* from the outset. The novel begins with John Walden's return to his hometown—however, John does not return as "John Walden," but rather as "John Warwick," as is announced in capital letters in the second paragraph of the novel (quoting the hotel registry) and explained in the ensuing reunion scene with his mother: "From Bulwer's novel, he had read the story of Warwick the Kingmaker, and upon leaving home had chosen it for his own. He was a new man, but he had the blood of an old race, and he would select for his own one of its worthy names" (287).[21] Similarly, when Rena comes to live with him, he announces that "henceforth she must be known as Miss Warwick, dropping the old name with the old life" (296). Going further, he changes Rena's first name as well, turning to another novel of English history, Walter Scott's *Ivanhoe* (1819) for the similar-sounding but very differently signifying name of Ivanhoe's bride, Lady Rowena.

Throughout the novel, John and Rena's names index their racialized identity. The narrator's practice of always referring to John as John Warwick, as opposed to Walden, acknowledges the success of his self-fashioning as a white man, whereas the narrator's refusal to call John's sister "Rowena" reflects the temporary achievement of this social identity and the limited purchase her time living as a white person has on her self-conception. To be sure, this purchase is limited but real, as the narrator also makes clear with reference to her name: "Miss Rowena Warwick could never again become quite the Rena Walden who had left the house behind the cedars no more than a year and a half before" (409). Rena herself uses her name to indicate this liminal, conflicted state when she writes to George to refuse his request to meet after he has broken off their engagement: "You are white, and you have given me to understand that I am black" (438), she writes, and in keeping with this nuanced formulation she signs her letter "Yours very truly, Rowena Walden." This play with Rena's name continues until the novel's last line, which indicates powerfully that, no matter how split Rena's sense of self is in life, in death her social identity is clear. The novel ends with the answer to George's question "Who's dead?": "A young cullud 'oman, suh . . . Mis' Molly Walden's daughter Rena" (461). For these characters, then, to have a name taken from nineteenth-century British literature is to be (recognized as) white, and to be white is to have a name taken from nineteenth-century British literature.

As we have seen in previous chapters, nineteenth-century British literature served some of Chesnutt's predecessors and contemporaries as a resource in their efforts to promote African American identity and solidarity. In *The House Behind the Cedars*, by contrast, this literature serves as a resource for characters who reject such an identity and are uninterested in such solidarity. But John's relationship to nineteenth-century British literature is neither purely instrumental for him nor purely ironic for the novel. On the contrary, this literature is also inspirational: for John in particular, the literature he reads is not merely a tool to help him achieve his goals but also contributes significantly to the development of those goals in the first place. Thus, from the very beginning of the novel, Chesnutt emphasizes the centrality of reading to John's childhood as he experienced and remembers it: in the early reunion scene with his mother, the first statement John makes that is not in direct response to something she says is, "There are the dear old books; have they been read since I went away?" (279), and his most common memory of his childhood is of being "sprawled upon the hearth . . . reading, by the light of a blazing pine-knot or lump of resin, some volume from the bookcase in the hall" (287). The books are also at the core of his remembered relationship with Rena—he greets her by saying "You're the little sister I used to read stories to" (280)—and they have stood in for him in his absence: "I've kep' 'em dusted clean, an' kep the moths an' the bugs out," his mother explains, "for I hoped you'd come back some day, an knowd you'd like to find 'em all in their places, jus' like you left 'em" (279).

As Molly's pathetic statement indicates, however, the books that stand in for John in his absence also stand for his absence. The past to which the books connect John is a past defined by a longing to escape his home, to consign it to the past, and his youthful reading is bound up intimately with that longing and that escape. This dynamic is articulated more fully later in the novel, in a chapter that breaks from the narrative's chronological organization to stage its own return to the past. After recounting Molly's history, Chesnutt begins his sketch of John's youth with the watershed incident in which John learns of his stigma: in 1855, at the age of fifteen, "the white boys on the street" with whom he plays, and from whom "no external sign . . . mark[s] him off," inform he that he is "black," and beat him for denying it (373). This scene is followed immediately by an extended description of John's childhood reading and its effect on him. The source of John's reading material is that "small but remarkable collection of books" mentioned earlier in the novel but which, we now learn in a crucial further piece of information, was left in his home by his father—"the distinguished gentleman who did not give his name to Mis' Molly's children" (373). Chesnutt identifies the volumes in this collection in some detail:

Among the books were a volume of Fielding's complete works, in fine print, set in double columns; a set of Bulwer's novels; a collection of everything that Walter Scott—the literary idol of the South—had ever written; Beaumont and Fletcher's plays, cheek by jowl with the history of the virtuous Clarissa Harlowe; the Spectator and Tristram

Shandy, Robinson Crusoe and the Arabian Nights. On these secluded shelves Roderick Random, Don Quixote, and Gil Blas for a long time ceased their wanderings, the Pilgrim's Progress was suspended, Milton's mighty harmonies were dumb, and Shakespeare reigned over a silent kingdom. (374)

This literature fascinates and transports the young John:

he discovered the library, . . . and found in it the portal of a new world, peopled with strange and marvelous beings. Lying prone upon the floor of the shaded front piazza, behind the fragrant garden, he followed the fortunes of Tom Jones and Sophia; he wept over the fate of Eugene Aram; he penetrated with Richard the Lion-heart into Saladin's tent, with Gil Blas into the robbers' cave; he flew through the air on the magic carpet or the enchanted horse, or tied with Sindbad to the roc's leg. (374)

No mere diversion, John's reading transforms him: having "tasted of the fruit of the Tree of Knowledge," he loses any sense of "contentment" with his lot and comes to believe that "happiness lay far beyond the sphere where he was born" (375). This account of John's reading is accordingly followed immediately by the narration of his first concrete step toward escaping that sphere, as he successfully appeals for help to a leading citizen of the town, Judge Straight, to whom he announces his desire to be a lawyer and his intention to live as the white man he considers himself to be.

Chesnutt portrays the young John's refusal to be defined and constrained by an arbitrary, oppressive racial designation, as well as the role his reading plays in cultivating this defiant attitude, with sympathy and understanding. However, not only does the novel show the costs of John's actions—costs borne primarily by his mother and sister—but it also implicates the very literature that inspires John to "[demand] entrance to the golden gate of opportunity, which society barred to all who bore the blood of the despised race" (378) in the barring of that gate. As we have seen, Chesnutt interrupts his cataloging of John's library to label Walter Scott "the literary idol of the South" (374), and he develops this point more fully in an earlier scene depicting the Clarence Social Club's annual tournament. Modeled on the tournament scene in *Ivanhoe*, these "bloodless imitations" (298) stand as a testament to what Chesnutt describes as "the influence of Walter Scott . . . upon the old South" (298): "The South before the war was essentially feudal," the narrator explains, "and Scott's novels of chivalry appealed forcefully to the feudal heart" (298).[22] It is at this historically diminished, politically reactionary, doubly nostalgic (because nostalgic for the antebellum South as much as for a mythical English past) event that "Rowena Warwick" is chosen by George Tryon as the Queen of Love and Beauty (and chosen, we might add over the other "six Rebeccas and eight Rowenas" present [302]). This triumph is thus rendered as dubious by its setting as by its consequences.[23]

Despite his Scott-fueled aspirations, John himself seems to cast a satirical eye on southern society's most egregious self-mythologizing: his ostensible argument for the superiority of the Clarence tournament over its model leads another spectator to accuse him of being "the least bit heretical about our chivalry—or else . . . a little too deep for me" (299). Nonetheless, John remains unequivocally committed to succeeding in this society; despite any failings, it remains for him what Tom McDonald might call the only party in town.

The same might be said for Chesnutt himself: although John represents a road not taken by his creator—who considered and rejected the idea of passing for white—Chesnutt also sought to succeed in the white world. Also like his character, Chesnutt finds models in nineteenth-century British literature. However, Chesnutt's engagement with that literature far exceeds that of his character in its variety, extent, and sophistication, and bespeaks an attitude toward that literature as complex as the attitude toward the promotion of African American identity and solidarity with which it is entangled. Like John, though, Chesnutt drops hints that his attitude toward this literature may be "the least bit heretical"—hints, like John's, that have proved "too deep" for his readers insofar as they have gone largely unrecognized. As we shall see, Chesnutt does eventually bring his deep game to the surface, but not in *The House Behind the Cedars*, nor indeed in any other work published in his lifetime.

As in "The Wife of His Youth," I am suggesting, nineteenth-century British literature not only plays a key role in characters' efforts to negotiate their relationships to their own past—to break from or remain loyal to it, to be cut off from or trapped by it, to choose among or be unable to choose among its constituent elements—but also plays a further, non-identical but equally key role in Chesnutt's depiction of these efforts. These distinct levels of engagement are most dramatically on display in the episode that, for different reasons, Richard Brodhead has identified as the novel's "primal scene": the depiction of John's childhood reading, discussed above. As Brodhead notes, this scene "is set at the bookcase that stands for [John and

Rena's] absent white father";[24] what has gone unnoticed is that this scene not only depicts literary affiliations but enacts one of its own. In fact, it rewrites another primal scene featuring another absent (white) father.

Describing his youthful suffering under his step-father's cruel treatment, David Copperfield declares, "I believe I should have been almost stupefied but for one circumstance":

> It was this. My father had left a small collection of books in a little room up stairs, to which I had access (for it adjoined my own) and which nobody else in our house ever troubled. From that blessed little room, Roderick Random, Peregrine Pickle, Humphrey Clinker, Tom Jones, The Vicar of Wakefield, Don Quixote, Gil Blas, and Robinson Crusoe, came out, a glorious host, to keep me company. They kept alive my fancy, and my hope of something beyond that place and time,—they, and the Arabian Nights, and the Tales of the Genii,—and did me no harm; for whatever harm was in some of them was not there for me; I knew nothing of it. . . . It is curious to me how I could ever have consoled myself under my small troubles (which were great troubles to me), by impersonating my favorite characters in them—as I did—and by putting Mr. and Miss Murdstone into all the bad ones—which I did too. I have been Tom Jones (a child's Tom Jones, a harmless creature) for a week together. I have sustained my own idea of Roderick Random for a month at a stretch, I believe. . . .
>
> This was my only and my constant comfort. When I think of it, the picture always rises in my mind, of a summer evening, the boys at play in the churchyard, and I sitting on my bed, reading as if for life.[25]

The echoes of this well-known passage in *The House Behind the Cedars* are unmistakable. Just as the young David turns to his dead father's collection of books, "which nobody else in our house ever troubled," so too does the young John turn to his own dead father's collection of books, "which for several years had been without a reader." The collections contain many of the same books: *Tom Jones, Roderick Random, Don Quixote, Gil Blas, Robinson Crusoe, Arabian Nights*. Both accounts emphasize the readerly experience of identification—"I have been Tom Jones"; "[John] flew through the air on the magic carpet"—and both stress the impact of the characters' reading on their dreams for the future: David's books give him "hope of something beyond that place and time," while John's open "the portal of a new world" and lead him to believe that "happiness lay far beyond the sphere where he was born."

Thus, while John's reading shapes his aspirations and leads him to model himself on a character from a Victorian novel, Chesnutt's depiction of this *Bildung*—the very process by which John arrives at those aspirations and identifications—finds its own model in a Victorian novel. Chesnutt shifts the emphasis from consolation to discontent and adds Scott and Bulwer Lytton to the reading list, but these departures from his Dickensian template do not seem particularly charged. Moreover, Chesnutt's very transporting or transposition of the passage accords fully with the spirit of the passage itself, which is about acts of literary transport; the depicted acts may be readerly rather than writerly, but the passage's emphasis on the active role of the readerly imagination diminishes the importance of this distinction. Just as David Copperfield "sustained [his] own idea of Roderick Random for a month at a stretch," so too does Chesnutt sustain his own idea of David Copperfield.[26]

But Chesnutt's idea of David Copperfield is not identical to Dickens's, and the most salient differences between the two characters have to do precisely with the "sustaining" of ideas and identities. These differences underwrite two key revisions Chesnutt makes to Dickens's passage. The first of these is paradoxically so basic as to be easily overlooked: the shift in narration from first- to third-person. This shift reflects the fact that David writes an autobiography and John does not, and this fundamental difference indicates in turn the gap between their respective relationships with their past. That is, the adult David's writing of his autobiography (even one which "he never meant to be Published on any account," as the wrappers of the novel's original monthly parts had it) reflects his investment in remembering and memorializing his childhood, and his desire to view and make sense of his life as a whole; by contrast, John does not write an autobiography because he seeks to distance himself from his childhood and efface any record of it. David may be unsure "Whether I shall turn out to be the hero of my own life,"[27] but John is ultimately not even the protagonist of the novel he inhabits, as he is able to sustain his own idea of himself only by cutting all ties with the social world it depicts.

Remarkably, though, Chesnutt's sustained "idea" or version of David happens to be Dickens's own, unsustained idea of David as well: just as the library scene in *The House Behind the Cedars* is preceded by John being informed that he is "black," the library scene in *David Copperfield* is preceded by David "having made a Mulatto of myself"—a feat David accomplishes "by getting the dirt of the slate into the pores of my skin" while doing his lessons.[28] If John Walden is a mulatto David Copperfield, then, so too is

David Copperfield, at least briefly. Or rather: but only briefly. David's use of this word hints at a self-pitying parallel between the abuse he receives at the hands of his step-father and her sister and the treatment of American slaves, and the proximity of this image to David's account of his reading perhaps gestures toward Frederick Douglass's account of the role of literacy in his struggle to survive and escape slavery.[29] But these connections are not developed. Chesnutt's other key revision of Dickens, then, is to literalize his metaphor, and to explore at length an identity the Victorian author invokes only momentarily—and hardly ever invokes at all: this is one of only two, equally fleeting appearances of the word *mulatto* in any of Dickens's novels.[30]

The deliberateness with which Chesnutt seizes on what we might term the "mulatto moment" in *David Copperfield* is underscored—and the stakes of this reworking are clarified—by his invocation of another such moment in the same scene. Immediately after explaining that John's reading leads him to believe that "happiness lay far beyond the sphere where he was born," the narrator states, "The blood of his white fathers, the heirs of the ages, cried out for its own, and after the manner of that blood set about getting the object of its desire" (375). This ambiguously focalized sentence alludes to a line in Tennyson's 1842 poem "Locksley Hall": "I the heir of all the ages, in the foremost files of time."[31] Brief as it is, this allusion does a good deal of work.[32] For John, the line speaks to his claiming of his white ancestry and to the privileged status that makes white ancestry worth claiming. It looks both back in time and ahead, in a manner that recalls and extends the logic of his adoption of the name Warwick: "He was a new man, but he had the blood of an old race" (287); in Tennyson's construction, it is the very age of this race that makes for the individual's newness, that positions him to lead the way into the future.

However, if we return this line to its original context, its resonance changes. The speaker of Tennyson's poem, embittered by the loss of the woman he loves to a wealthier suitor, imagines abandoning the civilized world for a tropical island, where "I will take some savage woman, she shall rear my dusky race" (l. 168). After imagining his mixed-race children frolicking in the natural world, "Not with blinded eyesight poring over miserable books" (l. 172), the speaker recoils from this vision—

I, to herd with narrow foreheads, vacant of our glorious gains,
Like a beast with lower pleasures, like a beast with lower pains!
Mated with a squalid savage—what to me were sun or clime?
(ll. 175–77)

It is here that the speaker reasserts his identity as "the heir of all the ages." Thus, the very passage John lights upon to assert his whiteness, his connection to his "white fathers," signals the rejection or even negation of mixed-race progeny such as himself. John's father has taken the course the speaker of the poem imagines but disavows, taking (what that speaker would view as) "some savage woman" as the mother of his children. Tennyson himself wrote a sequel to the poem, in which the speaker addresses his grandson, and *The House Behind the Cedars*, published fifty-eight years after "Locksley Hall," stands as a kind of alternative "Locksley Hall Sixty Years After."[33]

Thus, rather than African Americanize Victorian works in the manner of Hannah Crafts or George Henry Boker or Frances Harper—that is, rather than use a Victorian text about white characters as a model or template for his own texts about black characters—Chesnutt homes in on Victorian texts that invoke and flirt with such parallels themselves—or rather, homes in with remarkable precision on texts that invoke not black but rather mixed-race identities. How are we to read this pattern? Insofar as Chesnutt's echoes and allusions invoke the mixed-race identity John seeks to escape, there is a definite irony here at the character's expense.

John's very choice of "Warwick" as a name reinforces this irony—not because Bulwer Lytton figures Warwick as a mulatto, but rather because John's literary self-renaming recalls the famous real-life precedent of Frederick Douglass, especially given Chesnutt's alignment of Bulwer Lytton with Scott. We are given no reason to believe that John would have been aware of this precedent—certainly no work in which it is described is included in his youthful library. However, the episode would have been fresh in Chesnutt's mind, as he had recounted it in the biography of Douglass he published in 1899, the year before *The House Behind the Cedars* came out:

> In New York [after escaping from slavery] he had called himself Frederick Johnson; but, finding when he reached New Bedford that a considerable portion of the colored population of the city already rejoiced in this familiar designation, he fell in with the suggestion of his host, who had been reading Scott's Lady of the Lake, and traced an analogy between the runaway slave and the fugitive chieftain, that the new freeman should call himself Douglass, after the noble Scot of that name. The choice proved not inappropriate, for this modern Douglass fought as valiantly in his own cause and with his own weapons as ever any Douglas [*sic*] fought with flashing steel in border foray.[34]

Just as John's association with works by Dickens and Tennyson paradoxically reinforces his identity as mixed race, then, so too does his choice of a name, meant to facilitate his abandonment of his mother's race and embrace of a white identity, align him with the mixed-race Douglass, whose comparable choice marks his opposite commitment.

Yet Chesnutt's irony cuts against the Victorian authors as much as it does against Chesnutt's own character. By writing a version of David Copperfield who really is a mulatto—that is, by literalizing a figure Dickens is only interested in, and barely interested in, as a figure—Chesnutt does not follow Dickens's lead or even simply redeploy the latter's work for his own purposes, but instead points up the limitations of Dickens's vision and sympathies. Indeed, the juxtaposition with the allusion to Tennyson casts Dickens's practice as a milder version of "Locksley Hall"'s vision of mixed-race progeny: the figure of the mulatto is not invoked in *David Copperfield* in order to be rejected in disgust, as for the speaker of the poem, but is invoked nonetheless as a symbol of abjection and as shadow to the story's real substance and focus. Critics such as Susan Meyer and Jennifer Devere Brody have taught us to recognize the figurative violence Victorian literature does to people of color by reducing them to the status of figures, or otherwise marginalizing them—by refusing, we might say, to sustain the idea of these characters.[35] Charles Chesnutt's rewriting of Victorian literature's mulatto moments—his insistence on sustaining the idea—signals and acts upon a similar recognition. "I wish I could write like Dickens," the teenage Chesnutt wrote in his journal in 1875, "but alas! I can't."[36] In *The House Behind the Cedars* the adult Chesnutt found a way to fulfill, cancel, and surpass that desire.

Despite the close resemblance between the formative scenes of childhood reading in *The House Behind the Cedars* and *David Copperfield*, John Walden's and David Copperfield's stories diverge sharply. Put differently, the close resemblance between these scenes highlights the differences between the characters: David's momentarily darkened skin notwithstanding, *The House Behind the Cedars* suggests that to be a mulatto David Copperfield is to live a life very unlike David Copperfield's. To sustain the conceit of a mulatto David Copperfield, in other words, is to abandon the parallels between the two characters, since John's youthful reading inspires him to break from his childhood traumas—to lead a discontinuous life—whereas David finds in his reading the tools to integrate his. However, it is the character in *The House Behind the Cedars* who aspires to lead a continuous life and is doomed to lead such a life—John's sister, Rena—who bears the most sustained resemblance to Victorian predecessors. The mulatto-minded Victorian intertextuality that underwrites the "primal scene" of John's life shapes and shadows his sister Rena's story as a whole, in a less concentrated but more pervasive way.[37]

Consideration of this intertextuality is important not only because it captures a formative aspect of the novel that has gone largely unrecognized—and not only because it illuminates the novel's Victorian intertexts as well—but also because it makes newly compelling the part of the novel critics often deem weakest: its treatment of Rena, and in particular the fact that she dies. For these critics, Rena's death makes her a disappointingly conventional "tragic mulatta," and represents Chesnutt's capitulation to the expectations of the white literary marketplace. In a typical expression of this view, for example, Matthew Wilson writes that *"The House Behind the Cedars* is the most conventional of the three novels published in Chesnutt's lifetime in its willingness to accommodate itself to its genre, to what William L. Andrews has termed 'the protocols of "tragic mulatta" fiction,' the racialized genre of the novel par excellence for a white audience at the turn of the century."[38] Whatever the merit of such claims regarding the novel's resemblance to existing American novels (and these claims rarely descend from their invocations of generic convention to the identification and discussion of specific precursor texts), my argument is that in its depiction of Rena, as in its depiction of John, *The House Behind the Cedars* is also in dialogue with a series of Victorian novels, and it is through this dialogue that the novel's literary-historical intervention emerges most fully.

Even more so than his portrayal of John, Chesnutt's depiction of Rena shows that while his characters inhabit nineteenth-century British novels, they do not inhabit novels of their own choosing, or in the manner they choose. This is partly due to the difference racial status makes, as we have just seen with John and will see again with Rena. However, and somewhat paradoxically, it is also because that tradition includes powerfully sympathetic representations of characters whose stories resemble Rena's. In his dialogue with nineteenth-century British literature, Chesnutt shows himself equally alert to the existence of such representations and to their limitations.

Even *Ivanhoe*, the novel Chesnutt links most closely to southern white society's values and self-conception, shows the victims and costs of that society's constitution. Chesnutt alludes to this aspect of Scott's novel in a scene in which the literary and historical antecedents of Rena's assumed name are noted. Directly preceding George's discovery of Rena's "true" identity, this discussion points not to the end of *Ivanhoe*'s relevance to her identity or story but rather to the refinement of that relevance, an improvement of its fit to her situation: George's announcement that his beloved is "a Miss Rowena Warwick" sparks the following exchange:

> "A good, strong old English name," observed the doctor.
> "The heroine of 'Ivanhoe'!" exclaimed Miss Harriet.
> "Warwick the Kingmaker!" said Miss Mary. "Is she tall and fair, and dignified and stately?"
> "She is tall, dark rather than fair, and full of tender grace and sweet humility."
> "She should have been named Rebecca instead of Rowena," rejoined Miss Mary, who was well up in her Scott. (358)

Miss Mary is right: Rena proves to resemble more closely the Jewess Rebecca than she does the Saxon Rowena, not only because of her complexion and manner but also because she is a member of an oppressed minority— and because, like Rebecca, the man she loves will not marry her because of this status. Read thus, *Ivanhoe* makes plain the barriers Rena faces.[39]

To John and Rena's—especially Rena's—misfortune, the Walden siblings obviously do not read *Ivanhoe* thus. The novel's sole reference to Rena's own reading (as opposed to her brother's reading to her) might be taken to suggest that Rena has read novels too credulously: "But would her lover still love her, if he knew all? She had read some of the novels in the bookcase in her mother's hall, and others at boarding school. She had read that love was a conqueror, that neither life nor death, nor creed nor caste, could stay his triumphant course" (318). However, the example of *Ivanhoe* suggests instead that her mistake as a reader is misidentification: love does overcome obstacles in *Ivanhoe*—just not the obstacle that most resembles her own.

To identify with Rebecca as opposed to Rowena arguably requires one to read against the grain of Scott's novel, but such reading practices did exist at the time. In fact, Rena could have found an exact model in a novel published in the period between John's departure from the family home and her own arrival at boarding school. "I'm determined to read no more books where the blond-haired women carry away all the happiness," *The Mill on the Floss*'s Maggie Tulliver famously declares. "If you could give me some story, now, where the dark woman triumphs, it would restore the balance. I want to avenge Rebecca and Flora MacIvor, and Minna and all the rest of the dark unhappy ones."[40]

As Maggie's protest makes plain, criticism of (some of) the prejudices inscribed in nineteenth-century British literature is also inscribed in that literature, as are at least the seeds of counternarratives. And while *The House Behind the Cedars* is silent on the question of whether Rena has read *The Mill on the Floss*, let alone read it well, the novel gives abundant clues that her creator has done so and is alert to this element of immanent critique. But Chesnutt does not give us the story Maggie asks for any more than George Eliot does: refusing to fulfill that wish, he gives Maggie's own story to Rena.

The significant echoes of *The Mill on the Floss* in *The House Behind the Cedars* begin with the similarly structured titles—titles that reflect the similarly central role of the protagonists' childhood home, not only as a home but as a site of fraught departures and returns. Crucial to both novels is an older brother–younger sister relationship that generates crises of familial loyalty. Tom Tulliver represents the "continuous life" Maggie alternately cherishes and chafes against ("I desire no future that will break the ties of the past. . . . I can do nothing willingly that will divide me always from him"),[41] whereas John models and engineers Rena's (failed) break from the past ("Thus for the time being was severed the last tie that bound Rena to her narrow past, and for some time to come the places and the people who had known her once were to know her no more").[42] In both cases, though, the brothers are much less conflicted in their ambitions and desires and much more successful in achieving them, and in both novels the sister's final return home estranges her from her brother, with Rena refusing John's invitation to again move away from her mother's home ("I left her once . . . and it brought pain and sorrow to all three of us. . . . I will not leave her here to die alone")[43] and Maggie's return unmarried from her scandalous outing with Stephen Guest leading her brother to cut off contact with her (until their dying reconciliation). Unlike Rena, Maggie cannot live in her childhood home, since it is now her brother's. However, she, along with her mother, is taken in by Bob Jakin, the loyal working-class admirer who has worshiped her since childhood, and *The House Behind the Cedars* features a very similar character, Frank Fowler: like Bob, Frank provides intermittent but lifelong support to the woman he adores, including when she is abandoned by her older brother as well as separated from her erstwhile lover.

Rena's resemblance to Maggie is clinched by her death, and it is in his treatment of this death that Chesnutt comes closest to openly alluding to *The Mill on the Floss*. The threat of drowning hangs over both novels: early in Eliot's novel, Maggie's mother declares, "where's the use o' my telling you to keep away from the water? You'll tumble in and be drownded some day,"[44] and of course this prophecy is fulfilled in the flood that ends the novel. Similarly, Frank saves Rena from drowning as a child, and two mentions of a possible flood are so extraneous to the narrative that they beg to be read as foreshadowing: Rena's mother reports to her in passing in a letter that "there has been a big freshet in the river, and it looked at one time as if the new bridge would be washed away" (330); soon thereafter, a minor character comments, "There was a freshet here a few weeks ago . . . and they had to open the flood-gates and let the water out of the mill pond, for if the dam had broken, as it did twenty years ago, it would have washed the pillars from under the judge's office and let it down in the creek" (340). This repetition primes the reader to expect a *Mill*-like cataclysm—and perhaps, through its juxtaposition of the words "mill" and "flood," to think of Eliot's novel itself. The expectation of a fatal flood is fulfilled in the antepenultimate chapter, titled "In Deep Waters"; while the waters that kill Rena ultimately prove metaphorical rather than symbolic, this is barely so: although she does not literally drown, she is carried to her deathbed after being found "lying unconscious in the edge of the swamp" after this chapter's violent storm, in which "the rain fell in torrents" (448). Like Maggie, Rena dies a death that releases her from her double bind and brings the novel to an abrupt close.

Just as John is a mulatto David Copperfield, then, so too is Rena a mulatta Maggie Tulliver. And just as John's Victorian-novel predecessor is not himself a mulatto but is described as resembling one, the same is true of Rena's: according to Mrs. Tulliver, Maggie has "brown skin as makes her look like a mulatter."[45] This ostensible mulattaness, unlike David's, does not wash off, and it is what leads Maggie to identify with Rebecca instead of Rowena. Eliot does not explicitly develop this analogy any more than Dickens does, but the permanence of Maggie's brown skin does correspond with the more lasting resemblance of her story to Rena's.

In literalizing and sustaining the idea of Maggie Tulliver as mulatta, then, Chesnutt departs much less dramatically from his intertext than he does when sustaining the idea of David Copperfield as mulatto. This commonality between female protagonists suggests the determining role of gender in the scenarios conjured in both novels—even as Mrs. Tulliver's comment hints at George Eliot's awareness of the abiding relevance of racial dynamics, and the tragic-mulatta trope in particular, to the stories she wants to tell (as discussed in the previous chapter). At the same time, Chesnutt's elaboration of the parallels between stories shows his own alertness to Eliot's hint, and his own recognition of the relevance of Eliot's project to his own.

The echoes of *The Mill on the Floss* make it clear that even or especially when Rena fails to secure her place in the traditional society represented for her by Scott and Bulwer Lytton, Chesnutt is working in the tradition of the British novel. Put differently, notwithstanding nineteenth-century British literature's association with whiteness in the eyes of Chesnutt's characters, Rena is never more of a Victorian novel heroine than when she is no longer attempting to pass as white—when she is no longer willing or able to break from her past, when she is attempting to both return and move on after this attempt fails, when she dies. To be sure, very few prominent Victorian novels end with the death of a female protagonist, and indeed such an ending is rare enough to have been controversial (rather than trite, as critics today often view the fate of "tragic mulattas"). But *The Mill on the Floss* is one of two Victorian novels that famously end not only with the female protagonist's death but with her death at the very sort of impasse Rena's story reaches (which raises them to the level of tragedy), and *The House Behind the Cedars* is in dialogue with both. As Jay Saunders Redding observed in his pioneering work on African American literature:

> Rena faces the same problem that faced Hardy's Tess—whether to disclose her secret (of Negro blood) on the chance that her happiness would not be destroyed thereby. Like Tess, she sees the problem as a moral issue. The Hardian flavor is strong: the primary sin which was, however, not her sin, the struggle between the desire for happiness and the propulsion to truth, the innumerable circumstances that work for and against, and finally, the stark, bare tragedy and the resolution in death.[46]

Published in 1891, just nine years before *The House Behind the Cedars, Tess of the d'Urbervilles* conducts its own, more ostentatious interrogation of the literary tradition it nonetheless (and thereby) extends. Chesnutt's engagement with Hardy's novel reinforces this dynamic, as his use of *Tess* aligns it with the earlier novels Chesnutt himself both builds on and critiques. In other words, the presence of the near-contemporaneous *Tess* in Chesnutt's novel suggests the continued authority and even currency of the tradition Chesnutt is working with and on. And a finer-grained comparison of *Tess* and *The House Behind the Cedars* shows that this presence is even greater than Redding indicates. For example, like Angel Clare, who recoils from Tess when he learns of her sexual history despite being an "advanced and well-meaning young man,"[47] George Tryon breaks from Rena when he learns her racial ancestry despite his "liberality, of which he had spoken so nobly and so sincerely" (362). Just as Angel "looked upon [Tess] as a species of impostor, a guilty woman in the guise of an innocent one,"[48] George thinks of "the fraud of which he had been made the victim[:] A negro girl had been foisted upon him for a white woman" (362).

In both cases, moreover, this line between tainted sexuality and tainted ancestry blurs: Angel tells Tess, "I cannot help associating your decline as a family with this other fact—of your want of firmness,"[49] while Rena's physical collapse upon George's discovery of her mixed-race parentage leads to her being described tellingly as "the young woman who had fallen" (361). And yet in both cases the man eventually attempts to restore the relationship, but too late: by the time Angel finds Tess, she has returned to Alec d'Urberville and is in a state of death-in-life—"his original Tess had spiritually ceased to recognize the body before him as hers—allowing it to drift, like a corpse upon the current, in a direction dissociated from its living will"[50]—while by the time George arrives in Patesville to tell Rena "that he loved her, that she was all the world to him, that he had come to marry her, and take her away where they might be happy together" (461), she is already dead.

What Redding calls "the Hardian flavor" of *The House Behind the Cedars* is also discernible in Chesnutt's prose at the level of phrase and sentence. It is perhaps strongest in this final chapter, when the narrator pulls back from the image of Frank sobbing over the delirious, dying Rena:

> Meantime the sun shone on as brightly as before, the mocking-bird sang yet more joyously. A gentle breeze sprang up and wafted the odor of bay and jessamine past them on its wings. The grand triumphal sweep of nature's onward march recked nothing of life's little tragedies. (458)[51]

This bitterly ironic zoom-out to record the natural world's indifference to human suffering is a classic Hardian move, as when Hardy pivots away from Alec d'Urberville's rape of Tess to note the "gentle roosting birds" and "hopping rabbits and hares."[52] Indeed, Chesnutt seems to have paid particularly close attention to that famous scene: for example, the narrator's statement that Rena "was yet to learn that the innocent suffer with the guilty, and feel the punishment the more keenly because unmerited. She had yet to learn that the old Mosaic formula, 'The sins of the fathers shall be visited upon the children,' was graven more indelibly upon the heart of the race than upon the tables of Sinai" (318), recalls (while shifting the emphasis of) Hardy's "But though to visit the sins of the fathers upon the children may be a morality good enough for divinities, it is scorned by average human nature; and it therefore does not mend the matter."[53] Chesnutt similarly incorporates while tweaking the sentiment expressed in the next sentence from this passage: "As Tess's own people down in those retreats are never tired of saying among each other in their fatalistic way: 'It was to be'"[54] echoes in the suggestion that "From some ancestral source [Rena] had derived a strain of the passive fatalism by which alone one can submit uncomplainingly to the inevitable" (328).

In a striking convergence, Maggie Tulliver, Tess Durbeyfield/d'Urberville, and Rena Walden/Warwick all descend into "the valley of humiliation."[55] While it would be a stretch to read Chesnutt's use of Bunyan's evocative phrase as alluding to Eliot or Hardy (let alone both), the three authors' shared recourse to this image—which appears almost nowhere else in now-canonical Victorian fiction[56]—further attests to Chesnutt's place in this lineage.[57] Or rather, Chesnutt himself helps construct and make visible a transatlantic, interracial lineage in which the novelistic treatment of scandals of fallenness and mixed-race ancestry (interracial lineage) are mutually informed and illuminating. Unlike Maggie, Tess is not compared to a mulatta, but Chesnutt's reworking of Hardy's novel shows how much she too is "like a mulatter," for reasons other than the color of her skin. Indeed, Chesnutt newly motivates a prominent yet seemingly insignificant detail in *Tess*: Tess's native village, we learn in the very first sentence of the novel, is located in the "Vale of Blakemore or Blackmoor." While the existence of alternative names for the locale speaks to the lingering orality of its inhabitants' culture, the actual content of the variant opens up Hardy's provincially anchored story to a more global and interracial horizon. The nearly identical variant name "Blackmoor," we might say, hints punningly at the possibility of a variant story that is also nearly identical—only more black (if not the story of a "blackamoor"). With *The House Behind the Cedars*, Chesnutt provides such a story.[58]

In his depiction of Rena as in his depiction of John, Chesnutt is not only extending the tradition of the British novel but also at times working athwart or against it. In light of what we have seen with regard to Eliot and Hardy, we should keep in mind that this tradition itself is characterized by or even formed through continuity, revision, and critique; nonetheless, the distinctive revisions Chesnutt enacts and the insights these revisions in turn afford are not necessarily present (elsewhere) within this tradition. Moreover, at times the critical edge of these revisions seems particularly sharp. With the treatment of Rena as with that of John, this sharper edge emerges when Chesnutt moves from literalizing figurative mulattoes to invoking or reworking a Victorian text that depicts, or flirts with depicting, an actual mixed-race character. In Rena's story, this intertextual role—which we saw played by "Locksley Hall" in John's narrative—is filled by the novel that portrays the most notorious (if ambiguously) mixed-race character in Victorian literature: *Jane Eyre*.

As with "Locksley Hall," Chesnutt signals this intertextual engagement through an allusion, although this latter allusion—and the sustained connection it hints at—seems to have gone unrecognized (as have the links to *David Copperfield* and *The Mill on the Floss*). The explicit allusion comes in the name Chesnutt assigns Rena's romantic rival, who is a more caste-appropriate choice for the man she loves: Blanche. Perhaps the too-obvious racial signification of this name has kept critics from reading it as an allusion to Blanche Ingram, Rochester's supposed love-interest in *Jane Eyre*. In both novels, though, the protagonists' engagements are broken off not because of the would-be groom's preference for a Blanche but rather because of the discovery of a "creole" (370), in the person of Bertha Mason or Rena herself. Moreover, the post-broken-off-engagement phase of Rena's story tracks Jane's: after Jane's engagement falls through, her flight from temptation leads her to strangers who turn out to be her kin—cousins with whom she comes to share "sisterly love";[59] after Rena's own engagement falls through, Rena gains a new sense of kinship with her "rediscovered people," whom she views with the "sympathy of a sister" (396). Jane takes a job teaching peasant girls in a remote village schoolhouse, keeping busy by day and "rush[ing] into strange dreams at night . . . dreams where . . . I still again and again met Mr Rochester,"[60] while Rena takes a position as the teacher at a small rural school for black children, "her absorption in the work . . . keep[ing] at a distance the spectre of her lost love," although "her dreams she could not control" (430). At this stage of the narrative, Jane seems to have replaced Maggie and Tess as Rena's closest precursor.

Of course, Rena's fate differs dramatically from Jane's. Yet this divergence is precisely to the point: the ending Brontë engineers for Jane is not available, and emphatically not available, for Rena. It is not available because while the death of Jane Eyre's "dark double" (as Sandra Gilbert and Susan Gubar famously labeled Bertha) clears the way for Jane's marriage to Rochester, Rena is her own dark double, a status paradoxically only possible because she is not "dark" in pigmentation.[61] The idea of a mulatta Jane Eyre proves unsustainable because Jane's ultimate fate depends on the fact that she is not a mulatta (or at least not a "creole"). *Jane Eyre* was perhaps the nineteenth-century novel's most celebrated and influential disseminator of the conviction that, as we have seen, Rena acquires from her own reading of fiction: "that love was a conqueror, that neither life nor death, nor creed nor caste, could stay his triumphant course" (318). Over half a century before *Wide Sargasso Sea*, *The House Behind the Cedars* reworks Brontë's novel to put the lie to this claim. Reader, she died.

In considering Chesnutt's response to *Jane Eyre*, moreover, we should also note that the "she" who dies is not the Bertha-figure *instead of* the Jane-figure, but rather a character who embodies both these figures. This revision might be read as reflecting a generic switch from a gothic externalization or splitting of aspects of identity to a more realist mode of internalized tension. Viewed in the context of Chesnutt's inscription and expansion of Victorian literature's "mulatto moments" more generally, however, it can be seen to register a fundamental difference in the very conception of the mulatto assumed and promoted by British and American literature. More specifically, what Chesnutt makes visible is a basic but easily overlooked difference in visibility: when Maggie Tulliver and David Copperfield are compared to mulattoes, the basis for the comparison is the darkness of their skin. By contrast, to be a mulatto in *The House Behind the Cedars*, as so often in American literature, means potentially being light-skinned enough to live as a white person: there is "no external sign to mark [them] off" (373). As he transforms the narrative role of the mulatto/a from figure and foil to protagonist, then, Chesnutt does not just criticize and correct for the marginalization and instrumentalization of mulattoes in Victorian fiction. He also uses the mulatto to undermine the very purpose it serves in that fiction, whether casually or concertedly: to reinforce what Irene Tucker calls "the logic of racial self-evidence."[62]

In the preceding account of *The House Behind the Cedars*'s transatlantic, cross-racial intertextuality, works that are alluded to faintly if at all emerge as equal or greater in importance than those that are explicitly referenced by name. One way to understand this disparity would be to view novels such as *David Copperfield* and *The Mill on the Floss* as sources Chesnutt sought to move beyond and leave behind; on this account, the detectable traces of their presence reflect his failure to fully transmute or transcend his influences. However, the multiple drafts of the novel Chesnutt wrote over a period of years tell a different story: as he wrote and rewrote the novel, Chesnutt consistently revised it in ways that strengthened its parallels with, and (thereby) sharpened its departures from, nineteenth-century British literature. In other words, his process of composition reveals a pattern not of increasing separation but rather of heightened engagement. It suggests that instead of looking to nineteenth-century British literature for models to adapt to a new context or for new purposes, Chesnutt was actively probing the nature and limits (and the nature of the limits) of this literature's relevance to the stories he wanted to tell.

This is true with regard to the depictions of both Rena and John. In early versions of the novel, entitled "Rena," Rena has no brother and does not try to pass as white.[63] She marries the character, Wain, whom she resists in the final version, but then learns that he is already married, at which point she returns home to die. Thus most of the aspects of the novel that will recall *The Mill on the Floss* are not yet present, from the title to the crucial sibling relationship to the structuring tension between loyalty to one's childhood home and desires that would cut one off from that home.[64] Similarly, in a version of the novel closer to the published form, John is now present and the story of Rena's abortive relationship with George Tryon is largely in place, but there is no ersatz *Ivanhoe* tournament scene and Rena's post-engagement experience has not yet acquired its *Jane Eyre*–like trajectory, as instead of discovering a sense of kinship and becoming a teacher, Rena recovers at her mother's home for six months and then meets and marries Wain.[65]

Most striking of all is the evolution of the Copperfieldian scene of reading. No late addition, a version of this scene is present from early drafts of the novel—even before the inclusion of John as a major character, and thus even before the revisionary engagement with the (male) bildungsroman in which this scene figures so prominently. In these drafts, the novel is a first-person narrative narrated not by a main character but rather by a visitor to the town where Rena grows up. In the first chapter, the narrator explains that he came to know Rena and her mother because of the family's collection of books, which constituted "the most striking personal evidence" of Rena's white father that "remained about the house": this "library," the narrator says, was "the chief attraction that drew me to Mis' Molly's."[66] The narrator then provides a description of the library's contents that overlaps to a large extent with the version in *The House Behind the Cedars*, from the opening specification of a volume of Fielding "in fine print," followed by mentions of Bulwer and Scott (although the latter not yet identified as "the literary idol of the South" and represented by a hefty four volumes but not

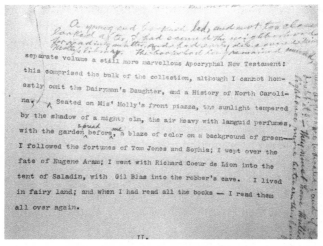

4.1. Manuscript page of "Rena," copy 3 (early draft of *The House Behind the Cedars*). Fisk University, John Hope and Aurelia E. Franklin Library, Special Collections, Charles W. Chesnutt Collection, box 9, folder 4.

a complete set—details that reflect the greater role he plays in the final version), to the listing of all the same books that the final version shares with *David Copperfield*. The narrator describes his experience reading these books in terms that will be reassigned almost verbatim to describe John's experience: "Seated on Mis' Molly's front piazza . . . I followed the fortunes of Tom Jones and Sophia; I wept over the fate of Eugene Aram; I went with Richard Coeur de Lion into the tent of Saladin, and with Gil Blas into the robber's cave."[67] (Recall the published version: "Lying prone upon the floor of the shaded front piazza, behind the fragrant garden, he followed the fortunes of Tom Jones and Sophia; he wept over the fate of Eugene Aram; he penetrated with Richard the Lion-heart into Saladin's tent, with Gil Blas into the robbers' cave; he flew through the air on the magic carpet or the enchanted horse, or tied with Sindbad to the roc's leg" [374].) (See figure 4.1)

The most obvious difference between these two accounts is syntactic—the switch from first- to third-person. Paradoxically, however, the switch away from *David Copperfield*'s first-person narration corresponds to a heightening of the parallel between the scenes and the readers: the adult narrator has no prior connection to this library, whereas for the young John as for the young David the books belonged to his father—in both cases, moreover, a father the boy never knew. In keeping with this change, *The House Behind the Cedars* recalls *David Copperfield* in explicitly assigning this childhood reading a formative role in the reader's life, whereas in the early draft the passage (and chapter) end anticlimactically with the narrator's summary statement that "I lived in fairy land; and when I had read all the books—I read them all over again."[68] Finally, it is only in Chesnutt's reworking of his initial reworking of *David Copperfield*'s scene of reading that David's self-description as a "Mulatto" comes into play, both because John is a mulatto and because his initiation into this identity, like David's self-description, immediately precedes this scene. Chesnutt's revisions thus amplify both the scope and force of his engagement with Victorian literature.

THE *QUARRY*'S QUARRY

The composition history of *The House Behind the Cedars* suggests the deliberateness and care with which Chesnutt aligned his novel with specific nineteenth-century British texts, in particular texts with "mulatto moments," and did so in order to explore and reveal the difference it makes to expand—that is, sustain the idea of—these moments. And yet in the face of all this effort and ingenuity on Chesnutt's part, one is forced to acknowledge an uncomfortable fact: these aspects of the novel have gone largely undetected for over a century. However, Chesnutt's subsequent career suggests that he himself noticed and responded to his readers' apparent failure to pick up on his elaborate but largely submerged dialogue with nineteenth-century British literature. After *The House Behind the Cedars*, no longer will Chesnutt engage in such extensive and subtle intertextual play.[69] Ultimately, though, instead of simply abandoning the critical and creative intertextuality of his first published novel, he makes its stakes newly visible by converting its sly grappling with Victorian literature into grand gestures.

Thus, the title of Chesnutt's next novel, *The Marrow of Tradition* (1901), again bears a relationship to a nineteenth-century British text, but instead of a subtle resemblance (*The House Behind the Cedars* / *The Mill on the Floss*) we get a direct quotation. Ensuring that his readers attach the phrase to its source, Chesnutt uses the poem from which it is drawn as his epigraph:

> I like you and your book, ingenious Hone!
> In whose capacious all-embracing leaves
> The very marrow of tradition's shown.
>   CHARLES LAMB
>   To the Editor of the Every-Day Book.

Ironically, however, what this citation helps make visible is the looseness of the match between source-text and novel: Chesnutt's repurposing of Lamb's resonant phrase seems neither closely linked to nor a pointed departure from the original context. Although the significance of the title is somewhat obscure, Chesnutt seems to replace Lamb's positively valued, implicitly literary tradition with the South's crippling history of racial prejudice and oppression as the "tradition" in question. Tempting as it may be to see this shift as implying a link between the two traditions, especially when viewed through the lens of *The House Behind the Cedars*'s treatment of the South's "literary idol" Walter Scott, the novel itself does not develop this idea.

In the last novel Chesnutt published in his lifetime, *The Colonel's Dream* (1905), nineteenth-century British literature is mentioned as casually and fleetingly as that literature typically treats mulattoes: one character is shown reading *Jane Eyre*, but the novel serves her mainly as a means of avoiding eye contact with another character, and Brontë's novel has no particular resonance in the novel as a whole.[70] However, the last novel Chesnutt wrote, *The Quarry* (written in 1928 but not published until 1999) strikingly renews and extends *The House Behind the Cedar*'s intertextual strategies. Revisionary tropes we have teased out of the earlier novel are brought to the surface in the later one, in a manner that makes especially clear the combination of homage and aggression that marks Chesnutt's career-long engagement with Victorian literature and brings this engagement to a fitting conclusion.

The Quarry returns to the familiar themes of racial identification and racial uplift but manages to scramble and upend the usual narratives. Raised by his adoptive parents to be a race leader, the protagonist, Donald Glover, resists opportunities to pass as white or, alternately, to take up residence in England and live a largely post-racial life among the aristocracy. In a stunning variation on the unwitting-passing plot I discuss in chapter 3, Donald (like the title character of Chesnutt's other posthumously published late novel, *Paul Marchand, F.M.C.*) discovers that he is not in fact of mixed-race ancestry but rather entirely white. In other words, he has been unwittingly passing as African American. Decisively severing racial identity and solidarity from descent, Chesnutt has his protagonist choose to "remain"—or simply remain—African American: "Circumstances had made him one of a certain group. He had been reared as one of them. He had been taught to see things as they saw them, he had shared their joys, their griefs, their hopes and their fears—in fact he had become psychologically and spiritually one of them. . . . He could only desert this group at the sacrifice of love and loyalty and the whole setup of his life."[71]

As is so often the case in novels where racial identification and solidarity are at stake, the protagonist's choice of a race correlates with his choice of a mate. In a manner we have come more specifically to identify with Chesnutt, these choices also involve a relationship to nineteenth-century British literature. Donald's own "views concerning women" are formed through his reading of Victorian fiction, indeed of a very Chesnuttian canon: "Dickens, Thackeray, Bulwer Lytton, George Eliot, Thomas Hardy."[72] And in developing his romance plot, Chesnutt returns to another of the novels he reworked in *The House Behind the Cedars* (and mentioned in *The Colonel's Dream*): as in *The House Behind the Cedars*, one of the love interests is named Blanche—Lady Blanche, in this case, for she is an English aristocrat, and as such represents Donald's potential abandonment of racial uplift (even before he knows his real parentage) for a cushy life abroad. Also as in *The House Behind the Cedars*, the blatant symbolism of the name "Blanche" threatens to muffle the echo of *Jane Eyre*. In *The Quarry*, though, Chesnutt meets this threat head on: Donald passes over Blanche in favor of a darker woman named—yes—Bertha.

Yet Chesnutt's reworking of his predecessors is more complex than the mere choice of a Bertha over a Blanche suggests. Heightening the literary stakes of Donald's choice of a wife, Chesnutt stresses the Victorian-novel associations in ways that offer a more radical revision of literary history. To choose Lady Blanche Merrivale and her life in England, the novel makes plain, would also mean choosing Victorian literature, and indeed an especially conservative vision of that literature. In the manner we have come to expect, Chesnutt forges this link through his depiction of a party: extending his own tradition of the party Tom McDonald crashes, Mr. Ryder's ball, and the ersatz *Ivanhoe* tournament, Chesnutt sends Donald with Lady Blanche to a garden party. Thoroughly charmed, Donald "could not imagine anything more genuinely hospitable and friendly," and he praises the party accordingly: "It was the ideal garden party that Trollope wrote about and Marcus Stone painted. It might have furnished the setting for Barchester Towers."[73] It is this welcoming world Donald ultimately rejects, and we can see this rejection as a fitting conclusion to a trajectory that began with Tom McDonald's embarrassing experience at the party to which he was not invited.

As an ambivalent literary guest, however, Chesnutt goes one step further. In rejecting this world, Donald rejects Lady Blanche as well—but Lady Blanche herself, it turns out, "has some dark blood."[74] This twist attenuates her status as an emblem of whiteness. Surprisingly, though, it also ends up reinforcing her connection to the Victorian novel. For if with the introduction of a character named Bertha, Chesnutt alludes to the most famous (possible) mulatta in Victorian literature, with Lady Blanche Merrivale he brings in perhaps the second most famous:

> Lady Merrivale was well read in English literature, and Donald discovered during the conversation that their tastes were quite similar. Among the Victorian novelists she was most fond of Thackeray.
>
> "I ought to be," she said, "for one of my ancestors appears in Vanity Fair. She was the original of Miss Schwartz, the West Indian fellow pupil of Becky Sharp at Miss Wilkinson's Academy."[75]

While Lady Merrivale's references to *Vanity Fair* are cavalier in their sloppiness—the name of Becky Sharp's West Indian fellow pupil is Miss Swartz, and the academy they attend is run by Miss Pinkerton—Chesnutt's citation is stunning in its audacity. Returning to the very novel that inspired both the dream of authorship and the anxiety of exclusion almost half a century earlier, Chesnutt now switches the vectors of chronology and influence. Whereas before he literalized figurative mulattoes, in this passage he works a kind of ontological reversal whereby Thackeray's marginalized, literal mulatta is revealed as a fiction within—a copy derived from—the "original" world of Chesnutt's fiction. Here indeed is the revenge of the "dark"—and not so dark—"unhappy ones": Victorian fiction itself, at least for a moment, stands revealed as an African American fiction, the figment of Charles Chesnutt's imagination.

CHAPTER FIVE

CULTURAL TRANSMISSION AND
TRANSGRESSION: PAULINE HOPKINS

Immediately after helping a young man and woman escape from slave trad-
ers to the relative safety of the camp of the revolutionary abolitionist John
Brown, the young English lawyer Warren Maxwell is captured by a mob
of "Southern desperadoes."[1] The mob ties Maxwell to a stake and prepares
to burn him to death, being careful not to pile the wood "as high as his
knees, for a slow fire steadily increased, would prolong the enjoyment"
(368). As the flames rise Maxwell heroically maintains his determination
"to die and make no moan to please and gratify the crowd," even as "the
sweat of physical anguish and faintness moved in drops on his forehead"
and his open shirt shows "the beating pulse in the white brawn" of his
chest (370). At the last minute, though, Maxwell is saved by the arrival of
"State constables" led by a Colonel Titus, who berates the mob: "'Fools!,'
he shouted, . . . 'what are you doing?'" (371). The grounds for the Colonel's
objection are not moral but rather geopolitical: "Thomson," he says to the
leader of the mob, "I gave you credit for having more sense. This man is a
British subject. How are we to impress the world with our fair and impar-
tial dealing with all mankind, and the slavery question in particular, if you
and a lot more hot-headed galoots go to work and call us liars by breaking
the slate [i.e., the law]?" (372).

This scene occurs halfway through Pauline E. Hopkins's *Winona: A Tale
of Negro Life in the South and Southwest*, published serially in the *Colored
American Magazine* in 1902, the third of four novels Hopkins published in
quick succession at the turn of the century. Hopkins—who has emerged
alongside Charles Chesnutt as the most widely studied African American

fiction writer of the period—has nothing in common with her character Colonel Titus, with one exception: an appreciation of the decisive importance of Britishness. Even before the colonel's arrival, the scene has foregrounded Maxwell's national identity: his capture interrupts a reverie about his "peaceful English home"—"He could see the beautiful avenues of noble trees, and the rambling, mass-covered manse; he could see the kindly patrician face of his father, and his brothers and sisters smiled at him from every bush" (360–61)—and his "scorn" for his captors is intensified by thoughts of "the British idea of fair play" (368).

Winona's conclusion turns on the antithesis between the United States and this idealized vision of British character and society, making plain its centrality to the ideological work of the novel: Maxwell has come to the States to find the heir to an English estate, and this heir turns out to be the novel's title character, the daughter of a fugitive slave and a man who has been living as an Indian chief but is in fact (or originally) an English aristocrat. Winona and Maxwell marry and move to England, where "American caste prejudice could not touch them" and she is "worshipped" as "the last beautiful representative of an ancient family" (435). The novel's closing vignette drives home the significance of its utopian fantasy of England as a color-blind, post-racial society, as back in the U.S. an African American character interprets "the story of Winona's strange fortunes" as meaning "we's bound to be free," explaining "Dar's dat gal, she's got black blood nuff in her to put her on de block in this fersaken country, but over dar she's a lady with de top crus' of de crus'. Somethin's gwine happen" (436).

The strategic anglophilia of *Winona* is impossible to miss, but Hopkins's investment in this anglophilia is rendered all the more striking when one compares her novel to the novel that served as the model for the dramatic scene with which we began. *The White Islander*, an 1893 novel by Mary Hartwell Catherwood, tells the story of an English fur trader, Alexander Henry, who falls in love with a young French orphan, Marie, who has been raised by Chippewas on Mackinac Island. Henry's life is saved during an Indian raid by a Chippewa, Wawatam, who is also Marie's protector—but when Wawatam realizes that Henry and Marie have fallen in love, he captures Henry and plans to burn him at the stake, per the alleged Chippewa custom of roasting and eating one's enemies. Henry's life is saved at the last minute by the arrival of a Frenchman, M. Cadotte, who had married into the tribe. "'Fools of Chippewas,' he shouted, 'what are you doing?'"[2]

As with the transfer of M. Cadotte's words to Colonel Titus's mouth, all the details of the attempted burning of Warren Maxwell at the stake quoted in the first paragraph above, and many more besides, are drawn directly from *The White Islander*.[3] What is especially striking about Hopkins's adaptation of Catherwood's novel, though, is that even as Hopkins borrows freely and often verbatim from her source, she abandons its racial and national investments—replacing its virulently racist depiction of Native Americans with a more positive one while reassigning their villainous actions (minus the cannibalism) to a southern white rabble; omitting its French characters; and, most obviously, making central the category of the African American, which is entirely absent from *The White Islander*—with one exception: in both novels, the heroic male protagonist and love interest is English.[4] Hopkins not only adopts this valorization of Englishness wholesale but even amplifies it; the references to British fair play and the Englishman's idyllic native home, for example, are her own contribution.

As we shall have occasion to see throughout this chapter, the manner in which Hopkins makes use of *The White Islander* is no isolated instance. On the contrary, the unacknowledged borrowing from other texts—at times verbatim or with minimal reworking, at times with more extensive reimagining—is a recurrent feature of Hopkins's compositional practice. Like Colonel Titus with regard to the burning of Warren Maxwell, my interest is more in the geopolitics of this practice than in its morality—or more precisely, in how this practice enters into the geopolitics of Hopkins's work, and in particular into her attitude toward Britain and her relations with Victorian literature. From this perspective, as significant as the anglophilia that informs Hopkins's use of *The White Islander* is the fact that this novel itself is not British: Mary Hartwell Catherwood was an American writer who spent her life in the Midwest,[5] and *The White Islander* was published in New York. As this suggests, the archive from which Hopkins draws is not itself exclusively or particularly British.

As we shall also see, however, the Britishness of certain texts, as well as their depiction of Englishness or Britishness, can play a significant role in their selection and treatment by Hopkins. In *Winona* itself, for example, the novel's anglophilia both inspires and delimits her engagement with British literature. Winona knows her father as White Eagle, but he is originally "Henry Carlingford, heir to the great Carlingford estates" (426). As Hopkins biographer Lois Brown notes, although there was a prominent English politician in the last quarter of the nineteenth century named Baron Carlingford, this name can also be read as an allusion to Margaret Oliphant's *Chronicles of Carlingford*, a series of works Oliphant began publishing in the early 1860s. Noting that both *Winona* and *The Chronicles of Carlingford*—and especially the first story in the series, "The Executor" (1861)—"revolve around tangled plots of thwarted inheritance, unexpected bequests, and family reunion," and that "both have similarly named characters," Brown argues that Hopkins "was influenced heavily" by Oliphant.[6] Shifting the emphasis, I would suggest that the similarities Brown identifies highlight the gap between Oliphant's work and Hopkins's, and that Hopkins alludes to Oliphant precisely to highlight the gap between the societies each depicts.

Like *Winona*, "The Executor" tells the story of an effort to locate an heir. Eschewing the kind of genealogical revelation crucial to *Winona* (and all Hopkins's novels), however, "The Executor" never does find the mysterious heir or explain why the deceased had chosen to leave her money to this unknown individual. Instead, the rather stolid, middle-aged lawyer who has been charged to locate the heir ends up falling in love (if that is not too strong a term for the moderate nature of the feelings on display in the story) with the young woman whose expectations have been dashed by this will. What makes "The Executor" an especially striking intertext for *Winona*, though, is the name of this lawyer: John Brown. Lois Brown argues that the introduction of this name in the opening lines of the story gives them "an additional and explosive meaning" to "an American reader like Hopkins," who "immediately would have thought of the insurrectionist John Brown, the leader of the raid on Harper's Ferry who figures prominently in . . . *Winona*."[7] This is undoubtedly correct, but the two John Browns could not have less in common, and in sending us back to Oliphant's story with her mention of Carlingford, Hopkins is not inviting us to see what the stories share but, on the contrary, to appreciate how different they are.

What would have been striking to an American reader like Hopkins, in other words, is that the gap between Britain and the U.S. is so great that in a story published in Britain in May 1861—weeks after the start of the Civil War—the name "John Brown" would apparently not call to mind the American insurrectionist who had been executed a year and a half earlier, but instead could signify as one of the plainest, least resonant names imaginable. For Winona and her English husband, as we have seen, "American caste prejudice could not touch them in their home beyond the sea" (435); Oliphant's deployment of the name "John Brown" makes it seem as if even news of that prejudice does not reach beyond the sea. Hopkins's allusion to *The Chronicles of Carlingford* thus captures that work's near-irrelevance to the concerns of "a tale of Negro life in the South and Southwest," an irrelevance *Winona* celebrates. "A long story full of deep interest might be written concerning the subsequent fortunes of John Brown and his sons and their trusty followers," Hopkins writes at the end of the novel, "a story

of hardships, ruined homes and persecutions, and retribution to their per-
secutors, after all, through the happenings of the Civil War. But with these
events we are all familiar" (435). "Carlingford," for Hopkins, names a world
where we are not "all familiar" with these events, where we are free from
such familiarity because freed from the racist order that occasions them.[8]

We saw in the previous chapter that Charles Chesnutt—Hopkins's nearly
exact contemporary—was deeply, systematically engaged with British literature as such, especially an emerging canon of nineteenth-century British
literature.[9] By contrast, Hopkins often seems to draw on and engage indis-
criminately with work originating in both the U.S. and Britain, even as she
is consistently alert to the representation of British society in texts of any origin. As the example of "Carlingford" suggests, however, Hopkins at times
makes careful and suggestive use of Victorian literature. Ranging across all
her novels but focusing in particular on her first, *Contending Forces*, and her
last, *Of One Blood*, this chapter will show that Hopkins's engagement with
Victorian authors and texts is much more extensive and substantive than
has previously been recognized, and that this engagement informs those
aspects of her work critics have deemed central to her achievement.

In particular, we will see that Hopkins uses Victorian literature in ways
that amplify the counternormative, even transgressive currents of her work,
with regard to her treatment of gender and sexuality as well as race. In addition, we will see that Hopkins's deployment of Victorian literature does not
depart or distract from her contribution to and engagement with African
American literature, but on the contrary must be understood as part of that
contribution and engagement. Indeed, one of the most striking features
of Hopkins's intertextual and appropriative relationship to Victorian literature is that the Victorian authors she engages with in especially sustained
and complex ways are the very ones who figure most explicitly in Charles
Chesnutt's work, as we saw in the last chapter: Alfred, Lord Tennyson and
Edward Bulwer Lytton. These authors matter to Hopkins in part, I will
argue, because they matter to Chesnutt, and her engagement with them is
at the same time and thereby an engagement with Chesnutt as well.[10]

YOKED: TENNYSON AND *CONTENDING FORCES*

Pauline Hopkins's first novel, *Contending Forces: A Romance Illustrative of
Negro Life North and South*, was published in Boston in 1900 by the Colored
Co-Operative Publishing Company. The novel begins with a preface in
which the author justifies her literary effort by stating her desire to help

"raise the stigma of degradation from my race" and asserting that "the simple, homely tale . . . cements the bond of brotherhood among all classes and all complexions" (13). In increasingly forceful terms, she declares that

> Fiction is of great value to any people as a preserver of manners and customs—religious, political and social. It is a record of growth and development from generation to generation. *No one will do this for us; we must ourselves develop the men and women who will faithfully portray the inmost thoughts and feelings of the Negro with all the fire and romance which lie dormant in our history,* and, as yet, unrecognized by writers of the Anglo-Saxon race. (13–14; original emphasis)

The novel that follows is divided into two parts. The opening four chapters (about one-sixth of the book) recount the tragic consequences that ensue for the family of a wealthy British slave-owner, Charles Montfort, after they move from Bermuda to North Carolina in 1790: fearing Montfort plans to free his slaves and suspecting his wife of having "Negro blood" (45), a suspicion the novel never confirms or refutes, the local whites kill Montfort and whip his wife, driving her to suicide. Their two sons are enslaved, but the young Charles is purchased by an Englishman who promises to free him, and Jesse escapes to New England and becomes "absorbed" into the "negro" race (69–70).

The novel then jumps ahead to present-day Boston to follow the fortunes of Jesse's descendants: Ma Smith, who runs a lodging house, and her two children in young adulthood, Will and Dora. Much of the novel's plot revolves around a beautiful and mysterious lodger named Sappho, who turns out to be hiding her past as a victim of sexual violence—and also hiding the son that resulted from that rape. Sappho becomes close to both Dora and Will, and eventually accepts Will's marriage proposal, while keeping her past a secret. However, a blackmail attempt leads her to flee Boston, and three years pass before Will finds her in New Orleans. Meanwhile, Will has emerged as an eloquent advocate of DuBoisian racial uplift, and the Smith family has been reunited with the white English descendant of Charles Montfort, Mr. Withington, who embraces his African American relatives and restores the family's wealth to them. The novel concludes with the newly married Sappho and Will, accompanied by Sappho's son, Will's mother, and Dora and her husband and daughter, onboard a ship to England to visit Mr. Withington. Looking to the future, Sappho and Will plan "to work together to bring joy to hearts crushed by despair" (401).

In addition to its preface, *Contending Forces* contains several other paratextual elements absent from Hopkins's subsequent, serialized novels (all of which appeared in the *Colored American Magazine,* where Hopkins also worked as an editor). Along with the epigraphs and chapter titles, some of which are themselves quotations, the novel includes more intercalated quotations than Hopkins's later novels, making *Contending Forces* the most allusive and in that sense "literary" of her novels. All the writers Hopkins cites are white, and almost none is contemporary. Among American writers, she gravitates toward poets associated with the antislavery cause, such as William Cullen Bryant, Henry Wadsworth Longfellow, and John Greenleaf Whittier, and takes as the epigraph to the book a passage from Ralph Waldo Emerson's "Address on Emancipation in the British West Indies." From British literature, Hopkins's sources include Shakespeare and several of the most familiar eighteenth-century poems associated with antislavery or offering sympathetic portrayals of the downtrodden and dispossessed: William Cowper's "The Task," Oliver Goldsmith's "The Deserted Village," Thomas Gray's "Elegy Written in a Country Church-Yard."

Aside from one African Americanizing allusion to Robert Louis Stevenson—Will Smith declares that "the Negro . . . *is the Hyde who torments the Dr. Jekyll of the white man's refined civilization!*" (272, original italics)— Hopkins only cites one Victorian author: Tennyson. And despite the almost complete lack of political or aesthetic engagement with slavery or the poor on the part of the recently deceased poet laureate (Tennyson died in 1892), Hopkins cites him more frequently than she does any other author. She quotes Tennyson's poetry some eleven times, in passages drawn from five different poems and ranging in length from a phrase to five lines. (Whittier is a distant second, at five citations.) These citations occur in chapter titles, chapter epigraphs (the only place where the poet's name actually appears), within the narrative itself, and, most strikingly, at the very end of the novel. Immediately after describing the newlyweds' aspirations, the novel concludes with one of the most prominently placed citations of Victorian literature in the African American literary tradition:

> They [Sappho and Will] stood upon the deck that night long after the others had retired to their staterooms, watching the receding shores with hearts filled with emotion too deep for words.
> "My wife, my life. O, we will walk this world
> Yoked in all exercise of noble end,
> And so through those dark gates across the wild

That no man knows.

. . . .

Lay thy sweet hands in mine and trust to me." (401–2)

Giving the final word—literally—to another writer is an extravagant gesture few novelists risk. (In fact, a novel-ending quotation like this is so rare that we do not have a standard name for it; following Gérard Genette, I will call it a *terminal epigraph*.)[11] Yet as far as I can determine, no critic has ever asked why Hopkins chose to end *Contending Forces* with this passage from Tennyson's 1847 poem *The Princess: A Medley*, or what difference this terminal epigraph makes to our understanding of the novel. This is so even though readings of *Contending Forces* almost invariably address the novel's ending in terms of plot, treating it as a major interpretive crux. Critics have been particularly interested in the implications of the novel's concluding marriages for the racial and sexual politics of the novel as a whole. They have also discussed the characters' departure from the United States (however temporary) as the culmination of the novel's comparative treatment of American and British (or more generally European) culture and society.[12] Yet one can read virtually everything that has been written on *Contending Forces* without seeing its final lines quoted or even referenced.[13]

Even given the general neglect of the Victorian presence in African American literature that this book seeks to correct, this gap in the criticism is worth pondering. Perhaps, instead of seeing the terminal epigraph as a particularly insistent intertextual gambit, critics view these lines as merely tacked on—a flourish presumably intended to demonstrate the author's cultural literacy, but one that adds nothing to the narrative to which it is appended. The recurrent citations of Tennyson throughout the novel suggest on the contrary that Hopkins's choice of a terminal epigraph is no mere afterthought but rather part of the design of the novel as a whole—however, this entire pattern of citation has also gone unremarked. I suspect this silent treatment reflects two specific concerns about Hopkins's turn to Tennyson: this turn seems to go against the novelist's own declared commitment to African American expression as articulated in her preface, and it also seems to reinforce the strain of conventional sentimentality many critics find disappointing—or, alternately, to work against the ways critics who defend Hopkins from this charge see her as revising and even radicalizing the conventional marriage plot.

Even if these views were valid, of course, they would be worth articulating. I will argue, however, that the novel's use of Tennyson, as capped by its terminal epigraph, is neither mere window-dressing nor evidence of a retrograde conservatism on Hopkins's part. Counterintuitive as it may seem, Hopkins mobilizes Tennyson in *Contending Forces* to put the novel in dialogue with other writings by African Americans and to further its challenge to existing racial and sexual norms.

The allusions to Tennyson in *Contending Forces* cluster primarily around the figure of Sappho. There are no such allusions (that I have detected) in the novel's first section, depicting the earlier generation of Montforts, and the first one occurs in the first passage in which Sappho's appearance is described:

> Tall and fair, with hair of a golden cast, aquiline nose, rosebud mouth, soft brown eyes veiled by long, dark lashes which swept her cheek, just now covered with a delicate rose flush, she burst upon them—a combination of "queen rose and lily in one." (107)

Hopkins here alludes to a line from the well-known song in *Maud: A Mono-drama* (1855), "Come into the garden, Maud": "Queen lily and rose in one." On two more occasions in *Contending Forces,* Hopkins uses slightly altered lines from Tennyson to describe Sappho's appearance, both times drawing from the description of Helen of Troy in "A Dream of Fair Women": "'The starlike beauty of immortal eyes,' fringed by long, curling lashes, flashed at [the smitten Will] from the four corners of his dingy room" (169–70; Hopkins substitutes "beauty" for "sorrows"), and "Gowned in a pure white china silk with a bunch of her favorite Jacks in her corsage, she moved 'a daughter of the gods divinely fair'" (202; the original line reads ". . . divinely tall / And most divinely fair").

These allusions to common Tennysonian tags perform an important function as markers of cultural literacy. In doing so, moreover and somewhat paradoxically, the use of slightly altered quotations bespeaks a casualness and familiarity that only enhances the effect.[14] At the same time, the allusions, brief and commonplace as they are, may not seem to do extensive work for Hopkins with regard to description or characterization. Yet there are hints that her investment in these allusions goes further. Their sheer multiplicity suggests a more-than-casual insistence on Hopkins's part on aligning her female protagonists with Tennysonian ideals of beauty, and it is important that two of the passages cited reference complexion: "Queen lily and rose" and "divinely fair." Hopkins continues this practice in her next novel, *Hagar's Daughter,* quoting—indeed, again misquoting—the same stanza of *Maud* when introducing the light-skinned, mixed-race title character of that work, Jewel Bowen.[15]

While Sappho's light complexion puts her in a long line of mulattas, tragic and—as we saw in chapter 3—increasingly otherwise, the association with Tennyson and especially the citations of "A Dream of Fair Women" suggest that Hopkins is also locating her more specifically in relation to Chesnutt's recent "The Wife of His Youth" (first published in the *Atlantic Monthly* in July 1898). As we saw in the last chapter, the protagonist of that story rifles through his beloved copy of Tennyson's poems to find appropriate lines with which to toast his intended fiancée, and among the passages he lights upon is the one from "A Dream of Fair Women" that includes the line "a daughter of the gods divinely tall / And most divinely fair." With her repeated use of Tennyson to describe her heroine, Hopkins courts the risk of seeming not so much to have been influenced by Chesnutt as being a second Mr. Ryder herself. Indeed, the situation she conjures comes much closer to Mr. Ryder's dream scenario than does the one Chesnutt provides him with: whereas Mr. Ryder is forced to acknowledge the limited applicability of Tennyson's language to the woman he is courting—"Mrs. Dixon was the palest lady he expected at the ball [but] she was of a rather ruddy complexion"—Sappho is so fair that the applicability of Tennyson's lines to her is unqualified.

Hopkins's Ryder-like rewriting of "The Wife of His Youth" goes further: whereas references to Tennyson in Chesnutt's story (if not, as I argue, Tennyson's relevance to the story) end with—are ended by—the unwonted arrival of the dark-skinned and aged "wife of his youth," the romance between Sappho and Will not only begins but also proceeds and culminates quite explicitly under the sign of Tennyson. Hopkins cites the poet at four key junctures in their relationship: when Will falls in love, when Sappho accepts his marriage proposal, when the two are permanently reunited after a long separation, and, as we have seen, when the two embark on their voyage to England and life together as a married couple. Hopkins's systematic citations of Tennyson serve to mark the progress of this relationship and to reinforce connections and contrasts between particular moments in the narrative.

Thus, the chapter in which Will is shown falling in love with Sappho— "love had come to Smith like a flood sweeping all barriers before it" (169)— not only contains the passing invocation of "The starlike beauty of immortal eyes," noted above, but also grants Tennyson a much more prominent place:

the chapter is called "'Love Took Up the Harp of Life'" (in quotation marks, to signal its status as an allusion), and the passage from "Locksley Hall" containing this phrase serves as epigraph:

Love took up the glass of Time, and turn'd it in his glowing hands;
Every moment, lightly shaken, ran itself in golden sands.
Love took up the harp of Life, and smote on all the chords with might.
—TENNYSON (166)[16]

When Will proposes to Sappho, Hopkins turns to Tennyson to mark the moment Sappho accepts him, quoting for the first time from *The Princess*—as we saw, the same poem she cites to end the novel. (I will return to both these passages below.) Similarly, when Sappho and Will are reunited after their three-year-long separation, Hopkins again calls on Tennyson to mark this climax:

She saw and recognized him at the same instant. With a mighty cry of joy and thanksgiving he clasped her in his arms.
   "O, that 'twere possible,
      After long grief and pain,
To find the arms of my true love
      Round me once again!" (394)

Here Hopkins quotes again from *Maud*. In doing so, she not only aligns this moment with the other turning points in the romance plot but also links it to another moment in the novel when she cites this particular poem. This passage comes three chapters earlier, when Hopkins is depicting John Langley's tormented reaction to his failed blackmail of Sappho (which has led to her separation from Will):

What if the girl should defy him—expose him! He cursed his own folly, her beauty, his own infatuation. Turn as he would, he could not shut out the beautiful, despairing face.
   "And there rises ever a passionate cry
From underneath in the darkened land" (334)

The paired citations of *Maud*, both inserted into the narrative without narratorial comment or syntactic connection, reinforce the symmetry and thus the contrast between Langley's downward spiral and Sappho and

Will's joyful reunion. In addition, this latter citation of Tennyson recalls the earlier one in which Will too sees Sappho everywhere ("'The starlike beauty of immortal eyes,' fringed by long, curling lashes, flashed at him from the four corners of his dingy room").

Citations of Tennyson thus form a web of cross-references within the novel, highlighting and reinforcing the patterning that structures the narrative. The result—a romance plot culminating in marriage to a light-skinned woman and carried out from start to finish under the sign of Tennyson—reads as the triumph of Mr. Ryder's vision, or Hopkins's revenge on his behalf.

By the same token, however, even as attention to Hopkins's use of Tennyson thus reveals another dimension of her artistry and another way in which she is in dialogue with other African American writers, this attention seems also to reinforce an understanding of *Contending Forces* as beholden to bourgeois values and forms and accepting of the racial status quo—as, precisely, Mr. Ryder's triumph. In fact, though, a closer look at the passages in which Hopkins invokes Tennyson and the passages she invokes leads to a quite different conclusion. Hopkins's use of Tennyson contributes to the challenges she poses to social norms with regard to both race and sexuality. Sometimes—especially with regard to race—this involves brushing Tennyson against the grain, but more often—with regard to sexuality—it means seizing on counternormative impulses already present within the poet's oeuvre.

As a rule, insofar as Hopkins uses Tennyson to reinforce her romance plot, she is not being true to him, and insofar as she is true to him, she uses him to destabilize that plot. This pattern begins with her use of "Locksley Hall" to frame her narration of Will's initial love for Sappho. As discussed in the last chapter when considering Chesnutt's exactly contemporaneous use of this poem in *The House Behind the Cedars*, the speaker of "Locksley Hall" fantasizes at one point about abandoning the civilized world for a tropical island where, he says, "I will take some savage woman, she shall rear my dusky race" (l. 168). Although Tennyson does not necessarily endorse the views of his speaker, nothing about the poem anticipates or invites the granting of subjectivity or narrative centrality to members of such "dusky race[s]," who serve solely as imaginary props in the speaker's psychodrama. By mining such a poem for imagery to describe the love of a (mixed-race) African American man for a (mixed-race) African American woman, then, Hopkins extends the literary and affective franchise in ways that "Locksley Hall" not only fails to imagine but also arguably makes harder to envision.

Such contrarian appropriation recalls the use made of *Bleak House* by both Frederick Douglass and Hannah Crafts, as discussed in chapter 1.

On this reading, Hopkins's use of Tennyson in framing her romance plot aligns with the understanding of that plot developed by such critics as Hazel Carby and Ann duCille: according to these critics, the seeming conventionality of the novel's romance plot, and of its concluding marriage in particular, is belied by the unconventionality of its participants, especially Sappho—a mixed-race survivor of rape with a son who is the product of that rape. Hopkins's use of "Locksley Hall" captures this radical recalibration, as the "savage woman [who] shall rear my dusky race" is transformed from racist trope to romantic heroine and wife as virtuous as she is beautiful.[17]

Contending Forces makes plain the far-reaching political implications of this revision of the referent and reach of Tennyson's poetry in one of the scenes citing "A Dream of Fair Women." Instead of marking a key moment in the romance plot as do the other quotations, this allusion occurs in a passage seemingly designed to model the ideal reaction of a white reader to the novel itself. Describing the impression Sappho makes at a church fair at which "many influential whites were present in order to display their philanthropic interest in the welfare of the colored people" (201), Hopkins writes:

> Occasionally [Sappho] would leave her seat and mingle with the crowd. Gowned in a pure white china silk with a bunch of her favorite Jacks in her corsage, she moved "a daughter of the gods divinely fair." And many a thought came into the heart of one learned doctor as he gazed on the child [Alphonse] and the beautiful girl [Sappho], and then upon faces ebony-hued but bright and sparkling with the light of freedom and intelligence. In that moment a cloud passed from before his mental vision, and he beheld in all its hideousness the cankering sore which is eating into the heart of republican principles and stamping the lie upon the Constitution. (202)

Recognition of the applicability of Tennyson's language to Sappho leads directly and immediately to recognition of the injustice of the existing racial order in the United States. This dual recognition may depend at first on the fairness of Sappho's complexion, but it explicitly encompasses her "ebony-hued" brethren as well—even as this means going beyond or athwart Tennyson's own aesthetic (let alone political) program.

With "A Dream of Fair Women" as with "Locksley Hall," then, where Chesnutt highlights the irony and dissonance generated by African

American (or mixed-race) attempts to lay claim to Tennyson, Hopkins willfully doubles down on this allegiance. And while Hopkins could not yet have read *The House Behind the Cedars* (with its allusion to "Locksley Hall") when she was writing *Contending Forces*, the passage in which she cites "A Dream of Fair Women" reads as a pointed response to "The Wife of His Youth." Not only does Hopkins cite a line also cited in the story, but she also reworks and even verbally echoes the key scene in which that citation occurs: in the story, Mr. Ryder's application of Tennyson's words to his intended wife, Mrs. Dixon (even as he worries about her ruddiness), is interrupted and derailed by the arrival of the wife of his antebellum, enslaved youth, who is "very black" and looks around with "very bright and restless eyes" ("Wife," 105). In the novel, as we have just seen, the application of these same words to Sappho flows smoothly into sympathetic consideration of "faces ebony-hued but bright and sparkling" (202). Ultimately, then, *Contending Forces* is not Mr. Ryder's triumph after all: in this scene as in the novel as a whole, Hopkins refuses to follow him in opposing an appreciation for light-skinned beauty to African American solidarity and a commitment to racial justice, and she aligns Mr. Ryder's beloved Tennyson not with this opposition but instead with this refusal.

Just as Hopkins's use of Tennyson recalls and revises that of a leading contemporary African American fiction writer, so too does it recall and revise that of a leading contemporary African American lecturer and essayist, Anna Julia Cooper. Thus, Hopkins's seemingly paradoxical recourse to the English poet after asserting the need for African Americans to express and represent themselves recalls the opening gambit of Cooper's 1892 collection of essays, *A Voice from the South*, discussed in the introduction. As we saw, Cooper begins her preface by decrying the absence from public discourse of "the sadly expectant Black Woman," who has been, she writes,

> An infant crying in the night,
> An infant crying for the light;
> And with *no language—but a cry*.[18]

Cooper also anticipates Hopkins in enlisting Tennyson in her attempt to combat prejudice and empower African American women through the strategic embrace of bourgeois respectability and ostensibly conservative gendered norms and values.[19] Indeed, the poem Hopkins cites most prominently—in her terminal epigraph—is the same one that Cooper excerpts most extensively. Turning to *The Princess* in her chapter on "The Higher Education of Women," Cooper offers up a lengthy passage in support of her contention that "the feminine factor can have its proper effect only through women's development and education so that she may fitly and intelligently stamp her force on the forces of her day, and add her modicum to the riches of the world's thought":

> For woman's cause is man's: they rise or sink
> Together, dwarfed or godlike, bond or free:
> For she that out of Lethe scales with man
> The shining steps of nature, shares with man
> His nights, his days, moves with him to one goal.
> If she be small, slight-natured, miserable,
> How shall men grow?
>   . . . Let her make herself her own
> To give or keep, to live and learn and be
> All that not harms distinctive womanhood.
> For woman is not undeveloped man
> But diverse: could we make her as the man
> Sweet love were slain; his dearest bond is this,
> Not like to like, but like in difference.
> Yet in the long years liker must they grow;
> The man be more of woman, she of man;
> He gain in sweetness and in moral height,
> Nor lose the wrestling thews that throw the world;
> She mental breadth, nor fail in childward care,
> Nor lose the childlike in the larger mind;
> Till at the last she set herself to man,
> Like perfect music unto noble words.[20]

Cooper leverages this passage to forward her argument for increasing access to higher education for women—even though in the poem itself this vision follows from the abandonment of such aspirations.[21] In direct contrast to Hopkins, however, Cooper explicitly refuses Tennyson—and the Tennyson of *The Princess* in particular—the last word. "I might close," Cooper writes,

> with a glowing prediction of what the twentieth century may expect from this heritage of twin forces—the masculine battered and

toil-worn as a grim veteran after centuries of warfare, but still strong, active and vigorous, ready to help with his hard-won experience the young recruit rejoicing in her newly found freedom, who so confidently places her hand in his with mutual pledges to redeem the ages.

> And so the twain upon the skirts of time,
> Sit side by side, full-summed in all their powers,
> Dispensing harvest, sowing the To-be,
> Self-reverent each and reverencing each.[22]

Yet instead of closing with these additional lines from *The Princess*, Cooper continues: "Fain would I follow them, but duty is nearer home." This duty, she explains, is "THE HIGHER EDUCATION OF COLORED WOMEN," which she goes on to discuss without further reference to Tennyson.[23]

Cooper thus seems to recognize a limit to Tennyson's applicability that Hopkins does not. Yet rather than signaling greater conventionality, let alone deference, Hopkins's refusal to explicitly move beyond Tennyson reflects instead her greater boldness in harnessing his poetry to her own ends. This boldness comes more fully into focus if we consider more closely the relationship between the poems she cites and the narrative contexts into which she inserts them. When we do so, we quickly discover that the novel's apparent alignment of several of his poems with its romance plot—Hopkins's use of Tennyson's poems to mark the stations of that plot—at times ignores or belies the plots of those poems themselves.

For example, while Hopkins's use of "Locksley Hall" challenges that poem's racial assumptions, it also breaks from that poem's narrative, which describes a failed romance: the embittered speaker loses his beloved to a wealthier suitor. Arguably, the lines Hopkins cites had already taken on a life of their own in Anglo-American print culture and did not necessarily invoke that original narrative context. However, the same gap between poem and novel opens up when Sappho and Will are reunited at the end of the novel: as we have seen, Hopkins quotes lines from *Maud*—"O, that 'twere possible, / After long grief and pain, / To find the arms of my true love / Round me once again!" (394)—at the very moment Will's arms are around Sappho "After long grief and pain." But in *Maud* such a reunion is decidedly *not* possible, because the speaker's beloved is dead. The syntax of this passage—"O, that 'twere possible"—makes it more difficult for the reader to ignore the extent of Hopkins's recontextualization, while the very fact that she makes the same switch twice suggests that she may be doing so by design.

But why? One might understand Hopkins's ostentatious perversion or reversal of the original context of the passages she cites as broadcasting her willingness and ability to do as she likes with her sources, despite and in contrast to their original author's intentions. However, another possibility is that Hopkins is drawn to Tennyson precisely for his portrayals of failed relationships and unruly passions, and that she is interested in mobilizing these aspects of his work. These explanations are not mutually exclusive, but it is the latter one that proves more revealing (and requires more defending): as I will show, Tennyson serves in *Contending Forces* not to mark and shore up the normalizing trajectory of the novel's romance plot but on the contrary to destabilize this plot and amplify the novel's counternormative energies.

Support for this reading comes from the use Hopkins makes of yet another Tennyson poem, the early, relatively obscure "Ballad of Oriana" (1830). This poem supplies the title for chapter XIX of the novel—"The Bitter Arrow"—and its epigraph: "O, breaking heart that will not break, / Oriana! / O, pale, pale face so sweet and meek, / Oriana! / —Tennyson" (323). In this instance, though, not only the mood evoked by these particular lines but also the situation of the poem as a whole finds its clear corollary within the novel. The speaker of the poem is brokenhearted because he has inadvertently killed the woman he loves with an errant arrow while in combat outside the castle wall upon which she stands: "The bitter arrow went aside, / . . . / And pierced thy heart, my love, my bride."[24] The corresponding chapter of *Contending Forces* describes John Langley's remorse after his failed attempt to blackmail Sappho into sleeping with him. These are hardly identical scenarios, but the end of the chapter makes clear the parallel between the two by emphasizing John's awareness of his responsibility for his own suffering: "His own hand had wrought this ruin to himself, said his heart and conscience" (339). Hopkins's use of "The Ballad of Oriana" thus shows that sometimes, at least, she means to evoke the entire Tennyson poem she cites, and it confirms as well that she does not associate the poet solely with the achievement and celebration of matrimony.

Taking our cue from this example, we can read the invocations of Tennyson at key moments of Sappho and Will's romance as troubling that narrative—that is, as hinting at the possibility of counternarratives and counterenergies and, in the awkwardness of intertextual fit, at the effort of normalization required to make the characters fit this conventional narrative. Hopkins's use of Tennyson, I am suggesting, may appear to contradict but in fact contributes to the aspect of the novel analyzed most fully by Siobhan Somerville: the extent to which Hopkins not only "borrowed from nineteenth-century romance conventions, in which the narrative works toward a heterosexual resolution in marriage," as other critics have emphasized, but also depicts "a certain anxiety surround[ing] the subject of heterosexual marriage" and uses "scenes of female homoeroticism [to] structure the narrative in important ways." As Somerville shows, in both the treatment of the relationship between Sappho and Dora and of that between the minor characters Sarah Ann White and Ophelia Davis, "Hopkins portrays female couples as potential sites for the expression of desire and identification, at the same time that she contains their threat to the narrative's overall heterosexual trajectory."[25] While the unfulfilled desires of the male speakers of "Locksley Hall," *Maud,* and "The Ballad of Oriana" are directed toward conventional, heterosexual objects, the fact that these desires go unfulfilled even as (with the former two) Hopkins applies them to Will and Sappho's relationship hints at the possibility of alternatives to the matrimonial trajectory.

Hopkins's choice of "Sappho" as a name also hints at such alternatives, as Somerville explores.[26] But so too does the choice of the name "Dora," thanks to the novel's insistent Tennysonianism. Tennyson's "Dora," a self-described "English idyl" first published in 1842, is not among his better-known poems today, but its transatlantic popularity in the nineteenth century is suggested by its publication history: in addition to appearing in collected editions of Tennyson's verse, "Dora" was included in multiple editions of Boston-based Ticknor and Fields's *Favorite Authors: A Companion-Book of Prose and Poetry* (starting in 1860), and Boston publishers Lee and Shepard issued a freestanding, illustrated edition of "Dora" in 1887, despite the poem's brevity (167 lines). The possibility that Hopkins had the poem in mind when she chose the name "Dora" and expected her readers to as well is heightened by her choice of the name "Will," for Tennyson's "Dora" also tells the story of a Dora and a William. Their story is by no means identical to the one Hopkins tells, but the affinities are suggestive and in keeping with the counternormative pattern I have identified.

Tennyson's Dora and William are not sister and brother, but almost: they are first cousins who are raised together by William's father. Moreover, while Dora is amenable to her uncle's desire that she and William marry, William is not, precisely because "He had been always with her in the house" and therefore "Thought not of Dora"—which is to say, he thought of her as a sister, not a love interest.[27] William breaks with his father, marries another woman, fathers a son, and dies in the space of thirty lines, and the remainder of the poem narrates the reconciliation of the surviving parties (Dora, her uncle, William's widow Mary, and the child). The poem concludes:

> So those four abode
> Within one house together; and as years
> Went forward, Mary took another mate;
> But Dora lived unmarried till her death. (ll. 164–67)

This story and its conclusion differ from those of *Contending Forces*, and indeed in one respect the two Doras are polar opposites: Dora Smith says of her fiancé, "I know I'll get tired of him" (122), whereas Tennyson's Dora spectacularly fulfills the truism Sappho voices: "A woman loves one man, and is true to him through all eternity" (122). Yet the hint of incest in the poem suggests the non-normativity of the earlier Dora's desire too, and more importantly, she manages to fulfill Sappho's truism in such a way as to achieve the escape from heterosexual coupling the later one longs for. Hopkins's frequent recourse to Tennyson encourages the reading of her Dora's name as an allusion to the poet's, and thus as adumbrating an alternative to the conventional, normative fate Dora Smith unsuccessfully resists.

Ironically, the poem Hopkins calls upon that offers the most overt resistance to matrimony and imagines most fully unconventional alternatives to it nonetheless does conclude with marriage —like *Contending Forces* itself. In *The Princess*, a group of young friends who have gathered at a country estate make up a story about the establishment and fate of an all-female community; a series of seven men narrate the tale: led by Princess Ida, a group of women found and inhabit a university from which men are banned, but which is infiltrated by the neighboring kingdom's prince, to whom Ida's father has promised her. War between the kingdoms turns the feminist scholars into marriageable nurses, their separatist project is abandoned, and Ida ultimately accepts the prince's proposal. In the words of Eve Kosofsky Sedgwick, this tale thus "begins with the astonishing vision of a feminist separatist community, and ends with one of the age's definitive articulations of the cult of the angel in the house."[28]

Like *The Princess*, *Contending Forces* opens up the possibility of a break from the normative heterosexual matrimonial narrative and offers glimpses of a female homoerotic alternative, only to back away from and shut down these possibilities. As Alan Sinfield among others has argued, however, "although Tennyson may try eventually to close down the challenge [to gender categories he poses], he is playing a risky game, one which is likely to leave uncomfortable residues."[29] Hopkins, I am suggesting, seizes on this aspect of Tennyson's work to amplify and keep open similar challenges, despite and against the overarching narrative trajectory of her novel. Thus, when she cites *The Princess* at a key moment of capitulation to this trajectory, her citation may seem, at a casual glance, to stabilize this trajectory, but it also and predominantly reinforces this sense of capitulation:

> [Sappho] was carried away by the vehemence of his wooing. All obstacles seemed, indeed, but trifles before this all-absorbing, passionate, eager warmth of youth's first love. . . . She felt drawn out of herself as she looked into the eyes of love and met the luminous light which transfigured the face of her lover.
> "Ask me no more; thy fate and mine are sealed:
> I strove against the stream and all in vain;
> Let the great river take me in the main:
> No more, dear love, for at a touch I yield;
>   Ask me no more."
> Silently she turned to him and placed the other hand within his clasp, and burst into a tempest of weeping. (312)[30]

Hopkins here quotes the last of the six interpolated songs Tennyson added to the poem soon after its initial publication. These songs are voiced not by the male narrators but by their female companions, and as Sedgwick notes, they are "often at an odd or even subversive angle to what is manifestly supposed to be going on."[31] "Ask me no more" appears right at the point where "everything was changed," the women's "sanctuary violated, / . . . their fair college turned to hospital,"[32] and while at a glance these lines may suggest a conventional feminine submissiveness,[33] it is also possible to read them, in Alisa Clapp-Itnyre's words, as "a tragic song of forced love" that calls into question the poem's supposed happy ending and suggests that "from the women's viewpoint . . . Ida's marriage—and the many like it coerced by men and not truly chosen by women—truly is a defeat."[34] Given the progressive ideological work performed by Hopkins's representation of Sappho as suitable for bourgeois marriage, it would be wrong to see the character's capitulation here as affirming the dominant patriarchal order in the way Princess Ida's does. Instead, Hopkins uses Tennyson to keep alive an awareness that this achievement has its costs and sacrifices.

The same is true of the novel's terminal epigraph. *Contending Forces* ends with the words the central narrative of *The Princess* ends with, as the prince addresses his bride. Unlike *Contending Forces*, however, *The Princess* as a whole does not end with these words but rather returns to the poem's frame. When it does so, the very men who have made up the story, and who comfortably inhabit the gendered social order it arrives at, immediately register dissatisfaction with its outcome: "I wish she had not yielded!" exclaims Walter, the host.[35] Hopkins does not cite this wish, but the double-voiced role Tennyson has played throughout the novel gives it a ghostly presence.[36]

To be sure, an effect this subtle is easily missed (or disputed). But Hopkins makes it easier to see (and harder to dismiss) by using Tennyson to generate a similar but more overt irony at a parallel moment in her next novel, *Hagar's Daughter*. As noted above, Hopkins turns to the same section of *Maud* that she uses to introduce Sappho to introduce the later novel's light-skinned title character, Jewel Bowen. Similarly, just as Hopkins uses Tennyson to mark the reunion of Sappho and Will Smith after a long separation, so too does the other citation of Tennyson in the later novel mark Jewel's reunion with her husband, Cuthbert Sumner:

"Look thro' mine eyes with thine, true wife,
Round my true heart thine arms entwine;
My other dearer life in life,
Look thro' my very soul with thine!"[37]

This passage from "The Miller's Daughter" recalls the terminal epigraph from *Contending Forces*. Yet unlike that passage from *The Princess*, the celebration of marital union here is unequivocally endorsed in the poem from which it is drawn, which looks back lovingly on a lifelong partnership. However, just as Hopkins slyly cites Tennyson poems about failed or explicitly disappointing relationships when depicting an ostensibly successful romance in the earlier novel, so too does this reference to a successful marriage quickly prove ironic, as the relationship between Jewel and Sumner is about to collapse. It does so for a reason Hopkins has just foreshadowed: the lines from Tennyson appear immediately after Sumner says, "I am thankful that Mrs. Bowen is only your step-mother" and the narrator describes the two as "drift[ing] back into their lovers' talk once more" (269). But Mrs. Bowen—who, it has recently emerged, is a mixed-race former slave named Hagar—is in fact Jewel's birth mother, and the revelation of this relationship shortly after the husband-wife reunion leads very quickly to their separation and Jewel's death. In both novels, then, the meaning of these citations of Tennyson depends on the gap between the romantic scenarios in the poems Hopkins cites and those of the narratives she constructs.

In addition to completing a pattern of allusion within the novel it concludes, the terminal epigraph to *Contending Forces* also affiliates the novel—or cements its affiliation—with two other novels that also conclude with this rare device: Frances E. W. Harper's *Iola Leroy* (1892), the concluding "Note" of which ends with a stanza of Harper's own poem "A Brighter Coming Day," and George Eliot's *Daniel Deronda* (1876), which ends with lines from Milton's *Samson Agonistes*. As we saw in chapter 3, these latter novels are already linked to one another by their shared use of the plot of unwitting passing and voluntary racial re-identification—a plot Eliot pioneered in her earlier work, *The Spanish Gypsy*, a sentence from which Harper echoes nearly word for word in her concluding "Note." Hopkins does not reproduce that precise plot, but her use of a terminal epigraph underscores her novel's participation in this transatlantic tradition of racial-uplift literature. At the same time, while *Contending Forces* has more in common with *Iola Leroy* than it does with *Daniel Deronda*—and Hopkins's novel has long been read in relation to Harper's—Hopkins's concluding invocation of Tennyson more closely resembles Eliot's of Milton. *Contending Forces*'s terminal epigraph serves most revealingly, then, to strengthen and clarify the novel's relationship to Eliot's novel.[38]

For the male protagonists of both *Daniel Deronda* and *Contending Forces*, a stigmatized racial identity comes to serve as a source of vocation, but the two characters arrive at this aspiration by way of very different paths. Similarly, the women these men marry, Mirah Lapidoth and Sappho Clark, both overcome histories of sexual victimization bound up in some way with their racial identity as Jew and African American, respectively, but again the specifics differ greatly. Nonetheless, and as the shared device of the terminal epigraph highlights, the endings of the two novels are quite similar, in terms of both plot and tone. Both novels end not quite with the wedding of its central romantic couple but instead with their subsequent departure for an overseas destination: Daniel and Mirah are headed to Palestine, Will and Sappho to England. In both cases, the happiness of the newlyweds is tempered—in the former case, by the death of Mirah's brother and Daniel's spiritual guide Mordecai, in the latter by "chasten[ing]" thoughts of "sorrow and self-sacrifice" and "hearts crushed by despair" (401)—and the expression of great feeling takes the form of silence: the narration in *Contending*

Forces ends with Will and Sappho "watching the receding shores with hearts filled with emotion too deep for words" (402), while the lines from Milton with which *Daniel Deronda* ends conclude that

"Nothing is here for tears, nothing to wail
Or knock the breast . . .
. . . nothing but well and fair,
And what may quiet us in a death so noble."[39]

Yet this moment of greatest convergence between the two novels also pinpoints a key difference between them. *Daniel Deronda* ends with departure *from* England, whereas *Contending Forces* ends with departure *for* England. This does not simply reflect the difference between the two novels' settings: Daniel and Mirah do not so much leave England as abandon it to what the novel represents as its materialist torpor and lack of idealism, whereas *Contending Forces* describes England (and Europe more generally) as a prejudice-free zone where African Americans can flourish, associating "on equal terms with men of the highest culture" (389), their dignity respected and their rights vindicated. Ironically, then, in this instance Hopkins's strategic anglophilia drives a wedge between her work and that of the most distinguished Victorian novelist who demonstrates an interest in racial uplift at all comparable to her own.

Although my primary emphasis throughout this book is on conscious acts of citation, positioning, and repurposing, I am not claiming that Hopkins necessarily had Eliot in mind (or had even read her) when composing the ending of her novel; the insights made available by the juxtaposition of these two terminal epigraphs do not depend on reading the later one as an allusion or response to the earlier one. However, I do want to argue that Hopkins had another, much less exalted Victorian novel in mind when she chose her terminal epigraph: *The Temptation of Dulce Carruthers*, by Constance E. C. Weigall. Like Mary Hartwell Catherwood's *The White Islander*, this novel attracted limited notice when it was new and has been forgotten by literary history but evidently caught Hopkins's eye and served as a resource for the writing of her own fiction.

Published serially in 1891 in *Cassell's Family Magazine* (a London-based periodical that circulated in the U.S. in the form of an "American Edition") and issued in book form in Britain shortly thereafter, *The Temptation of Dulce Carruthers* tells the story of a "very lovely girl" from an old family of modest means living in "a typical Cornish village."[40] Dulce falls in love with "Jack Mordaunt, the rising young village doctor," and the two become engaged.[41] However, Dulce has her head turned when she visits aristocratic relatives in London (from whom her family had been estranged), breaks her engagement to Jack, and becomes engaged to a wealthy lord instead. In time, though, Dulce overcomes this temptation and breaks off her new engagement, and eventually she is reunited with her true love—who is no longer a poor doctor, thanks to an unexpected inheritance (as she learns only after she has confessed her love).

This highly conventional Victorian female bildungsroman has little in common with *Contending Forces*. Both novels do conclude with a wedding that occurs almost immediately after the man, who has become wealthy, tracks down the woman, who has been in hiding—"'My darling—my own Dulce—always mine!' [Jack] said. 'Why did you try and run away from me? Didn't you know that I should search the wide world through to find you?'" (459); "Why did you leave me, Sappho," asks Will. "Had you no confidence in my love for you?" (395)—but these are fairly generic plot elements. However, this is how *The Temptation of Dulce Carruthers* ends:

> When Dr. and Mrs. Mordaunt [the newlywed Dulce and her husband] had lost sight of the old home in the trees, and had waved their last farewells to their friends, Jack leaned forward to kiss away his wife's tears.
>
> "Don't cry, my darling," he said tenderly. "Our new life is going to be so bright and full of happiness, please God—
>
> > 'My wife, my life, oh! we will walk this world,
> > Yoked in all exercise of noble end,
> > And then thro' those dark gates across the wild
> > That no man knows. . . .
> > Lay thy sweet hands in mine, and trust to me!'"
> > THE END[42]

This is the exact same quotation *Contending Forces* ends with (save for Hopkins's substitution of "so" for Weigall's—and Tennyson's—"then" as the second word of the third line). It is particularly telling that both novels omit the same two-and-a-half lines and mark this omission with an ellipsis. Hopkins almost certainly borrowed her terminal epigraph from Weigall.[43]

The discovery of Hopkins's model raises the possibility that her familiarity with the quoted passage from Tennyson is secondhand and limited, and her terminal epigraph's connection to those of Harper and Eliot indirect or attenuated. Can we still read this citation of Tennyson as performing the work of allusion and affiliation I have attributed to it? Hopkins's appropriative compositional practice often raises such questions, especially for accounts (such as this one) interested in Hopkins's agency as an author, and perhaps most acutely when she borrows allusions and citations. For example, the end of the introductory description of Bermuda in the first chapter of *Contending Forces* reads:

> . . . and thus Shakespeare's magic island of Prospero and Miranda has
> become, indeed, to the traveler
> > The spot of earth uncurst,
> > To show how all things were created first. (21–22)

Any claims one might want to make for the work performed by the allusion to *The Tempest* and the quotation from Edmund Waller's "Battle of the Summer Islands" would not be automatically negated, but might well need to be reevaluated and perhaps differently inflected, when one learns that Hopkins evidently borrowed both from Arnold Kennedy's 1898 history, the *Story of The West Indies*.[44] I do not mean to suggest, however, that such discoveries leave us asking what to make of a diminished thing, but rather that they need to be factored into the analysis. By doing so we may even come to see Hopkins's work as even richer and stranger than we had realized.

This is the case with regard to Hopkins's use of Weigall (and we will see this pattern again when we turn to her final novel, *Of One Blood*). The discovery that Hopkins's terminal epigraph is identical to Weigall's does not negate or undo the patterns and echoes I have identified; on the contrary, comparison of the two novels reinforces these patterns and makes these echoes all the more resounding. This is most obviously the case with regard to *Daniel Deronda*: the failure of Weigall's terminal epigraph to establish or reveal any meaningful relationship between her novel and Eliot's does not call into question that between *Contending Forces* and *Daniel Deronda* but instead sets it in relief. It is also the case with regard to Tennyson's role throughout *Contending Forces*. This is not because Tennyson plays no role in *Dulce Carruthers* prior to the terminal epigraph, but rather because Hopkins radicalizes the role he does play there, as capped by his appearance in the terminal epigraph.

Like Hopkins, Weigall threads references to Tennyson throughout her novel, although with the exception of the terminal epigraph these occur on the level of diegesis (as opposed to narrative and paratextual discourse in

Hopkins): early in her stay in London, Dulce is shown "taking up a volume of Tennyson, [and becoming] enthralled in his exquisite 'Idylls,' until the sound of the gong summoned her to breakfast" (72); later she is again seen absorbed in her volume, "revelling" in a "Tennyson dreamland" (193); Dulce sings the song "Tears, idle tears," from *Maud*, charming Lord Melvell even as she feels she is "singing the dirge of her own past life" (169); and Dulce's sister is wooed by a man who sings "Come into the garden, Maud" (451). The predominant use of Tennyson in the novel, then, is to signal resistance within a courtship plot. This is most obviously the case when Weigall calls attention to the opposition between Dulce's experience of "Tears, idle tears" and that of her suitor. Yet it also holds true for Dulce's immersive reading of Tennyson, which might be taken to reflect the immaturity and romanticism that make her vulnerable to "temptation," but which Weigall also counterposes to Lord Melvell's courtship: when her grandmother enters her boudoir to tell her that Lord Melvell has come to court her, Dulce is "so absorbed in her book that she [does] not hear the opening of the door," and the grandmother's announcement of his romantic interest abruptly awakens her "from the Tennyson dreamland in which she had been revelling" and leaves her "bewildered" (193).

But Dulce's resistance to Lord Melvell's courtship is ultimately in the service of the morally pure and ideologically correct romantic match with which the novel concludes. The terminal epigraph merely clinches this alignment of Tennyson with propriety and true romance. *Dulce Carruthers* thus shows what a more normative use of Tennyson looks like, while also suggesting how Hopkins arrived at her own, counternormative use: by seizing on this deployment of Tennyson to mark a character's resistance within a particular romance plot and subtly redirecting it to adumbrate resistance to the heterosexual marriage plot as such.[45]

Hopkins's decision to use Tennyson as she does in *Contending Forces* is clearly overdetermined. And there is yet another reason why he is an appropriate choice, whether or not this too served as motivation for the novelist: as we have begun to see, Hopkins does not hesitate to borrow freely and verbatim from other texts, and Tennyson himself was repeatedly described as engaging in similar compositional practices. James McCune Smith's argument in the pages of *Frederick Douglass' Paper* that Tennyson plagiarized "The Charge of the Light Brigade" from an African war chant (discussed in chapter 2) is an early example of this recurrent accusation. The fullest elaboration of Tennyson's supposed "obligations to his predecessors" came in 1891, with the London publication of John Churton Collins's *Illustrations of Tennyson,* an expansion of a two-part essay, "A New Study of Tennyson," that appeared in 1880 in the *Cornhill* in Britain and in *Littell's Living Age* in the U.S.[46] In these works Collins sought to demonstrate that Tennyson's "genius" is "essentially imitative and reflective."[47] He illustrates the poet's "wondrous assimilative skill" with a long catalog of examples, while somewhat disingenuously dismissing the possibility that his critical efforts might be "construed into an insinuation of plagiarism against a great and noble poet."[48]

While it is unlikely that Hopkins read McCune Smith's column,[49] she may have known Collins's work. Her familiarity with it is suggested most strongly by the six-line excerpt from "Lancelot and Elaine" she cites in her last novel, *Of One Blood:* her version of this passage is identical to Collins's, which is distinguished by its use of two elisions, one a half-line long and the other a line and a half.[50] *Contending Forces* also seems to pick up where "A New Study of Tennyson" leaves off: Collins concludes by comparing Tennyson's poetry to

> the enchanted island in Shakspeare [*sic*]:
> > Full of echoes,
> > Sounds and sweet airs, that give delight.[51]

As we have seen, Hopkins makes this same "enchanted island"—"Shakespeare's magic island of Prospero and Miranda" (21–22)—the setting for the opening section of *Contending Forces*. In addition to literalizing this metaphor, though, she also makes the allusive, assimilative method it figures her own, while adding Tennyson himself as a major source of the echoes that fill her own text.

Whether or not Hopkins herself was aware of Collins's work in particular or contemporary discussion of Tennyson's "assimilative" practices more generally, our own recognition of these practices serves as a salutary reminder that the uses these two writers made of other texts exist along a continuum—and if not at the same spot along that continuum, also not at opposite poles. Moreover, which writer is closer to which end of the continuum varies from case to case: Hopkins's choice of the names Dora and William, I have argued, can be read as alluding to Tennyson's "Dora," but "Dora" itself was identified in the nineteenth century as perhaps the poem by the laureate bearing the greatest and most problematically unacknowledged obligation to a predecessor. A detailed account of the many parallels between "Dora" and Mary Mitford's story "Dora Cresswell" appeared by 1866 and was still considered worth noting in a literary periodical in 1904;[52] in his *Illustrations*, Collins states that "the whole plot of the poem . . . to the minutest details is taken from a prose story of Miss Mitford's," and he puzzles over why Tennyson fails to acknowledge this debt.[53]

Tennyson marked up his own copy of Collins's study with comments like "nonsense" and "not known to me,"[54] but he was sensitive enough to the charge regarding "Dora" that eventually he did add a footnote acknowledging that debt (while also seeking to delimit its extent).[55] This note is among those Tennyson wrote for an edition of his work that was first published posthumously, and one of the statements with which he prefaced those notes is especially suggestive in the present context. "Many of the parallelisms here given are accidental," he avers, and goes on to explain that

> The same idea must often occur independently to two men looking on the same aspects of Nature. There is a wholesome page in Eckermann's "Conversations with Goethe," where one or the other (I have not the book by me) remarks that the prosaic mind finds plagiarism in passages that only prove "the common brotherhood of man."[56]

This brief passage is wonderfully self-divided. Tennyson seeks to back up his claim that "the same idea must often occur independently to two men" by citing an authority, but then cannot recall which of two men deserves credit for the remark he cites, as if to suggest that since the same idea may have occurred independently to each of them, it hardly matters. It is also by no means clear that either Goethe or Eckermann makes the remark attributed to one or the other in the book Tennyson names; perhaps, if the "prosaic mind" finds plagiarism everywhere, to the poetic mind passages are not even identical to themselves? Tennyson ends by putting the phrase "the common brotherhood of man" in quotation marks, but this is a common phrase that hardly seems to need attribution—or rather, since we don't get that attribution, hardly seems to need this acknowledgment of the need for attribution. Moreover, it may be that Tennyson is quoting himself here, since he uses this phrase in his play *The Promise of May*.

The seesawing on display in this passage suggests the strains involved in Tennyson's effort to preserve a notion of originality by dissociating it from a model of uniqueness that has proved untenable, at least with regard to his own practice. Yet as unstable as this balancing act is, the poet's conflicted commitment to both proprietary authorship and "the common

brotherhood of man" finds enormous resonance throughout Pauline Hopkins's work. Its fullest expression, though, comes in her final novel, *Of One
Blood*, which—as its title suggests—is centrally concerned with the possible "common brotherhood of man," and which is also Hopkins's most
palimpsestic novel, the one most fully constructed through the reworking
and repurposing and verbatim reproduction of other texts: according to
Geoffrey Sanborn, "at least seventy-two passages, amounting to 18 percent
of the novel as a whole, are more or less transcribed, without attribution,
from other texts."[57] If for Tennyson, then, the common brotherhood of man
disproves charges of plagiarism in favor of parallelisms, Hopkins by contrast
will deploy plagiarism itself (or something closely akin to it) to help prove
that common brotherhood.[58]

But even as Hopkins embraces and extends this ostensibly Tennysonian
model of creativity, she shifts her attention to another Victorian author.
Like Tennyson in *Contending Forces*, this author will play a dual, contradictory role in *Of One Blood* and thereby reinforce a counternarrative that
runs athwart the novel's ostensible trajectory—a trajectory his work was
seemingly incorporated to propel onward. In this instance, I will argue, this
contradiction is best explained by the fact that in her last novel as in her first
one, Hopkins's most complex engagement with a Victorian author is also
and thereby an engagement with the work of Charles Chesnutt.

OF ONE BLOOD'S SONGS OF THE PAST

Of One Blood; or, The Hidden Self was published serially in the *Colored American Magazine* between November 1902 and November 1903. The novel
tells the story of Reuel Briggs, a young medical student in Boston who is
passing as white. After a number of melodramatic and mystical episodes—
including Reuel's "re-animation after seeming death" (37) of a beautiful
member of the Fisk Jubilee Singers, Dianthe Lusk, who also appears to him
as an apparition, and who becomes his wife but turns out to be his sister—
Reuel goes to Africa as medical officer on an expedition to find "the ancient
Ethiopian capital Meroe" (87). Instead of ruins, Reuel discovers a hidden
city, Telassar, in which this ancient civilization remains alive, and where
Reuel himself is recognized as Ergamenes, the hereditary king of this people. The novel's closing paragraphs report that Reuel, married to a "virgin
queen" (130) who bears a remarkable resemblance to Dianthe (who has died
in a complicated subplot), "spends his days in teaching his people all that

he has learned in years of contact with modern culture," even as he worries about "the advance of mighty nations penetrating the dark, mysterious forests of his native land" (193). Proclaiming that "none save Omnipotence can solve the problem," Hopkins ends the novel with the declaration that "Caste prejudice, race pride, boundless wealth, scintillating intellects refined by all the arts of the intellectual world, are but puppets in His hand, for His promises stand, and He will prove His words, 'Of one blood have I made all races of men'" (193).

Many critics have discussed *Of One Blood*'s generic eclecticism, fractured structure, and outlandish plot, all of which have increasingly come to be seen as calculated—or, to shift idioms, as features, not bugs. In perhaps the most fully developed account of the novel as an intervention in literary history, Laura Doyle has argued that Hopkins's "gothic tale is also a metacommentary on the Atlantic literary gothic" and, further, that "by way of her gothic yet Africanist epic, Hopkins has turned inside out the epic tales of the Anglo-Atlantic written by Catharine Maria Sedgwick, Nathaniel Hawthorne, and George Eliot."[59] More recently, shifting the focus to Hopkins's many verbatim and near-verbatim borrowings from other texts, Geoffrey Sanborn has argued that Hopkins is intent on "locating herself within various existing traditions of popular writing . . . by relocating bits and pieces of that writing into *Of One Blood*," and that her relationship to her sources "is remarkably nonagonistic."[60] Viewing the sheer abundance of Hopkins's borrowings as reason to dismiss the idea that she might be "'signifyin(g) on'—ironically repeating and revising her sources," Sanborn draws on poststructuralist conceptualizations of intertextuality to argue instead that Hopkins's "plagiaristic" technique "amplifies the unowned, unownable flowing of language, the babbling of the intertextual brook."[61]

Genuinely illuminating as they are, the analyses of both Doyle and Sanborn tend to flatten out differences within Hopkins's intertextual practices of particular interest here, and to constrict the range of ways Hopkins can be seen as working on or with her sources. More specifically, Hopkins's view of the literary tradition is not as monolithic as Doyle's account suggests, nor her attitude toward it as consistently oppositional; similarly, the use Hopkins makes of texts she "plagiarizes" is more varied and dialogic than Sanborn allows, and not as uniformly hostile to notions of proprietary authorship and determinate origins as his account implies. These nuanced distinctions all come into play in the novel's climactic scene of cultural transmission, a scene that features Hopkins's most provocative—and perplexing—engagement with Victorian literature.

Reuel initially makes sense of what he sees and learns in Africa by taking as his frame of reference a central text in the Western canon, *Paradise Lost:* when he learns the name of the city of Telassar, he recalls the lines "where the sons of Eden long before / Dwelt in Telassar" (114), and when he first gazes on Telassar and the surrounding countryside, he sees it as "the very embodiment" of Milton's description of Eden, thirteen lines of which he quotes "in his thoughts" (118). Immediately after this long citation, however, the narrative marks the limitations of Reuel's knowledge and perspective—and, by extension, of the literary tradition he relies upon: "Come, we will go down into the city," Telassar's leader Ai says to Reuel. "You who know the wonders of modern life at its zenith, tell me what lesson you learn from the wonders of a civilization which had its zenith six thousand years before Christ's birth" (119). When Reuel is then hailed as "Ergamenes" by "the assembled multitude" (121), he reaches as far beyond the Western literary tradition as he can to make sense of his baffling situation, but to no avail: "What is the meaning of this strange happening, more like a scene from the Arabian nights? Who is Ergamenes?" (122).

Reuel's new, deeper understanding of his own identity, along with knowledge of his people's history and heritage, come through his introduction to the Ethiopians' own cultural texts, which take the form of song and recitation:

[F]rom the hidden recesses the musicians came forth, and kneeling before Reuel, one began a song in blank verse, telling the story of Ergamenes and his kingdom.

"Hail, oh, hail Ergamenes!
The dimmest sea-cave below thee,
    The farthest sky-arch above,
In their innermost stillness know thee,
    And heave with the birth of Love.
    "All hail!
We are thine, all thine, forevermore;
Not a leaf on the laughing shore,
Not a wave on the heaving sea,
    Nor a single sigh
    In the boundless sky,
But is vowed evermore to thee!"[62]
"Son of a fallen dynasty, outcast of a sunken people, upon your breast is a lotus lily, God's mark to prove your race and descent . . ." (122–23)

This account continues in prose, with two more extended sections in verse, as the minstrels recount the history of their civilization and call upon Ergamenes to lead it back to its "ancient glory" (126). Thanks to this "song of the past of Ethiopia" (127), Reuel can finally make sense of his mother's mysterious behavior during his childhood and understands the origins of his "occult powers" (126), and he becomes aware of "how great a destiny was his" (125).

Focusing on the extensive use Hopkins makes of the work of William Wells Brown in *Hagar's Daughter*, Holly Jackson has argued that Hopkins treats "print culture as an alternate vehicle for identity transmission and historical continuity in lieu of blood-based conceptions of lineage and reproduction tainted with socioscientific racism."[63] The later novel changes this equation. Within *Of One Blood*, we see here, Hopkins depicts blood-based lineage and reproduction not as being replaced but rather supplemented, and not by print culture but by an oral culture represented as coextensive with that lineage. But there is a further twist to this scenario, for this scene not only narrates but also enacts a process of cultural transmission—one that is difficult to square with the event depicted: except for its first line, the verse cited above is lifted verbatim from Edward Bulwer Lytton's 1834 novel *The Last Days of Pompeii*, as is the phrase "Son of a fallen dynasty, outcast of a sunken people."[64] So too is the second of the three extended verse sections:

Once more the measure changed, and another voice took up the story in verse:

"Who will assume the bays
   That the hero wore?
Wreaths on the Tomb of Days
   Gone evermore!
Who shall disturb the brave
Or one leaf of their holy grave?
The laurel is vow'd to them,
Leave the bay on its sacred stem!
But hope, the rose, the unfading rose,
Alike for slave and freeman grows!

"On the summit, worn and hoary,
Of Lybia's solemn hills,
The tramp of the brave is still!

And still is the poisoned dart,
In the pulse of the mighty hearts,
Whose very blood was glory!

Who will assume the bays
    That the hero wore?
Wreaths on the Tomb of Days
    Gone evermore!" (125)

This final stanza is repeated at the end of the third, concluding verse passage. The first two of that passage's three stanzas are not taken from *The Last Days of Pompeii*—instead, they are taken from another nineteenth-century British novel, *Exiles in Babylon; or, Children of Light* (1864), by Charlotte Maria Tucker, who published under the initials "A.L.O.E." ("A Lady of England"):

"You come from afar
    From the land of the stranger,
The dreadful in war,
    The daring in danger;
Before him our plain
    Like Eden is lying;
Behind him remain
    But the wasted and dying.

"The weak finds not ruth,[65]
    Nor the patriot glory;
No hope for the youth,
    And no rest for the hoary;
O'er Ethiop's lost plains
    The victor's sword flashes,
Her sons are in chains,
    And her temples in ashes!" (127)

The one substantive revision Hopkins makes to these passages is the substitution of African place names for those in the original: "Lybia's" replaces "Phyle's" in the second Bulwer Lytton passage, and Tucker's "Judah's" becomes "Ethiop's." Much of the musicians' recitation is also taken from these two novels: for example, a long paragraph describing Babylon comes virtually verbatim from *Exiles in Babylon* (a novel that retells the biblical story of

Daniel), and a paragraph describing the downfall of the Ethiopian people—
"Stiff-necked, haughty, no conscience but that of intellect, awed not by
God's laws . . . God has punished us as he promised" (126)—is adapted
somewhat more freely from *The Last Days.*

There is an obvious tension—if not an outright contradiction—between
the act of cultural transmission this scene depicts and that which it constitutes: Reuel listens to the words of an ancient African oral culture, whereas
the reader reads words drawn from recent Anglo-American print culture.
The alternative to this reliance on the words of other writers, of course,
would not have been for Hopkins to transcribe the actual song of imaginary Ethiopians, but rather to write it herself. But the particularities of the
scenario Hopkins depicts, combined with the race—the whiteness—of the
authors whose works she borrows, render this inevitable gap between diegesis and poiesis—the reality within the fictional world and the reality of its
making—unusually fraught and potentially disablingly ironic: the story and
song Reuel listens to are those of a distinct people with an unbroken lineage
stretching back millennia, whereas those the reader reads are an idiosyn-
cratic mélange of Victorian texts. This tension is especially pronounced with
regard to the verse: whereas much of the recited narrative covers ground
known to the West, such as the account of Babylon, the verse sections do not
convey information but instead serve a more incantatory, bardic function.
They are the collective expression of the culture to which Reuel is being
introduced and into which he is being inducted. And they are the work of
Edward Bulwer Lytton and "A Lady of England." How can this fact not undermine the scene's narrative purpose and ideological investments?

One might argue, following Geoffrey Sanborn, that Hopkins is interested purely in the resonance of the passages she "plagiarizes" and not in
their provenance, and that what we have here is another example of her
treating language as flowing "unowned" and "unownable."[66] Yet such a
reading would not solve the problem presented by this scene but on the
contrary reinscribes it, since the scene itself promotes a much more linear
model of textual transmission: the voice Reuel listens to is represented as
transindividual but decidedly not transcultural, and the very transindividu-
ality the song displays and promotes is in the service of determinate origins,
not unbounded circulation. From this perspective, then, Hopkins's formal
practice still contradicts the models of genealogy and cultural transmission
on display in the scene.

Alternatively, we might read Hopkins's formal practice as revealing uncomfortable truths the narrative seeks to hide: that its vision of African

civilization is a westernized construct, that the model of cultural identity and continuity on display is an unsustainable myth. Yet another of *Of One Blood*'s driving commitments is precisely to the revelation of uncomfortable truths, and in particular uncomfortable truths about origins. The novel treats the inevitability of such revelations as an epistemological rule: early in the novel, Dianthe is led by "the hand of mysticism" to a page in a Bible in which "the following quotation from the twelfth chapter of Luke [is underscored]: 'For there is nothing covered that shall not be revealed'" (73), and this passage is repeated virtually verbatim late in the novel, with Aubrey as the reader, and with the quotation extended: "For there is nothing covered that shall not be revealed, neither hid that shall not be known" (168). The secret most immediately at issue in these scenes is these characters' (shared) ancestry—it is their mother, Mira, who has underlined the passage and whose apparition points it out to Dianthe—but the absolute nature of the dictum itself suggests a more expansive applicability. Its applicability to Hopkins's appropriative compositional practice in particular is driven home by the fact that this passage itself is appropriated from a midcentury novella by the Anglo-American spiritualist writer Emma Hardinge titled "L'Improvvisatore"—the text from which Hopkins borrows most extensively in composing her novel.[67]

To be sure, Hopkins's readers were unlikely to have noticed the vast majority of her borrowings, some of which are quite short and most of which are from ephemeral periodical literature or fairly obscure books—such as *Exiles in Babylon* and "L'Improvvisatore." It is also the case, however, that she does not seem intent on avoiding such notice: several passages, for example, rely heavily on *Casa Braccio*, a recent novel (1894) by a relatively well-known, widely reviewed American author, F. Marion Crawford. Hopkins's opening physical description of Reuel Briggs's appearance even echoes that of a character with the teasingly similar name "Paul Griggs" (who appears in more than one of Crawford's novels).[68] In a partial citational gesture, Hopkins also puts one lifted sentence in quotation marks (even as she alters it), but without identifying her source.[69]

Among Hopkins's many sources, *The Last Days of Pompeii* stands out not only as likely the most destabilizing (given what we have seen of the challenges it presents) but also paradoxically as the most recognizable. Several factors combine to grant Bulwer Lytton's novel its uniquely visible status among Hopkins's sources. The first is the novel's own visibility in turn-of-the-century American culture: as William St. Clair and Annika Bautz have shown, "in terms of literary history seen as a parade of authors and first publications, the *Last Days* is a work of 1834," but "in terms of readership and influence . . . its glory days are the late-Victorian and pre-1914 generation"; the novel "reached mass readerships" in both Britain and the United States in the 1890s.[70] This cultural visibility is matched by the passages' visibility on the page: the large chunks of appropriated verse are set off from the surrounding text. And finally, Hopkins even mentions Pompeii in the novel: the final paragraph of the chapter preceding the one with the passages from *Last Days* describes Reuel enjoying "a repast of fruit, game and wine, served him on curious golden dishes that resembled the specimens taken from ruined Pompeii" (116). At a minimum, we can say that this mention of Pompeii is not the work of a writer interested in covering her tracks. Going further, though, at a time when *The Last Days of Pompeii* served as the primary lens through which many people viewed the ancient site, we might well read this reference to "specimens taken from ruined Pompeii" as a winking allusion to the poetic "specimens" Hopkins herself is about to take from Bulwer Lytton's *Pompeii*.

A closer look at these "specimens" themselves, moreover, suggests that their main appeal for Hopkins lay less in their actual content than in their provenance. Thus, the first verse passage is introduced as "telling the story of Ergamenes and his kingdom," but in fact this passage postpones the story, and offers up a vow of eternal fealty on the part of the natural world that seems a somewhat awkward fit for the occasion. Similarly, the later song is presumably meant to herald the arrival of a new "hero"—"Who will assume the bays / That the hero wore?"—but instead suggests that no hero is arriving: "Wreaths on the Tomb of Days / Gone evermore! / . . . / Leave the bay on its sacred stem!" Indeed, the song Hopkins excerpts and adapts here is called "The Apology for Pleasure," and the second stanza, which Hopkins omits, makes even more plain its gist: "If hope is lost and Freedom fled, / The more excuse for Pleasure."[71]

In addition to this omission, along with that of the final stanza, Hopkins makes one small tweak to improve the fit: nudging the song from nostalgic hedonism to political optimism—restoring "hope," as it were—Hopkins changes Bulwer Lytton's "But *this*, the rose, the fading rose, / Alike for slave and freeman grows!" to "But *hope*, the rose, the unfading rose, / Alike for slave and freeman grows!" (190, 125; emphasis added). This revision suggests that Hopkins is aware of the mismatch between texts but is determined nonetheless to find a place for Bulwer Lytton's novel in her own.

The Last Days of Pompeii is better understood, then, less as a source Hopkins draws on than as an intertext she seeks to bring into dialogue or even align with *Of One Blood*. One reason she might want to do so is adumbrated by a pair of other phrases she borrows from Bulwer Lytton's novel in this chapter. The beginning of the recitation cited above—"Son of a fallen dynasty, outcast of a sunken people"—comes from the novel, as does the explanation within the recitation of the Ethiopian people as having fallen because they had "no conscience but that of intellect [and were] awed not by God's laws" (126). In *Last Days*, these descriptors apply to the character who is of most obvious relevance to *Of One Blood*: Arbaces, an Egyptian priest. One of the main characters in *Last Days*, Arbaces argues for Egypt's foundational role for Western civilization: "From Egypt came all the knowledge of the world: from Egypt came the lore of Athens, and the profound policy of Crete; from Egypt came those early and mysterious tribes which . . . possessed all the arts of wisdom and the graces of intellectual life."[72] *Of One Blood* offers up a comparable, if slightly different, historiography: "Babylon and Egypt," its archaeologist Professor Stone explains, "acted as the pioneers of mankind in the untrodden fields of knowledge" (98), but he also represents Ethiopian civilization as antedating Egypt's (even while insisting on a racial kinship between the two peoples), and the novel emphasizes this civilization's early achievements but, unlike Arbaces, not any enduring influence. Still, of all the English novels that had themselves proved enduring at the moment Hopkins was writing, *The Last Days of Pompeii* is perhaps unique for its inclusion of such an Afrocentric view of civilization—let alone the articulation of such a view by a "formidable and profound" African spokesman.[73]

Even as Hopkins brings Bulwer Lytton's novel into play, however, it is not at all clear how she means to position her novel in relation to his. To some extent, *Of One Blood* can be understood as a corrective to *Last Days*: Bulwer Lytton's Arbaces is a powerful, charismatic figure, but he is also the novel's villain. Irredeemably vicious and cruel, the character inspires a memorable, corresponding cruelty in his creator. Not content to simply kill off Arbaces by having a statue fall on him when Vesuvius erupts, Bulwer Lytton then treats the reader to the spectacle of Arbaces' "ghastly face [which] seemed to emerge, without limbs or trunk, from the huge fragments of the shattered column—a face of unutterable pain, agony and despair!" (417), and then gloats over this death: "So perished the wise Magician—the great Arbaces— the Hermes of the Burning Belt—the last of the royalty of Egypt!" (417). *Of One Blood* transforms this fate: Reuel, like Arbaces, is "son of a fallen dynasty, outcast of a sunken people," but if the royalty of Egypt dies off in the earlier novel, that of Ethiopia lives on triumphantly in the later one.

Satisfyingly antithetical as this revision may be, Hopkins refuses to maintain a consistent distance from or stance toward Bulwer Lytton. The irony of using a description of Arbaces' genealogical and historical place to describe Reuel is abandoned a few paragraphs later when Bulwer Lytton's analysis of Arbaces' "villainy"—"The conscience of Arbaces was solely of the intellect—it was awed by no moral laws"[74]—becomes the recitation's explanation for the Ethiopian people's downfall: "Stiff-necked, haughty, no conscience but that of intellect, awed not by God's laws, worshipping Mammon, sensual, unbelieving, God has punished us as he promised in the beginning" (126).[75] The lingering impression, then, is as much of strategic blindness to the earlier novel's racism as of a strongly revisionary, let alone subversive, impulse.

Within the history of African Americanizing deployments of Victorian literature, this strategy recalls that of Frederick Douglass and Hannah Crafts: as we saw in chapter 1, Douglass and Crafts do not protest *Bleak House*'s hostility toward those who concern themselves with the condition of Africans and American slaves but instead simply ignore it while enlisting the novel for their own purposes. Hopkins's most significant precursor, however, is her most immediate one: Charles Chesnutt. As we saw in the previous chapter, the work of Edward Bulwer Lytton is accorded a prominent role in *The House Behind the Cedars*: Bulwer Lytton's novels are among the books that make up the young John Walden's formative reading, and John takes the name Warwick from Bulwer Lytton's *The Last of the Barons* when he decides to live as a white man. The sheer fact that both Chesnutt and Hopkins make use of Bulwer Lytton is notable, but more striking and revealing is the fact that the two writers assign him symmetrical roles.

In both *The House Behind the Cedars* and *Of One Blood*, novels by Bulwer Lytton participate in a process of cultural transmission that supplements and circumscribes biological genealogy. More specifically, in both texts, novels by Bulwer Lytton facilitate the mixed-race male protagonist's affirmation of a racialized identity, an affirmation marked by a change in name. Crucially, however, these parallel trajectories go in opposite directions, as John Warwick né Walden identifies with his patrilineal whiteness while Reuel Briggs cum Ergamenes assumes the full privilege and responsibility of his matrilineal blackness. *The Last of the Barons* serves Chesnutt's character as an inspiration and resource for living as white, whereas *The Last Days of Pompeii* helps educate and acculturate Hopkins's as an Ethiopian. This divergence builds on the difference in content between the two Bulwer Lytton novels, but the neatness of this antithesis has much less to do with those novels than with the novels in which they are put to use. By the same token, this symmetry suggests that Hopkins turns to Bulwer Lytton to enter into dialogue with Chesnutt as much as with Bulwer Lytton himself.

What is the nature of this dialogue? As we have seen, the comparable yet contrasting role Bulwer Lytton plays in the two novels highlights the novelists' shared interest in both biological and cultural genealogies and the relationship between the two—and more basically, the male protagonists' opposite narrative trajectories. But this latter opposition does not reflect opposing ideological stances on the part of the two authors: both treat the desire of a mixed-race character to live as white with understanding, but neither can be said to endorse such a choice. The two authors' common ground with regard to racial identity and racial mixing is further suggested by the similarities between *The House Behind the Cedars* and Hopkins's second novel, *Hagar's Daughter:* both offer a version of the tragic-mulatta plot in which the revelation to the mulatta's white beloved (fiancé or husband) of her racial status leads to her abandonment and death, and both novels are hostile not to interracial romance per se but rather to the prejudice that destroys it.

Any real daylight between Chesnutt's and Hopkins's ideological stances may have more to do with the role of English culture and literature in the construction and maintenance of the system the two oppose on similar grounds. That is, Hopkins is not using Bulwer Lytton to position herself in relation to Chesnutt so much as repositioning—recuperating—Bulwer Lytton himself. Or rather, in recuperating Bulwer Lytton she is in fact positioning herself in relation to Chesnutt—and especially in relation to his treatment of Bulwer Lytton and British culture more generally. For while Chesnutt's relationship to British literature, as we have seen, is nuanced and multifaceted, the explicit representation of that literature in *The House Behind the Cedars* foregrounds its use to reproduce and perpetuate the racist order of the American South (as in the adoption of a model of chivalry derived from the fiction of Walter Scott).[76] Whereas Hopkins, as we have also seen, chooses to represent Britain and its culture as free from racial prejudice. This attitude is more overtly on display in *Winona* and *Contending Forces*, but, I am suggesting, it also underwrites the revisionary use she makes of Bulwer Lytton—revisionary, that is, of the use made of that Victorian author by her African American contemporary.

The final step in this rehabilitation of Bulwer Lytton occurs not in *Of One Blood* but elsewhere in the pages of the *Colored American*, a few months after the novel finished its run. In the March 1904 issue of the magazine, near the

5.1. Edward Bulwer Lytton in the table of contents of *The Colored American*, March 1904.

very end of Hopkins's time as editor and contributor—and, indeed, as an author of fiction—the name "Edward Bulwer Lytton" appears in the table of contents, listed alongside Hopkins herself writing under her own name and two pseudonyms (Sarah A. Allen and J. Shirley Shadrach), a number of other contemporary African American writers, and another mid-Victorian writer, but one with sterling abolitionist credentials—Harriet Martineau, whose 1841 historical novel *The Hour and the Man*, about Toussaint Louverture, was being serialized in the *Colored American*. (See figure 5.1)

The Bulwer Lytton piece Hopkins reprints is a short poem entitled "The Kingdom of God," which begins:

There is no unbelief;
Whoever plants a seed beneath the sod
And waits to see it push away the clod,
    He trusts in God.[77]

As this opening suggests, the poem (which is only four stanzas long) has no explicit racial content and reads as anodyne inspirational verse. Appearing on the bottom half of a page, the top part of which is taken up by the end of a long, unrelated article ("Camp Life, Tenth U.S. Cavalry," by Albert S. Lowe), the poem practically announces its own status as filler. It is unassuming in virtually every way, except for the fact of Bulwer Lytton's authorship. But this authorship is what matters, as Hopkins hereby recruits the author whom Charles Chesnutt linked so closely to John Walden's rejection of an African American identity to the ranks of contributors to a magazine "devoted to the interests of the colored race."[78]

This enlistment of Bulwer Lytton neatly reverses the role assigned the aristocratic English author in *The House Behind the Cedars*, even though it may not completely defuse any lingering sense of the incongruousness of his presence in *Of One Blood*. However, his appearance in the *Colored American Magazine* does something even more impressive: it manages to capture Hopkins's dual commitment to the importance of the authorial signature, on the one hand, and to a model of authorship as borrowing, reworking, and redeployment, on the other; *and* her dual commitment to an idealized vision of English culture and society, on the one hand, and to a transnational archive of sources and intertexts, on the other. Bulwer Lytton's appearance in the magazine does all this for the paradoxical reason that Bulwer Lytton did not in fact write "The Kingdom of God": while often ascribed to him or some other Victorian writer—Charles Kingsley, Elizabeth Barrett Browning—the poem was actually the work of an American Quaker, Elizabeth York Case (or so it seems).[79] In a final, fitting irony, then, not an act of African Americanizing appropriation but instead one of Victorianizing misattribution cements Bulwer Lytton's place in African American culture and caps Pauline Hopkins's engagement with Victorian literature.

CHAPTER SIX

THE CITATIONAL SOUL OF
BLACK FOLK: W.E.B. DU BOIS

Strolling through New York's Lower East Side one day early in the twentieth century, a young Russian Jewish immigrant impulsively purchases *The
Souls of Black Folk*, having been attracted by the title. So moved by W.E.B.
Du Bois's recently published book is the twenty-four-year old D. Tabak
that he writes a letter of gratitude to the author, urging Du Bois to "keep
up the noble work you do" and attempting to convey the jumble of emo-
tions he experienced while reading: "I was over powered by a peculiar
pain that was so much akin to bliss, indignation stirring my blood, yet,
somehow, being glad of that—growing furious at times, overcome with
shame and disgrace, yet, from underneath all this, up swelled a keen sense
of inner delight." "Heavens," exclaims Tabak, "who could describe in ade-
quate terms that Satanic blending of both pain of a bleeding heart and joy
[of] the gods?"[1]

A number of scholars have commented on this letter, which Du Bois
saved and which bears vivid witness to the impact his seminal work was
capable of having on its earliest readers across racial and ethnic lines.[2] Of
particular interest here, though, is the little-noted sentence following, and
implicitly answering, the seemingly rhetorical question posed by Tabak
("Heavens who could describe . . . ?"). "But lo," he continues, "all this inner
agitation culminated to [*sic*] 'tears, idle tears.'"[3] At a loss for words, Tabak
calls on Tennyson.

This allusion on the part of a recent (if obviously bookish) immigrant
to an English-speaking country suggests the continued currency of this
phrase from one of Tennyson's most popular lyrics a half-century after its

publication. But this turn to Tennyson by no means signals a turn away from Du Bois's book. On the contrary, Tabak's allusion shows that his sensitivity as a reader of *Souls* extends beyond its argument and pathos to include its range of references as well: Du Bois himself quotes and alludes to Tennyson several times, along with a number of other nineteenth-century British poets.

The Souls of Black Folk is widely recognized, in Eric Sundquist's words, as "the preeminent modern text of African American cultural consciousness,"[4] and its deployment of nineteenth-century British literature is both prominent and provocative. It therefore stands as the fitting culmination of the history traced in this book. Unlike most of the intertextual engagements we have examined thus far, however, Du Bois's citations have been widely noted and discussed. Moreover, Du Bois himself tends to attract the adjective "Victorian" as a descriptor—of his intellectual formation, his prose style, his aesthetic, his morality—with greater frequency than virtually any other figure in the African American literary and intellectual tradition. Nonetheless, I will show, critics have been too quick to generalize about the presence of nineteenth-century British literature in *Souls*. They have rarely asked why Du Bois selected the specific authors, texts, and passages he cites or how these citations contribute to and intervene in a tradition of African American citation and intertextuality. Addressing these questions not only nuances our understanding of Du Bois's rhetorical strategy but also leads us to reconsider a seemingly settled question in the scholarship on *Souls*: the role Du Bois assigns culture in the fight for racial equality.

As this chapter will also show, even as *The Souls of Black Folk* extends the tradition of African Americanization traced here and gives it its most visible expression, it also marks a turning point: when later African American writers engage with Victorian literature, they will not be engaging with it as contemporary, and when they engage with contemporary literature, they will not be engaging with Victorian literature. We will see this shift occurring within the pages of *Souls* itself, as Du Bois supplements his citations of no-longer-contemporary nineteenth-century poets who have a history of African American citation with citations of younger, turn-of-the-century poets. However, Du Bois himself never stops citing Victorian literature, and I end the chapter with an account of a late lecture in which he revisits and reworks his citational strategy in *Souls* by way of one of the most unlikely and spectacular African Americanizations of Victorian literature ever undertaken.

Published in 1903, *The Souls of Black Folk* flouts generic and disciplinary boundaries by bringing together lightly revised versions of Du Bois's recently published historical and sociological articles along with several new chapters, including a short story and a memoir. Du Bois frames the book with a brief "Forethought" and "Afterthought," and prefaces each of its fourteen chapters with a pair of epigraphs. Among the most famous paratexts in African American literary history, these formally innovative dual epigraphs consist in every case of lines of verse, typically identified by author, followed by several measures of unidentified musical notation drawn from African American folk songs and spirituals, which Du Bois calls "Sorrow Songs."[5] Eleven of the fourteen verse epigraphs are drawn from the work of white, nineteenth-century and turn-of-the-century poets: Americans James Russell Lowell, William Vaughn Moody, and John Greenleaf Whittier; and British writers Elizabeth Barrett Browning (who appears twice), Lord Byron, Edward FitzGerald (as translator of Omar Khayyám), William Sharp (under his pseudonym, Fiona Macleod), Algernon Swinburne, Arthur Symons, and Tennyson. In addition, one epigraph is from the Song of Solomon, and one, in German, from Friedrich Schiller's play *The Maid of Orleans*. The verse epigraph for the last chapter, "The Sorrow Songs," is taken from one of the songs themselves. (See figure 6.1)

Du Bois offers little explicit guidance on how to interpret the epigraphs. In the book's "Forethought," he explains that "Before each chapter, as now printed, stands a bar of the Sorrow Songs,—some echo of haunting melody from the only American music which welled up from black souls in the dark past" (6). At the beginning of the chapter on the Sorrow Songs he again notes, "before each thought that I have written in this book I have set a phrase, a haunting echo of these weird old songs in which the soul of the black slave spoke to men" (154–55), and in the course of that chapter he identifies the specific songs cited in various chapter epigraphs. But Du Bois says nothing about the verse epigraphs or about the pairings he constructs.[6]

Despite this reticence, critics universally agree that the paired epigraphs do more than merely reinforce the book's coherence as a book (as opposed to the more miscellaneous collection of "essays and sketches" indicated by the book's subtitle): the epigraphs perform rhetorical and ideological work that speaks to some of the central concerns of *Souls*. And differences of emphasis and nuance notwithstanding, a standard interpretation has emerged. This critical consensus emphasizes the profound gap between verse and musical epigraphs: they are described, variously (or not so variously), as "appearing to be from bizarrely different realms,"[7] "appear[ing] as autonomous fragments from opposing worlds,"[8] "not simply from different genres but virtually from different worlds (or at the least from radically segregated

THE

SOULS OF BLACK FOLK.

I

OF OUR SPIRITUAL STRIVINGS

> O water, voice of my heart, crying in the sand,
>   All night long crying with a mournful cry,
> As I lie and listen, and cannot understand
>   The voice of my heart in my side or the voice of the sea,
>   O water, crying for rest, is it I, is it I?
>   All night long the water is crying to me.
>
> Unresting water, there shall never be rest
>   Till the last-moon droop and the last tide fail,
> And the fire of the end begin to burn in the west;
>   And the heart shall be weary and wonder and cry like the sea,
>   All life long crying without avail,
>   As the water all night long is crying to me.
>   ARTHUR SYMONS.

BETWEEN me and the other world there is
ever an unasked question: unasked by some
through feelings of delicacy; by others through
the difficulty of rightly framing it. All, nevertheless,
flutter round it. They approach me in a half-hesitant
sort of way, eye me curiously or compassionately,
and then, instead of saying directly, How does it feel
to be a problem? they say, I know an excellent

1

6.1. Dual epigraphs to chapter 1 of *The Souls of
Black Folk.*

traditions, audiences, and cultures),"[9] a "blunt dialectical challenge" marking "the gulf between black and white America."[10]

Crucially, however, critics also tend to see the pairing of the epigraphs as graphically modeling the overcoming of this gap. Versions of this argument tend to invoke two of the book's most famous passages: Du Bois's assertion that "the end of [the Negro's] striving is to be a co-worker in the kingdom of culture" (11), and his celebrated vision of the sociability of culture, which comes at the end of the chapter on "the training of black men":

> I sit with Shakespeare and he winces not. Across the color line I move
> arm in arm with Balzac and Dumas, where smiling men and welcom-
> ing women glide in gilded halls. From out the caves of evening that
> swing between the strong-limbed earth and the tracery of the stars, I
> summon Aristotle and Aurelius and what soul I will, and they come

all graciously with no scorn nor condescension. So, wed with Truth, I
dwell above the Veil. (74)

According to Eric Sundquist, "[this] well-known passage defined a world in
which the alternating epigraphs would be in communion, not in conflict,
in which the Western and African traditions might harmoniously coexist."[11]
In a similar vein, Ross Posnock asserts that the "paired epigraphs . . . represent the 'kingdom [of culture]' itself in miniature as a utopian realm above
the Veil where sorrow songs and Swinburne dwell together 'un-colored.'"[12]

For these critics, then, the form of *The Souls of Black Folk*'s paired epigraphs neatly enacts the book's argument about culture. As I will show,
however, this reading flattens out differences among the verse epigraphs
themselves, which are hardly the uniform collection of Arnoldian touch-
stones critics often take them for. It also fails to situate the epigraphs within
the history of African American citational practices. The poems and poets
cited vary greatly with regard to their cultural standing and signification,
on the one hand, and their distance from African American history and
the African American literary tradition, on the other. Moreover, the tradition Du Bois extends and tropes on is not simply one of African American
citation but rather of *African Americanizing* citation: that is, as we have seen
throughout this book, citations (and other forms of intertextuality) that assign African American contents or referents to the texts and passages cited.
These principles of selection and forms of deployment give the epigraphs
different valences—different from one another and different from that usually ascribed to them.

SOULS AND THE AFRICAN AMERICAN TRADITION OF CITATION

Two factors in particular regarding the verse epigraphs have not received
their due: the familiarity of some and the contemporaneity of others. To
start with the former, we should note that fully half of the verse epigraphs
in *The Souls of Black Folk* would not have seemed out of place in the pages
of *Frederick Douglass' Paper* a half-century earlier: those quoting Lowell,
Whittier, Barrett Browning (twice), Byron, and Tennyson (as well as the
Bible). This fact alone suggests that talk of the distance or even opposition
between verse and musical epigraphs has been overstated. Most obviously,
Lowell's "The Present Crisis" and Whittier's "Howard at Atlanta" are hardly
"force[d] to bear witness to slavery," as one critic claims: the former is one of

the most famous antislavery poems and the latter is about emancipation.[13] Similarly, while neither of the poems Du Bois cites by Elizabeth Barrett Browning—"A Vision of Poets" and "A Romance of the Ganges"—is about race or slavery, Barrett Browning herself was also identified with the abolitionist movement thanks to the two poems she published in the antislavery annual *The Liberty Bell*, "The Runaway Slave at Pilgrim's Point" and "The Curse of a Nation." These writers and their work were associated with an interracial fight for racial justice, not a rarefied realm of high culture removed from the lives of "black folk."

Two of the other nineteenth-century British poets Du Bois cites in addition to Barrett Browning—Byron and Tennyson—occupy a different position, but not the remote one to which Du Bois's critics tend to assign them. Unlike Lowell, Whittier, and Barrett Browning, these poets did not write about American slavery, but both were familiar presences in the writing and oratory of African Americans addressing issues of race—as we have seen at length with regard to Tennyson, and as we shall see for Byron as well, especially for the particular passage Du Bois cites. In citing these writers, then, Du Bois extends an existing tradition of African American citational practice.

Moreover, Du Bois does not simply join this tradition: he also references and tropes on it. In other words, his verse epigraphs—especially those by Byron and Tennyson—not only extend but also evoke an African American literary and rhetorical tradition, just as the musical epigraphs evoke an African American folk tradition. Indeed, I would go so far as to suggest that the paired epigraphs juxtapose *these* traditions, as much as black and white ones. From this perspective, the merger they epitomize is not interracial but intraracial, and the lines they cross are those of class and education, not color: that between the Byron- and Tennyson-citing Talented Tenth and the sorrow-song-composing black folk, a major concern throughout the book.[14]

The self-consciousness with which Du Bois uses Byron and Tennyson to summon an African American tradition of citation—and to associate this tradition with the black elite—is suggested by these poets' appearance at the head of the two chapters in the book most explicitly concerned with the question of African American leadership: the Byron epigraph introduces the chapter devoted to Booker T. Washington, whom Du Bois challenges, while the Tennyson epigraph introduces that on Alexander Crummell, whom Du Bois eulogizes and implicitly positions himself as succeeding. These citations herald and contribute to this self-positioning.

Chapter 3 of *Souls*, "Of Mr. Booker T. Washington and Others," famously criticizes Washington for his willingness to accept civil inferiority for African Americans and his advocacy of mechanical training as opposed to what Du Bois calls "the higher education of Negro youth" (40). The chapter's verse epigraph reads:

From birth till death enslaved; in word, in deed, unmanned!

. . . .

Hereditary bondsmen! Know ye not
Who would be free themselves must strike the blow?
                                        Byron.
    (34)

In *Childe Harold's Pilgrimage*, these lines refer to Greece. As Eric Sundquist was perhaps the first to note, however, the use of the latter two lines to rally African Americans to the cause of their own liberation began by the 1830s, when the lines circulated in African American and abolitionist newspapers.[15] Henry Highland Garnet quotes them in his 1843 "Address to the Slaves of the United States," and Martin Delany used them as the motto for a newspaper he published in the 1840s. Frederick Douglass used them as a chapter epigraph in his novella "The Heroic Slave"; quotes them again in his second autobiography, *My Bondage and My Freedom*, where they are also quoted in James McCune Smith's introduction; and quotes them yet again in his third autobiography, the *Life and Times of Frederick Douglass*.[16]

In citing Byron's incitement, then, Du Bois does not reach outside an African American tradition but takes his place in the line of writers and leaders who have cited this passage before him. Indeed, it is this tradition of citation he is citing, as much as the poem itself. In other words, the epigraph is a meta-epigraph, and it signifies not only that Du Bois sits with Byron, who winces not, but also that he stands with Garnet and Delaney and Douglass.

Or perhaps not quite *with* these African American predecessors, but in relation to them. Du Bois signifies upon and distinguishes himself from this tradition in two ways. First, he expands the usual citation to include another line from the poem, from two stanzas earlier: "From birth till death enslaved; in word, in deed, unmanned" (34). The addition of this line suggests that Du Bois has returned to the original poem as his source, and thus implies that even as Du Bois's use of Byron references that of prior African Americans, his familiarity with Byron is not fully mediated by that history. Second, Du Bois breaks from prior citations of Byron by giving the lines an ironic twist. Robert Gooding-Williams (who is perhaps the first critic to note Du Bois's expansion of the conventional citation) reads the extended citation as opposing Washington's ostensible submissiveness, as captured by the first line, to the more defiant stance advocated by Du Bois and represented by the latter two lines.[17] However, one of Du Bois's final criticisms of Washington is that "his doctrine has tended to make the whites . . . shift the burden of the Negro problem to the Negro's shoulders and stand aside as critical and rather pessimistic spectators." "In fact," Du Bois continues, "the burden belongs to the nation," and the notion that the Negro's "future rise depends primarily on his own efforts" is "a dangerous half-truth" (45, 44).[18] It is thus Washington, not Du Bois, who gets aligned here with Byronic initiative and autonomy. The blow Du Bois himself strikes is against the historically uniform embrace of Byron's lines by those who cite it. By the same token, insofar as Byron is not fully absorbed into the African American tradition here, the co-presence of his verse with bars of a Sorrow Song ("A Great Camp-Meeting in the Promised Land") exemplifies the biracial effort Du Bois demands as much as the desired result of such efforts.

Du Bois's epigraphic citation of Tennyson similarly participates in an African American history of citation while at the same time establishing a certain distance between Du Bois and a race leader with whom he ostensibly aligns himself. Here, though, this distancing involves citational practices themselves and the cultural politics they imply. Du Bois uses lines from "The Passing of Arthur" (part of *Idylls of the King*) as the verse epigraph for his elegiac chapter on Alexander Crummell, the African-nationalist intellectual and activist who died in 1898:

Then from the Dawn it seemed there came, but faint
As from beyond the limit of the world,
Like the last echo born of a great cry,
Sounds, as if some fair city were one voice
Around a king returning from his wars.
                                Tennyson.
   (134)

The extent to which Crummell's life and death echo King Arthur's may seem as faint as the echo these lines describe, yet the location of the epigraph asks us to view Arthur as a figure for Crummell. Although Du Bois does not develop the analogy at length in a biographical sketch that focuses on Crummell's blackness as the defining fact of his life—the source of the challenges he faced and the focus of his life's work—he returns to it in the chapter's closing paragraph: just as Tennyson's lines describe the disappearance of the barge carrying Arthur's body, so too does Du Bois conclude with a vision of Crummell "gliding" into "that dim world beyond," greeted by a different "King,—a dark and pierced Jew." The echoing "great cry" greeting Arthur is itself echoed in the "singing" of "the morning stars" greeting Crummell, and with which the chapter ends (142).

However bold this appropriative citation of "The Passing of Arthur" is in its particulars, by 1903 the African Americanizing deployment of Tennyson is also a well-established practice—a practice, as we have seen, with a long history, and which in the decade or so preceding Du Bois's book includes such prominent examples as Anna Julia Cooper's *A Voice from the South* (1892), Paul Laurence Dunbar's "The Colored Soldiers" (1895), and Pauline Hopkins's *Contending Forces* (1901). The resemblance between the roles assigned Tennyson in *Souls* and *Contending Forces* is especially striking given the difference in genre between the two works: just as turning points in Hopkins's romance plot are marked by citations of Tennyson, as we saw in the previous chapter, so too are key moments in Du Bois's historical narrative.[19] Thus, Du Bois calls upon Tennyson not only when enacting the implicit passing of the torch from Crummell to himself but also, of more profound import, to figure both the origins of American slavery and its abolition: with devastating understatement, he writes of the initial establishment of slavery in the New World, "some one had blundered" (30), and he writes that slaves mistakenly looked forward to Emancipation as the "one divine event" that would bring "the end of all doubt and disappointment" (12). The former allusion, as noted in chapter 2, transforms Tennyson's blunt characterization of a miscommunicated order in "The Charge of the Light Brigade" into a tragicomic euphemism for one of the most momentous events in world history; the latter allusion gives specific content to the studied vagueness of the concluding lines of *In Memoriam*: "one far-off divine event, / To which the whole creation moves."[20]

When articulating his own more positive vision of the future, Du Bois again turns to *In Memoriam*: concluding a chapter on southern labor relations, he proclaims that "Only by a union of intelligence and sympathy across the color-line in this critical period of the Republic shall justice and right triumph,—

'That mind and soul according well,
May make one music as before,
　　But vaster.'" (118–19)

Here again, Du Bois gives new, and newly racial, meaning to Tennyson's
language to evoke a key (future) moment in race relations, transforming the
poet's call for an end to the tension between knowledge and religious reverence into an image of interracial harmony.[21] It is no wonder that D. Tabak
was moved to cite Tennyson to capture the effect of reading *Souls*.

Yet Du Bois's epigraphic citation of Tennyson does not align him with
Alexander Crummell himself—not quite. Du Bois departs in a subtle but
significant way from Crummell's own typical citational practice and the
relationship between race and culture it implies. Crummell is one of the
most inveterate African American quoters of British literature in the nineteenth century, but he has not been a focus of this book because he does not
typically repurpose or transpose the passages he quotes—that is, he rarely
assigns them new, let alone specifically African American, referents. For
example, when Crummell quotes William Wordsworth on "Splendor in the
grass, and glory in the flower," he does so to embroider his own description
of "the attractiveness and charm of nature." When he quotes Tennyson on
"The blind hysterics of the Celt," he is talking about the Irish.[22] As this latter
example suggests, when Crummell does attend to the treatment of race and
ethnicity in nineteenth-century British literature, he tends simply to admire
it or call on its authority. Thus, he quotes in full "the touching Sonnet of
Wordsworth . . . on the occasion of the cruel exile of Negroes from France"
and writes that Nature's "conserving power which tends everywhere to fixity of type . . . reminds us of the lines of Tennyson:

Are God and nature, then, at strife,
That nature lends such evil dreams?
So careful of the type she seems,
So careless of the single life."[23]

In contrast to Crummell, and as we have been seeing, when Du Bois cites
nineteenth-century British poetry he frequently does so in such a way as to
give the poetry a racial or specifically African American meaning or referent it does not already have—in short, he African Americanizes it. Even as
the implicit comparison of Crummell's death to that of Tennyson's Arthur
works to honor Crummell and elevate his stature, then, it also marks Du

Bois's break from his predecessor. His repurposing of British literature signals a more dialogic relationship to that literature than Crummell's, and
a more race-conscious view of culture than what the paired epigraphs are
often read as symbolizing.

Both Du Bois's difference from Crummell and the implications of this
difference—which is to say, the implications of Du Bois's African Americanizing use of nineteenth-century British literature—regarding Du Bois's
view of the relationship between race and culture, are made clearer by his
references to Wordsworth's "Intimations" ode. Whereas, as we have just seen,
Crummell takes the ode on its own terms, Du Bois gives Wordsworth's universalizing account of childhood and maturation social, and explicitly racial,
content. Recounting Crummell's youthful aspirations, Du Bois writes, "And
then from that Vision Splendid all the glory faded slowly away"; he concludes the paragraph containing that phrase, "even then the burden had not
lifted from that heart, for there had passed a glory from the earth"; and he repeats this phrase at the end of the following paragraph: "and then across his
dream gleamed some faint after-glow of that first fair vision of youth—only
an after-glow, for there had passed a glory from the earth" (137–38). Du Bois
echoes several famous passages from Wordsworth's poem—"The Youth . . .
by the vision splendid / Is on his way attended; / At length the Man perceives
it die away, / And fade into the light of common day"; "But yet I know,
where'er I go, / That there hath pass'd away a glory from the earth"; "Whither
is fled the visionary gleam? / Where is it now, the glory and the dream?"[24]
However, the falling off Du Bois allusively uses Wordsworth's language to
describe is not the inevitable result of growing up but rather the product of
racial discrimination: Crummell's vision fades and a glory passes from the
earth because Crummell's initial attempts to become a priest are met with
the response, "It is all very natural—it is even commendable; but the General
Theological Seminary of the Episcopal Church cannot admit a Negro" (137).

Du Bois's assignment of specific historical content to Wordsworth's aggressively departicularizing paradigm might seem to brush the ode against
the grain; however, the point of this racializing redirection is not to demys-
tify the poem's false universalizing or accuse it of bad faith (as readers raised
on the hermeneutics of suspicion might be quick to assume). Instead, Du
Bois calls upon and reworks Wordsworth's mythmaking to reinforce his
own.[25] This use of the "Intimations" ode picks up on and extends the use Du
Bois makes of the same poem in an autobiographical passage at the beginning of *Souls*. Writing of his childhood, Du Bois remarks, "The shades of the
prison-house closed round about us all." Continuing, however, he introduces

a distinction absent from Wordsworth's ode: "walls strait and stubborn to the whitest, but relentlessly narrow, tall, and unscalable to sons of night who must plod darkly on in resignation" (10). Du Bois seeks here neither simply to inhabit nor to escape the prison-house of Wordsworth's language, but instead to do both at once—that is, to grant the poem universal applicability while also using it to articulate a specifically black experience.[26]

The relevance of such finely parsed intertextuality to the central concerns of *The Souls of Black Folk* is suggested by this passage's specific location in the first chapter. The sentence revising Wordsworth is followed immediately by the famous passage in which Du Bois ascribes a "double-consciousness" to African Americans—the "sense of always looking at one's self through the eyes of others" and state of "two-ness"—American and Negro—he hopes to see superseded by the "merging" of this "double self into a better and truer self" in which "neither of the older selves [would] be lost" (11). Neither the existing form of subjectivity nor its desired replacement is directly analogous to the doubled vision required by the preceding intertextuality, yet the very shape of Du Bois's discussion suggests that his treatment of Wordsworth anticipates and paves the way for their articulation. The fact that the discussion of double consciousness culminates in the declaration, "This, then, is the end of his striving: to be a co-worker in the kingdom of culture" (11), reinforces this connection between his vision of African American selfhood and the recalibration of Wordsworth that precedes it.

Strikingly, Du Bois's later evocation of a cultural sphere free from racial prejudice is also preceded by allusive play with nineteenth-century British poetry, and the connection between these latter passages is less ambiguous. In the last sentence of the paragraph immediately preceding the pronouncement "I sit with Shakespeare and he winces not," Du Bois, describing educated black men, avers that "to themselves in these the days that try their souls, the chance to soar in the dim blue air above the smoke is to their finer spirits boon and guerdon for what they lose on earth by being black" (73). This image looks ahead to the following paragraph's utopian realm "above the Veil"; at the same time, though, it also looks back to the chapter's verse epigraph:

Why, if the Soul can fling the Dust aside,
And naked on the Air of Heaven ride,
　　Were't not a Shame—were't not a Shame for him
In this clay carcase crippled to abide?
　　　　　　Omar Khayyám (FitzGerald) (62)

Like the epigraph, the sentence near the end of the chapter celebrates the transcendence of bodily materiality. Even as it echoes the epigraph, though, the later sentence also introduces a racial dimension into the dynamic the poem describes—"for 'clay,'" Du Bois in effect says, "read: 'black.'" As he did with Wordsworth's ode, Du Bois turns Khayyám's metaphysical lament into a sociohistorical one. Here, though, this move is paradoxical, as Du Bois imports race into a poem to make it into a poem about leaving race behind. In other words, rather than emblematizing a realm where racism or even race itself does not exist, the epigraph depicts—that is, is made to depict— the desire for and aspiration toward such a realm. The educated black man reading FitzGerald's Omar Khayyám the way Du Bois reads him does not so much dwell above the Veil or soar in the dim blue air above the smoke as find in the poem an image of his very desire to do so.

These African Americanizing allusions to Tennyson, Wordsworth, and FitzGerald within the body of the text suggest that Du Bois's use of nineteenth-century British poetry in general, including the epigraphs, conforms less to the utopian vision of culture evoked at moments within *The Souls of Black Folk* than to the view he later articulated in his essay "Criteria of Negro Art." There Du Bois notoriously declares that "all Art is propaganda and ever must be," and claims that "whatever art I have for writing has been used always for propaganda for gaining the right of black folk to love and enjoy."[27] As Ross Posnock emphasizes, however, Du Bois does not thereby choose politics over aesthetics but instead "radically defamiliarizes propaganda by giving it the function of restoring beauty to an impoverished American culture."[28] According to Posnock, Du Bois's article "is intended as a wedge against premature closure"[29] of the battle against racism by those who might see the ability of African Americans to produce beautiful art as reason to declare victory in, as Du Bois puts it, "the eternal struggle along the color line"[30]: as Du Bois asserts, "the Beauty of Truth and Freedom which shall some day be our heritage and the heritage of all civilized men is not in our hands yet."[31] While Du Bois credits the NAACP with promoting this view in the 1920s, I am arguing that this same view animates his use of nineteenth-century British poetry in *Souls* two decades earlier—its use, that is, to conduct that ongoing struggle.

Du Bois strengthens the connection between *The Souls of Black Folk* and "Criteria of Negro Art" by ending the later text with a quotation from one of the same poets deployed in *Souls*, William Vaughn Moody. In the final section of the essay, Du Bois argues that while "the ultimate art coming from black folk is going to be just as beautiful, and beautiful largely in the same ways, as the art that comes from white folk," in the meantime "the point today" is not therefore to view art in a color-blind way but rather to use art to "compell recognition" of the humanity of "black folk." Only when that recognition comes, he continues, will it be time to view their art as timeless: "when through art they compell recognition then let the world discover if it will that their art is as new as it is old and as old as new." Ending on an evocative note, he concludes by describing and quoting a scene from Moody's play *The Fire-Bringer* in which the sight of the heavens brings the cry, "It is the stars, it is the ancient stars, it is the young and everlasting stars!"[32]

Despite the congruence between the two texts, however, the weaponized view of art articulated most explicitly in "Criteria" is undoubtedly in tension with the vision of culture as a timeless realm of cross-racial respect and sociability so powerfully evoked by the "I sit with Shakespeare and he winces not" passage. At the same time, though, the later essay highlights and clarifies the underappreciated twist Du Bois's argument takes at the end of that famous passage. After laying out his vision of what it would look like to "dwell above the Veil," Du Bois continues the paragraph, and concludes the chapter, with a series of pointed questions:

> Is this the life you grudge us, O knightly America? Is this the life you long to change into the dull red hideousness of Georgia? Are you so afraid lest peering from this high Pisgah, between Philistine and Amalekite, we sight the Promised Land? (74)

Up until the last sentence, it seems as if the realm of culture Du Bois has been describing is itself the Promised Land. Here, though, this realm becomes instead the mountaintop from which one can view that Promised Land. Presumably, this place makes the Promised Land visible by serving as its harbinger or type. Yet insofar as it is *not* itself the Promised Land, this place also serves—like the passage from the *Rubáiyát* as reworked in the preceding paragraph—as a reminder that one does not yet inhabit it.

SOULS AND THE CONTEMPORARY LITERARY FIELD

Du Bois's use of culture to signify both ongoing struggle and transcendence— that is, his use of poems as "propaganda" in the ongoing antiracist effort to destroy cultural and political barriers as well as to shadow forth the prize for such efforts—helps explain the presence and role of another group of verse epigraphs in *Souls*. This group's distinctiveness as a group has in fact rarely been recognized, thanks to the widespread tendency to view the epigraphs as symbolizing an established, monolithic Western canon or tradition. Just as the prior association of several of the poems and poets with African American writing, oratory, and print culture has been obscured by this tendency, so too has the sheer *contemporaneity* of others. Du Bois cites four living poets—Macleod (Sharp), Moody, Swinburne, and Symons— all of whom, except Swinburne, were members of his own generation.[33] These living, active writers inhabit—and signify—the actual present tense rather than the historical present tense of the "I sit with Shakespeare and he winces not" passage.

When Du Bois quotes Moody in "Criteria of Negro Art," he does not name the poet but instead identifies him as "a classmate" he once had: the two were both at Harvard in the early 1890s.[34] Yet even before Du Bois calls on Moody and his two other contemporaries for epigraphs in *Souls*, he already "dwells" with all three of them: not "above the Veil" or (only) on campus in Cambridge but rather in the pages of American periodicals. Not only were the poems he cites by all three poets quite recently published, but in addition they all appeared in the very magazines in which his own articles were appearing, including several of the pieces that became chapters in *The Souls of Black Folk*. Thus, Moody's "The Brute" first appeared in 1901 in the *Atlantic*, which published versions of five of Du Bois's chapters between 1897 and 1902, and books by Symons and Macleod containing the poems Du Bois cites ("The Crying of Water" and "Dim Face of Beauty," respectively) were reviewed together in 1902 in *The Dial*, which had published one of Du Bois's chapters the previous year. In a coincidence too remarkable to be dismissed as a coincidence, this review quotes in full, on the same page, both of the short lyrics Du Bois uses. (See figure 6.2)

The review from which Du Bois (presumably) took the Symons and Macleod poems points toward another common denominator linking Macleod, Moody, Swinburne, and Symons beyond the sheer fact of being alive at the time Du Bois was writing: all four poets received the strong endorsement of the author of that review, William Morton Payne. A prominent, Chicago-based literary critic at the turn of the century and the regular reviewer of poetry and fiction for *The Dial* for many years, Payne was also a leading champion of both the young Moody and the aging Swinburne (whose reputation remained contested at the time): in a review in *The Dial* in 1900, for example, Payne called Swinburne "the greatest [poet] that remains to us," author of "upwards of a score of volumes of the noblest poetry to which after year plays upon the strings of sense, and runs the whole gamut of carnal passion until, satiety being achieved, he can find no nobler refuge than a nauseating mixture of faint sensuality and religious mysticism. As long as he can hold to it, the motto of his song seems to be that of these lines from "Liber Amoris" — lines that derive directly from Baudelaire:

> "What's virtue, Bianca? Have we not
> Agreed the word should be forgot,
> That ours be every dear device
> And all the subtleties of vice,
> And, in diverse imaginings,
> The savour of forbidden things,"

Our quotation must close abruptly with the comma, because what follows is unfit for decent print. But even this sort of thing is better than the mawkish religiosity of the mood that succeeds.

> "O Most High! I will pray, look down through the seven
>   Passionate veils of heaven,
> Out of eternal peace, where the world's desire
> Enfolds thee in veils of fire;
> Holy of Holies, the immaculate Lamb,
> Behold me, the thing I am!
> I, the redeemed of thy blood, the bought with a price,
> The reward of thy sacrifice,
> I, who walk with thy saints in a robe of white,
> And who worship thee day and night,
> Behold me, the thing I am, and do thou beat back
> These feet that burn on my track."

The feet are those of the dogs of sensual desire, but there is no real repentance in the prayer, only a subtler form of the self-indulgence that has brought this pitiful soul to so pitiful a pass. The unwholesome character of these poems by Mr. Symons has to be emphasized because their verbal magic is potent to charm even when they glorify what is most base in human nature. How pure and true a poet Mr. Symons can be at his best may be illustrated by these lovely verses written at Montserrat:

> "Peace waits among the hills;
> I have drunk peace,
> Here, where the blue air fills
> The great cup of the hills,
> And fills with peace.
>
> "Between the earth and sky,
> I have seen the earth
> Like a dark cloud go by,
> And fade out of the sky;
> There was no more earth.
>
> "Here, where the Holy Graal
> Brought secret light
> Once, from beyond the veil,
> I, seeing no Holy Graal,
> See divine light.
>
> "Light fills the hills with God,
> Wind with his breath,
> And here, in his abode,
> Light, wind, and air praise God,
> And this poor breath."

One more lyric, representing the author's latest work, must be quoted. It is called "The Crying of Water."

> "O water, voice of my heart, crying in the sand,
> All night long crying with a mournful cry,
> As I lie and listen, and cannot understand

> The voice of my heart in my side or the voice of the sea,
> O water, crying for rest, is it I, is it I?
> All night long the water is crying to me.
>
> "Unresting water, there shall never be rest
> Till the last moon droop and the last tide fail,
> And the fire of the end begin to burn in the west;
> And the heart shall be weary and wonder and cry like the sea,
> All life long crying without avail,
> As the water all night long is crying to me."

This seems to us one of the most beautiful things in English song; its tender pathos is fairly matched by the subtle music of the verse, and the result is quite beyond criticism. A very slender sheaf of such verse as this would outweigh all the contents of these two substantial volumes.

In the metrical freedom as well as in the natural imagery of the later work of Mr. Symons the attentive ear may catch echoes, not alone of Verlaine and his fellows, but also of the neo-Celtic movement in English poetry. Let us set by the side of the poem last quoted this stanza by another writer:

> "O sands of my heart, what wind moans low along thy
>   shadowy shore?
> Is that the deep sea-heart I hear with the dying sob at its
>   core?
> Each dim lost wave that lapses is like a closing door:
> 'Tis closing doors they hear at last who soon shall hear no
>   more,
> Who soon shall hear no more."

The two poems might have been written by the same hand, yet the one just illustrated is the work, not of Mr. Arthur Symons, but of Miss "Fiona Macleod." We take it from a recent selection of her songs, containing pieces both old and new, and entitled "From the Hills of Dream." Having made the one extract for the purpose of indicating a parallelism of sentiment and artistic method, we will make one more for the sake of its own sheer loveliness.

> "Dim face of Beauty haunting all the world,
> Fair face of Beauty all too fair to see,
> Where the lost stars adown the heavens are hurled,
>   There, there alone for thee
>   May white peace be.
>
> "For here where all the dreams of men are whirled
> Like sere torn leaves of autumn to and fro,
> There is no place for thee in all the world,
>   Who driftest as a star,
>   Beyond, afar.
>
> "Beauty, sad face of Beauty, Mystery, Wonder,
> What are these dreams to foolish babbling men —
> Who cry with little noises 'neath the thunders
>   Of ages ground to sand,
>   To a little sand."

Simplicity of diction, subtlety of thought, and absolute sincerity are the qualities which give distinction to the poetry of Mrs. Alice Meynell. She publishes little because she is too severe a censor of her own work to allow it to stream forth unrestrained. Her own artistic conscience must be satisfied, and then the reader may say what he will. Her "Later Poems" constitute a volume even more slender than the earlier "Poems" that won the applause of such critics as Ruskin, Rossetti, and

6.2. "Recent Poetry" review in *The Dial*, showing two poems used as epigraphs in *Souls*, May 1, 1902.

the English tongue has given utterance"[35]; and in a 1901 review Payne declared of Moody that "no other new poet of the past score of years, either in America or in England, has displayed a finer promise upon the occasion of his first appearance."[36] Payne's visibility may well have been at its height when Du Bois was compiling *The Souls of Black Folk*, as three collections of the critic's literary articles from *The Dial* were published in 1902, the year before *Souls* appeared. These collections were published by A. C. McClurg, the same press that published *Souls* (and *The Dial*).

Whether or not Du Bois's own taste was shaped by Payne, then, his sense of what was esteemed or fashionable in the literary world into which he was launching his book certainly seems to have been. By the same token, he could be confident that his readers would share in his recognition of these poets' standing in the contemporary literary field. Unlike, say, Aristotle and Aurelius, their cultural currency resided precisely in their currentness.[37] In citing these poets, then, Du Bois does not lay claim to the cultural past but rather displays his familiarity and identification with the cultural present. He positions himself—and the sorrow songs with which he pairs these poems—in the realm of cultural and political history in the making.

The terms in which Payne writes about these poems also shed light on Du Bois's selections and on their relationships to other verse epigraphs and the musical epigraphs in *Souls*. The poem by Moody that heads the chapter "Of the Quest of the Golden Fleece," "The Brute," depicts the historical struggle to harness the force of machinery personified by its title character and thus seems broadly relevant to that chapter's treatment of the sharecropping system.[38] More relevant still, however, are the terms in which Payne praises Moody in his 1901 *Dial* review, writing with particular reference to Moody's poems protesting U.S. imperial expansion: in "a period of inexpressible sadness to Americans who have been taught to cherish the teachings of Washington and Jefferson, of Sumner and Lincoln," Payne laments, "How we have longed for the indignant words of protest that our Whittier or our Emerson or our Lowell would have voiced had their lives reached down to this unhappy time!" "But," he continues, "in reading Mr. Moody's 'Ode in Time of Hesitation' and his lines 'On a Soldier Fallen in the Philippines,' we are almost consoled for the silence of the prophet-voices that appealed so powerfully to the moral consciousness of the generation before our own."[39] Du Bois thus follows Payne in locating Moody in a specifically American poetic/prophetic tradition identified closely (though not exclusively) with the antislavery movement.

By contrast, Du Bois's use of the Symons and Macleod poems both follows and departs from their treatment by Payne. Payne's review praises Symons's "The Crying of Water," which serves as the verse epigraph to the first chapter of *Souls*, as "one of the most beautiful things in English song," with "its tender pathos . . . fairly matched by the subtle music of the verse"; similarly, the review chooses "Dim Face of Beauty" from "a recent selection of [Macleod's] songs . . . for the sake of its own sheer loveliness."[40] These formulations repeat and underscore the historical identification of lyric poems with or as "songs." This identification suggests a greater formal kinship between the verse and musical epigraphs than is acknowledged by accounts that read the two kinds of epigraphs as representing opposed literate and oral cultures. To notice this kinship is not to deny all differences between these cultures, nor indeed to minimize the gulf between the sociohistorical reality out of which the sorrow songs and these tenderly pathetic lyrics emerged. However, this kinship, as foregrounded by Payne's language, suggests that Du Bois chose poems that in some respect reached across these gulfs, whether through their subject matter, history of citation, or, as here, their formal properties.

In one key respect, though, Du Bois's deployment of these poems runs athwart Payne's characterization of them. We can hear in that characterization the influence of Victorian critic Walter Pater, who argued that

> [poetry] may find a noble and quite legitimate function in the conveyance of moral or political aspiration, as often in the poetry of Victor Hugo. . . . But the ideal types of poetry are those in which this distinction [between the matter and the form] is reduced to its *minimum*; so that lyrical poetry, precisely because in it we are least able to detach the matter from the form, without a deduction of something from that matter itself, is, at least artistically, the highest and most complete form of poetry. And the very perfection of such poetry often appears to depend, in part, on a certain suppression or vagueness of mere subject, so that the meaning reaches us through ways not distinctly traceable by the understanding.[41]

Payne follows Pater in valuing the lyrics he selects for their inextricability of matter and form and their "vagueness of mere subject." Du Bois himself embraces vagueness "as a political and aesthetic project" in *Souls*, as Ross Posnock has shown, and this stance helps account for his selection of these particular poems.[42] Yet however much Du Bois values the evocativeness and defamiliarizing power of vagueness, ultimately he places that vagueness in the service of capturing and conveying "the strange meaning of being black here in the dawning of the Twentieth Century," as the first sentence of the book's "Forethought" announces.[43] Thus, by recontextualizing Symons's poem, Du Bois assigns a new cause for or meaning to its expression of sorrow—or rather, assigns it a specific cause and meaning for the first time.

Indeed, insofar as the most immediate new context Du Bois provides for his verse epigraphs is the bars of music from the sorrow songs (that for "The Crying of Water" is "Nobody Knows the Trouble I've Seen"), he can be seen as reimagining the famous dictum with which Pater summarizes the view expressed above: *"all art constantly aspires towards the condition of music."*[44] In other words, whereas Du Bois's practice, as captured by his own corresponding dictum—"all art is propaganda"—might seem to contradict Pater's claim, it can also be seen as rendering it ironically true, by redefining "the condition of music"—at least this music—as "the articulate message of the slave to the world," music that tells "of death and suffering and unvoiced longing toward a true world."[45] The epigraphic movement from poetry to musical notation thus enacts a miniature Paterian narrative—from poetry to music—but in so doing combines this aspiration with "the conveyance of moral or political aspiration" against which Pater opposes it.[46] In citing such poets as Symons and Macleod, then, Du Bois aligns himself with contemporary literature and aesthetic doctrine even as he subtly manipulates them to serve his own agenda.

VICTORIAN AFTERLIFE: "THE VISION OF PHILLIS"

The recognizable contemporariness of the literature Du Bois cites, I have argued, is crucial to the effects he seeks. In thus expanding his archive from earlier nineteenth-century poets to include more recent works, Du Bois extends the practice of engagement with contemporary literature that played such an important role for virtually all earlier African Americanizers of Victorian literature. But in so doing he also signals the beginning of the end of this phenomenon, at least in its major phase, as a gap opens up between the Victorian and the contemporary. The sheer passage of time changes the nature and reduces the frequency, centrality, and intensity of African American engagements with Victorian literature. This falling off is greatly exacerbated by the rapid decline of Victorian literature's critical reputation, on the one hand, and by the more gradual (and fitful) rise of a commitment to an autonomous African American literary tradition, on the other.

Du Bois himself acknowledges in 1945 that "It is not today fashionable to quote the poet of the Victorian Age." Yet he makes that acknowledgment even as he quotes "Locksley Hall,"[47] and Du Bois never stopped citing Victorian literature and drawing on it as a stylistic resource. One of the most notable examples comes in his 1928 novel *Dark Princess*, which not only references *In Memoriam*'s "far-off divine event," as noted earlier, but also includes a pastiche of the opening paragraphs of *Bleak House:*

> London. . . . Fog everywhere. Fog up the river, where it flows among green aits and meadows; fog down the river, where it rolls defiled among the tiers of shipping, and the waterside pollutions of a great (and dirty) city. Fog on the Essex marshes, fog on the Kentish heights.[48]

> Fall. Fall of leaf and sigh of wind. . . . Fall on the vast gray-green Atlantic, where waves of all waters heave and groan toward bitter storms to come. Fall in the crowded streets of New York. Fall in the heart of the world.[49]

This rewriting recalls Hannah Crafts's even closer reworking of the same passage in *The Bondwoman's Narrative*, as discussed in chapter 1 ("Gloom everywhere. Gloom up the Potomac")—a striking coincidence, but presumably not another example of Du Bois's metacitationality, since there is no evidence that he was familiar with Crafts's unpublished manuscript.

Unlike Crafts's pastiche, moreover, Du Bois's is not part of a sustained engagement with Dickens's novel, and *Dark Princess* as a whole is much less invested in the protocols of Victorian realism than was Du Bois's earlier novel, *The Quest of the Silver Fleece* (1911).[50] Du Bois's later allusions often stand as isolated grace notes—although, given his evolving political stance, these notes are sometimes quite jarring. For example, in his last editorial for *The Crisis*, in 1934, Du Bois embraces voluntary segregation and decries "drowning our originality in imitation of mediocre white folks," yet (as noted in my introduction) he does so using terms borrowed from Thomas Carlyle: "In this period of frustration and disappointment," he writes, "we must turn from negation to affirmation, from the ever-lasting 'No' to the ever-lasting 'Yes.'" Perhaps it is enough for Du Bois that the author of *Sartor Resartus*— not only white but also obnoxiously racist, even by the standards of his own time—was not "mediocre," but here the productive tension of so many of Du Bois's citations threatens to give way to disabling contradiction.[51]

A remarkable 1941 lecture by Du Bois flirts with a similar contradiction and—if we can read into the piece's near-total absence from Du Bois criticism (despite its inclusion by Eric Sundquist in the Oxford *W.E.B. Du Bois Reader*)—has largely been written off for succumbing to it. However, here Du Bois returns, I will argue, to his strategy in *The Souls of Black Folk* of granting Victorian literature a prominent role in his writing not out of a habit that has lost its purchase but instead precisely to revisit and revise his own earlier practice. Just as Du Bois's citations of nineteenth-century British literature in *Souls* were in some cases meta-citations—citations of prior African American citations of that literature and indeed of an entire practice of citation—this late example performs a kind of auto-meta-intertextuality, an intertextual exercise in dialogue with Du Bois's own earlier such exercises. This piece thus proves less a belated instance of the African Americanization of Victorian literature than a self-conscious return and reflective limit case.

Participating in the seventy-fifth anniversary celebration of Fisk University as perhaps its most celebrated alumnus, Du Bois delivered a lecture titled "The Vision of Phillis the Blessed: An Allegory of Negro American Literature in the Eighteenth and Nineteenth Centuries." He begins the lecture by quoting the opening stanza of Dante Gabriel Rossetti's "The Blessed Damozel":

The blessed Damozel leaned out
     From the gold bar of Heaven:
Her eyes were deeper than the depth
     Of waters stilled at even;
She had three lilies in her hand
     And the stars in her hair were seven.[52]

He then declares, rather remarkably, "I find in these well-known verses of Rossetti a text upon which to build a brief review of the literature of American Negroes before the twentieth century" (328). (See figure 6.3)

As Du Bois clearly expects his listeners to know (judging from his characterization of the lines he quotes as "well-known"), "The Blessed Damozel" is a kind of "inverted elegy"[53] in which a young woman in heaven grieves over her separation from her still-living lover—or, alternately, in which a bereaved young man imagines his dead beloved thus grieving.[54] The relevance of such a poem to Du Bois's announced topic is not self-evident

10 —

FISK NEWS

The Vision of Phillis the Blessed

*An allegory of Negro American Literature in the Eighteenth and
Nineteenth Centuries; set down for the Seventy-fifth
Anniversary of Fisk University, 1941
By* W. E. BURGHARDT DU BOIS, 1888

DR. W. E. B. DU BOIS

The blessed Damozel leaned out
From the gold bar of Heaven:
Her eyes were deeper than the depth
Of waters stilled at even;
She had three lilies in her hand
And the stars in her hair were
seven.

I find in these well-known verses
of Rossetti, a text upon which to
build a brief review of the literature
of American Negroes before the
twentieth century. In 1754 there was
born in West Africa a little black girl
who was miraculously lifted across
the wide Atlantic and set down as a
servant to a pious well-read New England woman.

"I was a poor little outcast and a
stranger when she took me in, not
only into her house, but I presently
became a sharer in her most tender
affections. I was treated by her more
like her child than her servant."

Phillis was a child of seven when
she landed in Boston; old enough to
know the beginnings of life; the first
patterns of her ancestral culture;
she remembered her mother pouring
libations before the rising sun; she
sensed the contrast between tropical
Africa and bleak New England. From
portrait and description we know her
as frail and slight, with little hands
and feet, thin lips, small nose and
wide temples. Her skin was darkly
brown, velvet and glossy. Her hair,
tight-curled, grasped her high round
head like a close woven cap of tendrils. Her eyes were large and
black—

Her eyes were deeper than the
depth,
Of waters stilled at even.

Her gift of verse in a foreign tongue and a stilted repressed culture
was not great and yet it was there.
She sang to the Earl of Dartmouth
when the stump act was repealed;—

Should you, my lord, while you
peruse my song,
Wonder from whence my love of
freedom sprung;
Whence flow those wishes for
the common good,
By feeling hearts alone best understood—
I, young in life, by seeming cruel
fate,

Was snatched from Afric's
fancied happy seat.
What pangs excruciating must
molest,
What sorrows labour in my parents' breast!
Steeled was that soul, and by no
misery moved,
That from a father seized his
babe beloved:
Such, such my case.

She made a strange and lonesome
figure in the America of the day just
before the Revolution—calm and correct without, silent. Her deep sense of
religion and evangelical patois veiled
her more human soul to us as it did
to Thomas Jefferson. Yet within
must have bloomed and sung a world
of Phantasy. It is these imagined
visions of Phillis, in the long days of
her childhood wonder, her first happiness of young womanhood and the
hard long martyrdom of her after
years that made her Phillis the Blessed. There was in Phillis just the suggestion—not more—of something fey,
wild and elemental, sternly repressed,
confined so that the inner soul never
burst through, only the transmuted
echo—refined. (she loved the word)
not crude, not brash:

Before my mortal eyes,
The lightnings blaze across the
vaulted skies,
And, as the thunder shakes the
heav'nly plains,
A deep felt horror thrills through
all my veins.
When gentler strains demand thy
graceful song,
The length'ning lines moves lan-
guishing along.

Was Phillis blessed? Yes! with se-
curity and affection, with education
beyond her status, by contact with
cultured folk. Surely this is the beginning of blessing; and then with
sorrow and bereavement, with poverty
and hunger, with death and pain. Only
Love was lacking—love and its loss.
Reverence, affection, friendship—all
these were hers; but she was a love-
less child, woman and wife. Lacking
this miracle, she could never be a
Saint—but she was Phillis the Blessed.

Always a certain sense of mystery
lurked in the furtherest reaches of

Phillis' consciousness — the miracle
of her sudden transport to this far
land; the hoarse voice of the Visions,
the dire deep Visions, thus floated
and drifted, loomed and died in her
thoughts and dreams. In the only
home she knew—and the only friends
she had, she was always partly a
stranger. Only her phantasy was
real, only her dreams were true. She
could not help but have visions—prophetic visions,—she who in a single
childhood, had encompassed the ends
of earth.

She loved flowers and saw but few:
buttercups and daisies, arbutus and
violets; less often, a rose. She dimly
remembered riots of blooms; purple
wisteria, flowering bougainvillea, orange poinciana and crimson poinset-
tas; but she shrank from these—
thither lay riot and revolt and wild
desire and hate; and she shrunk within herself—peace, quiet, silence was
her way; only she yearned for quiet
lilies; and the stars in her hair were
seven.

The stars were her friends, her old
and trusted friends. They alone knew
her tall ghost mother, and sisters;—
Were there sisters and brothers? She
thought so, but they were dim and
vague. But her tall straight mother,
she was real. So were the stars.
Some stars were gone—a little jewel-
ed cross from the south was lost as
she was; others were misplaced. But
she knew them and loved them. They
were hers. Mornings they sang together.

Looking out from her own singular
and narrow corner of the world, Phillis must have had visions of the souls
and voices, who, coming after her,
continued and fulfilled her promise
and tradition—David Walker and his
bitter cry; the lilt of love that sang
in Armand Lanusse; the busy chroni-
cle of George Williams; the labored
tales of Wells Brown; Alberry Whitman trying desperately to sing; and
finally the grown and finished figures
of Charles Waddell Chestnutt, master
of fiction; and Paul Laurence Dunbar,
the Song of Songs.

6.3. W.E.B. Du Bois, "The Vision of Phillis the Blessed," *Fisk News*, May 1941. Fisk
University, John Hope and Aurelia E. Franklin Library, Special Collections.

(to put it mildly), but Du Bois is quick to develop his conceit. Beginning his history with a discussion of Phillis Wheatley that includes biographical information and examples of her poetry, he repeatedly applies lines from "The Blessed Damozel" to "Phillis the Blessed," as he calls her: describing her appearance, for example, he writes, "Her skin was darkly brown, velvet and glossy. Her hair, tight-curled, grasped her high round head like a close woven cap of tendrils. Her eyes were large and black—

> Her eyes were deeper than the depth,
> Of waters stilled at even." (328)

"Build[ing]" on Rossetti's imagery, Du Bois assigns meaning of his own devising to the three lilies in the damozel's hands, writing, "I seem to see her there . . . one hundred sixty-five years ago, with hands holding the three lilies of her thought; the tall white lily of her faith . . . ; the tiger lily . . . typifying her inward frightened revolt; and finally the little purple flower of her sorrow" (330).

Similarly, if more spectacularly, Du Bois aggressively allegorizes the stars in the damozel's hair. Incorporating Rossetti's line into his own prose, he describes how seven singing stars "came down and nestled in [Phillis's] hair—her stiff and crinkly close-curled hair; so the stars in her hair were seven," and goes on to explain that these seven stars are African American writers "who, coming after her, continued and fulfilled her promise and tra-dition." "One by one," Du Bois continues, these writers "leapt heavenward like thin flames; and over the birth of each, Phillis shivered with appeal and longing, and before her eyes the Visions passed" (332)—alluding here to a later passage from Rossetti's poem, in which the blessed damozel watches as the souls of lovers newly reunited by death "mounting up to God / Went by her like thin flames" (ll. 41–42).

In the middle part of the lecture, Du Bois briefly sketches the contribu-tions of his chosen seven writers: David Walker, Armand Lanusse, George Williams, William Wells Brown, Alberry Whitman, Charles Chesnutt, and Paul Laurence Dunbar. This section is largely free of allusions to Rossetti. Toward the end of the lecture, though, he returns to both Wheatley and Rossetti, as he sketches a portrait of Phillis on her deathbed: "She lay stark and stiff, thin as a skeleton, worn to a shadow, her little dark hands crossed on her flat chest, clasping three lilies. Her crinkled hair formed a dim halo about her head. Yet . . . she did not die; she rose again and lived incarnate in Paul Laurence Dunbar. Again that soul of song lived in a thin, black body and behind eyes 'Deeper than the depth / Of waters stilled at even'" (341). Soon thereafter, the lecture concludes as it began, with Du Bois quoting Rossetti's opening stanza.

Viewed in isolation, Du Bois's flamboyant allegorical gambit seems random if not bizarre, and more likely to distract from his narrative than to organize and punctuate it. When we view the lecture through the lens this book has sought to construct, however, we can see that Du Bois is both revisiting his own prior practice and extending a strand of the African American literary tradition he celebrates—that is, its very history of African Americanizing Victorian literature. In particular, "The Vision of Phillis" offers both an explicitation and elaboration of the intertextual strategy of *The Souls of Black Folk*, on the one hand, and a supplement or corrective to it, on the other.

Du Bois invites comparison of his lecture to his most famous book in several ways. Most obviously, his prefatory quotation of Victorian poetry recalls the verse epigraphs of *The Souls of Black Folk* structurally—that is, by virtue of its position as a prefatory quotation. Although Rossetti is not cited in the earlier work, his turn-of-the-century reception and reputation align him closely with several of the Victorian and fin-de-siècle poets Du Bois does cite. As we have seen, for example, Du Bois's selections of recent poetry correspond with the critical judgments of William Morton Payne, and in his 1901 review of William Vaughn Moody's work, Payne asserts that only two books of poetry so great as "to constitute an event in literature, or to set its writer among the enduring poets of his age" had appeared "In the memory of men now in their middle or advancing years": Swinburne's *Poems and Ballads* (the volume in which "Itylus," the source of one of the verse epigraphs in *Souls*, appears) in 1866 and Rossetti's *Poems* (the volume in which "The Blessed Damozel" was first published in book form) in 1870.[55] The Pre-Raphaelite poet was also often viewed as a forerunner of the aestheticist movement with which several of Du Bois's choices were associated, and the two youngest British poets Du Bois called upon for epigraphs, William Sharp (Fiona Macleod) and Arthur Symons, both wrote appreciative books about him.[56]

In choosing "The Blessed Damozel," Du Bois also returns to the topoi of Heaven, the heavens, and the afterlife shared by several of the verse epigraphs in *Souls*—in particular, those by FitzGerald, Macleod, and Tennyson. Du Bois's intertextuality is at its most layered and precise here: for example, leaning out from Heaven, the blessed damozel is imagined as having a voice "like the voice the stars / Had when they sang together"; similarly, Du Bois envisions Wheatley leaning out from Heaven as "the morning stars . . . sang together." But even as Du Bois echoes Rossetti here, the added specification that it is the *morning* stars that are singing (an image that originates in the Book of Job) recalls as well a passage in *The Souls of Black Folk*—recalls, in fact, the passage that most closely anticipates the scenario of "Phillis the Blessed," the final paragraph of the chapter on Alexander Crummell: as we saw, Du Bois pictures Crummell, like Wheatley, in Heaven; in doing so alludes to and reworks a Victorian poem (Tennyson's "Passing of Arthur"); and ends with the image of "the morning stars . . . singing."[57]

The specific ways in which Du Bois reworks Rossetti's depiction of Heaven and the central figure of its blessed inhabitant not only recall but also flesh out the earlier book's allusive and revisionary practices. They also pack a greater critical punch. For example, in "The Blessed Damozel," as Antony Harrison observes, "Symbolism full of potentially Christian meaning— such as the seven stars in the Damozel's hair and the three lilies in her hand—are drained of all such meaning and become merely ornamental."[58] Du Bois's bold assignment of meaning to these symbols highlights this void and fills it, just as he anchors and gives specific content to the vague longings of Symons and Macleod. While the obvious arbitrariness of Du Bois's allegorizing of the stars and lilies seems playful rather than critical, other tweaks and reworkings are more pointed, and more barbed than those in *Souls*. Thus, Du Bois's racialization of the image of confinement in the "Intimations" ode is echoed and intensified by his tweaking of Rossetti's comparable image of a barrier: whereas "the blessed damozel leaned out / From the gold bar of Heaven," Wheatley "leaned out and then as now Heaven was barred with gold" (330). "Without lay poverty, darkness and dirt," Du Bois adds, "without crawled crime and disease, while within the angels sang." Like the blessed damozel, "Phillis yearned down from heaven to earth," but she does so not out of desire for her lover but rather because she is "striving to lift the soul of a people" (330). According to Harrison, Rossetti's poems "manipulate palimpsests parodically in order . . . to resist the social actuality which obsessed his contemporaries."[59] Du Bois reverses this process, using Rossetti's own method to restore "social actuality" to the poem.

Similarly, whereas Du Bois's use of King Arthur as a figure for Alexander Crummell does not emphasize the cross-racial nature of this identification, Du Bois repeatedly highlights a racially coded difference between the Blessed Damozel and Phillis the Blessed. Again and again, he calls attention to Phillis Wheatley's hair, which he describes as "tight curled . . . like a close woven cap of tendrils," and "stiff and crinkly close-curled." Pre-Raphaelite

6.4. Dante Gabriel Rossetti, *The Blessed Damozel*, 1871–78. Oil on canvas, 53 ⅞″ × 38″. Harvard Art Museums / Fogg Museum, Bequest of Grenville L. Winthrop, 1943.202. Photo: Imaging Department © President and Fellows of Harvard College.

hair this is not; the Blessed Damozel's hair, we learn in the second stanza of the poem, "lay along her back" and "Was yellow like ripe corn" (ll. 11–12). Here, then, the mismatch between poem and lecture not only indexes Du Bois's will to allegorical power but also makes visible the racial specificity of the poem's ideal of beauty.[60] (See figures 6.4, 6.5)

In addition to opening up a greater critical distance between his own writing and a chosen Victorian intertext than he did in *Souls* even as he extends the citational practice of the earlier work, Du Bois also turns his attention to a body of work conspicuously absent from that book: African American literature itself. Although Phillis Wheatley is mentioned in passing in *Souls*, Du Bois's championing of the Sorrow Songs seems to leave him no room, rhetorically, in which to situate—let alone celebrate—an African

6.5. Frontispiece portrait of Phillis Wheatley, from Wheatley, *Poems on Various Subjects, Religious and Moral* (London: Printed for A. Bell, 1773).

American literary tradition. "The Vision of Phillis" can thus be understood as supplementing *Souls* by sketching that tradition. From this perspective, the use of the epigraph-like Victorian poem—paired now not with a Sorrow Song but with Phillis Wheatley and indeed the lecture's whole series of African American writers—signals the work's corrective relationship to its predecessor.

In combination, though, these two departures from *Souls*—greater critical distance from the cited white-authored text and new focus on African American authors—raise a question: Why continue to grant nineteenth-century British literature such a prominent role? To be sure, Du Bois's stance cannot be mistaken for that of William Stanley Braithwaite's cloying poem "To Dante Gabriel Rossetti" (1908), which proclaims, "I salute thee . . . Master . . . as the one faultless voice / In the praise of Beauty blown / Since Keats' lips were turned to stone."[61] Yet although Du Bois's reworking of Rossetti contains an element of critique, the lecture's very conceit runs the risk of positioning African American literature as secondary and of suggesting that, when it comes to aesthetic value, Rossetti's "gold bar" remains the gold standard.

By way of contrast, consider the argument Alice Dunbar Nelson makes in her 1922 essay "Negro Literature for Negro Pupils." Using imagery that does not allude to but resonates with "The Blessed Damozel," Dunbar Nelson objects that "for two generations we have given brown and black children a blonde ideal of beauty to worship, a milk-white literature to assimilate, and a pearly Paradise to anticipate, in which their dark faces would be hopelessly out of place."[62] Like Dunbar Nelson, Du Bois sees how "milk-white literature" can promote racially exclusive norms and ideals; unlike Dunbar Nelson, however, Du Bois refuses to set "milk-white literature" aside, even when celebrating the creative achievements of African Americans.

Of course, it is precisely through his use of "The Blessed Damozel" that Du Bois is able to put "The Vision of Phillis" in dialogue with his earlier work, as we have seen. And if this dialogue revises the earlier practice, it does not reject outright that practice or the vision of culture bound up with it: Du Bois remains committed to an ideal of culture as integrated and free from prejudice, sharing the "dream" he ascribes to Wheatley of "a day . . . when it would be natural to see folk of all races mingling in a democracy of culture" (335). But his use of "The Blessed Damozel" also helps specify just what such "mingling" looks like to Du Bois.[63]

Despite his implicit criticism of Rossetti and the blatant arbitrariness of his allegorizing, there are elements of the poem that clearly appeal to Du Bois. Indeed, the very liberties Du Bois takes with the poem are in keeping with its spirit, and that of Rossetti's artistic practice more generally, which Antony Harrison has characterized as "*seriously* parodic"—that is, combining sincerity and parody—in its treatment of its source and intertexts.[64] Du Bois, we might say, is doing to Rossetti's poem what Rossetti, in an evocative phrase, once described himself as doing to a poem by Tennyson: "allegoriz[ing] on one's own hook on the subject of the poem, without killing, for oneself and everyone, a distinct idea of the poet's."[65]

Nor is Du Bois true to his source only insofar as he departs from it. On the contrary, two "distinct idea[s]" from the poem, one formal and one philosophical, make their presence felt in the lecture. Formally, the structure of the lecture recapitulates and makes explicit the implied structure of the poem: both are acts of projection, specifically a man attributing thoughts to a dead woman imagined to be in Heaven. Philosophically, Rossetti's version of Heaven itself as a site of yearning corresponds to Du Bois's understanding of culture as a site of struggle and striving as well as the goal of such striving—both the Promised Land and Pisgah, the place from which one gazes on the Promised Land. Moreover, whereas in *Souls* Du Bois flirted with the notion of a Heaven where bodies and blackness are left behind (for example, by way of his allusive play with the *Rubáiyát*), his commitment here to a specifically African American literary tradition jibes better with Rossetti's notoriously physical version of Heaven (in which bodies are not left behind, as the Blessed Damozel's bosom warms the bar and wilts the flowers she holds).

Instead of moving past "The Blessed Damozel" once the work of critique is done, then, Du Bois continues to "mingle" with it. He repeatedly cites key lines from it, giving them an incantatory quality while palimpsestically superimposing a new meaning on them. As in *The Souls of Black Folk* but more ostentatiously, he leverages his intertext to reinforce his own mythmaking. The success of this technique is suggested by a report in the same commemorative Fisk newsletter in which the lecture was published. According to this report, Du Bois's listeners were neither puzzled by his gambit nor knowingly appreciative of his irony: they were "spellbound."[66]

Mingling Rossetti's language and imagery with his own to weave his spell, Du Bois thus manages to simultaneously acknowledge and transcend the incongruity between the Blessed Damozel and Phillis the Blessed. In a final flourish, he ends his lecture by conjuring a lingering image of the "darkly brown" foundational figure of the African American literary tradition—and does so by reproducing verbatim the Victorian image of yellow-haired beauty with which he began. Following Du Bois's lead, I will conclude with this doubled vision of Heaven, which stands as the very apotheosis of the African Americanizing practices traced in this book.

> And so the story ends. . . . Last night and each night:
>   The blessed Damozel leaned out
>   From the gold bar of Heaven:
>   Her eyes were deeper than the depth
>   Of waters stilled at even;
>   She had three lilies in her hand
>   And the stars in her hair were seven. (342)

AFTER DU BOIS

This study makes no claim to comprehensiveness. I have focused on citational and appropriative acts most likely—due to their elaborateness, insightfulness, or sheer unexpectedness—to challenge and deepen our understanding of Victorian literature and of African American literature and print culture as well as the relationship between the two; and I have highlighted the work done on and with Victorian literature by now-canonical figures in particular to show that these textual encounters are not a marginal phenomenon but on the contrary helped shape the African American literary tradition. However, given the size of the archive of African American literature and print culture, on the one hand, and the many possible forms of citation and appropriation (not all of which are readily apparent) on the other, there is every reason to believe that further research will reveal this history of engagement to be even richer and more revelatory than I have been able to show here.

Yet even a more fully fleshed-out account of the African Americanization of Victorian literature will, I suspect, continue to show this phenomenon as flourishing primarily in the second half of the nineteenth and early years of the twentieth century. As argued in the previous chapter, Victorian literature becomes less distinctive and less significant a presence in African American literature and print culture after the end of the Victorian era. This is not surprising, since both the prestige and popularity of most Victorian literature—and of Victorian literature as a category—diminished rapidly in the first half of the twentieth century, thanks in good part to the rise of modernism; with the loss of its contemporaneity, Victorian literature came to seem not timeless but passé. Moreover, when twentieth-century African American writers looked abroad for cultures that seemed freer from racial prejudice or even the pressures of racialized identity than the U.S., their gaze shifted from Britain elsewhere. As Brent Hayes Edwards has shown, France in particular took on this role, while also becoming the privileged site of black internationalism, with Paris viewed as "a special space for black transnational interaction, exchange, and dialogue."[1] Beginning with the Harlem Renaissance, notions of racial authenticity also reinforced this turn away from Victorian literature, not only for its whiteness but also for its association with gentility and middle-class values. As discussed in the introduction, these same attitudes have shaped the dominant critical reception of the Victorian presence in African American literature and print culture until quite recently.

Among the writers associated with the Harlem Renaissance itself, the one who does the most to extend this Victorian presence is Jessie Redmon Fauset, literary editor of *The Crisis* and a close associate of Du Bois. Fauset's first novel, *There Is Confusion* (1924), takes its title and epigraph ("There is confusion worse than death, / Trouble on trouble; pain on pain") from Tennyson's "The Lotos-Eaters," and allusions to this passage within the novel recall the use Du Bois made of "The Charge of the Light Brigade" and *In Memoriam* in *The Souls of Black Folk*: "It is amazing into what confusion slavery threw American life," remarks one character late in the novel.[2] Like Du Bois, then, Fauset uses a Tennysonian phrase from a very different context to describe the institution of slavery. Fauset, though, also keeps the phrase's original context in play: this comment comes in a conversation between American soldiers in Europe during World War I, and the novel's attention to soldiers at war and soldiers returning home further motivates the use of "The Lotos-Eaters."

More intriguingly, in *There Is Confusion* Fauset also alludes to a Victorian novel with which Charles Chesnutt is in dialogue in *The House Behind the Cedars* (as I argued in chapter 4)—as is Du Bois in *The Quest of the Silver Fleece* (as I have argued elsewhere): *The Mill on the Floss*.[3] One of the plotlines in Fauset's novel tracks the balked relationship between a young working-class woman and a young man from a more well-to-do, respectable family that disapproves of the match. This is of course a generic novelistic scenario (albeit not one that had been explored many times with African American characters at the time Fauset is writing) and as such does not automatically call to mind Eliot's novel. By naming her characters Maggie and Philip, however, Fauset invites comparison of the relationship she depicts to that between Maggie Tulliver—she of the "brown skin as makes her look like a mulatter"—and Philip Wakem, the sensitive, artistic son of the lawyer who is Maggie's father's sworn enemy.[4]

Although Maggie Ellersley and Philip Marshall are black—and although Fauset herself will famously be criticized by Alain Locke as "mid-Victorian"[5]—Fauset seems less interested in African Americanizing this mid-Victorian novel than in updating it. That is, her novel's general focus on the role of racial prejudice and loyalties in determining individual destinies notwithstanding, Fauset is less interested in exploring what difference this racial difference makes to the story she and Eliot both tell than in exploring what difference the difference in era makes. Maggie Tulliver ends her engagement to Philip Wakem with a scandalous trip down the river with another man, but she does not consummate that (or any) relationship; by contrast, Maggie Ellersley reacts to a cruel letter from Philip Marshall's sister seeking to break off her engagement ("Philip Marshall cannot marry a hair-dresser!" [87]) by rushing into marriage with a violent gambler—a marriage, moreover, that quickly ends in divorce. Maggie Tulliver can find no way to escape the predicament created by her supposed sexual history; the divorced Maggie Ellersley leaves for France to work at a leave-center for Negro soldiers, where she finds contentment for the first time. Maggie Tulliver feels admiration and pity but not romantic love for Philip Wakem, who is disabled (he is hunchbacked); when Maggie Ellersley and Philip Marshall are by chance reunited in France, her love for him is only intensified by the fact that he has been wounded and gassed—"She did not want him ill, but she adored his weakness, it gave her her first chance . . . to pay back, instead of always taking" (263)—and the two marry, even though Philip is dying. None of these differences reflect the fact that Eliot's characters are white and Fauset's are black. Fauset's relative formal conservatism notwithstanding, most of *There Is Confusion*—in particular, the plot of divorce and remarriage, Maggie Ellersley's greater economic independence, and the role played by war in shaping the characters' lives—reflects the fact that the novel was published in 1924 rather than 1860.

It is telling that Fauset did not take issue with Alain Locke's scorn for the mid-Victorian, even as she angrily rejected this epithet's applicability to herself. Indeed, in a story published the year before *There Is Confusion*, Fauset acknowledged the declining currency of one quintessential Victorian writer, even as she cites him: "He was living at this time in the last years of the nineties," her narrator remarks of one character, "and so was given to much reading of Tennyson. Angélique made him think of the Miller's daughter, who had 'grown so dear, so dear.'"[6] While Robert Browning's "Two in the Campagna" serves as a touchstone in her second novel, *Plum Bun* (1929), Fauset's references to Victorian literature in her later novels are often framed by similar periodizing and modernizing gestures—for example, the narrator of *The Chinaberry Tree* (1931) notes that "once the frequent quoting of the *Rubáiyát* marked a person as possessing a certain amount of literary perspicuity"—and such references are virtually absent from her last novel, *Comedy: American Style* (1933).[7]

By and large, Victorian literature has not attracted particular attention from African American novelists writing more recently than Fauset. We might take as emblematic of the relationship of post–Harlem Renaissance literature to Victorian literature that displayed by one of the most celebrated novels by an African American, Ralph Ellison's *Invisible Man* (1952). Although *Invisible Man* borrows its title from H. G. Wells's 1897 novel *The Invisible Man*, Ellison seems entirely uninterested in establishing any kind of intertextual relationship to Wells's work. On the rare occasion when Ellison does mention Victorian literature in his critical and autobiographical essays, he is careful to limit its influence on him as a writer: "*Wuthering Heights* had caused me an agony of unexpressible emotion, and the same was true of *Jude the Obscure*, but *The Waste Land* seized my mind." Despite the fact that Ellison himself became a novelist and not a poet, he identifies the reading of this poem, rather than the earlier novels, as the turning point in his relationship to literature, "the real transition to writing."[8]

Yet the overall trend represented by Ellison notwithstanding, Victorian literature and the history of African American engagement with that literature may still have a productive and provocative role to play in contemporary literature by African American writers, as suggested by two recent novels. Not coincidentally, I would argue, these novels court controversy, with both of them depicting and occupying fraught positions with regard to the African American literary tradition and African American identity more generally. The earlier of these novels, Percival Everett's *Erasure* (2001), tells the teasingly semi-autobiographical story of a novelist, Thelonious Ellison, who resists being defined as black and rejects the notion that his subject should be "the African American experience" or that his writing should be viewed "as an exercise in racial self-expression."[9] Yet as the voicing of this resistance indicates (and as the protagonist's first and last names emphasize), the novel does not escape this frame of reference but rather takes the frustrated desire to escape it as its subject: thus, instead of his usual postmodernist pastiches, the narrator writes a parody of a ghetto novel that, taken straight, achieves critical and commercial success. This strand of the novel is free of references to Victorian literature. However, another narrative strand of *Erasure* tracks Ellison's efforts to come to terms with the death of his parents, and a Victorian text makes a striking cameo at a key moment: reading through a box of his father's private papers, which consist mainly of letters revealing that his father had had a wartime affair with a British nurse—an affair resulting in the birth of a daughter—the narrator comes across "A very small, leather-bound book": "*Silas Marner* by George Eliot." This is, he comments, "An odd book to find," but he discovers "pressed in its pages . . . a small flower, pink and white."[10]

Coming as it does in a scene of emotionally loaded narrative revelation, this intertextual gesture begs to be read as meaningful. And coming as it does in a novel intent on contesting narrow definitions of the sources and subjects of fiction by African Americans—"I didn't write as an act of testimony or social indignation . . . and I did not write out of a so-called family tradition of oral storytelling"[11]—the choice of this Victorian staple of the twentieth-century canon and school curriculum makes sense as a possible nod to and renewal of the history of African American engagement with Victorian literature: although this history is by no means one of uniform opposition to the writerly motives and sources *Erasure* disdains here, it does model the freedom of literary association and appropriation claimed by Everett.[12] Ironically, however, the narrator reports that "The pages between which the little flower was pressed seemed to have no significance or bearing on anything," and the reader (at least, this reader) can do no better at motivating Everett's choice of this "curiously chosen novel," except to point to this recalcitrance itself.[13] In other words, efforts to relate the particularities of Eliot's fable of "the Weaver of Raveloe" (to quote the book's subtitle) to *Erasure* seem as forced and unconvincing as the narrator's extrapolation from the handwriting in the letters that "that nurse had had small but strong hands with trimmed nails, a weaver's hands perhaps."[14] Everett introduces *Silas Marner* into the novel, it would seem, precisely to stymie and mock conventional interpretive protocols.

Insofar as *Erasure* bears out its narrator's contention that the Victorian text he encounters has "no significance or bearing on anything," this novel might serve as a fitting endpoint to the narrative constructed in *Reaping Something New*: the tradition of engagement tracked here is resurrected, only to be decisively put to rest. As Everett himself knows full well, however, a gesture such as his does not end a tradition but instead sustains it (if only "under erasure"); as his narrator muses in another context, "maybe I have misunderstood my experiments all along, propping up, as if propping up is needed, the artistic traditions that I have pretended to challenge."[15] This tension between propping up and challenging the presence of Victorian literature in African American literature is even more pronounced in another, even more recent novel, Paul Beatty's *The Sellout* (2015). Strikingly, this novel not only includes several prominent references to Victorian literature but also depicts their African Americanization.

In fact, Beatty homes in on practices, authors, and even one key text highlighted in the present book with uncanny precision. In doing so, Beatty does not seek to turn back the clock; rather, he takes turning back the clock as his topic, to consider how much has and has not changed over time for African Americans, for better and for worse. Thus, in this ferocious send-up of African American pieties and stereotypes alike (the first sentence of which is, "This may be hard to believe, coming from a black man, but I've never stolen anything"[16]), the unnamed narrator humors his aging neighbor Hominy Jenkins (supposedly one of the Little Rascals) by treating him as a slave and attempts to restore a sense of identity and community to his hometown by bringing back segregation. The name of this hometown is Dickens.

In addition to this place name (to which I will return), *The Sellout* references Victorian literature in two scenes. In both, characters African Americanize that literature—that is, they rewrite it with black characters and (stereotypically) black cultural referents. In the later scene, all we see are the reworked titles of Victorian novels, but the earlier scene includes twenty-seven lines of rewritten verse. Thinking back to his childhood, the narrator describes witnessing the birth of gangster rap—the brainchild, we are informed, of a neighborhood crack dealer when "hallucinating high on his own supply and Alfred Lord Tennyson's brooding lyricism" (37). A pastiche of "The Charge of the Light Brigade" (I am tempted to add: of course) titled "The Charge of the Light-Skinned Spade," the rap begins at the beginning of the poem with "Half a liter, half a liter, / Half a liter onward / All in the alley of Death"; features lines like "Niggers to the right of them, / niggers to the left of them," and "Theirs not to reason what the fuck, / Theirs but to shoot and duck"; and continues on to the end of the poem: "When can their shine and buzz fade? / Oh the buckwild charge they made! / . . . / Respect the charge of the Light-skinned Spade / The noble now empty Olde English Eight Hundred" (38–39).

As with the use of "The Charge of the Light Brigade" in *The Fresh Prince of Bel-Air* (discussed in chapter 2), Beatty's choice of Tennyson's poem is likely determined more by the poem's remarkably unfaded currency in the culture at large than by the specific history of African American engagement I trace; indeed, rather than hint at these historical links, Beatty underscores and plays for laughs the incongruity between the occasion and diction of

Tennyson's poem and that of Carl "Kilo G" Garfield. If it is not immediately clear whether the joke here is on Tennyson or gangster rap (or both), it may be because Beatty's real target is neither, but instead the very concerns over racial authenticity, cross-racial appropriation, and aesthetic value an origin story such as this one might be expected to raise. "The Charge of the Light Brigade" is the perfect vehicle for mounting this critique, since, as we have seen, the poem has been enlisted in this discourse from the moment of its publication.

The trope of rewriting Victorian texts with African American content returns briefly later in *The Sellout*. Here Beatty's target is the pedagogical impulse to render such texts, now understood as "classics" or "the Canon" (165), relevant to African Americans and free of racism—an impulse, Beatty suggests, that only reinscribes that racism and serves the self-promoting ends of would-be race leaders. Thus, the narrator's nemesis Foy Cheshire—the character who dubs the narrator "the Sellout" for the perceived inadequacy of his commitment to black culture—begins by replacing "the repugnant 'n-word'" in *Huckleberry Finn* with "warrior" and "improv[ing] Jim's diction" (95), and soon is promoting a curriculum featuring such titles as *Uncle Tom's Condo* and *The Point Guard in the Rye* alongside *Measured Expectations* and *Middlemarch Middle of April, I'll Have Your Money—I Swear* (165, 217). Although Beatty's inclusion of both British and American titles might suggest that the Victorianness of these latter two works is not significant, these novels—especially Eliot's—stand out here as the only ones mentioned (aside from Stowe's, an easily accounted-for exception) that are not standard middle-school or high-school texts (indeed, Beatty also mentions *The Great Blacksby* and *The Old Black Man and the Inflatable Winnie the Pooh Swimming Pool* [165, 217]). *The Sellout* thus registers the particular affinity of African Americanizers for Victorian literature—an affinity the disdainful narrator perhaps has in mind when he names one of the strains of marijuana he grows "Anglophobia" (64).

Yet Beatty himself seems to extend the tradition of engagement he mocks, not only by mocking it but also, as noted above, by naming the Compton-like "ghetto community on the southern outskirts of Los Angeles" in which the story is set "Dickens" (27). The scene of virtually all the novel's action, Dickens is also at the center of its plot. As the narrator explains, the municipality's bad reputation and the effect of this reputation on the property values of nearby neighborhoods have led to its "disappearance" (57): "One clear South Central morning," he recounts, "we awoke to find that . . . the signs that said Welcome to the City of Dickens were gone" (58);

this "erasure" is so complete that Internet searches for "Dickens" almost exclusively turn up "references to 'Dickens, Charles John Huffam'" (57, 58). The narrative tracks the narrator's attempt to "Bring back Dickens," including literally putting "Dickens . . . back on the map" (78, 284).

Why Dickens? The one specific allusion to Dickens's writings in *The Sellout* (beyond the mention of *Measured Expectations*) offers an answer: presenting his plan to bring back Dickens to a neighborhood group, the narrator draws a box and labels the inside "Dickens" and "The Worst of Times," and the outside "White America" and "The Best of Times" (99).[17] However, Beatty does not develop the analogy between his novel and *A Tale of Two Cities* any further, as if to keep his distance from the African Americanizing practices he depicts. The relationship between African American and Victorian literature here remains unsettled and under negotiation.

The Sellout thus resonates provocatively with the tradition traced in this book and stands as a timely warning against consigning it entirely to the past. It is an especially fitting text with which to conclude this study, however, not only because it keeps this tradition alive but also because it does so, in part, by allegorizing its renewal or recovery: "Bring back Dickens." Taking my own cue, then, from the appropriative spirit characteristic of this tradition of engagement, from Frederick Douglass's reprinting and Hannah Crafts's reworking of *Bleak House* to W.E.B. Du Bois's transformation of "The Blessed Damozel," I will end by proposing that we read *The Sellout* as an allegory of the present volume itself—which has sought to direct searches for Dickens (and other Victorian authors) toward African American locations, and to advance understanding of African American literature and print culture by putting Victorian literature back on the map.

NOTES

INTRODUCTION: THE AFRICAN AMERICANIZATION OF VICTORIAN LITERATURE

1. James A. Snead, "Repetition as a Figure of Black Culture," in Henry Louis Gates Jr., ed., *Black Literature and Literary Theory* (New York: Methuen, 1984), 59.

2. In a sympathetic discussion of my approach, Rebecca L. Walkowitz writes, "Hack calls his methodology 'close reading at a distance,' but his procedure involves something more like distant reading up close since he is interested above all in the dynamics of reception: how an original text with 'intrinsic features' travels from one political context to another, and how it is deployed in each of those contexts." As I hope emerges more clearly here, though, my commitment to detailed textual analysis and my frequent attention to what "the dynamics of reception" for a particular text can tell us about that text's "intrinsic features" motivates (and hopefully justifies) my continued use of the term "close reading at a distance." Moreover, as I emphasize below but only hint at in the articles Walkowitz cites, I also use "close reading at a distance" to characterize the practices of the writers and editors I am studying. Rebecca L. Walkowitz, *Born Translated: The Contemporary Novel in an Age of World Literature* (New York: Columbia University Press, 2015), 87. (Walkowitz cites the phrase "intrinsic features" from Daniel Hack, "Close Reading at a Distance: The African Americanization of *Bleak House*," *Critical Inquiry* 34, no. 4 [Summer 2008]: 730.)

   An interpretive dialectic akin to that which I am proposing here animates some versions of adaptation studies; see, for example, Linda Hutcheon, *A Theory of Adaptation* (New York: Routledge, 2006). Unlike the present book, however, adaptation studies tends to focus on translation from one medium to another (such as from novel to film) as well as on a more limited range of intertextual relationships; for example, Hutcheon's influential account defines its ambit as "openly acknowledged and extended reworkings of particular other texts"; Ibid., 16.

3. Franco Moretti, "Conjectures on World Literature," *New Left Review* 1 (January–February 2000): 57. For a comparison of my method (as laid out in

the previously published article-versions of chapter 1 of this book) to Moretti's, and the articulation of her own, somewhat different version of "close reading at a distance" responsive to the distinctive material conditions and formal features of contemporary fiction, see Walkowitz, *Born Translated: The Contemporary Novel in an Age of World Literature*, 83–91, esp. 86–87.

4. Anna Julia Cooper, *The Voice of Anna Julia Cooper: Including a Voice from the South and Other Important Essays, Papers, and Letters*, ed. Charles C. Lemert and Esme Bhan (Lanham, Maryland: Rowman & Littlefield, 1998), 51.

5. Ibid., 52.

6. Ibid.

7. Henry Louis Gates Jr., "Foreword: In Her Own Write," in *Schomburg Library of Nineteenth-Century Black Women Writers* (New York: Oxford UP, 1988), vii.

8. Gates, "Foreword: In Her Own Write," xviii.

9. Henry Louis Gates Jr. and Nellie Y. McKay, "Introduction: Talking Books," in *Norton Anthology of African American Literature*, 2nd ed. (New York: Norton, 2004), xlv. For the way Gates's model both points toward and defers attention to "literary multiracialism," see Kenneth Warren, *Black and White Strangers: Race and American Literary Realism* (Chicago: U of Chicago P, 1993), 18–19.

10. Henry Louis Gates Jr., *The Signifying Monkey: A Theory of Afro-American Literary Criticism* (New York: Oxford UP, 1988), xxii.

11. Gates, *Signifying Monkey*, 122. See Kenneth Warren, *So Black and Blue: Ralph Ellison and the Occasion of Criticism* (Chicago: U of Chicago P, 2003), for a discussion of this tension in Gates's critical program, 18–19. For a recent roundtable on the legacy and historical significance of *The Signifying Monkey*, see *Early American Literature* 50, no. 3 (2015).

12. Gates, *The Signifying Monkey*, 114, quoting Du Bois in *The Crisis* 41 (June 1934): 182.

13. See Frances Smith Foster, *Written by Herself: Literary Production by African American Women, 1746–1892* (Bloomington: Indiana UP, 1993); Ann DuCille, *The Coupling Convention: Sex, Text, and Tradition in Black Women's Fiction* (New York: Oxford UP, 1993); and Carla L. Peterson, *"Doers of the Word": African-American Women Speakers & Writers in the North (1830–1880)*, (New Brunswick, NJ: Rutgers UP, 1995). See also Kari J. Winter, *Subjects of Slavery, Agents of Change: Women and Power in Gothic Novels and Slave Narratives, 1790–1865* (Athens: U of Georgia P, 1992), which takes a largely comparative approach. In an intriguing glimpse of the reach of one Victorian novel, though, Winter records that "At least one slave mother in the 1860s named her daughter Jane Eyre" (92).

14. Paul Gilroy, *The Black Atlantic: Modernity and Double Consciousness* (Cambridge, MA: Harvard UP, 1993). See also Brent Hayes Edwards, *The Practice of Diaspora: Literature, Translation, and the Rise of Black Internationalism* (Cambridge, MA: Harvard UP, 2003).

15. Ross Posnock, *Color and Culture: Black Writers and the Making of the Modern Intellectual* (Cambridge, MA: Harvard UP, 1998), 300; W.E.B. Du Bois, *The Souls of Black Folk* (New York: Norton, 1999), 74.

16. See, for example, William W. Cook and James Tatum, *African American Writers and Classical Tradition* (Chicago: U of Chicago P, 2010); and Dennis Looney,

Freedom Readers: The African American Reception of Dante Alighieri and the Divine Comedy (Notre Dame, IN: U of Notre Dame P, 2011)

17. Laura Doyle, *Freedom's Empire: Race and the Rise of the Novel in Atlantic Modernity, 1640–1940* (Durham, NC: Duke UP, 2008); Elisa Tamarkin, *Anglophilia: Deference, Devotion, and Antebellum America* (Chicago: U of Chicago P, 2008); Elizabeth Young, *Black Frankenstein: The Making of an American Metaphor* (New York: NYU Press, 2008). I am also indebted to work on transatlantic literary traffic that does not focus on African American participation in this traffic, including Meredith L. McGill, *American Literature and the Culture of Reprinting, 1834–1853* (Philadelphia: U of Pennsylvania P, 2003); McGill, ed., *The Traffic in Poems: Nineteenth-Century Poetry and Transatlantic Exchange* (New Brunswick, NJ: Rutgers UP, 2008); and Amanda Claybaugh, *The Novel of Purpose: Literature and Social Reform in the Anglo-American World* (Ithaca, NY: Cornell UP, 2008). Such transatlanticist work serves as a corrective to the long history of critical efforts to assert and define the distinctiveness of American literature by minimizing the role of transatlantic exchange or framing any dialogue as fundamentally antagonistic. For an overview and critique of this history, along with a pioneering effort to move beyond it, see Paul Giles, *Transatlantic Insurrections: British Culture and the Formation of American Literature, 1730–1860* (Philadelphia: U of Pennsylvania Press, 2001). Illuminating brief surveys and analyses of the transatlanticist turn in Victorian and nineteenth-century American literary studies include Linda K. Hughes and Sarah R. Robbins, "Introduction: Tracing Currents and Joining Conversations," in *Teaching Transatlanticism: Resources for Teaching Nineteenth-Century Anglo-American Print Culture* (Edinburgh: Edinburgh UP, 2015); John Picker, "Current Thinking: On Transatlantic Victorianism," *Victorian Literature and Culture* 39 (2011): 595–603; and Joseph Rezek, "What We Need from Transatlantic Studies," *American Literary History* 26, no. 4 (2014): 791–803.

18. Several studies have addressed other aspects of African American interest in Victorian culture. See, in particular, Wilson Jeremiah Moses, *The Golden Age of Black Nationalism, 1850–1925* (New York: Oxford UP, 1978); Tamarkin, *Anglophilia*; and Vanessa D. Dickerson, *Dark Victorians* (Urbana, IL: U of Illinois P, 2008). Moses's intellectual history characterizes black nationalism as "a genteel tradition in English letters" and shows its interest in "preserving Anglo-American values and transmitting them, in modified form, to the black community" (11). Focusing on the antebellum period, Tamarkin argues that African Americans' "extravagant fixation on aspects of British culture far removed from, and far surpassing, the political imperatives of abolition itself" (180) reflects both a more widespread American anglophilia and a more specific view of Britain as a site of freedom from antislavery (and not only from slavery)—a site, that is, where African Americans were free to cultivate interests unrelated to abolition or race. Dickerson surveys the attitudes toward Britain of nineteenth-century African Americans who visited that country and briefly discusses African American responses to Thomas Carlyle.

19. Here I take issue with the implicit logic underwriting Kenneth Warren's claim that "the turn to diasporic, transatlantic, global and other frames indicates a dim

awareness that the boundary creating [African American literature as a distinct entity] has eroded": writers sometimes reach across boundaries in the course of their efforts to build a distinct tradition, and the very ways in which they reach across boundaries can themselves form such a tradition. Kenneth Warren, *What Was African American Literature?* (Cambridge, MA: Harvard UP, 2011), 8.

20. "The Everlasting No" and "The Everlasting Yea" are central concepts (and chapter titles) in Carlyle's *Sartor Resartus* (1834). The notoriety of Carlyle's views regarding blacks and slavery in the early twentieth century is evidenced by Kelly Miller's 1906 article on "The Artistic Gifts of the Negro," in which Miller states, "The Dogma of Carlyle, that 'the Negro is useful to God's creation only as a servant,' still finds wide acceptance." It is also worth noting that later in the same essay Miller calls the singing of slaves on plantations "the smothered voice of a race crying in the wilderness, 'with no language, but a cry'": Cooper may or may not have been the first to bring Tennyson's line to bear on the experience of African Americans, but she was definitely not the last. Kelly Miller, "The Artistic Gifts of the Negro," *Voice of the Negro* (Atlanta), 1 April 1906, 252–57; 252, 253.

21. DuCille, *The Coupling Convention*, 3.

22. Warren, *What Was African American Literature?*, 120.

23. There is no need to rehearse here the long Western history of denigrating and denying the intellectual and artistic abilities of both blacks and women, but as a reminder of the currency of these attitudes, we might turn briefly to Victorian England's greatest theorist of and spokesman for culture, Matthew Arnold. Arnold visited Oberlin College in Ohio in 1884, at which time Anna Julia Cooper was one of three African American female students at the school. Cooper and her friend and classmate Mary Church Terrell both later provided pertinent vignettes of this visit: Cooper, in "The Higher Education of Women," one of the essays collected in *A Voice from the South*, reports that after Arnold lectured, he remarked with surprise "that the young women in the audience . . . 'paid as close attention as the men, *all the way through*'" (81). Terrell, in her autobiography, describes Arnold's reaction when he learns that Terrell, whom he hears read and translate a Greek passage, is "of African descent": "Thereupon Mr. Arnold expressed the greatest surprise imaginable, because, he said, he thought the tongue of the African was so thick he could not be taught to pronounce the Greek correctly" (*A Colored Woman in a White World* [Washington, DC: Ransdell, 1940], 41).

24. Nella Larsen, *"Quicksand" and "Passing"* (New Brunswick, NJ: Rutgers UP, 1986), 75.

25. Chesnutt uses the relevant lines of Lamb's poem "To the Editor of the Every-Day Book" as the epigraph to *The Marrow of Tradition*. Epigraphs are an important site of African American engagement with Victorian literature, as we shall see in chapters 5 and 6.

26. Joseph Rezek, "What We Need from Transatlantic Studies," *American Literary History* 26, no. 4 (2014): 791–803; 793, 794. According to Rezek, however, "Because work in this mode situates national stories in Atlantic contexts . . . its intervention ultimately lies within the historiography of a single nation" (794). By contrast, I argue that the recovery of the tradition I trace contributes to our understanding of both Victorian and African American literature.

27. Alfred, Lord Tennyson, *In Memoriam A.H.H.*, section LIV, 1–2. Tennyson, *The Poems of Tennyson*, ed. Christopher Ricks (London: Longmans, 1969).
28. Ibid., l. 17.
29. G. Haven, "Modern Literature," *Christian Recorder*, 23 March 1861. The article notes that it is reprinted from the *Methodist Quarterly*.
30. Cooper engages in a similar kind of play in one of her epigraphs to the second half of her book. There she quotes a passage she attributes to "Felix Holt": "The greatest question in the world is how to give every man a man's share in what goes on in life—we want a freeman's share, and that is to think and speak and act about what concerns us all, and see whether these fine gentlemen who undertake to govern us are doing the best they can for us" (120). The substitution of the titular character's name for the author's, while itself curious, also suggests that these words are spoken by that character—but they are not. Nor, for that matter, are they spoken by a character with whom Felix aligns himself, or whose politics are endorsed by the novel.
31. Frances Smith Foster, ed., *A Brighter Coming Day: A Frances Ellen Watkins Harper Reader* (New York: The Feminist Press at CUNY, 1990), 62. Emphasis added by way of example.
32. Cooper, *The Voice of Anna Julia Cooper*, 115.
33. Ibid.
34. In a rare example of critical attention to this pattern, Cornel West notes that Du Bois's citation of the late Victorian Arthur Symons's poem "The Crying of Water" in the first chapter epigraph in *The Souls of Black Folk* "seems to echo the opening" of Cooper's book. Cornel West, "Black Strivings in a Twilight Civilization," in Henry Louis Gates Jr. and Cornel West, *The Future of the Race* (New York: Alfred A. Knopf, 1996), 191.
35. Tennyson, *In Memoriam A.H.H.*, section LIV, 5–7, 9.
36. Elizabeth Barrett Browning, "The Runaway Slave at Pilgrim's Point," section IV, l. 4–7. Barrett Browning, *Poems*, 4th ed. (London: Chapman & Hall, 1856), 2: 130.
37. Cooper, *The Voice of Anna Julia Cooper*, 50.
38. For a recent, virtually unprecedented sustained treatment of the poem (which was based on a tale in Boccaccio's *Decameron*, as Eliot notes in the poem itself), see Wendy S. Williams, *George Eliot, Poetess* (Burlington, VT: Ashgate, 2014), 92–105.
39. In her 1895 essay "The New Negro Woman," Mrs. Booker T. Washington asserts that "Women of all races had a friend in George Eliot," quotes Eliot, and explains that "We are a race of servants, not in the low sense of this word, but in the highest and purest sense, and, in our serving, let us keep these beautiful lines of the servant of all women as our guide." Mrs. Washington almost certainly took these lines from Cooper's epigraph: she quotes the exact same lines as Cooper, with the same elision and, tellingly, the same misquotation of "inward pang" as "inward pangs." Here, then, is also a neat example of the self-perpetuating quality of the African American engagement with Victorian literature. Mrs. Booker T. Washington, "The New Negro Woman," in Edward E. Hale, ed., *Lend a Hand: A Record of Progress*, v. 15, October 1895, 254–60.

40. My emphasis on contemporaneity distinguishes my approach from the influential transnational work of Wai-chee Dimock, who challenges what she sees as the insularity of nineteenth-century American literary studies by advocating "a scale enlargement along the temporal axis." Dimock sees this enlargement as also expanding literary study's "spatial compass." However, by treating the latter expansion as a function of the former, her model makes it is difficult to gain purchase on—or even recognize—the specific dynamics governing and generated by engagements with literary works felt to be of or near one's own historical moment. Dimock, *Through Other Continents: American Literature Across Deep Time* (Princeton: Princeton UP, 2008), 4.

    In emphasizing the importance of contemporaneity or near-contemporaneity, my argument recalls the pioneering transatlanticist work of Robert Weisbuch, who states flatly that for American writers in what he calls "the Age of Emerson," "Contemporaries matter most." (Robert Weisbuch, *Atlantic Double-Cross: American Literature and British Influence in the Age of Emerson* [Chicago: U of Chicago P, 1986], 16.) They do so, according to Weisbuch, because American writers saw their British counterparts as "monopoliz[ing] the attention of the American reading public and prov[ing] the attraction of the British way" (16). American resentment over this popularity and prestige produced what Weisbuch sees as a "basic pattern of aggressive, parodic response" (15). However, Weisbuch focuses exclusively on white writers. As we are seeing, whatever the merit of his argument for his chosen examples, the very different social and political situation of African American writers encouraged a very different and more complex attitude—or rather, range of attitudes—toward contemporary British literature and culture.

41. See William St. Clair, *The Reading Nation in the Romantic Period* (Cambridge: Cambridge UP, 2004).

42. Simon Gikandi, "The Embarrassment of Victorianism: Colonial Subjects and the Lure of Englishness," in *Victorian Afterlife: Postmodern Culture Rewrites the Nineteenth Century,* ed. John Kucich and Dianne F. Sadoff (Minneapolis: U of Minnesota P, 2000), 157–85; 158, 182.

43. For a wide-ranging history of this subject, see Joan Shelley Rubin, *Songs of Ourselves: The Uses of Poetry in America* (Cambridge, MA: Belknap Press of Harvard UP, 2007).

44. I borrow the term "diegetic transposition" from Gérard Genette, *Palimpsests: Literature in the Second Degree,* trans. Channa Newman and Claude Doubinsky (Lincoln: U of Nebraska P, 1997), 296.

45. For an extensive list of "key terms of interculturality in current use," see Susan Stanford Friedman, "One Hand Clapping: Colonialism, Postcolonialism, and the Spatio/Temporal Boundaries of Modernism," in *Translocal Modernisms: International Perspectives* (New York: Peter Lang, 2008), 11–40: 22–23. Oddly, Friedman's list does not include "afterlives." Two books published at the turn of the present century gave this term currency in Victorian literary studies. *Victorian Afterlife: Postmodern Culture Rewrites the Nineteenth Century* is a collection of essays edited by John Kucich and Dianne F. Sadoff focusing mainly on the Victorian revivalism of the 1980s and 1990s; the editors do not address their

choice of "afterlife" for their title, and the term is not used prominently in the book itself. Robert Douglas-Fairhurst does highlight the term itself in his study of the Victorians' own discourse of influence, *Victorian Afterlives: The Shaping of Influence in Nineteenth-Century Literature* (New York: Oxford UP, 2002). Douglas-Fairhurst's usage of "afterlives" is at times more literal-minded than mine, as one of his topics is the Victorian interest in posthumous influence. The term seems to have had less currency in African American literary studies; as of this writing, a Google search of the term "African American afterlives" turns up only references to the present study.

46. With this emphasis on contemporaneity and the recent past, I do not mean to challenge the interest or value of a work's later afterlives, but rather to specify my focus and underscore the role of historical proximity or distance in determining a response's nature and significance. The recently constituted field of neo-Victorian studies takes as its focus late-twentieth- and twenty-first-century returns to the Victorian; in addition to Kucich and Sadoff, *Victorian Afterlife*, see, for example, the journal *Neo-Victorian Studies* (neovictorianstudies.com) and Ann Heilmann and Mark Llewellyn, *Neo-Victorianism: The Victorians in the Twenty-First Century, 1999–2009* (New York: Palgrave Macmillan, 2010).

47. To date, the most robust case for an African American influence on Victorian literature comes in Julia Sun-Joo Lee's provocative *The American Slave Narrative and the Victorian Novel* (New York: Oxford UP, 2010). I find Lee's identification of shared tropes and narrative strategies more persuasive than her arguments for direct influence. I discuss Lee's argument more fully in my review of her book: Hack, *"The American Slave Narrative and the Victorian Novel"* (review), *Victorian Studies* 53, no. 2 (Winter 2011): 325–27.

CHAPTER ONE: CLOSE READING *BLEAK HOUSE* AT A DISTANCE

1. [Edmund Quincy?], "The Jerry Rescue Meeting," *Liberator*, 7 October 1853, 158.
2. For a telling example of the limitations of an approach that abandons textual interpretation even as it seeks to determine a text's cultural impact, see the chapter "Frankenstein" in William St. Clair's magisterial, and in many ways invaluable, *The Reading Nation in the Romantic Period* (Cambridge UP, 2004). Sophisticated and meticulous as he is in his efforts to "elucidate and model the factors which determined which constituencies of readers had access to which printed texts at which times" (8–9), St. Clair nonetheless feels free to claim that Mary Shelley's notoriously slippery and reinterpretable text has a "plain meaning" (373) and "explicit message" (368), claims he supports with little more than a two-sentence summary of the plot and a statement by Percy Shelley. In relying on Percy Shelley, moreover, St. Clair takes it for granted that Mary and Percy agreed about "the meaning and message of the work" (358) and, further, that the work carried the meaning and message they intended it to carry. St. Clair ignores the large body of criticism vigorously interrogating both these assumptions.
3. See Benedict Anderson, *Imagined Communities: Reflections on the Origin and Spread of Nationalism* (London: Verso, 1983).

4. *Frederick Douglass' Paper*, 16 December 1853; "Prospectus to the Eighth Volume of *Frederick Douglass' Paper*," 15 December 1854.

5. To note Griffiths's role is not to distance Douglass from the paper's choices; he himself stresses that the *Paper* should be read "as its name imports, as Frederick Douglass' paper, in the fullest sense." "Prospectus to the Eighth Volume of *Frederick Douglass' Paper*," 15 December 1854.

6. Almost its entirety: on a couple of occasions, *Douglass' Paper* ends a weekly installment midchapter and fails to include the remainder of the chapter in the next installment, but these seem like minor oversights. For a detailed inventory of the paper's literary content, see Patsy Brewington Perry, "The Literary Content of *Frederick Douglass's Paper* through 1860," *CLA Journal* 17 (1973): 214–29. Perry emphasizes Douglass's desire to enrich his readers' lives by exposing them to "good literature," whatever its source, along with his desire to support "budding black poets who needed an appreciative audience" (214, 221). More recently, Elizabeth McHenry has emphasized the political implications of Douglass's integrationist policy, arguing that "Douglass's placement of the work of the most celebrated white European and European American writers next to that of black writers insisted on the equality of their literary, cultural, and artistic pursuits," and on the "transracial" nature of literary talent. See *Forgotten Readers: Recovering the Lost History of African American Literary Societies* (Durham, NC: Duke UP, 2002), 116, 126.

7. *Frederick Douglass' Paper*, 8 April 1852.

8. "'Bleak House,'" *Commonwealth* (Boston), 25 March 1852.

9. "'The Bleak House,'" *Commonwealth* (Boston), 20 March 1852.

10. "The New Story by Dickens," *Commonwealth* (Boston), 19 March 1852.

11. "Dickens," *Commonwealth* (Boston), 2 April 1852.

12. Douglass, *My Bondage and My Freedom* (New York: Penguin, 2003), 304.

13. By contrast, the politics of *Harper's* was much closer to that of the novel. See Thomas H. Lilly, "Contexts of Reception and Interpretation of the United States Serializations of *Uncle Tom's Cabin* (1851–1852) and *Bleak House* (1852–1853)" (PhD diss., Emory University, 2003), 75–110.

14. Charles Dickens, *Bleak House*, ed. George Ford and Sylvère Monod (New York: Norton, 1977), 38; hereafter abbreviated *BH*.

15. Indeed, female British abolitionists purchased Douglass's freedom, and his paper tracks abolitionist activities in Britain and regularly thanks its "kind trans-Atlantic Anti-Slavery friends." *Frederick Douglass' Paper*, 16 June 1854.

16. See James Buzard, *Disorienting Fiction: The Autoethnographic Work of Nineteenth-Century British Novels* (Princeton: Princeton UP, 2005), 105–56, for an extended analysis of the ways *Bleak House* opposes "British consequential ground" to "'place-less, unrepresentable reaches of unmeaning or unvalue" (116).

17. Frederick Douglass, "The Meaning of July Fourth for the Negro," in *Frederick Douglass: Selected Speeches and Writings*, ed. Philip S. Foner, adapted by Yuval Taylor (Chicago: U of Chicago P, 1999), 205.

18. Esther's statement appeared in the 10 June 1852 issue, and Douglass's speech in the 9 July 1852 issue.

19. *Frederick Douglass' Paper*, 24 September 1852.

20. "'Bleak House,'" *The Commonwealth* (Boston), 25 March 1852, 2.
21. Lord Denman, *"Uncle Tom's Cabin, Bleak House,* Slavery and the Slave Trade" (London: Longman, Brown, Green and Longmans, 1853), 5.
22. Denman, *"Uncle Tom's Cabin,"* p. 7.
23. Dickens to Mrs. Cropper, 20 December 1852, quoted in Harry Stone, "Charles Dickens and Harriet Beecher Stowe," *Nineteenth-Century Fiction* 12, no. 3 (1957): 195.
24. Letter to the *Times* (signed "Common Sense"), 2 December 1852, 6.
25. It is interesting to note that Dickens chose not to respond to Denman's charge in the preface to *Bleak House* (first published with the novel's final monthly part), even as he used this preface to defend the novel against criticism of its depictions of the Court of Chancery and of spontaneous human combustion. We might speculate that Dickens's silence reflects his awareness of both the strength of Denman's case, on the one hand, and the relative harmlessness of this charge, on the other: from Dickens's perspective, in other words, even if Denman is right, this would not undermine the novel's social criticism or Dickens's authority to mount such criticism, as the other objections threaten to do. For more on the stakes of Dickens's defense of his treatment of spontaneous human combustion, see Daniel Hack, *The Material Interests of the Victorian Novel* (Charlottesville: U of Virginia P, 2005), 37–61.
26. David Brown, *The Planter; or, Thirteen Years in the South, by a Northern Man* (Philadelphia: H. Hooker, 1853), 274.
27. Brown, *The Planter*, 11.
28. Despite the promise that "Our readers may depend upon having the successive numbers promptly as they come to hand," the *Commonwealth* discontinued publication after running the first five monthly parts, apparently without comment. The novel may have been sacrificed to the increased coverage of the increasingly turbulent political scene leading up to the presidential election that fall. It may also be significant that Elizur Wright had been replaced as editor by this point.
29. "Literary Notices," *Frederick Douglass' Paper*, 22 July 1853.
30. "Literary Notices," *Frederick Douglass' Paper*, 29 April 1852.
31. We should note a similar strategy at work in *Douglass' Paper*'s embrace of *Uncle Tom's Cabin* itself: as Robert S. Levine has shown in some detail, in working to "publicize, promote, and shape the reception of Stowe's novel," Douglass acted as "a creatively appropriative reader" of a work whose politics did not entirely mesh with his own, for instance in its advocacy of Liberian colonization. Levine, *Martin Delany, Frederick Douglass, and the Politics of Representative Identity* (Chapel Hill: U of North Carolina P, 1997), 72–73. In the only previous, extended analysis I know of of Douglass's reprinting of *Bleak House*, Elizabeth McHenry reads this notice as "highlighting [a] tension" between the two novels deriving from "the timing of [their] publication," which, she argues, "seemed to have put them in direct competition with one another." "In this implied contest," she writes, "*Uncle Tom's Cabin* was the definitive victor; while *Bleak House* inspired little critical commentary [in *Douglass' Paper*], letters to the newspaper concerning the literary and political merits of Stowe's novel abounded" (McHenry, *Forgotten Readers*, 126). As the notice makes clear, though, the two

works were not direct competitors, since *Uncle Tom's Cabin* completed its run as *Bleak House* began its own, and book publication of Stowe's novel preceded that of Dickens's by a full year and a half.

32. "Uncle Tom's Cabin in England," *Frederick Douglass' Paper*, 15 October 1852. The connection between Stowe and Dickens was strengthened by the fact that Stowe spent part of 1852 traveling in Britain. *Douglass' Paper* reports frequently on this triumphant tour, informing readers, for instance, that at a dinner given by the Lord Mayor of London at which Stowe was present, "Justice Talfourd made an oration complimentary to Mrs. Stowe, to which Charles Dickens replied in the name of that lady." *Frederick Douglass' Paper*, 20 May 1853.

33. Dickens's own reaction to *Uncle Tom's Cabin* was mixed, whether because or despite of his recognition of a certain kinship: in one letter he writes of Stowe's novel, "I seem to see a writer with whom I am very intimate (and whom nobody can possibly admire more than myself) peeping very often through the thinness of the paper." Dickens to Mrs. Richard Watson, 22 November 1852. Charles Dickens, *Letters*, ed. Madeline House and Graham Storey (Oxford: Clarendon Press, 1965–2002), 6: 808.

34. *Frederick Douglass' Paper*, 26 May 1854; 27 August 1852.

35. *Frederick Douglass' Paper*, 17 June 1852; 1 July 1852. This correspondent goes on to pepper his discussion of Liberty Party politics with references to the novel and two weeks later sends another communication from what he calls "Growlery, No. 2."

36. "Literary Notices," *Frederick Douglass' Paper*, 1 September 1854.

37. Buzard, *Disorienting Fiction*, 123. The scene ends with the narrator intoning: "Dead, your Majesty. Dead, my lords and gentlemen. Dead, Right Reverends and Wrong Reverends of every order. Dead, men and women, born with Heavenly compassion in your hearts. And dying thus around us every day" (*Bleak House*, 572).

38. The marking of the final phrase here suggests that Griffiths is alluding to, and aligning *Bleak House* with, the Victorian journalist Henry Mayhew's proto-sociological study *London Labour and the London Poor*, published in 1851.

39. Buzard, *Disorienting Fiction*, 153; "Literary Notices," *Frederick Douglass' Paper*, 3 June 1853.

40. The poem appeared in *Douglass' Paper* on 2 February 1855. Although no source is given, *Douglass' Paper* might have picked it up from either the *National Anti-Slavery Standard*, where it appeared on 6 January 1855, or the *Liberator*, where it appeared on 19 January 1855. In the *National Anti-Slavery Standard*, the poem carries the dateline "Oswego, December 5, 1854," and is credited to the *Albany Atlas*; in the *Liberator*, the poem is headed "From the Albany Atlas, Dec. 27." I have not been able to find any further information about this poem.

41. *Frederick Douglass' Paper*, 2 February 1855.

42. *Frederick Douglass' Paper*, 4 March 1854. Rpt. from the *Evening Journal*.

43. Buzard, *Disorienting Fiction*, 147.

44. Sarah Luria, "Racial Equality Begins at Home: Frederick Douglass's Challenge to American Domesticity," in *The American Home: Material Culture, Domestic Space, and Family Life*, ed. Eleanor McD. Thompson (Winterthur, DE: Henry

Francis du Pont Winterthur Museum,1998): 25–43, 33–34. *Bleak House* seems to have been one of the few novels Douglass owned at the time of his death in 1895; an undated edition, possibly from the early 1870s, is listed in William L. Petrie, ed., *Bibliography of the Frederick Douglass Library at Cedar Hill* (Ft. Washington, MD: Silesia, 1995), 179.

45. Gregg Hecimovich has recently argued that "Hannah Crafts" is the pseudonym of an escaped slave named Hannah Bond; as of this writing, though, he has yet to publish his findings. See Julie Bosman, "Professor Says He Has Solved a Mystery Over a Slave's Novel," *New York Times*, 19 September 2013, A1. Definitive knowledge of the race of the author of *The Bondwoman's Narrative* would allow us to determine whether she belongs to the African American tradition of African Americanizing Victorian literature that forms the main focus of this book, or instead stands as the very rare non–African American writer to engage in such an African Americanization. However, the analysis of *The Bondwoman's Narrative* undertaken here does not hinge on that knowledge.

46. David D. Kirkpatrick, "On Long-Lost Pages, a Female Slave's Voice," *New York Times*, 11 November 2001.

47. Much of the critical work on *The Bondwoman's Narrative* published to date appears in Henry Louis Gates Jr. and Hollis Robbins, eds., *In Search of Hannah Crafts: Critical Essays on "The Bondwoman's Narrative"* (New York: Basic Books, 2004). Of the volume's twenty-seven essays and reviews, two offer extended discussions of the novel's relationship to *Bleak House:* Hollis Robbins's "Blackening *Bleak House:* Hannah Crafts's *The Bondwoman's Narrative*" and William Gleason's "'I Dwell Now in a Neat Little Cottage': Architecture, Race, and Desire in *The Bondwoman's Narrative*." Gill Ballinger, Tim Lustig, and Dale Townshend offer the most sustained and nuanced account to date of *The Bondwoman's Narrative*'s intertextuality, in particular as it bears on this concept's central role in African American literary criticism. Oddly, however, the authors premise their argument on Crafts's presumed identity as an African American, which they simply take for granted, even as they criticize Henry Louis Gates Jr. for making essentializing claims about the authenticity of Crafts's voice. See Ballinger, Lustig, and Townsend, "Missing Intertexts: Hannah Crafts's *The Bondwoman's Narrative* and African American Literary History," *Journal of American Studies* 39 (2005): 207–37. More recent work that brings together *Bleak House* and *The Bondwoman's Narrative* includes Rachel Teukolsky, "Pictures in Bleak Houses: Slavery and the Aesthetics of Transatlantic Reform," *ELH* 76, no. 2 (2009): 491–522; and Rebecca Soares, "Literary Graftings: Hannah Crafts's *The Bondwoman's Narrative* and the Nineteenth-Century Transatlantic Reader," *Victorian Periodicals Review* 44, no. 1 (2011): 1–23.

48. Hannah Crafts, *The Bondwoman's Narrative*, ed. Henry Louis Gates Jr. (New York: Warner Books, 2003), 161–62; hereafter abbreviated *BN*. I cite the paperback edition because it includes more extensive documentation of the novel's relationship to *Bleak House* than does the previous year's cloth edition.

49. "Closely modeled" in the sense we should be used to by now, with much of the language used to describe him, much of his dialogue, and many of his actions lifted directly from Dickens. For example, Tulkinghorn is "an old-fashioned old

gentleman" who is "rusty to look at" (*BH*, 13), while Trappe is "a rusty seedy old-fashioned gentleman" (*BN*, 28), and just as when Tulkinghorn visits Chesney Wold he stays in "a turret chamber . . . plainly but comfortably furnished, and having an old-fashioned business air" (*BH*, 146), Trappe stays in "a plainly furnished chamber on the second story, old-fashioned like himself and having a quiet impassive air" (*BN*, 32–33) when he is a guest at the estate where Hannah serves as waiting maid to her mistress. Much like Tulkinghorn, Trappe uses his knowledge of a secret concerning the mistress of the estate to control her actions until she flees and eventually dies—Lady Dedlock dying at the gate of the graveyard of which she has asked, "Is this place of abomination, consecrated ground?" (*BH*, 202), Hannah's mistress buried in a grave of which Hannah says, "I know not whether it was consecrated ground" (*BN*, 104). The parallels are reinforced by shared dialogue: "I am rather surprised by the course you have taken" (*BH*, 580) becomes "you must be aware that I could not approve of the course you have taken' (*BN*, 37); "It is no longer your secret. Excuse me. That is just the mistake. It is my secret, in trust for Sir Leicester and the family" (*BH*, 581) becomes "It is not your secret, but mine, and may be your husband's before another day" (*BN*, 38–39); "'I have no more to say.' 'Excuse me, Lady Dedlock, if I add, a little more to hear'" (*BH*, 510) becomes "'I have no more to say.' 'But a little more to hear,' he replied" (*BN*, 41); and so on.

50. Many though not all of these debts are identified in the annotations to the 2003 paperback edition of the novel. However, these annotations are incomplete and sometimes misleading.

51. For the most thorough documentation of Brown's plagiarism, see Geoffrey Sanborn, "'People Will Pay to Hear the Drama': Plagiarism in *Clotel*," *African American Review* 45 (2012): 65–82. According to Sanborn, "The primary purpose of the plagiarism in *Clotel* is . . . to enable [Brown] to shift hard from one linguistic register to another" (72). Although *The Bondwoman's Narrative*'s use of *Bleak House* also produces an occasional shift in register, Crafts's sustained reliance on and engagement with a single text bears little resemblance to Brown's characteristic "unpredictable movement from idiom to idiom" (69).

52. Frank J. Webb, *The Garies and Their Friends* (Baltimore, MD: Johns Hopkins UP, 1997), 15. Samuel Otter suggests that "the names 'Esther' and 'Caddy' evoke the striving outsiders in the recently published *Bleak House*, and Webb reworks Dickens's concerns with deportment and respectability." *Philadelphia Stories: America's Literature of Race and Freedom* (New York: Oxford UP, 2010), 226.

53. The subtitle of *Uncle Tom's Cabin* is of course "Life Among the Lowly."

54. J. R. Johnson, "Uncle William's Pulpit," *Frederick Douglass' Paper*, 30 July 1852.

55. For an explicit, knowing engagement with these protocols, see chapter 2, below. The closest parallel to Crafts's practice may be that of Pauline Hopkins, discussed in chapter 5, below. As we shall see, Hopkins also borrows extensively, often verbatim, and without attribution, from other texts—texts, moreover, that evince little or no interest in African Americans—and while these texts are less ubiquitous than *Bleak House*, they are not always obscure.

56. Cf. Bruce Robbins, "Telescopic Philanthropy: Professionalism and Responsibility in *Bleak House*," *Nation and Narration*, ed. Homi Bhabha (London: Routledge, 1990), 213–30.

57. Recall that it is the threat of a forced "marriage" that finally inspires the normally dutiful Hannah to escape to the North. The representation of slavery as a threat to the family is common in sentimental antislavery discourse.

58. Hilary M. Schor, *Dickens and the Daughter of the House* (New York: Cambridge UP, 2000), 101–23.

59. This is not a unique transposition: the depiction of a woman's scandalous sexual history in British fiction will again serve as model or intertext for the depiction of a woman's scandalous racial ancestry in Charles Chesnutt's *The House Behind the Cedars*, discussed in chapter 4, below.

60. Ironically, it is only because she has been separated from her mother that Hannah's mistress is able to live part of her life as free. However, this is hardly an irony the novel invites us to savor, as it is careful to note that part of her tragedy (even before her flight leads to imprisonment, madness, and death) is that as a girl she was "taught . . . to consider her mother as dead," when in fact she was "a slave then toiling in the cotton feilds [*sic*] of Georgia" (*BN*, 45).

61. The version of mother/daughter reunification in *The Bondwoman's Narrative*, so different from that in *Bleak House*, recalls a similar moment in the very novel with which Douglass sought to align *Bleak House*, *Uncle Tom's Cabin* (Cassie's reunion with Eliza). This resemblance is noted in Jean Fagan Yellin, "*The Bondwoman's Narrative* and *Uncle Tom's Cabin*," in *In Search of Hannah Crafts*, 114.

62. Charlotte Brontë, *Villette* (Harmondsworth: Penguin, 1979), 596. The editors of *The Bondwoman's Narrative* do not note this echo.

63. Ballinger, Lustig, and Townsend conclude similarly that "Hannah's individual 'becoming,' rather than being compromised by the Dickensian example, is acted out at the level of the text" (237). However, the authors' conflation here of author (Crafts) and narrator (Hannah) undercuts their claims for the text's constitutive intertextuality and produces a certain incoherence in their argument. This is perhaps more easily seen in an earlier passage, when they describe "Hannah, patterning herself on Esther" [p. 227]—as if it were the character, rather than the author, who had read *Bleak House*. These slips reflect the authors' lingering tendency to read the text as autobiographically referential. The novel's intertextual relationship to *Bleak House* does not rule out this possibility, but it does compromise and complicate any such referentiality in ways the authors fail to address.

64. See, for example, Robert S. Levine's claim that Crafts's Trappe "is clearly modeled on [*The Scarlet Letter*'s] Chillingworth"; as discussed above, Trappe is much more clearly modeled on *Bleak House*'s Tulkinghorn—but the persuasive connection Levine makes between Trappe and Chillingworth invites us to notice and rethink the links among all three. See Robert S. Levine, "Trappe(d): Race and Genealogical Haunting in *The Bondwoman's Narrative*," in *In Search of Hannah Crafts*, 279.

65. Charles Dickens to William Charles Macready, 17 March 1848. Charles Dickens, *Letters*, ed. Madeline House and Graham Storey (Oxford: Clarendon Press, 1965–), 5: 262–63. The editors of Dickens's letters suggest that Dickens "probably had one of the American edns, containing a very grim and aggressive-looking head and shoulders portrait as frontispiece, as against the comparatively relaxed portrait in the English edns" (263n). However, the portrait in the first American edition of the *Narrative*, at least, is not at all "aggressive-looking," but rather shows

Douglass seated, dressed formally, arms crossed, looking very much the gentle-man. It seems at least as likely that Douglass looked too civilized for Dickens's taste as too barbaric, but it is impossible to say with any confidence what inspired his reaction. I am grateful to Julia Lee for calling my attention to this letter.

CHAPTER TWO: (RE-)RACIALIZING "THE CHARGE OF THE LIGHT BRIGADE"

1. I thank Jason Camlot for alerting me to this episode. In another relatively re-cent indication of its endurance, "The Light Brigade" was one of the very few Victorian poems performed at the finals of the Poetry Foundation's 2008 Po-etry Out Loud National Recitation Contest. See http://www.poetryoutloud.org /news/2008%20POL%20Finals%20Program.pdf.
2. Jerome J. McGann, "Tennyson and the Histories of Criticism," in *The Beauty of Inflections* (New York: Oxford UP, 1985), 191.
3. See, for example, Trudi Tate, "On Not Knowing Why: Memorializing the Light Brigade," in *Literature, Science, Psychoanalysis, 1830–1870: Essays in Honour of Gillian Beer*, ed. Helen Small and Trudi Tate (New York: Oxford UP, 2003), 160–80; and Kathryn Ledbetter, *Tennyson and Victorian Periodicals: Commodities in Context* (Burlington, VT: Ashgate, 2007), 121–27.
4. McGann, *Beauty of Inflections*, 193.
5. Paul Giles, *Transatlantic Insurrections: British Culture and the Formation of Ameri-can Literature, 1730–1860* (Philadelphia: U of Pennsylvania P, 2001), 3.
6. Henry D. Thoreau, "A Plea for Captain John Brown" (1859 lecture, first published 1860), in *Reform Papers*, ed. Wendell Glick (Princeton: Princeton UP, 1973), 119.
7. Tennyson's appreciation of heroically "steady," sustained advances also governs his own, later response to John Brown—or at least "John Brown." In an 1880 diary entry, William Allingham records that:

   After dinner Tennyson called on [his son] Hallam to sing "John Brown," which he accordingly began in a strong bass voice, T. joining in (the first time I ever heard him try any musical performance), and sometimes thump-ing with his fists on the table—

   John Brown's body lies mouldering in the grave,
   But his soul is marching on!

   He urged Hallam to go on, saying, "I like it, I like it," but Hallam thought the noise too great, and drew off. The soul marching on delighted Tennyson (William Allingham, *William Allingham: A Diary, 1824–1889* [London: Mac-millan, 1907], 304).

8. "Multiple News Items," *Frederick Douglass' Paper*, 28 January 1853. A few months later *Douglass' Paper* printed excerpts from "The Brook" (from the newly pub-lished *Maud and Other Poems*), which do not readily lend themselves to a politi-cal reading.

9. "Fall of Sebastopol! The Allies Triumphant!!" *Frederick Douglass' Paper*, 5 October 1855.
10. Communipaw [James McCune Smith], "From Our New York Correspondent," *FDP*, 5 October 1855.
11. One major exception is *Bleak House*, as discussed in chapter 1, above.
12. John Stauffer, "Introduction," in *The Works of James McCune Smith, Black Intellectual and Abolitionist*, ed. Stauffer (New York: Oxford UP, 2006), xiii. For more information about Smith, see David W. Blight, "In Search of Learning, Liberty, and Self-Definition: James McCune Smith and the Ordeal of the Antebellum Black Intellectual," *Afro-Americans in New York Life and History* 9, no. 2 (July 1985): 7–25; and Stauffer, *The Black Hearts of Men: Radical Abolitionists and the Transformation of Race* (Cambridge, MA: Harvard UP, 2001).
13. Communipaw [James McCune Smith], "From Our New York Correspondent," *FDP*, 12 January 1855. This piece is reprinted in Smith, *The Works of James McCune Smith, Black Intellectual and Abolitionist*, ed. John Stauffer (New York: Oxford UP, 2006), 108–13.
14. This article was reprinted in chapter 4 of Gustave d'Alaux, *L'Empereur Soulouque et Son Empire* (Paris: Michel Lévy Frères, 1856), 63–78. For a more recent discussion of the history and meaning of this chant, see David Geggus, "Haitian Voodoo in the Eighteenth Century: Language, Culture, Resistance," *Jahrbuch für Geschichte von Staat, Wirtschaft und Gesellschaft Lateinamerikas* 28 (1991): 21–51.
15. According to Ifeoma Kiddoe Nwankwo, "Whites' fear of the [Haitian] revolution and its presumably contagious nature forced people of African descent throughout the Americas, particularly those in the public and published eye, to name a relationship to the Haitian Revolution, in particular, and to a transnational idea of black community, in general." *Black Cosmopolitanism: Racial Consciousness and Transnational Identity in the Nineteenth-Century Americas* (Philadelphia, U of Pennsylvania P, 2005), 7. Smith's column belongs in this tradition, or rather signifies on it, as Smith gleefully raises this topic but at the same time refuses to be pinned down to a particular position.
16. For several other early American parodies, see Horace Perry Jones, "Southern Parodies on Tennyson's 'Charge of the Light Brigade,'" *Louisiana Studies* 11 (1972): 315–20. None of Jones's examples engage questions of race. The same is true of the various "Light Brigade" parodies collected in Walter Hamilton, *Parodies of the Works of English and American Authors*, vol. 1 (London: Reeves & Turner, 1884). The promisingly titled "Charge of the Black Brigade," printed in *Punch* in 1868, turns out to be about a meeting of clergymen.
17. For an illuminating account of Smith's column that reads his accusation against Tennyson in relation to the contemporaneous discourse on translation (as opposed to my focus on plagiarism), see Benjamin Fagan, "'Feebler than the Original': Translation and Early Black Transnationalism," *Transnational American Studies* (2012): 229–48.
18. The invocation of *Villette* is not as random as it might seem: Brontë's novel had only recently been published and was noticed in *Douglass' Paper*. See chapter 1 for Hannah Crafts's reworking of *Villette*'s final sentences in *The Bondwoman's Narrative*.

19. Poe's series of articles appeared in 1845, with a final return to the topic in 1850. See www.eapoe.org/people/longfehw.htm#criticism (1 May 2014) for a bibliography of these articles and links to most of them. For a helpful discussion of this episode, known as "the little Longfellow war," see McGill, *American Literature*, 204–17.

20. Communipaw [James McCune Smith], "From Our New York Correspondent," *FDP*, 15 December 1854; rpt. in Smith, *Works*, 104–7.

21. Years later, when again faced with the charge of plagiarism, Tennyson himself will feel it necessary to criticize such an approach: "I will answer for it that no modern poet can write a single line but among the innumerable authors of this world you will somewhere find a striking parallelism. It is the unimaginative man who thinks everything borrowed." Quoted in Eugene England, "Tuckerman and Tennyson: 'Two Friends . . . on Either Side the Atlantic,'" *New England Quarterly* 57, no. 2 (1984): 225–39, 234. I discuss additional accusations of plagiarism against Tennyson in chapter 5, below, where I compare his compositional practices to those of Pauline Hopkins.

22. Eric Lott, *Love and Theft: Blackface Minstrelsy and the American Working Class* (New York: Oxford UP, 1993), 4.

23. These quotations are taken from Lott, *Love and Theft*, 15.

24. *National Anti-Slavery Standard*, 23 December 1854.

25. Smith, *Works*, 120. Rpt. from *FDP*, 9 March 1855.

26. Ibid., 121, 120.

27. Ibid., 121.

28. By contrast, William Wilson ("Ethiop") rejected James McCune Smith's accusation that he had plagiarized Frederick Douglass and Charlotte Brontë, claiming in his own column two weeks later never to have read either of the works in question—claims made defiantly, with regard to *Villette*, and apologetically, with regard to Douglass's commencement address (Ethiop, "From Our Brooklyn Correspondent," *FDP*, 26 January 1855).

29. For an analysis of Boston's letter within the broader context of antebellum black debates over integration and nationalism, see Patrick Rael, *Black Identity and Black Protest in the Antebellum North* (Chapel Hill: UNC Press, 2002), 237–78, esp. 237–38.

30. Philip A. Bell [Cosmopolite, pseud.], "Letter to the Editor," *Frederick Douglass' Paper*, 20 April 1855.

31. The gap between Bell and Smith is underlined by Smith's own allusion to "The Rime of the Ancient Mariner" in *Douglass' Paper* three years later, where the same line is put to polemical use: "In the whole wide sea of human beings who go up to make the white population of the land, we see no hand stretched forth to succor or save us; we are

'Alone, alone, all alone.'" (Smith, *Works*, 172; rpt. from *FDP*, 16 April 1858)

Carla L. Peterson discusses the differences between Bell and Smith's understandings of culture and racial identity in similar terms (*Black Gotham: A Family History of African Americans in Nineteenth-Century New York City* [New Haven: Yale UP, 2011], 218–22).

32. Much was made of the exhibition in New York of the two paintings Bell discusses, with their presence taken as a sign of the growing cultural importance and sophistication of the United States. See, for example, "Editor's Easy Chair" in *Harper's New Monthly Magazine* (January 1855) and "Editorial Notes—the Fine Arts" in *Putnam's* (February 1855). Interestingly, *Harper's* views this art in the context of the Crimean War: "While Sebastopol engages the Allies—while Spain lies in ominous paralysis—while Germany leans toward the Danube and listens, aghast, for the distant thunder of war—the servants of the arts which demand peace and perish in war, turn their looks to us, and appeal to us as patrons" (267).

33. Before concluding that Smith got the process right but the source wrong, we should recall that Hallam himself got the source wrong: as Christopher Ricks notes, this precise phrase did not appear in the *Times* (Alfred Tennyson, *The Poems of Tennyson*, 2nd ed., ed. Christopher Ricks [Berkeley: U of California P, 1987], 508). For a meticulous account of the poem's composition history, see Edgar Shannon and Christopher Ricks, "'The Charge of the Light Brigade': The Creation of a Poem," *Studies in Bibliography* 38 (1985): 1–44. Shannon and Ricks conclude that "the imaginative impulse and a significant element of the phrasing were derived from *The Times*, but the poet's inspiration and discernment led him to refine away or to transform much of the original language" (32). Supplementing their analysis, Kathryn Ledbetter argues that "Tennyson was consuming more than the *Times* reports for his poem," and shows that "a reporter in the *Examiner* on 18 November surely lent more phrases": in particular, the line "Theirs but to do and die" obviously derives from that article's statement that the soldiers "went to their work to do and die" (Ledbetter, *Tennyson and Victorian Periodicals*, 125).

34. W. D. Paden first identified this source in *Tennyson in Egypt: A Study of the Imagery in His Earlier Work* (Lawrence: U of Kansas P, 1942), 140.

35. Quotations from "Anacaona" are taken from Christopher Ricks, ed., *The Poems of Tennyson*, 2nd ed. (Berkeley: U of California P, 1987), 1: 309–11.

36. Marcus Wood, ed., *The Poetry of Slavery: An Anglo-American Anthology, 1764–1865* (New York: Oxford UP, 2003), 313.

37. Samuel Whitchurch, "Hispaniola," in Wood, *Poetry of Slavery*, 175.

38. Hallam Tennyson, *Alfred Lord Tennyson, A Memoir* (New York: Macmillan, 1897), 1: 56.

39. Quoted in Ricks, *Poems of Tennyson*, 1: 308.

40. Alfred Tennyson to Richard Monckton Milnes, 8 or 9 January 1837, *The Letters of Alfred Lord Tennyson*, ed. Cecil Y. Lang and Edgar F. Shannon Jr., 3 vols. (Cambridge, MA: Harvard UP, 1981), 1: 149.

41. Washington Irving, *A History of the Life and Voyages of Christopher Columbus*, 3 vols. (New York: Cargill, 1828), 3: 146.

42. A. Dwight Culler, *The Poetry of Tennyson* (New Haven: Yale UP, 1977), 56.

43. James Eli Adams, *Dandies and Desert Saints: Styles of Victorian Masculinity* (Ithaca: Cornell UP, 1995), 118.

44. The link between Anacaona and Tennyson as composers of "areytos" is strengthened by the recurrence of a key phrase from "Anacaona" in "Morte d'Arthur"

(written 1833–34 and published 1842): just as Anacaona sings "her wild carol" (73), the barge carrying Arthur away is compared to "some full-breasted swan / That, fluting a wild carol ere her death, / Ruffles her pure cold plume, and takes the flood / With swarthy webs" (266–69). Perhaps the similarity of Arthur's destination, "the island-valley of Avilion," to happy Anacaona's Xaraguay— Avilion "lies / Deep-meadowed, happy, fair with orchard-lawns / And bowery hollows crowned with summer sea" (259–63)—recalled the phrase "wild carol" to Tennyson's mind.

45. W. D. Paden identifies and analyzes this tendency in Tennyson's early work in *Tennyson in Egypt.*

46. Alan Sinfield argues that, "Finding imaginative impetus marginalized theoretically and politically in Britain, [Tennyson] invested it in remote places." *Alfred Tennyson* (New York: Blackwell, 1986), 39. Extending this insight, David G. Riede argues that while Tennyson's "flights from the center tend to be associated with transgression, with kinds of experience forbidden to an English gentleman . . . the kinds of transgressive experience Tennyson imagines *are* at the center of British imperial culture" ("Tennyson's Poetics of Melancholy and the Imperial Imagination," *Studies in English Literature, 1500–1900*, 40, no. 4 [2000]: 659–78, 668). James Eli Adams argues that these poems flirt with "the possibility that one might surrender to desire, and thereby unsettle the triumphant masculine conquest of self and circumstance" (*Dandies and Desert Saints*, 117).

47. In an important exception to this rule, Christopher Ricks has argued that the force of "The Light Brigade" lies in the poet's "own envious yearning" for the "assured simplicity" of the soldiers' willingness to "do and die" without "reason[ing] why": "In the heroic futility of the Charge of the Light Brigade, he found a perfect emblem of something which his father's death and his own early misery led him always to envisage: a situation in which it was not merely condonable but actually honourable to commit suicide." My analysis reinforces this argument while giving it a more social dimension. Ricks, *Tennyson*, 2nd ed., 231.

48. McGann, *Beauty of Inflections*, 198; Tate, "On Not Knowing Why," p. 167.

49. *Oxford English Dictionary*, "Wild," def. 5, 6, 7.

50. Shannon and Ricks argue that "wild" (which, they note, is one of very few adjectives in the poem) would have been "damaging" had Tennyson not "qualified" it by making it "fall away from the echoing companion line . . . : 'Honour the charge they made!' (53)" (31, 31n55). This analysis registers the oddness of Tennyson's word-choice without offering a reading of the word itself.

51. Tennyson's 1856 substitution of "he" for "Nolan," the one individual named in the poem, can also be seen as furthering this strategy. Robert Douglas-Fairhurst notes this revision as well when making the somewhat different argument that the poem "is especially alive to the idea that the news it reports should be of a more lasting significance than occasional verse usually provides" (*Victorian Afterlives*, 191).

52. See, for example, the recitations reported in "Mr. John H. Smith's Reading, in Sansom St. Hall," *Christian Recorder*, 4 February 1865; and "Letter from Alexandria, Va.," *Christian Recorder*, 11 July 1868.

53. Alice Dunbar-Nelson, "Negro Literature for Negro Pupils," *Southern Workman* 51, no. 2 (February 1922): 59–63; 60, 63.

54. Marcus Garvey, *The Philosophy and Opinions of Marcus Garvey, Part 2* (Paterson, NJ: Frank Cass, 1925), 201. The Black Star Line was founded in 1919.

55. Ironically, Tennyson himself was supportive of the South in the Civil War. In a letter written a month after President Lincoln issued the Emancipation Proclamation, Tennyson decried its "selfishness" and declared, "the loosing of all the Demonism in the [Confederate] states whatever their Treason or their imagined Treason I cannot for a moment tolerate." However, he was not publicly outspoken, and his son Hallam soft-pedaled his position in his posthumous *Memoir* (1897), stating that his father "had always looked forward anxiously to the total abolition of slavery: but he had hoped that it might be accomplished gradually and peacefully." Alfred, Lord Tennyson, letter to the Duchess of Argyll, 11 November 1862, *Letters of Alfred Lord Tennyson*, vol. 2, 318, 318n2.

56. "Letter from Alexandria, Va.," *Christian Recorder*, 11 July 1868.

57. "Mr. John H. Smith's Reading, in Sansom St. Hall," *Christian Recorder*, 4 February 1865.

58. George Henry Boker, "The Black Regiment," in *"Words for the Hour": A New Anthology of American Civil War Poetry*, ed. Faith Barrett and Cristanne Miller (Amherst: U of Massachusetts P, 2005), 112–14.

59. Similarly, Dunbar-Nelson includes Boker's poem in her anthology *The Dunbar Speaker and Entertainer, containing the Best Prose and Poetic selections by and about the Negro Race* (Naperville, IL: J. L. Nichols, 1920), but she marks his name and several others with an asterisk to indicate that they are "members of the Caucasian Race."

60. Even before the Civil War, we find "Charge of the Border Ruffian Brigade," a pastiche in the *Provincial Freeman* mocking the cowardice of the proslavery mob that sacked Lawrence, Kansas. The authorship (or race of the author) of this anonymous poem is unknown. "Charge of the Border Ruffian Brigade," *Provincial Freeman*, 19 July 1856.

61. James Madison Bell, "The Day and the War," in *The Poetical Works of James Madison Bell* (Lansing, MI: Wynkoop, Hallenbeck, Crawford, 1901), 71.

62. Bell, "The Day and the War," pp. 65, 73.

63. Bell, "The Day and the War," p. 73, emphasis added. The word "All" is italicized in all the anthologized versions of the poem I have seen, but the copies of the original 1864 pamphlet and the 1901 edition I have consulted (one of each) do not italicize it.

64. Bell, "The Day and the War," p. 57.

65. Bell, "The Day and the War," p. 80.

66. James Madison Bell and Philip A. Bell do not seem to have been related. Both were living in San Francisco in the 1860s, which helps account for their collaboration.

67. [Philip A. Bell], "Lisle Lester," *Elevator*, 28 July 1865. On Bell and the history of the *Elevator*, see chapter 3 of Eric Gardner, *Unexpected Places: Relocating Nineteenth-Century African American Literature* (Jackson, MS: UP of Mississippi, 2009).

68. For another example, see "The Battle of Port Hudson" (1900), by James Thomas Franklin, which returns to both the event George Henry Boker celebrates and the Tennysonian model he uses to do so: "A regiment black as night / Behold the cannon on their left / And cannons on their right"; "'Tis but the gaping jaws of death / The open gates of hell"; "And thro' the storm of shot and shell / Rushed into eternity." *Jessamine Poems* (Memphis, TN: n.p., 1900), 18–19.

69. Jennifer Terry, "'When Dey 'Listed Colored Soldiers': Paul Laurence Dunbar's Poetic Engagement with the Civil War, Masculinity, and Violence," *African American Review* 41, no. 2 (Summer 2007): 269–75, 269.

70. H. T. Kealing, "Titular Twaddle," *Christian Recorder*, 26 October 1882.

71. *The Souls of Black Folk* is the main focus of chapter 6, below.

72. Perhaps the first instance in which "The Light Brigade" is invoked to address this failure comes in Henry McNeal Turner's 1868 speech before the Georgia legislature. Speaking on behalf of the newly elected African American representatives whom the legislature is refusing to seat, Turner states: "We are in a position somewhat similar to that of the famous 'Light Brigade,' of which Tennyson says, they had

> 'Cannon to right of them,
> Cannon to left of them,
> Cannon in front of them,
> Volleyed and thundered.'"

"On the Eligibility of Colored Members to Seats in the Georgia Legislature" (1868), reprinted in *Respect Black: The Writings and Speeches of Henry McNeal Turner*, ed. Edwin S. Redkey (New York: Arno Press, 1971), 28.

73. W.E.B. Du Bois, *The Souls of Black Folk*, ed. Henry Louis Gates Jr. and Terri Hume Oliver (New York: Norton, 1999), 33.

74. Ibid., 30, emphasis added.

75. See Du Bois, *Writings*, 1317–18.

76. But never count out "The Charge of the Light Brigade": I discuss a quite recent African American reworking of the poem in my afterword, below.

CHAPTER THREE: AFFILIATING WITH GEORGE ELIOT

1. Mary Church Terrell, *A Colored Woman in a White World* (Washington, DC: Ransdell, 1940), 96.

2. Ibid.

3. Terrell's European diary is in the Mary Church Terrell Papers at the Library of Congress.

4. Terrell, *A Colored Woman in a White World*, 98.

5. Ibid., 99.

6. George Eliot, *Romola* (Harmondsworth: Penguin Books, 1980), 435, 431.

7. William Dean Howells, *An Imperative Duty* (Peterborough, Ontario: Broadview Press, 2010), 117.

8. Ibid., 45.

9. Ibid., 48.
10. Ibid., 55.
11. Ibid., 121.
12. For an overview of the changing fortunes of Eliot's reputation over time, see the introduction to David Carroll, ed., *George Eliot: The Critical Heritage* (London: Routledge & Kegan Paul, 1971). It is telling in the present context that this collection of contemporary reviews omits entirely reviews of Eliot's poetry.
13. I discuss the relationship between *The Mill on the Floss* and Fauset's *There Is Confusion* in the afterword, and that between *Mill* and Du Bois's *Quest of the Silver Fleece* in Daniel Hack, "The Last Victorian Novel: *The Quest of the Silver Fleece*, by W.E.B. Du Bois," in *The Oxford Handbook of the Victorian Novel*, ed. Lisa Rodensky (Oxford: Oxford UP, 2013), 759–60.
14. Herbert F. Tucker, *Epic: Britain's Heroic Muse, 1790–1910* (Oxford: Oxford UP, 2008), 414.
15. While the similarities between *The Spanish Gypsy* and *Daniel Deronda* have not gone unnoticed, no one has emphasized the uniqueness of their shared plot. For a probing comparison of the two works, see chapter 4 of Deborah Epstein Nord, *Gypsies and the British Imagination, 1807–1930* (New York: Columbia UP, 2008), 99–124.
16. In addition to the novels and stories discussed below, perhaps the most notable example is *Pointing the Way* (1908), by Sutton E. Griggs. The latest example I know of is Sinclair Lewis's 1947 novel *Kingsblood Royal*. I am grateful to Sharon Marcus for calling my attention to this book.
17. On the literary history of the "tragic mulatto/a" plot, see Eve Allegra Raimon, *The "Tragic Mulatta" Revisited: Race and Nationalism in Nineteenth-Century Antislavery Fiction* (New Brunswick, N.J.: Rutgers UP, 2004); Werner Sollors, *Neither Black nor White yet Both: Thematic Explorations of Interracial Literature* (New York: Oxford UP, 1997); and Teresa C. Zackodnik, *The Mulatta and the Politics of Race* (Jackson: UP of Mississippi, 2004). Eric Gardner identifies two "early examples of a discourse of mixed-race heroines running counter to the figure of the tragic mulatta—one in which the mixed-race heroine not only avoids a tragic end but actually embraces her genealogy, uses her visual racial indeterminacy to aid nation-building and self-empowerment, and finds fulfillment in a multi-racial family housed within the larger Black community," in "Coloring History and Mixing Race in Levina Urbino's *Sunshine in the Palace and Cottage* and Louise Heaven's *In Bonds*," *Legacy* 24, no. 2 (2007): 188.
18. Frances Ellen Watkins Harper, *Minnie's Sacrifice; Sowing and Reaping; Trial and Triumph: Three Rediscovered Novels*, ed. Frances Smith Foster, Black Women Writers Series (Boston: Beacon Press, 1994), 72.
19. Foster, "Introduction," xxx.
20. George Eliot, *Daniel Deronda*, ed. Terence Cave (London: Penguin, 1995), 657.
21. Harper, *Minnie's Sacrifice; Sowing and Reaping; Trial and Triumph*, 5.
22. Ibid., 91.
23. George Eliot, *The Spanish Gypsy*, ed. A. G. Van den Broek (London: Pickering & Chatto, 2008), I.2740–53. Further references will be included in the body of the text.
24. Harper, *Minnie's Sacrifice; Sowing and Reaping; Trial and Triumph*, 212.

25. Frances Ellen Watkins Harper, *Iola Leroy, or, Shadows Uplifted*, ed. Frances Smith Foster, The Schomburg Library of Nineteenth-Century Black Women Writers (Oxford: Oxford UP, 1988), 280.
26. Ibid., 271.
27. I return to these terminal epigraphs below, in chapter 5.
28. Harper, *Iola Leroy, or, Shadows Uplifted*, 265, 263, emphasis added.
29. Frances Ellen Watkins Harper, *A Brighter Coming Day: A Frances Ellen Watkins Harper Reader*, ed. Frances Smith Foster (New York : Feminist Press at the City University of New York, 1990), 222. This lecture, delivered at the Centennial Anniversary of the Pennsylvania Society for Promoting the Abolition of Slavery, was reprinted by Alice Dunbar-Nelson in her 1914 anthology *Masterpieces of Negro Eloquence* (published under the name Alice Moore Dunbar).
30. Ibid., 276.
31. Ibid., 278.
32. Harper, *Iola Leroy, or, Shadows Uplifted*, 274.
33. Kwame Anthony Appiah, *The Ethics of Identity* (Princeton, NJ: Princeton UP, 2005), 111.
34. Ibid., 112.
35. Emmett J. Scott, *Tuskegee and Its People: Their Ideals and Achievements*, ed. Booker T. Washington (New York: D. Appleton, 1905), 23–24.
36. David Kurnick, "Unspeakable George Eliot," *Victorian Literature and Culture* 38, no. 2 (September 2010): 504; Tucker, *Epic*, 423.
37. Tucker, *Epic*, 424. The logic that would lead to this preference for *The Spanish Gypsy* over *Daniel Deronda* is already evident in *Minnie's Sacrifice*, before the publication of Eliot's novel. When one of Harper's characters asserts "that the Jews and Negroes have one thing in common, and that is their power of endurance," another replies that "their origin and history have been different," because while "the Jews have a common ancestry and grand traditions, that have left alive their pride of race. . . . I do not think that the negro can trace with certainty his origin back to any of the older civilizations, and here for more than two hundred years his history has been a record of blood and tears, of ignorance, degradation, and slavery." Harper, *Minnie's Sacrifice; Sowing and Reaping; Trial and Triumph*, 30.
38. Fannie Barrier Williams, "Club Movement among Negro Women," in *Progress of a Race, or, The Remarkable Advancement of the American Negro from the Bondage of Slavery, Ignorance and Poverty to the Freedom of Citizenship, Intelligence, Affluence, Honor and Trust*, by J. W. Gibson and W. H. Crogman (Atlanta, GA: J. L. Nichols, 1902), 230.
39. Ibid., 231.
40. Ibid.
41. Fannie Barrier Williams, "After Many Days: A Christmas Story," in *Short Fiction by Black Women, 1900–1920*, ed. Elizabeth Ammons, The Schomburg Library of Nineteenth-Century Black Women Writers (Oxford: Oxford UP, 1991), 229.
42. Ibid., 231.
43. Ibid., 238.

44. For this reading of the story's ending, see Hanna Wallinger, *Pauline E. Hopkins: A Literary Biography* (Athens: U of Georgia P, 2005), 253.

45. *The Spanish Gypsy* is quoted at some length in a 1903 editorial in *The Colored American*, in another indication of the poem's currency in African American print culture at the time. This editorial, titled "Steadfastness," opens with an eight-line passage from the poem, one that includes epigrammatic lines that seem to have circulated widely in the culture at large: "never falter, no great deed is done / By falterers who ask for certainty," and "The greatest gift a hero leaves his race / Is to have been a hero" (I.3145–46, 3152–53). It is clearly Eliot's perceived cultural capital that is being called on here, for while the editorial proclaims, "What an inspiration for each one of us in these beautiful lines of George Eliot's," the ensuing argument that "much of the present discontent between mankind everywhere," including "the vexed 'Race Problem,'" could be easily settled "If the Church of Christ today would but follow the single teachings of their great leader, look upon God as their Father, and mankind as their brethren," finds little support in—indeed, is flatly contradicted by—Eliot's poem. "Steadfastness," *Colored American Magazine* (Boston), January 1903, 240.

46. Marie Louise Burgess-Ware, "Bernice, the Octoroon," in *Short Fiction by Black Women, 1900–1920*, ed. Elizabeth Ammons, The Schomburg Library of Nineteenth-Century Black Women Writers (Oxford: Oxford UP, 1991), 257.

47. Ibid., 275.

48. Harper, *Iola Leroy, or, Shadows Uplifted*, 219–20. In a similar intertextual convergence, Fannie Barrier Williams's title "After Many Days," while drawn from Ecclesiastes, may pick up its title from the penultimate chapter of Pauline Hopkins's *Contending Forces* (1900), where one character discovers he's been unwittingly passing (although as an Englishman he does not quite think of his discovered African American ancestry in these terms). I discuss Hopkins in chapter 5.

49. Henry James, "The Spanish Gypsy," *North American Review* 107 (1868): 630.

50. Ibid., 626.

51. John Morley, "The Spanish Gypsy," *Macmillan's Magazine* 18 (July 1868): 286.

52. Leslie Stephen, *George Eliot* (New York, London: Macmillan, 1902), 166.

53. William Dean Howells, "The Spanish Gypsy: A Poem," *Atlantic Monthly* 22 (September 1868): 383, 384.

54. Ibid., 383.

55. James, "The Spanish Gypsy," 625.

56. Howells, "The Spanish Gypsy: A Poem," 383.

57. We might note that *The Spanish Gypsy* also features a Jewish character, Sephardo, who similarly links communal loyalty to the sharing of a stigmatized status: Sephardo makes the general claim that "there's no such thing / As naked manhood. If the stars look down / On any mortal of our shape, whose strength / Is to judge all things without preference, / He is a monster, not a faithful man"; but he then moves immediately to his own specific case as a Jew: "While my heart beats, it shall wear livery— / My people's livery, whose yellow badge / Marks them for Christian scorn" (II.592–99).

58. Kwame Anthony Appiah, *Cosmopolitanism: Ethics in a World of Strangers* (New York: W.W. Norton, 2006), xviii, xvii.

59. Kwame Anthony Appiah, *Justice, Governance, Cosmopolitanism, and the Politics of Difference: Reconfigurations in a Transnational World; Distinguished W.E.B. Du Bois Lectures 2004/2005*, ed. Engelbert Habekost (Berlin: Humboldt University, 2007), 33.

60. In defense of Eliot's cosmopolitanism, focusing on *Daniel Deronda*, see Amanda Anderson, *The Powers of Distance: Cosmopolitanism and the Cultivation of Detachment* (Princeton, NJ: Princeton UP, 2001). For a more skeptical argument, focusing on *The Spanish Gypsy*, see Kurnick, "Unspeakable George Eliot."

61. Deborah Epstein Nord is the rare critic who does explore the role of stigma in Eliot's work. Nord offers an illuminating analysis of the association Eliot makes between unconventional femininity and membership in a stigmatized group. However, she tends to treat the latter as a figure for the former, rather than an object of interest in its own right for Eliot, as when she asks, "Why, in Eliot's scheme, are the contingencies of race or of some congenital marking necessary to make the argument for an unorthodox life?" Deborah Epstein Nord, "'Marks of Race': Gypsy Figures and Eccentric Femininity in Nineteenth-Century Women's Writing," *Victorian Studies* 41, no. 2 (Winter 1998): 205.

62. One important exception to this critical tendency is David Kurnick's reading of *The Spanish Gypsy*. Like Frances Harper, Kurnick highlights the "You paint us well" passage to explore the logic whereby the gypsies' abjection becomes reason to identify with them. However, in arguing further that "Eliot's concern in *The Spanish Gypsy* is precisely to work out a model of an affiliative politics that would not be guaranteed by religious, national, or cultural prestige" (504), Kurnick downplays those moments in the poem that look ahead to the future achievement of such prestige as a source of solidarity—the very moments seized upon by several African American writers.

63. James Buzard, *Disorienting Fiction: The Autoethnographic Work of Nineteenth-Century British Novels* (Princeton, NJ: Princeton UP, 2005), 294.

64. Ibid., 298.

65. Ibid.

66. Tucker, *Epic*, 414–15.

67. Ibid., 417.

68. Ibid., 424.

69. Ibid., 425.

70. Eliot, *Daniel Deronda*, 810.

71. Sylvia Kasey Marks, "A Brief Glance at George Eliot's 'The Spanish Gypsy,'" *Victorian Poetry* 21, no. 2 (1983): 189.

72. Bernard Semmel notes this pattern as well, but he argues that Fedalma resembles Eppie and Esther in "permitt[ing] sentiment to win over calculation." This is an odd claim, given how strongly Fedalma's love of Silva weighs against her choice to affiliate with the Zincali. Bernard Semmel, *George Eliot and the Politics of National Inheritance* (New York: Oxford UP, 1994), 112.

73. Tucker, *Epic*, 417.

74. Edward Wilmot Blyden, *The Origin and Purpose of African Colonization* (Washington, DC: American Colonization Society, 1883), 17. Blyden treats this passage as if it is in Eliot's own voice, rather than that of Theophrastus, the essayistic persona Eliot adopts in *Impressions*. Scholars continue to debate the extent to which the views expressed in *Impressions* reflect Eliot's own.

75. Eliot, *Daniel Deronda*, 534; Harper, *Iola Leroy*, 246.

76. Harper, *Iola Leroy*, 249.

77. Ibid., 249, 282.

78. "Bishop Turner," *The Freeman*, May 3, 1902, 4.

79. Ibid.

80. As noted above in chapter 1, a similar selectivity marked the reception of *Uncle Tom's Cabin* in *Frederick Douglass' Paper*, as Robert Levine has shown—in particular, Frederick Douglass found it worthwhile to endorse and align himself with Stowe's novel despite his rejection of its emigrationist conclusion. The revision of Eliot is more radical, however, insofar as the national-homeland strand is woven much more thoroughly into the fabric of *The Spanish Gypsy* and *Daniel Deronda* than it is in Stowe's novel. See Robert S. Levine, "*Uncle Tom's Cabin* in *Frederick Douglass' Paper*: An Analysis of Reception," *American Literature* 64, no. 1 (March 1992): 71–93.

81. Hazel V. Carby, *Reconstructing Womanhood: The Emergence of the Afro-American Woman Novelist* (New York: Oxford UP, 1987), 93.

82. For analysis of the interplay and tensions between political separatism and cultural assimilation in nineteenth- and early-twentieth-century black nationalism, see Wilson Jeremiah Moses, *The Golden Age of Black Nationalism, 1850–1925* (New York: Oxford UP, 1978).

83. Tucker, *Epic*, 216.

84. Walter Benn Michaels, *Our America: Nativism, Modernism, and Pluralism* (Durham: Duke UP, 1995), 116, 115, 117.

85. Ibid., 109.

86. Ibid., 115.

87. M. Giulia Fabi, *Passing and the Rise of the African American Novel* (Urbana: U of Illinois P, 2004), 93. Fabi does not cite Michaels but their discussions are similar, and both use James Weldon Johnson's *Autobiography of an Ex-Colored Man* as their main example of a novel about passing that displays the "personal identity" model of race. Michaels finds evidence for the presence of this model in that novel's concluding metaphor of race as a birthright—in choosing to live as a white man, the narrator says regretfully, "I cannot repress the thought that, after all, . . . I have sold my birthright for a mess of pottage"; the similarity of this conceptualization of race to Eliot's is suggested by Daniel Deronda's accusatory complaint to his mother when he learns that she has hidden his Jewish parentage from him: "How could you choose my birthright for me?" James Weldon Johnson, *The Autobiography of an Ex-Colored Man*, ed. William L. Andrews (London: Penguin Books, 1990), 154; Eliot, *Daniel Deronda*, 627.

88. Michaels, *Our America*, 117.

89. See, for example, Clare Cotugno, "Stowe, Eliot, and the Reform Aesthetic," in *Transatlantic Stowe: Harriet Beecher Stowe and European Culture*, ed. Denise Kohn, Sarah Meer, and Emily B. Todd (Iowa City: U of Iowa P, 2006), 111–30; Daniel Hack, "Transatlantic Eliot: African American Connections," in *A Companion to George Eliot*, ed. Amanda Anderson and Harry E. Shaw (Hoboken, NJ: John Wiley & Sons, 2013), 262–76; Kimberly Snyder Manganelli, *Transatlantic Spectacles of Race: The Tragic Mulatta and the Tragic Muse* (New Brunswick, NJ: Rutgers UP, 2012); Kenny Ralph Marotta, "The Literary Relationship of

George Eliot and Harriet Beecher Stowe" (PhD diss., Johns Hopkins University, 1974); Monika Mueller, *George Eliot U.S.: Transatlantic Literary and Cultural Perspectives* (Madison, NJ: Fairleigh Dickinson UP, 2005).

90. George Eliot, "Harriet Beecher Stowe's *Dred*, Charles Reade's *It Is Never Too Late to Mend* and Frederika Bremer's *Hertha*," in *Selected Essays, Poems and Other Writings*, ed. A. S. Byatt and Nicholas Warren (London: Penguin, 1990), 380. Eliot sent off her omnibus review including her review of *Dred* on September 19, 1856, and began working on her first published story, "The Sad Fortunes of the Reverend Amos Barton," three days later, on September 22.

91. Eliot, *The Spanish Gypsy*, 276.

92. Similarly, in *Daniel Deronda* Eliot hints glancingly at a connection between Deronda and enslaved Africans: "Grandcourt held that the Jamaican negro was a beastly sort of baptist Caliban; Deronda said that he had always felt a little with Caliban, who naturally had his own point of view and could sing a good song." Eliot, *Daniel Deronda*, 331.

93. Eliot first used this name in a letter to her publisher, John Blackwood, in February 1857, and it first appeared in print with the publication of *Scenes of Clerical Life* in January 1858. See George Eliot, *The George Eliot Letters*, ed. Gordon S. Haight (New Haven: Yale UP, 1954), 2: 292. According to Eliot's husband John Cross, "my wife told me the reason she fixed on this name was that George was Mr. Lewes's Christian name, and Eliot was a good mouth-filling, easily-pronounced word." John Cross, *George Eliot's Life as Related in Her Letters and Journals*, vol. 24 of *The Writings of George Eliot* (Boston: Houghton, Mifflin, 1909), 35. Blanche Colton Williams, in her 1936 biography of Eliot, appears to have been the first to claim that "Eliot" derived from "To L— I owe it," a speculation that has gained some currency. Blanche Colton Williams, *George Eliot; a Biography* (New York: Macmillan, 1936), 132. Ina Taylor notes that "A George Elliot (*sic*) had been the clerk in a neighboring parish which her father had dealings with, but more significantly there was a "George Eliot's Close' shown on one of the old maps of Chilver Coton, kept in her father's office at Griff House." Ina Taylor, *George Eliot: Woman of Contradictions* (London: Weidenfeld and Nicolson, 1989), 158.

94. A rare moment in *Daniel Deronda* when Eliot does refer to racial mixing suggests how quickly this topic can raise issues distinct from those that interest her most with regard to disempowered ethnic groups: in the dialogue about "the Jamaican negro" cited above, Deronda responds to one character's comment that "the blacks would be manageable enough if it were not for the half-breeds" by remarking that "the whites had to thank themselves for the half-breeds." Eliot, *Daniel Deronda*, 331.

CHAPTER FOUR: RACIAL MIXING AND TEXTUAL REMIXING:
CHARLES CHESNUTT

1. Charles W. Chesnutt, journal entry of 26 March 1881, in *The Journals of Charles W. Chesnutt*, ed. Richard H. Brodhead (Durham, NC: Duke University Press, 1993), 154–55.

2. Ibid., 155–56.
3. Ibid., 155.
4. Ibid., 156.
5. Ibid., 155n.87.
6. Chesnutt's alertness to Victorian literature's often-fleeting invocations and representations of mulattoes bears comparison to the attention Toni Morrison advocates to what she calls the "Africanist presence" in canonical American literature. As we shall see, however, unlike Morrison, Chesnutt conducts his investigation within his fiction itself and, in the process, not only holds this "mulatto presence" up for critical scrutiny but also turns it to account. Toni Morrison, *Playing in the Dark: Whiteness and the Literary Imagination* (New York: Vintage Books, 1993), 6.
7. Charles W. Chesnutt, "The Wife of His Youth," in *Stories, Novels & Essays*, ed. Werner Sollors (New York: Library of America, 2002), 101. Further references to this edition will be cited parenthetically in the text. "The Wife of His Youth" was first published in the *Atlantic Monthly* in 1898 and reprinted the following year in Chesnutt's collection *The Wife of His Youth and Other Stories of the Color Line*.
8. Alfred, Lord Tennyson, "A Dream of Fair Women," in *The Poems of Tennyson*, ed. Christopher Ricks (Harlow: Longmans, 1969), 445, ll. 91, 95–96. Further citations of Tennyson are from this edition. Chesnutt, "The Wife of His Youth," 95–96.
9. My reading of "The Wife of His Youth" picks up on Werner Sollors's argument that "Chesnutt does not quote Tennyson randomly or one-dimensionally" (230) and responds to his call for closer attention to this intertextual relationship. Sollors valuably points to Tennyson's portrayal of Cleopatra in "A Dream of Fair Women" as "swarthy" and "dusky" to argue that that poem "is not merely a white contrast for the colored world of Mr. Ryder," and similarly notes that the "pale" Margaret is eventually presented as "darker" than another woman, Adeline. Nonetheless, Mr. Ryder himself is not drawn to these passages. Werner Sollors, "Thematics Today," *Thematics: Interdisciplinary Studies*, ed. Max Louwerse and Willie van Peer (Philadelphia: John Benjamins, 2002), 217–35, 230.
10. For a reading of the story along these lines, see Eric J. Sundquist, *To Wake the Nations: Race in the Making of American Literature* (Cambridge, MA: Belknap Press of Harvard UP, 1993), 298–301.
11. Dean McWilliams, *Charles W. Chesnutt and the Fictions of Race* (Athens: U of Georgia P, 2002), 114.
12. Tennyson, *In Memoriam*, I.3–4. Werner Sollors also calls attention to this thematic tie between the story and Tennyson, noting that "the references to Tennyson's 'Guinevere,' . . . together with 'A Dream of Fair Maidens,' [sic] also direct us to the conflict of past and present." Sollors, *Beyond Ethnicity: Consent and Descent in American Culture* (New York: Oxford UP, 1986), 161.
13. Tennyson, "Enoch Arden," ll. 664, 699–700.
14. Tennyson, "Enoch Arden," l. 848; Chesnutt, "The Wife of His Youth," 112.
15. Tennyson, "Enoch Arden," l. 783.
16. I allude here, of course, to Tennyson's "The Lotos-Eaters" and "Ulysses."
17. Chesnutt, "The Wife of His Youth," 112.

18. Dean McWilliams, *Charles W. Chesnutt and the Fictions of Race*, 115–16.
19. Werner Sollors also identifies another possible Victorian intertext for this story, observing in passing that the name "'Liza-Jane" would seem to be an allusion to Thomas Hardy's *The Mayor of Casterbridge* (1886): the protagonist of that novel sells his wife and their daughter—whose name is Elizabeth-Jane—only to have them reappear years later, when he has risen in society. I discuss Hardy below, in relation to *The House Behind the Cedars*. Werner Sollors, "Thematics Today," in *Thematics: Interdisciplinary Studies*, ed. Max Louwerse and Willie van Peer (Philadelphia: John Benjamins, 2002), 229.
20. Chesnutt, *The House Behind the Cedars*, in *Stories, Novels & Essays*, 397. Further references to this text will be included parenthetically.
21. The novel in question is *The Last of the Barons* (1843). Though little read today, the fact that Chesnutt never provides the novel's title suggests its greater popularity at the time he is writing, and in fact multiple editions of the novel were published in the US in the 1890s. Bulwer Lytton depicts the fifteenth-century figure Warwick as "a man who stood colossal amidst the iron images of the Age—the greatest and the last of the old Norman chivalry—kinglier in pride, in state, in possessions, and in renown than the king himself" (Edward Bulwer Lytton, *Last of the Barons* [London: G Routledge and Sons, 1876], 22). Dean McWilliams suggests that John's choice of a name indicates that he "reads literature . . . poorly," since "his namesake's career ended with defeat, disgrace, and death." However, John's choice does not in fact foreshadow his own fate, which is much less dire: after Rena turns down his proposal that they leave the South and "start life over again," explaining "it will not be hard for me—I am young, and have means . . . [and] would have a larger outlook elsewhere" (388), John simply disappears from the novel. McWilliams, *Chesnutt and the Fictions of Race*, 135.
22. The locus classicus for this view of Scott and the South is chapter 46 of Mark Twain's *Life on the Mississippi* (1883).
23. In light of Chesnutt's irony here, the terms in which he is praised in the biographical sketch announcing the impending serialization of *The House Behind the Cedars* in the magazine *Self Culture* can be seen as exquisitely ill-chosen: stating that Chesnutt's "sympathies are all with the race which suffers so grievously from Anglo-Saxon pride and prejudice both North and South," the piece commends Chesnutt for "wield[ing] his pen as chivalrously in its behalf as ever knight of old wielded his sword." "Charles W. Chesnutt: A New Delineator of Southern Life," *Self Culture* 11 (July 1900), 409–11, 410–11.
24. Richard H. Brodhead, *Cultures of Letters: Scenes of Reading and Writing in Nineteenth-Century America* (Chicago: U of Chicago P, 1993), 207.
25. Charles Dickens, *David Copperfield* (London: Penguin Books, 1996), 59–60.
26. Chesnutt's high estimation of *David Copperfield* is suggested by a list of "Great characters in fiction" he includes in a speech on "The Writing of a Novel": three of the eleven characters he lists are from this one novel (David Copperfield, Micawber, Uriah Heep). As I am about to argue, however, and as is true of Chesnutt's relationship to Victorian literature in general, this esteem does not prevent Chesnutt from noticing and responding to the work's limitations with

regard to race. Chesnutt, "The Writing of a Novel," in *Charles W. Chesnutt: Essays and Speeches*, ed. Joseph R. McElrath Jr., Robert C. Leitz III, and Jesse S. Crisler (Stanford: Stanford UP, 1999), 551.

27. Dickens, *David Copperfield*, 11.
28. Dickens, *David Copperfield*, 59.
29. Recall, from chapter 1, that Dickens owned Douglass's *Narrative* and seems to have read it in the 1840s, before the composition of *David Copperfield*.
30. On one occasion in *Dombey and Son* (1844–46), the novel immediately preceding *David Copperfield*, the servant Susan Nipper complains of her treatment by describing herself as "a black slave and a mulotter." Susan is first introduced as "a short, brown, womanly girl of fourteen, with a little snub nose, and black eyes like jet beads," but Dickens offers no (further?) insinuation that she is in fact mixed race. Charles Dickens, *Dombey and Son* (London: Penguin Books, 1985), 108, 78.
31. Tennyson, "Locksley Hall," l. 178.
32. Werner Sollors was perhaps the first to note this allusion, in the Library of America edition of the novel, but its implications have gone unexplored.
33. Readers of the serial publication of *The House Behind the Cedars* would have been reminded of "Locksley Hall" and "Locksley Hall Sixty Years After" by an article "Tennyson in Two of His Poems—'Locksley Hall,'" which appeared in *Self Culture* in July 1900, the month before the novel's serialization began (and the same month the magazine ran its profile of Chesnutt, cited above).
34. Chesnutt, *Frederick Douglass* (Boston: Small, Maynard, 1899), 26.
35. Susan Meyer, "Colonialism and the Figurative Strategy of Jane Eyre," *Victorian Studies* 33, no. 2 (1990): 247–68; Jennifer DeVere Brody, *Impossible Purities: Blackness, Femininity, and Victorian Culture* (Durham: Duke UP, 1998).
36. Chesnutt, *The Journals of Charles W. Chesnutt*, 80.
37. For an alternative reading of Chesnutt's use of British literature, see Stacey Margolis, *The Public Life of Privacy in Nineteenth-Century American Literature* (Durham: Duke UP, 2005). Focusing in particular on *Ivanhoe* and Grace Aguilar's suggestively named *The Vale of Cedars*, Margolis argues provocatively that "In creating a fantasy of self-transformation, Chesnutt was drawing on a series of British conversion narratives in which Jews have the power to transform themselves into Christians" (113); conversion "makes identity . . . into a matter of individual choice" (113–14). Margolis acknowledges that "conversion was understood by many Victorian Jews (and is read by many critics) as a threat to cultural identity" but maintains that "its premise that identity is not simply announced by blood but can be changed entirely by the force of individual belief looks like a solution to the problem of segregation" (114). It seems odd, though, that the Jewish characters in both the Scott and Aguilar novels Margolis highlights as models for Chesnutt treat conversion not as a means to self-fulfillment but rather as a form of group- and even self-betrayal, and reject it accordingly. Moreover, conversion is a poor term or analogy for John's relationship to whiteness, since his personal sense of identity never changes: he always believes himself to be white.

38. Matthew Wilson, *Whiteness in the Novels of Charles W. Chesnutt* (Jackson: UP of Mississippi, 2004), 64. For a survey of influential articulations of this view, see Daniel Worden, "Birth in the Briar Patch: Charles W. Chesnutt and the Problem of Racial Identity," *Southern Literary Journal* 41, no. 2 (2009): 12–13.

39. M. Giulia Fabi argues that, by having Rena start out "with as promising a future as Scott's Rowena" but end up "as Rebecca," Chesnutt "merg[es] these opposed figures and traditional female narrative types into the same character" and thus "breaks the segregation of literary (and by implication social) roles" (M. Giulia Fabi, *Passing and the Rise of the African American Novel* [Urbana: U of Illinois P, 2001; 2004 ed., 158). I would argue, on the contrary, that Rena is a Rebecca masquerading or temporarily misrecognized as a Rowena—and of course her fate is much worse than Rebecca's: just as Rebecca ultimately refuses to give up her Jewish identity—"I may not change the faith of my fathers like a garment unsuited to the climate in which I seek to dwell"—and devotes herself to charitable works—"tending the sick, feeding the hungry, and relieving the distressed" (*Ivanhoe* [London: Penguin, 1984], 518)—so too will Rena resolve to "stay with my own people" (387) and "be of service" to them (396), but she is not allowed to live out this project. Her story thus suggests that no merger along the lines Fabi envisions is possible, and that segregation remains unbroken. For readings of the intertextual relationship between *The House Behind the Cedars* and *Ivanhoe* that emphasize the similarities between Rena and Rebecca, see Earle V. Bryant, "Charles Chesnutt's Southern Black Jew: Rena Walden's Masquerade in *The House Behind the Cedars*," *American Literary Realism, 1870–1910*, 3 (1999): 15–21; and Bill Hardwig, *Upon Provincialism: Southern Literature and National Periodical Culture* (Charlottesville: U of Virginia P, 2013), 36–43.

40. George Eliot, *The Mill on the Floss* (Peterborough, Ontario: Broadview, 2007), 348.

41. Ibid., 360.

42. Ibid., 297.

43. Ibid., 389.

44. Ibid., 57.

45. Ibid., 57.

46. Jay Saunders Redding, *To Make a Poet Black* (1939; rpt. Ithaca, NY: Cornell UP, 1988), 73.

47. Thomas Hardy, *Tess of the d'Urbervilles* (Boston: Bedford Books, 1998), 265.

48. Ibid., 233.

49. Ibid., 236.

50. Ibid., 367.

51. Chesnutt himself pairs these two doomed Victorian heroines in a late essay in which he lists four examples in support of his contention that "most of the interesting women in romance have sinned for love or for profit": "Beatrice Esmond, *Tess of the d'Urbervilles*, Maggie Tulliver in *The Mill on the Floss*, Anna Karenina." See "The Negro in Present Day Fiction" (1929), in *Charles W. Chesnutt: Essays and Speeches*, 524.

52. Hardy, *Tess of the d'Urbervilles*, 94. McWilliams also notes Chesnutt's narrator's adoption of a "cosmological perspective" here, but he reads the tone as

"exultant" rather than ironic and thus finds the scene "contradictory and confusing." McWilliams, *Charles W. Chesnutt and the Fictions of Race*, 145.

53. Hardy, *Tess of the d'Urbervilles*, 94. Citing a passage in *The House Behind the Cedars* featuring similar rhetoric, Eric Sundquist argues that "the novel is governed by the conventional requirement that Rena and John must, as Molly fears, do 'penance for her sin' and 'expiate as well the sins of their fathers.'" Attention to the novel's resemblance to *Tess* helps make plain the extent to which Chesnutt, like Hardy, does not simply accede to convention here but rather uses Rena's "conventional" suffering and death to protest the morality that sees these as just and makes them seem "inevitable." Comparison to *Tess* also underscores the gendering of the conventions at issue here, a point obscured by Sundquist's lumping together of Rena and John (as if each paid equally for their parents' sins). Sundquist, *To Wake the Nations*, 399.

54. Hardy, *Tess of the d'Urbervilles*, 95.

55. This is the title of Book Fourth of *The Mill on the Floss*; in *Tess*, Bunyan's phrase is applied most immediately to Angel Clare but in describing what he has in common with Tess, who has just been described as an "unhappy pilgrim herself" (140); *The House Behind the Cedars*, 454.

56. The only other novels that turn up in a search of the Nineteenth-Century Fiction database of 250 British novels from the period 1781–1901 are Scott's *Heart of Midlothian* and Hardy's *The Woodlanders*.

57. Garrett Stewart suggests that "the story of *The Mill on the Floss* is perhaps unique in Victorian fiction before Hardy . . . in its monolithic cruelty [and] its sense of devastated human potential—and not just squandered hopes, but possibilities actively laid waste by plot." This is a fair description of Rena's narrative as well. Stewart, *Novel Violence: A Narratography of Victorian Fiction* (Chicago: U of Chicago P, 2009), 132.

58. Chesnutt's incorporation of *The Mill on the Floss* and *Tess of the d'Urbervilles* into a literary lineage bringing together novels about both sexually compromised and mixed-race women was soon extended and cemented by W.E.B. Du Bois, in his 1911 novel *The Quest of the Silver Fleece*. See Hack, "The Last Victorian Novel."

59. Charlotte Brontë, *Jane Eyre* (London: Penguin, 1986), 432.

60. Ibid., 410.

61. Sandra Gilbert and Susan Gubar, *The Madwoman in the Attic: The Woman Writer and the Nineteenth-Century Literary Imagination* (New Haven: Yale UP, 1979), 360.

62. Irene Tucker, *The Moment of Racial Sight: A History* (Chicago: U of Chicago P, 2012), 18.

63. For a careful account of the novel's development through multiple drafts, see Robert P. Sedlack, "The Evolution of Charles Chesnutt's *The House Behind the Cedars*," *CLA Journal* 19, no. 2 (1975), 125–35.

64. "Rena," copy 3. Fisk University, John Hope and Aurelia E. Franklin Library, Special Collections, Charles W. Chesnutt Collection, box 9, folder 4.

65. "Rena," copy 4. Fisk University, John Hope and Aurelia E. Franklin Library, Special Collections, Charles W. Chesnutt Collection, box 9, folder 5.

66. "Rena," copy 3. Fisk University, John Hope and Aurelia E. Franklin Library, Special Collections, Charles W. Chesnutt Collection, box 9, folder 4, typescript p. 7.

67. Ibid., typescript p. 8.
68. Ibid. It is when he revises and expands this sentence, moreover, that Chesnutt adds the allusion to Tennyson: "When he had read all the books,—indeed, long before he had read them all,—he too had tasted of the fruit of the Tree of Knowledge: contentment took its flight, and happiness lay far beyond the sphere where he was born. The blood of his white fathers, the heirs of the ages, cried out for its own, and after the manner of that blood set about getting the object of its desire" (375).
69. Many critics have argued that the racial and racist imperatives of the literary marketplace pushed Chesnutt toward subtle forms of subversiveness in his early conjure tales. Summing up and extending this line of analysis, for example, Kenneth M. Price writes, "At the outset of [Chesnutt's] career, he wrote to allow certain readers to see his irony and others not." I am suggesting that a similar dynamic governs the intertextual ironies of *The House Behind the Cedars* as well. See Kenneth M. Price, "Charles Chesnutt, the *Atlantic Monthly*, and the Intersection of African-American Fiction and Elite Culture," in *Periodical Literature in Nineteenth-Century America*, ed. Kenneth M. Price and Susan Belasco Smith (Charlottesville, VA: UP of Virginia, 2000), 264.
70. See Leah Price, *How to Do Things with Books in Victorian Britain* (Princeton: Princeton UP, 2012), for a study of the uses of books for purposes other than reading, including the avoidance of eye contact.
71. Chesnutt, *The Quarry* (Princeton, NJ: Princeton UP, 1999), 277–78. For a discussion of Chesnutt's career-long "faith in consent as the mechanism for just human relation in sharp distinction to identitarian notions of blood," see Gregg D. Crane, *Race, Citizenship and Law in American Literature* (New York: Cambridge UP, 2002), 205.
72. Chesnutt, *The Quarry*, 75. Interestingly, from the present perspective, this passage comes just two sentences after the sole passage in the book that references its title: "Donald, all through his young manhood, was destined to be the quarry and not the hawk, the sought and not the seeker, the hunted and not the hunter" (75).
73. Ibid., 237.
74. Ibid., 192.
75. Ibid., 193.

CHAPTER FIVE: CULTURAL TRANSMISSION AND TRANSGRESSION: PAULINE HOPKINS

1. Pauline E. Hopkins, *The Magazine Novels of Pauline Hopkins* (New York; Oxford: Oxford University Press, 1988), 362. Further references to this edition are cited parenthetically within the text.
2. Mary Hartwell Catherwood, *The White Islander* (New York: Century, 1893), 155.
3. So too does the passage marking Winona and Maxwell's dawning realization of their love, which tracks that of Marie and Henry: "That chemistry of the spirit which draws two irresistibly together, through space and against time and

obstacles, kept them conscious only of each other" (357). The parallel passage in *The White Islander* begins, "That chemistry of the spirit which draws two irresistibly together, through space, through obstacles, through time,—which may work anguish to both, but must work because they exist,—kept these young creatures an instant conscious of nothing but each other" (91).

4. She does adopt the novel's interest in cross-national, cross-racial, cross-border relationships. In addition to the aspects of the novels already described, this is also evident in their opening settings and scenarios: just as the non-Indians Marie and George are raised by Indians on an island in the Great Lakes (in their case, Mackinac Island), so too are the non-Indians Winona and her stepbrother Judah raised among Indians on an island in the Great Lakes, Grand Island (technically in the Niagara River, between Buffalo and Canada).

5. Mary Hartwell Catherwood, "Mary Hartwell Catherwood Papers" (Chicago, Illinois, 1865–1945), The Newberry Library, http://mms.newberry.org/xml/xml _files/Catherwood.xml.

6. Lois Brown, *Pauline Elizabeth Hopkins: Black Daughter of the Revolution* (Chapel Hill: U of North Carolina P, 2008), 374.

7. Ibid.

8. So insignificant to Oliphant was the name "John Brown" that she herself misremembered it: in her autobiography, she describes "The Executor" as "something about a lawyer, John Brownlow." Margaret Oliphant, *The Autobiography of Margaret Oliphant*, ed. Elisabeth Jay (Peterborough, Ontario: Broadview Press, 2002), 135.

9. Chesnutt and Hopkins were born in 1858 and 1859, respectively, and their most active years of publication overlapped almost entirely: the first novel by each was published in the same month, October 1900, and by 1904 both authors had published virtually all the fiction they would publish in their lifetimes. They died two years apart, in 1932 and 1930, respectively. In addition, the work of both appeared mainly in Boston-based periodicals and presses, although Chesnutt wrote for a white-dominated market and Hopkins for a largely black one.

10. The coverage of Chesnutt in the *Colored American Magazine*, where Hopkins published most of her fiction and worked as an editor, makes clear his stature within African American literary circles at the time. A December 1901 appreciation by John Livingston Wright is titled "Charles W. Chesnutt. One of the Leading Novelists of the Race" and describes Chesnutt's work as "marked by feeling, understanding, grace, and polish." This piece argues that Chesnutt's special topic is the experience of light-skinned, mixed-race individuals, claiming that he has made "this hybrid race, . . . its mental anguish, its pitiful life, its heart-rending experiences" "singularly his own" field as a writer (John Livingston Wright, "Charles W. Chesnutt. One of the Leading Novelists of the Race," *Colored American Magazine*, December 1901, 153–57, quotes from 154).

11. Gérard Genette, *Paratexts: Thresholds of Interpretation* (Cambridge; New York: Cambridge University Press, 1997), 149. Hopkins was evidently fond of terminal epigraphs, as each of her four novels ends with the quotation of another text: her next novel, *Hagar's Daughter*, concludes with a chestnut from Longfellow's "My Lost Youth" ("A boy's will is the wind's will, / And the thoughts of youth

are long, long thoughts"); *Winona* ends with eight lines of a Negro spiritual, "My Way Is Cloudy," sung by one of the characters; and her final novel, *Of One Blood*, ends by quoting the biblical verse from which that novel draws its title: "He will prove his words, 'Of one blood have I made all races of men.'"

12. For a good summary of the questions raised by this departure, see Carla L. Peterson, "Commemorative Ceremonies and Invented Traditions: History, Memory, and Modernity in the 'New Negro' Novel of the Nadir," in *Post-Bellum, Pre-Harlem: African American Literature and Culture, 1877–1919*, ed. Barbara Mc-Caskill and Caroline Gebhard (New York: New York UP, 2006), 34–56, 45.

13. I should note as well that I find no mention of Hopkins's citations of Tennyson in the literature on Tennyson's afterlives, including Barbara Hardy, *Tennyson and the Novelists* (Lincoln: Tennyson Society, 1993); or John Morton, *Tennyson among the Novelists* (London; New York: Continuum, 2010).

14. Hopkins provides an example of such a (mis)quotation of Tennyson that, unlike the allusions under discussion here (as I am about to argue), does not seem to do additional work near the end of the last story she published in the *Colored American Magazine*, "As the Lord Lives, He Is One of Our Mother's Children": "soft and clear came the sound of distant church bells, calling to weekly prayer, like 'horns of Elfland softly blowing.'" Hopkins here alludes to a line from one of the songs in *The Princess*, "The horns of Elfland faintly blowing!" Pauline E. Hopkins, "As the Lord Lives, He Is One of Our Mother's Children," in *Short Fiction by Black Women, 1900–1920*, ed. Elizabeth Ammons, The Schomburg Library of Nineteenth-Century Black Women Writers (Oxford: Oxford University Press, 1991), 286. First published in the *Colored American Magazine* in November 1903. Tennyson, *Poems*, 783.

15. Hopkins writes "Inglass of satin, / And shimmer of pearls," a version of Tennyson's "In gloss of satin and glimmer of pearls" (*Magazine Novels*, 111). Lois Brown argues for the broader importance of *Maud* to *Hagar's Daughter*; see Brown, *Pauline Elizabeth Hopkins*, 355–58.

16. Five of the novel's twenty-two chapter titles are allusions: two to Tennyson, two to the Bible, and one to the Romantic-era British poet Thomas Campbell.

17. See Carby, *Reconstructing Womanhood*; Ann DuCille, *The Coupling Convention: Sex, Text, and Tradition in Black Women's Fiction* (New York: Oxford University Press, 1993).

18. Cooper, *The Voice of Anna Julia Cooper*, 51.

19. For an influential early analysis of this strategy in both Cooper and Hopkins, see Carby, *Reconstructing Womanhood*.

20. Cooper, *Voice*, 78–79 (Cooper's ellipsis).

21. Immediately after quoting Tennyson, Cooper offers historical examples of the "glowing effects" of "the higher education of women," and she begins with "Sappho, the bright, sweet singer of Lesbos" (79). Cooper thus provides an intriguing precedent for the conjunction of *The Princess* and Sappho in a fin-de-siècle book authored by an African American woman and explicitly committed to a project of African American expression and racial equality.

22. Cooper, *Voice*, 84.

23. Ibid.

24. Tennyson, "The Ballad of Oriana," ll. 36–42.
25. Siobhan Somerville, "Passing through the Closet in Pauline E. Hopkins's *Contending Forces*," *American Literature* 69, no. 1 (March 1997): 151, 159.
26. Ibid., 145–49.
27. Alfred, Lord Tennyson, "Dora," in *The Poems of Tennyson*, ed. Christopher Ricks (London: Longmans, 1969), ll. 7, 8.
28. Eve Kosofsky Sedgwick, *Between Men: English Literature and Male Homosocial Desire* (New York: Columbia UP, 1985), 120.
29. Alan Sinfield, *Alfred Tennyson* (New York: Blackwell, 1986), 136.
30. *Sic:* "in the main" should read "to the main"; this is probably a typo.
31. Sedgwick, *Between Men*, 132.
32. Alfred, Lord Tennyson, "The Princess," in *The Poems of Tennyson*, ed. Christopher Ricks (London: Longmans, 1969), section VI, l. 363; section VII, ll. 1–2.
33. "Thus, in her apparent defeat does she rise to the supreme height of her womanhood," as one nineteenth-century critic put it. See Samuel Edward Dawson, *A Study, with Critical and Explanatory Notes, of Lord Tennyson's Poem, The Princess*, 2nd ed. (Montreal: Dawson Bros., 1884), 33.
34. Alisa Clapp-Itnyre, "Marginalized Musical Interludes: Tennyson's Critique of Conventionality in *The Princess*," *Victorian Poetry* 38, no. 2 (2000): 240–41.
35. Alfred, Lord Tennyson, "The Princess," in *The Poems of Tennyson*, ed. Christopher Ricks (Harlow: Longmans, 1969), conclusion, l. 5.
36. My reading of the novel's ending thus aligns with that of Laura Doyle, who argues that "Although Hopkins ultimately directs the love relationships in her novel into strictly heterosexual channels, she nonetheless leaves the ripple of a homoerotic subcurrent." Moreover, Doyle is the rare critic to actually quote from Hopkins's citation of Tennyson (although she does not identify the source of the quotation). However, Doyle locates this "ripple" primarily in the person of Dora's daughter, who is named after Sappho, as against the texts of the Atlantic tradition Hopkins is in dialogue with. That is, Doyle sees Hopkins as disrupting and deconstructing this tradition, whereas I am arguing that she exploits oppositional and disruptive energies lodged within it. Laura Doyle, *Freedom's Empire: Race and the Rise of the Novel in Atlantic Modernity, 1640–1940* (Durham: Duke UP, 2008), 389. Similarly, Susan Gillman argues that the redemptiveness of past suffering represented by Sappho and Will's wedding is "ambivalently marked" by one character's description of it as "a fairy tale of love and chivalry such as we read of only in books" (398); on my account, this ambivalence is reinforced by that already on display within *The Princess*—the closest such "fairy tale" to hand. Susan Gillman, *Blood Talk: American Race Drama and the Culture of the Occult* (Chicago: U of Chicago P, 2003), 43.
37. Hopkins, *The Magazine Novels of Pauline Hopkins*, 269.
38. The one critic who has paid sustained attention to Hopkins's relationship to Eliot is Laura Doyle. As noted above, Doyle sees Hopkins's relationship to the literary tradition with which Doyle identifies Eliot as primarily disruptive. While Doyle successfully demonstrates the importance of bringing these authors into conversation and of reading Hopkins in the context of a transatlantic literary tradition, her specific claims are weakened at times by an inattention to

detail. Doyle argues, for example, that Hopkins cites Shakespeare early in *Contending Forces* to establish the literary tradition he represents as "the lineage *her* story disrupts" (373); but although Hopkins does mention Shakespeare, Doyle mistakenly attributes the lines of verse Hopkins cites to him, rather than their actual author, Edmund Waller. (A fuller analysis of that scene would also have to grapple with the fact that Hopkins borrows both her reference to *The Tempest* and Waller's lines from a book about the West Indies, as discussed below.) In describing the "nativist" project that she identifies with Eliot and which she sees Hopkins as deconstructing, Doyle emphasizes a supposed contradiction between Hopkins's citation of Goldsmith's celebration of "native charm" and the emphasis on racial mixing in the chapter for which his lines provide the epigraph; yet Goldsmith is contrasting "native charm" with "the gloss of art"— that is, "native" here does not mean "indigenous" but rather "unadorned, free from art, simple." Understood in these terms the supposed irony or tension of the citation melts away.

39. Eliot, *Daniel Deronda*, 811.
40. Constance E. C. Weigall, *The Temptation of Dulce Carruthers* (London: Cassell's family magazine, American edition, 1891), 31.
41. Ibid., 32.
42. Ibid., 460.
43. Remarkably, given how unusual terminal epigraphs are, there is yet another, earlier novel that also ends with these lines from *The Princess*: the southern U.S. author Augusta J. Evans's popular novel *St. Elmo* (1866). That novel also quotes the "Ask me no more" stanza Hopkins quotes. However, while Evans also omits part of the passage in her terminal epigraph, her omission (which goes unmarked) overlaps with but does not match that in *Contending Forces* and *The Temptation of Dulce Carruthers*. Thus, while Hopkins may have been aware of this earlier precedent, Weigall's more recent novel seems likely to have been her model.
44. Kennedy writes of Bermuda, "Under the touch of Shakespeare it became the magic island of Prospero and Miranda," and after further sketching the early history of European experience on the island he concludes this same paragraph by writing, "The story of the discovery reached England through others, and so favourable was their report that Bermuda ceased to be the 'still-vexed Bermoothes,' and became

The spot of earth uncurst
To show how all things were created first."

Arnold Kennedy, *The Story of the West Indies* (London: H. Marshall and Son, 1899), 52, 53.
45. As we would expect by now, Hopkins also departs from Weigall in offering up a more purely positive depiction of the English upper class. Lord Melvell is not a villain, but his very wealth and status constitute the "temptation" Dulce must learn to resist and renounce (even if they bear an uncomfortable resemblance to her reward for this renunciation). By contrast, Mr. Withington and the wealth he

possesses and conveys are treated as unambivalently good in *Contending Forces*, the novel's early attention to the history of slavery in Bermuda notwithstanding.

46. John Churton Collins, *Illustrations of Tennyson* (London: Chatto & Windus, 1891), 3.

47. Ibid., 2.

48. Ibid., 3, 4. Collins does explicitly credit one "serious charge of plagiarism" against Tennyson: the charge that his "Columbus" takes its "whole framework" as well as "many . . . ideas and details" from "Columbus at Seville," by Joseph Ellis. "If the resemblances between the poems are coincidences," Collins remarks, "it would be difficult to match coincidences so extraordinary in the whole history of literary parallels" (163).

49. Unlikely but not impossible. An article in the July 1904 issue of the *Colored American* titled "Our Literary Cult" includes a brief profile of McCune Smith, calling him "a champion of Titanic proportions" and asserting that "no writer we have since produced was more gifted by nature and acquired learning as a controversialist." "Our Literary Cult," *Colored American Magazine*, July 1904, 13–14, 13.

50. "In her right hand the lily, [in her left
   The letter]—all her bright hair streaming down—
   [And all the coverlid was cloth of gold
   Drawn to her waist,]—and she herself in white,
   All but her face, and that clear-featured face
   Was lovely, for she did not seem as dead,
   But fast asleep, and lay as tho' she smiled."

   Collins argues that "the points of resemblance" between this passage and one in Byron's *Corsair* "make it difficult to think that Tennyson has not borrowed from it." Pauline E. Hopkins, *Of One Blood; or, The Hidden Self* (New York: Washington Square Press, 2004), 166; Collins, *Illustrations of Tennyson*, 147–48.

51. John Churton Collins, "A New Study of Tennyson," *Cornhill Magazine* 42 (1880): 17–35, 35. Collins moves this comparison to the preface in *Illustrations*, viii.

52. See M. Syms, "Literary Parallels," *Athenaeum*, 1 September 1866, 271–72; "Notes," *The Academy and Literature*, 15 October 1904, 329–30.

53. Collins, *Illustrations of Tennyson*, 55.

54. Tennyson's annotated copy of "A New Study of Tennyson" is at the Tennyson Research Centre in Lincoln, UK. An image of a marked-up page can be found at www.bl.uk/collection-items/alfred-tennysons-notes-on-a-new-study-of-tennyson.

55. Alfred, Lord Tennyson, "Author's Prefatory Notes," in *The Works of Tennyson*, ed. Hallam, Lord Tennyson (London: Macmillan, 1907), 1: 391–92.

56. Ibid., 334.

57. Geoffrey Sanborn, "The Wind of Words: Plagiarism and Intertextuality in *Of One Blood*," *J19: The Journal of Nineteenth-Century Americanists* 3, no. 1 (2015): 68.

58. As Tennyson in particular would appreciate, these parallels and symmetry are "accidental": Tennyson's remarks were first published in the 1907–1908 edition of his poetry, more than four years after the publication of Hopkins's novel.

59. Doyle, *Freedom's Empire*, 267, 274.

60. Sanborn, "The Wind of Words," 73.

61. Ibid., 73, 84, 74.

62. Although this verse passage and those cited below are italicized in the edition I am citing, they are not italicized in the original version serialized in the *Colored American*. The introduction of italics arguably shades the implied relationship between the verse and the surrounding text, setting up a distinction between them lacking in the original version.

63. Holly Jackson, "Another Long Bridge: Reproduction and Reversion in *Hagar's Daughter*," in *Early African American Print Culture*, ed. Lara Langer Cohen and Jordan Alexander Stein (Philadelphia: U of Pennsylvania P, 2012), 202.

64. Edward Bulwer Lytton, *The Last Days of Pompeii* (New York: A. L. Burt, n.d.), 170, 137.

65. The edition I cite reads "truth," but this is a typographical error; the *Colored American*, like the novel Hopkins is borrowing from, reads "ruth."

66. Sanborn, "The Wind of Words," 74.

67. This story was (I believe) first published in the periodical *The Spiritual Age* and reprinted in Hardinge's collection *The Wildfire Club*, which was published in Boston in 1861. In fact, large chunks of the last five chapters of *Of One Blood*—dialogue, description, and the entire plot-line in which Dianthe tries to poison her husband and is instead poisoned by him and is momentarily reunited with Reuel before she dies—comes from Hardinge's story. Hopkins also borrows a long paragraph from this story in her previous novel, *Winona*.

68. Reuel Briggs:

No one could fail to notice the vast breadth of shoulder, the strong throat that upheld a plain face, the long limbs, the sinewy hands. His head was that of an athlete, with close-set ears, and covered with an abundance of black hair, straight and closely cut, thick and smooth; the nose was the aristocratic feature, although nearly spoiled by broad nostrils, of this remarkable young man; his skin was white, but of a tint suggesting olive, an almost sallow color which is a mark of strong, melancholic temperaments. (Hopkins, *Of One Blood*, 3.)

Paul Griggs:

No one could fail to notice the vast breadth of shoulder, the firm, columnar throat, and the small athlete's head with close-set ears. . . . The man's complexion was of that perfectly even but almost sallow colour which often belongs to very strong melancholic temperaments. . . . Dark, straight, closely cut hair grew thick and smooth as a priest's skull-cap, low on the forehead and far forward at the temples. . . . The nose was very thick between the eyes, relatively long, with unusually broad nostrils which ran upward from the point to the lean cheeks. (F. Marion Crawford, *Casa Braccio*, 253–55.)

69. Hopkins: "She had the glory of heaven in her voice, and in her face the fatal beauty of man's terrible sins" (Hopkins, *Of One Blood*, 52.) Crawford: ". . . fatal beauty of her dead mother's deadly sin" (Crawford, *Casa Braccio*, 331).

70. William St Clair and Annika Bautz, "Imperial Decadence: The Making of the Myths in Edward Bulwer Lytton's *The Last Days of Pompeii*," *Victorian Literature and Culture* 40, no. 2 (2012): 370, 387.

71. Bulwer Lytton, *The Last Days of Pompeii*, 190.

72. Ibid., 53.

73. Ibid., 140.

74. Ibid., 141.

75. This paragraph ends with another nonironic borrowing: a reference to Arbaces' statues as "those dread Theban monsters, whose majestic and passionless features the marble so well portrayed" becomes "Our sphinx, with passionless features, portrays the dumb suffering of our souls," and in each case this sentence is followed by two lines of verse: "Their look with the reach of past ages, was wise, / And the soul of eternity thought in their eyes" (145, 126). These lines are a slightly altered version of a description of Apollo in Leigh Hunt's "The Feast of Poets."

76. By the time he writes *The Quarry*, Chesnutt will offer a picture of a virtually color-blind English society not far off from Hopkins's, but that only comes two decades later.

77. Edward Bulwer Lytton, "The Kingdom of God," *Colored American Magazine*, March 1904, 208.

78. This phrase appears in the motto printed on the cover of each issue of the *Colored American*.

79. As it happens, Case herself would not have been out of place in the pages of the *Colored American*: in 1903 Case wrote a "Battle Hymn of Peace," set to the tune "John Brown," to celebrate the fiftieth anniversary of the Progressive Friends of Longwood, an organization with a long history of abolitionist, civil rights, and women's rights activism. For the history of this organization, see Albert J. Wahl, "The Progressive Friends of Longwood," *Bulletin of Friends Historical Association* 42, no. 1 (Spring 1953): 13–32. For Case's hymn, see *Proceedings of the Pennsylvania Yearly Meeting of Progressive Friends* (Kennet Square, Pennsylvania, 1903), 29–30. For Case's authorship of the poem attributed to Bulwer Lytton, see "The Story of a Poem," *Friends' Intelligencer*, 6 June 1903, 362.

　　There is no way of knowing if Hopkins herself knew she was perpetuating a misattribution, but it is worth noting that she made such misattributions something of a habit: the article Reuel Briggs reads that he attributes to Binet is actually the work of William James, as many scholars have noted, and while Hopkins's story "A Dash for Liberty" purports to be "Founded on an article written by Col. T. W. Higginson for the Atlantic Monthly, June 1861," it is in fact founded on a chapter from a book by William Wells Brown. For discussion of this latter switch, see John Cullen Gruesser, *Confluences: Postcolonialism, African American Literary Studies, and the Black Atlantic* (Athens: U of Georgia P, 2005), 80–81.

CHAPTER SIX: THE CITATIONAL SOUL OF BLACK FOLK: W.E.B. DU BOIS

1. W.E.B. Du Bois, *The Souls of Black Folk*, ed. David W. Blight and Robert Gooding-Williams (Boston: Bedford Books, 1997), 260.

2. See David L. Lewis, *W.E.B. Du Bois: Biography of a Race, 1868–1919* (New York: H. Holt, 1993), 294; Stephanie J. Shaw, *W.E.B. Du Bois and The Souls of Black Folk* (Chapel Hill: U of North Carolina P 2013), 159–60.

3. Du Bois, *The Souls of Black Folk*, 1997, 260.

4. Sundquist, *To Wake the Nations: Race in the Making of American Literature* (Cambridge, MA: Belknap Press of Harvard UP, 1993), 458.

5. Du Bois, *The Souls of Black Folk*, 1999, 6. Further references are to this edition, unless otherwise noted.

6. The passage just cited from the beginning of the Sorrow Songs chapter—"a phrase, a haunting echo of these weird old songs"—is arguably ambiguous enough to allow us to entertain the possibility that Du Bois is describing the verse epigraphs, rather than the bars of music, as the "phrase[s]" that echo the Sorrow Songs. Such a reading would put the Sorrow Songs in a position of priority and influence with regard to Western literature akin to that which James McCune Smith argues for in his reading of "The Charge of the Light Brigade" discussed in chapter 2, above. Although the similarity of Du Bois's phrasing here to that in his "Forethought"—where it is clearly the bars of music that he designates "echo[es] of haunting melody"—discourages such a reading, I shall argue that some of the chapter epigraphs should in fact be read as echoes of prior African American expressive acts, albeit ones that also take the form of citation.

7. Shelley Fisher Fishkin, "The Borderlands of Culture: Writing by W.E.B. Du Bois, James Agee, Tillie Olsen, and Gloria Anzaldúa," in *Literary Journalism in the Twentieth Century*, ed. Norman Sims (New York: Oxford UP, 1990), 140.

8. Nancy Bentley, "Literary Forms and Mass Culture, 1870–1920," in *The Cambridge History of American Literature: Prose Writing, 1860–1920*, ed. Sacvan Bercovitch (Cambridge University Press, 2005), 3: 282.

9. Ross Posnock, *Color and Culture: Black Writers and the Making of the Modern Intellectual* (Cambridge, MA: Harvard UP, 1998), 263.

10. Sundquist, *To Wake the Nations*, 468.

11. Ibid.

12. Posnock, *Color and Culture*, 263.

13. Alexander Weheliye, "In the Mix: Hearing the Souls of Black Folk," *Amerikastudien / American Studies* 45, no. 4 (1 January 2000): 553.

14. It is worth further noting that if, as I am arguing, in an important way the verse epigraphs are not solely or entirely "white," neither are the musical epigraphs purely "black": when Du Bois traces the development of the Sorrow Songs in the last chapter of the book, he explains that this development includes "a blending of Negro music with the music heard in the foster land," arguing that "The result is still distinctively Negro and the method of blending original, but the elements are both Negro and Caucasian" (Du Bois, *The Souls of Black Folk*, 1999, 158.).

15. Sundquist, *To Wake the Nations*, 496; see also Robert Gooding-Williams, *In the Shadow of Du Bois: Afro-Modern Political Thought in America* (Cambridge, MA: Harvard UP, 2009), 162–63.

16. Sundquist, *To Wake the Nations*, 496.

17. Gooding-Williams, *In the Shadow of Du Bois*, 162–63.
18. He continues, for "unless his striving be not simply seconded, but rather aroused and encouraged, by the initiative of the richer and wiser environing group, he cannot hope for great success" (44).
19. Hopkins seems to have been attentive to Du Bois's use of Tennyson in turn, and perhaps noticed the kinship with her own: in the installment of *Of One Blood* published five months after the publication of *Souls*, she too quotes a death scene from *Idylls*, comparing the near-death of her character Dianthe to the drowning of Elaine in "Lancelot and Elaine."
20. Alfred, Lord Tennyson, *In Memoriam*, "Epilogue," ll. 143–44. The allusion here may seem distant, but there can be little doubt that Du Bois had Tennyson's poem in mind here, as he explicitly cites the exact phrase—"one far-off divine event"—on at least two occasions contemporaneous with the 1897 publication of the article that became this chapter of *Souls* (and that contains this passage verbatim): in "The Conservation of Races," also from 1897, he writes that each race is "striving, each in its own way, to develop for civilization its particular message, its particular ideal, which shall help to guide the world nearer and nearer that perfection of human life for which we all long, that

    'one far off Divine event.'" (Du Bois, *The Souls of Black Folk*, 1999, 179)

    Similarly, in "Careers Open to College-Bred Negroes," Du Bois's 1898 commencement address at Fisk, he demands of his audience, "though toil, hard heavy toil, be the price of life, shall we not, young men and women, gladly work and sacrifice and serve

    'That one, far off, divine event,'

    Toward which the whole creation moves"? (W.E.B. Du Bois, *Writings* [New York, NY: The Library of America, 1986], 831–32.

    These uses prior to *Souls* do not African Americanize the "event" in question. By contrast, when Du Bois returned to the phrase in his 1928 novel *Dark Princess*, he again racializes it, albeit now it takes on a pan- (non-white) racial meaning, as in that novel's messianic conclusion, the title character declares that "The 'one far-off divine event' has come to pass." W.E.B. Du Bois, *Dark Princess: A Romance* (Jackson: UP of Mississippi, 1995), 297.
21. Ironically, though, this repurposing is itself unusually discordant, as the reader finds it difficult to align the dichotomies it sets up: presumably Tennyson's "mind and soul" align with Du Bois's "intelligence and sympathy," but it is not at all clear whether these qualities are themselves arrayed on opposite side of "the color-line"—and if so, which are assigned to blacks and which to whites? Alternately, if one reads the passage as suggesting that both blacks and whites need to unite intelligence/mind and sympathy/soul in order to make "justice and right triumph," this means that the passage's images of union no longer directly reference a racial union, which is now rather confusingly a second-order

phenomenon (that is, a union of black and white people who have themselves united intelligence and sympathy). Du Bois's inclusion of this citation despite its awkward fit underscores his commitment to his intertextual rhetorical strategy.

22. Alexander Crummell, *Civilization and Black Progress: Selected Writings of Alexander Crummell on the South*, ed. J. R. Oldfield (Charlottesville: Published for the Southern Texts Society by the UP of Virginia, 1995), 222, 122.

23. Ibid., 109, 168. In reading Tennyson's "type" as a synonym for "race," Crummell does tweak the poem's meaning, but he does not engage in the kind of radical recontextualization that has been our focus, and is Du Bois's habitual practice.

24. William Wordsworth, *Poems of William Wordsworth: Collected Reading Texts from the Cornell Wordsworth* (Penrith, UK: Humanities-Ebooks, 2009), 1: 712–17.

25. Robert Gooding-Williams also notes that "Du Bois adapts the Ode to the purposes of sociopolitical allegory." Relying on Marjorie Levinson's reading of the poem as an expression of Wordsworth's disillusionment with the French Revolution, he further suggests that "If Levinson is right, then the Ode lends itself to Du Bois's adaptation because it is already a sociopolitical allegory" (72). However, I see no hint that Du Bois himself read the poem in these terms. (For Levinson's interpretation of the poem, see Marjorie Levinson, *Wordsworth's Great Period Poems: Four Essays* (New York: Cambridge UP, 1986), 80–100.)

26. As with Du Bois's allusions to Tennyson's "far-off divine event," discussed above, this African Americanizing citation in *Souls* contrasts with Du Bois's racially unmarked citation of the poem in his Fisk commencement address "Careers Open to College-Bred Negroes." At the beginning of that address, he describes the graduates of the class of 1898 as having "been vouchsafed the vision splendid" and as "stand[ing] where once I stood,

'When meadow, grove, and stream,
    The earth, and every common sight,
To me did seem
Apparelled in celestial light,
The glory and the freshness of a dream.'" (Du Bois, *Writings*, 827)

27. Du Bois, "Criteria of Negro Art" (1926), in ibid., 1000.

28. Posnock, *Color and Culture*, 142.

29. Ibid., 143.

30. Du Bois, *Writings*, 998.

31. Ibid.

32. Ibid., 1002. The only place I have seen Du Bois's allusion identified is in the annotations to this article at the webdubois.org website: http://www.webdubois.org/dbCriteriaNArt.html.

33. Dates of birth: Sharp, 1855; Symons, 1865; Du Bois, 1868; Moody, 1869.

34. Du Bois, *Writings*, 1002.

35. William Morton Payne, "Recent Poetry," *The Dial*, 16 January 1900, 48. Payne also later edited a collection of Swinburne's poetry.

36. William Morton Payne, "The Poetry of Mr. Moody," *The Dial*, 1 June 1901, 365. By 1904 Payne is proposing that Moody is arguably "the most distinguished"

living American poet, "if quality alone were to be taken into account." William Morton Payne, "Recent American Poetry," *The Dial*, 16 March 1904, 108.

37. The same is arguably true of FitzGerald's *Rubáiyát*, which was published in 1859 but was at the height of its popularity when Du Bois was writing *Souls*—indeed, according to Erik Gray, "by the end of the nineteenth century it had become by far the best known and most popular poem in the English language" (Erik Gray, "Fitzgerald and the *Rubáiyát*, in and out of Time," *Victorian Poetry* 46, no. 1 (2008): 4; see also John D. Yohannan, "The Fin de Siècle Cult of FitzGerald's *Rubáiyát of Omar Khayyám*," *Review of National Literatures* 2 (1971): 74–91.)

38. Eric Sundquist makes this point in *To Wake the Nations*, 504.

39. Payne, "The Poetry of Mr. Moody," 368.

40. William Morton Payne, "Recent Poetry," *The Dial*, 1 May 1902, 318.

41. Walter Pater, *The Renaissance: Studies in Art and Poetry* (London; New York: Macmillan, 1888), 143.

42. Posnock, *Color and Culture*, 104. Posnock does not mention Pater (or Payne), instead associating vagueness with Du Bois's mentor William James.

43. Du Bois, *The Souls of Black Folk*, 1999, 5.

44. Pater, *The Renaissance*, 140.

45. Du Bois, *The Souls of Black Folk*, 1999, 156–57.

46. Inadvertent confirmation of the success of Du Bois's anti-Paterian appropriation comes from a poetry anthology published eight years after *The Souls of Black Folk*. *The Humbler Poets (second series): A Collection of Newspaper and Periodical Verse, 1885–1910* includes Symons's poem. However, as if following Du Bois's lead in transforming the poem's "vagueness of mere subject" into "the conveyance of moral or political aspiration," the anthology replaces Symons's title for his poem with the title of the chapter of *Souls* for which it serves as an epigraph: for "The Crying of Water," read "Our Spiritual Strivings." Wallace and Frances Rice, *The Humbler Poets (second series): A Collection of Newspaper and Periodical Verse, 1885–1910* (Chicago: A. C. McClurg, 1911), 251. It may not be a coincidence that this anthology was published by the same publisher as *The Souls of Black Folk*.

47. Discussing the Dumbarton Oaks conference at which the plan for the United Nations was formulated, Du Bois quotes Tennyson's speaker's vision of a future when "the war-drum throbb'd no longer, and the battle flags were furl'd, in the Parliament of man, the Federation of the World." W.E.B. Du Bois, *Color and Democracy: Colonies and Peace* (New York: Harcourt, Brace, 1945), 17.

48. Dickens, *Bleak House*, 5.

49. Du Bois, *Dark Princess*, 37.

50. For a reading of *The Quest of the Silver Fleece* in relation to Victorian fiction, see Hack, "The Last Victorian Novel: *The Quest of the Silver Fleece*, by W.E.B. Du Bois."

51. Vanessa Dickerson discusses Du Bois's interest in Carlyle in *Dark Victorians* (Urbana: U of Illinois P, 2008), 95–105.

52. W.E.B. Du Bois, *The Oxford W.E.B. Du Bois Reader*, ed. Eric J. Sundquist (New York: Oxford University Press, 1996), 328. (For unknown reasons this edition retitles the lecture "Phillis Wheatley and African American Culture.") Further

references to this edition will be included parenthetically in the text. Rossetti's poem was composed in 1847, first published in the Pre-Raphaelite journal *The Germ* in 1850, and first published in a book in 1870.

53. Antony H. Harrison, "Dante Rossetti: Parody and Ideology," *Studies in English Literature, 1500–1900* 29, no. 4 (1989): 749.

54. Both the currency of Rossetti's poem and the limits of that currency among educated African Americans a decade before Du Bois's lecture are suggested by an exchange in Jessie Redmon Fauset's 1931 novel *The Chinaberry Tree*:

> "Well, she wouldn't be leaning out of her window at this hour of night, would she, like the blesséd Damozel out of Heaven?"
> "I don't know anything about the blesséd Damozel," said Melissa, forgetting the Rossetti to which he'd introduced her . . ." (Jessie Redmon Fauset, *The Chinaberry Tree; a Novel of American Life* [New York: Negro UP, 1969], 258).

55. Payne, "The Poetry of Mr. Moody," 365. Payne notes that Moody does not quite measure up to this high mark.

56. See William Sharp, *Dante Gabriel Rossetti; a Record and a Study* (London: Macmillan, 1882); Arthur Symons, *Dante Gabriel Rossetti* (Paris: Librairie Artistique et Littéraire, 1909).

57. Du Bois, *The Souls of Black Folk*, 1999, 142.

58. Harrison, "Dante Rossetti: Parody and Ideology," 752.

59. Ibid., 746.

60. It is worth noting, however, that Rossetti's paintings (as opposed to his poetry) were often viewed as departing from "ideal paradigms of beauty," as Susan Casteras has documented. The terms in which one critic marked this departure are especially suggestive in the present context: writing in 1883, Theodore Watts-Dunton commented that "in certain heads the sensuous fulness of the lips became scarcely Caucasian." However, Du Bois gives no indication of being familiar with this reputation, let alone this specific characterization, and the only aspect of the damozel's appearance described in the poem is her long yellow hair. See Susan P. Casteras, "Pre-Raphaelite Challenges to Victorian Canons of Beauty," *The Huntington Library Quarterly* 55, no. 1 (1992): 13–35. Quotation from p. 29.

61. William Stanley Braithwaite, "To Dante Gabriel Rossetti," *The House of Falling Leaves: With Other Poems* (Boston: J. W. Luce, 1908), 45.

62. Alice Dunbar-Nelson, "Negro Literature for Negro Pupils," rpt. in Henry Louis Gates and Gene Andrew Jarrett, *The New Negro: Readings on Race, Representation, and African American Culture, 1892–1938* (Princeton, NJ: Princeton UP, 2007), 303.

63. Du Bois uses the same term in a key passage at the end of *Souls*, when he asks "Would America have been America without her Negro people?" explaining that "we have brought our three gifts and *mingled* them with yours: a gift of story and song . . . the gift of sweat and brawn . . . [and] a gift of the Spirit" (*The Souls of Black Folk*, 1999, 162–63, italics added).

64. Harrison, "Dante Rossetti," 753.

65. Rossetti to William Allingham, 23 January 1855, *Letters of Dante Gabriel Rossetti*, ed. Oswald Doughty and John Robert Wahl (Oxford: Clarendon Press, 1965), 1: 239.

66. Andrew J. Allison, "Fisk's Seventy-Fifth Anniversary: What Happened, Why, and Who Made It Happen," *Fisk News* 14 (May 1941): 5.

AFTERWORD: AFTER DU BOIS

1. Brent Hayes Edwards, *The Practice of Diaspora: Literature, Translation, and the Rise of Black Internationalism* (Cambridge, MA: Harvard UP, 2003), 5.

2. Jessie Redmon Fauset, *There Is Confusion* (Boston: Northeastern UP, 1989), 245. Further references to this edition will be given parenthetically in the text. Fauset puts this euphemistic phrasing in the mouth of a white character, Meriwether Bye, who meets and becomes friendly with his black relations. That character repeats this formulation at the very end of the novel, remarking, "I can see now that whatever slavery may have done for other men it has thrown the lives of all the Byes into confusion" (296).

3. Hack, "The Last Victorian Novel: *The Quest of the Silver Fleece*, by W.E.B. Du Bois."

4. George Eliot, *The Mill on the Floss*, ed. Oliver Lovesey (Peterborough, Ontario: Broadview Press, 2007), 57.

5. Review of *Comedy, American Style* in the journal *Opportunity*, cited in Leonard Harris and Charles Molesworth, *Alain L. Locke: Biography of a Philosopher* (Chicago: U of Chicago P, 2008), 271.

6. Jessie Redmon Fauset, "Double Trouble: A Story (pt. 2)," *The Crisis*, September 1923, 207.

7. Jessie Redmon Fauset, *The Chinaberry Tree: A Novel of American Life* (New York: Negro UP, 1969), 266.

8. Ralph Ellison, "Hidden Name and Complex Fate," in *The Collected Essays of Ralph Ellison*, ed. John F. Callahan (New York: Modern Library, 1995), 203, 202.

9. Percival L. Everett, *Erasure: A Novel* (Minneapolis: Graywolf Press, 2011), 2, 212.

10. Ibid., 146.

11. Ibid., 212.

12. For this canonical and curricular history, see Andrew Elfenbein, "The United States of Raveloe," *Modern Language Quarterly* 75, no. 2 (2014): 129–48.

13. Everett, *Erasure*, 147, 210.

14. Ibid., 209–10.

15. Ibid., 156.

16. Paul Beatty, *The Sellout* (New York: Farrar, Straus and Giroux, 2015), 3. Further references to this edition will be given parenthetically in the text.

17. Interestingly, Beatty writes that Dickens was "founded in 1868"; perhaps this is meant to situate its founding as immediately post-Civil War, but this date also offers a historical motivation for that choice of a name on the part of its (fictional, unrepresented) founders: Dickens conducted a very popular tour of the U.S. in 1867–68.

BIBLIOGRAPHY

Adams, James Eli. *Dandies and Desert Saints: Styles of Victorian Masculinity*. Ithaca: Cornell UP, 1995.

d'Alaux, Gustave. *L'Empereur Soulouque et Son Empire*. Paris: Michel Lévy Frères, 1856.

Allingham, William. *William Allingham: A Diary, 1824–1889*. London: Macmillan, 1907.

Allison, Andrew J. "Fisk's Seventy-Fifth Anniversary: What Happened, Why, and Who Made It Happen." *Fisk News* 14 (May 1941).

Anderson, Amanda. *The Powers of Distance: Cosmopolitanism and the Cultivation of Detachment*. Princeton, NJ: Princeton UP, 2001.

Anderson, Benedict. *Imagined Communities: Reflections on the Origin and Spread of Nationalism*. London: Verso, 1983.

Appiah, Kwame Anthony. *Cosmopolitanism: Ethics in a World of Strangers*. New York: W.W. Norton, 2006.

———. *The Ethics of Identity*. Princeton, NJ: Princeton UP, 2005.

———. *Justice, Governance, Cosmopolitanism, and the Politics of Difference: Reconfigurations in a Transnational World; Distinguished W.E.B. Du Bois Lectures 2004/2005*. Edited by Engelbert Habekost. Berlin: Humboldt University, 2007.

Ballinger, Gill, Tim Lustig, and Dale Townsend. "Missing Intertexts: Hannah Crafts's *The Bondwoman's Narrative* and African American Literary History." *Journal of American Studies* 39 (2005): 207–37.

Barrett, Faith, and Cristanne Miller, eds. *"Words for the Hour": A New Anthology of American Civil War Poetry*. Amherst: U of Massachusetts P, 2005.

Beatty, Paul. *The Sellout*. New York: Farrar, Straus and Giroux, 2015.

Bell, James Madison. *The Poetical Works of James Madison Bell*. Lansing, MI: Wynkoop, Hallenbeck, Crawford, 1901.

Bell, Philip A. [Cosmopolite, pseud.]. "Letter to the Editor." *Frederick Douglass' Paper*. 20 April 1855.

[Bell, Philip A.], "Lisle Lester," *Elevator*, 28 July 1865.

Bentley, Nancy. "Literary Forms and Mass Culture, 1870–1920." In *The Cambridge History of American Literature, Volume 3: Prose Writing, 1860–1920*, edited by Sacvan Bercovitch. New York: Cambridge UP, 2005.

"Bishop Turner." *The Freeman*. 3 May 1902.

Blight, David W. "In Search of Learning, Liberty, and Self-Definition: James McCune Smith and the Ordeal of the Antebellum Black Intellectual." *Afro-Americans in New York Life and History* 9, no. 2 (July 1985): 7–25.

Blyden, Edward Wilmot. *The Origin and Purpose of African Colonization.* Washington, DC: American Colonization Society, 1883.

Bosman, Julie. "Professor Says He Has Solved a Mystery Over a Slave's Novel," *New York Times*, 19 September 2013, A1.

Braithwaite, William Stanley. *The House of Falling Leaves: With Other Poems.* Boston: J. W. Luce, 1908.

Brodhead, Richard H. *Cultures of Letters: Scenes of Reading and Writing in Nineteenth-Century America.* Chicago: U of Chicago P, 1993.

Brody, Jennifer DeVere. *Impossible Purities: Blackness, Femininity, and Victorian Culture.* Durham, NC: Duke UP, 1998.

Brontë, Charlotte. *Villette.* 1853. Edited by Helen Cooper. London: Penguin, 2004.

Brown, David. *The Planter; or, Thirteen Years in the South, by a Northern Man.* Philadelphia: H. Hooker, 1853.

Brown, Lois. *Pauline Elizabeth Hopkins: Black Daughter of the Revolution.* Chapel Hill: U of North Carolina P, 2008.

Browning, Elizabeth Barrett. Poems. 3 vols. 4th ed. London: Chapman & Hall, 1856.

Bryant, Earle V. "Charles Chesnutt's Southern Black Jew: Rena Walden's Masquerade in *The House Behind the Cedars.*" *American Literary Realism, 1870–1910* 3 (1999): 15–21.

Bulwer Lytton, Edward. "The Kingdom of God." *Colored American Magazine.* March 1904.

———. *Last of the Barons.* 1843. London: G Routledge and Sons, 1876.

———. *The Last Days of Pompeii.* 1834. New York: A. L. Burt, n.d.

Burgess-Ware, Marie Louise. "Bernice, the Octoroon." 1903. In *Short Fiction by Black Women, 1900–1920*, edited by Elizabeth Ammons, 250–75. The Schomburg Library of Nineteenth-Century Black Women Writers. Oxford: Oxford UP, 1991.

Buzard, James. *Disorienting Fiction: The Autoethnographic Work of Nineteenth-Century British Novels.* Princeton, NJ: Princeton UP, 2005.

Carby, Hazel V. *Reconstructing Womanhood: The Emergence of the Afro-American Woman Novelist.* New York: Oxford UP, 1987.

Carroll, David, ed. *George Eliot: The Critical Heritage.* London: Routledge & Kegan Paul, 1971.

Casteras, Susan P. "Pre-Raphaelite Challenges to Victorian Canons of Beauty." *The Huntington Library Quarterly* 55, no. 1 (1992): 13–35.

Catherwood, Mary Hartwell. "Mary Hartwell Catherwood Papers." Chicago, Illinois, 1865–1945. The Newberry Library. http://mms.newberry.org/xml/xml_files/Catherwood.xml.

———. *The White Islander.* New York: Century, 1893.

"Charge of the Border Ruffian Brigade," *Provincial Freeman*, 19 July 1856.

"Charles W. Chesnutt: A New Delineator of Southern Life." *Self Culture* 11 (July 1900): 409–11.

Chesnutt, Charles W. *Charles W. Chesnutt: Essays and Speeches.* Edited by Joseph R. McElrath Jr., Robert C. Leitz III, and Jesse S. Crisler. Stanford, CA: Stanford UP, 1999.

————. *Frederick Douglass*. Boston: Small, Maynard, 1899.

————. *The Journals of Charles W. Chesnutt*. Edited by Richard H. Brodhead. Durham, NC: Duke UP, 1993.

————. *The Quarry*. Edited by Dean McWilliams. Princeton, NJ: Princeton UP, 1999.

————. "Rena." Fisk University, John Hope and Aurelia E. Franklin Library, Special Collections, Charles W. Chesnutt Collection.

————. *Stories, Novels and Essays*. Edited by Werner Sollors. New York: Library of America, 2002.

Christian Recorder. Philadelphia, PA, 1861–1960.

Clapp-Itnyre, Alisa. "Marginalized Musical Interludes: Tennyson's Critique of Conventionality in *The Princess*." *Victorian Poetry* 38, no. 2 (2000): 227–48.

Claybaugh, Amanda. *The Novel of Purpose: Literature and Social Reform in the Anglo-American World*. Ithaca, NY: Cornell UP, 2008.

Collins, John Churton. *Illustrations of Tennyson*. London: Chatto & Windus, 1891.

————. "A New Study of Tennyson." *Cornhill Magazine* 42 (1880): 17–35.

Cook, William W., and James Tatum. *African American Writers and Classical Tradition*. Chicago: U of Chicago P, 2010.

Cooper, Anna Julia. *The Voice of Anna Julia Cooper: Including A Voice from the South and Other Important Essays, Papers, and Letters*. Edited by Charles C. Lemert and Esme Bhan. Lanham, MD: Rowman & Littlefield, 1998.

Cotugno, Clare. "Stowe, Eliot, and the Reform Aesthetic." In *Transatlantic Stowe: Harriet Beecher Stowe and European Culture*, edited by Denise Kohn, Sarah Meer, and Emily B. Todd, 111–30. Iowa City: U of Iowa P, 2006.

Crafts, Hannah. *The Bondwoman's Narrative*. Edited by Henry Louis Gates Jr. New York: Warner Books, 2003.

Crawford, F. Marion. *Casa Braccio*. New York and London: Macmillan, 1895.

Cross, John. *George Eliot's Life as Related in Her Letters and Journals*. Vol. 24 of *The Writings of George Eliot*. Boston: Houghton, Mifflin, 1909.

Crummell, Alexander. *Civilization and Black Progress: Selected Writings of Alexander Crummell on the South*. Edited by J. R. Oldfield. Charlottesville: Published for the Southern Texts Society by the UP of Virginia, 1995.

Culler, A. Dwight. *The Poetry of Tennyson*. New Haven: Yale UP, 1977.

Dawson, Samuel Edward. *A Study, with Critical and Explanatory Notes, of Lord Tennyson's Poem, The Princess*. 2nd ed. Montreal: Dawson Bros., 1884.

Denman, Thomas Denman, Baron. "*Uncle Tom's Cabin, Bleak House*, Slavery and the Slave Trade." London: Longman, Brown, Green and Longmans, 1853.

Dickens, Charles. *Bleak House*. 1852–53. Edited by George H. Ford and Sylvère Monod. New York: Norton, 1977.

————. *David Copperfield*. 1849–50. London: Penguin Books, 1996.

————. *Dombey and Son*. 1846–48. Edited by Peter Fairclough. London: Penguin Books, 1985.

————. *Letters*. Edited by Madeline House and Graham Storey. Oxford: Clarendon Press, 1965–2002.

Dickerson, Vanessa D. *Dark Victorians*. Urbana: U of Illinois P, 2008.

Dimock, Wai-chee. *Through Other Continents: American Literature Across Deep Time*. Princeton: Princeton UP, 2008.

Douglas-Fairhurst Robert. *Victorian Afterlives: The Shaping of Influence in Nineteenth-Century Literature*. New York: Oxford UP, 2002.

Douglass, Frederick. *Frederick Douglass: Selected Speeches and Writings*. Edited by Philip S. Foner, adapted by Yuval Taylor. Chicago: U of Chicago P, 1999.

———. *My Bondage and My Freedom*. 1855. Edited by John David Smith. New York: Penguin, 2003.

Doyle, Laura. *Freedom's Empire: Race and the Rise of the Novel in Atlantic Modernity, 1640–1940*. Durham, NC: Duke UP, 2008.

Du Bois, W.E.B. *Color and Democracy: Colonies and Peace*. New York: Harcourt, Brace, 1945.

———. *Dark Princess: A Romance*. 1928. Jackson: UP of Mississippi, 1995.

———. *The Oxford W.E.B. Du Bois Reader*. Edited by Eric J. Sundquist. New York: Oxford UP, 1996.

———. *The Souls of Black Folk*. 1903. Edited by David W. Blight and Robert Gooding-Williams. Boston: Bedford Books, 1997.

———. *The Souls of Black Folk*. 1903. Edited by Henry Louis Gates Jr. and Terri Hume Oliver. New York: W. W. Norton, 1999.

———. *Writings*. Edited by Nathan Huggins. New York, NY: The Library of America, 1986.

DuCille, Ann. *The Coupling Convention: Sex, Text, and Tradition in Black Women's Fiction*. New York: Oxford UP, 1993.

Dunbar-Nelson, Alice. *The Dunbar Speaker and Entertainer, Containing the Best Prose and Poetic Selections by and about the Negro Race*. Naperville, IL: J. L. Nichols, 1920.

"Editorial Notes—the Fine Arts." *Putnam's*. February 1855.

"Editor's Easy Chair." *Harper's New Monthly Magazine*. January 1855.

Edwards, Brent Hayes. *The Practice of Diaspora: Literature, Translation, and the Rise of Black Internationalism*. Cambridge, MA: Harvard UP, 2003.

Elfenbein, Andrew. "The United States of Raveloe." *Modern Language Quarterly* 75, no. 2 (2014): 129–48.

Eliot, George. *Daniel Deronda*. 1876. Edited by Terence Cave. London: Penguin, 1995.

———. *The George Eliot Letters*. Edited by Gordon S. Haight. New Haven: Yale UP, 1954.

———. "Harriet Beecher Stowe's *Dred*, Charles Reade's *It Is Never Too Late to Mend* and Frederika Bremer's *Hertha*." 1856. In *Selected Essays, Poems and Other Writings*. Edited by A. S. Byatt and Nicholas Warren. London: Penguin, 1990.

———. *The Mill on the Floss*. 1860. Edited by Oliver Lovesey. Broadview Editions. Peterborough, Ontario: Broadview Press, 2007.

———. *Romola*. 1862–63. Edited by Andrew Sanders. Harmondsworth: Penguin Books, 1980.

———. *The Spanish Gypsy*. 1868. Edited by A. G. Van den Broek. London: Pickering & Chatto, 2008.

Ellison, Ralph. "Hidden Name and Complex Fate." In *The Collected Essays of Ralph Ellison*. Edited by John F. Callahan. New York: Modern Library, 1995.

England, Eugene. "Tuckerman and Tennyson: 'Two Friends . . . on Either Side the Atlantic." *New England Quarterly* 57, no. 2 (1984): 225–39.

Everett, Percival L. *Erasure: A Novel*. Minneapolis: Graywolf Press, 2011.

Fabi, M. Giulia. *Passing and the Rise of the African American Novel*. Urbana: U of Illinois P, 2004.

Fagan, Benjamin. "'Feebler than the Original': Translation and Early Black Transnationalism." In *Transnational American Studies*. Ed. Udo Hebel. (Heidelberg: WinterVerlag, 2012), 229–48.

Fauset, Jessie Redmon. *The Chinaberry Tree; a Novel of American Life*. 1931. New York: Negro Universities Press, 1969.

———. "Double Trouble: A Story (pt. 2)." *The Crisis*, September 1923.

———. *There Is Confusion*. 1924. Boston: Northeastern UP, 1989.

Fishkin, Shelley Fisher. "The Borderlands of Culture: Writing by W.E.B. Du Bois, James Agee, Tillie Olsen, and Gloria Anzaldúa." In *Literary Journalism in the Twentieth Century*, edited by Norman Sims, 133–82. New York: Oxford University Press, 1990.

Foster, Frances Smith. *Written by Herself: Literary Production by African American Women, 1746–1892*. Bloomington: Indiana UP, 1993.

Franklin, James Thomas. *Jessamine Poems*. Memphis, TN: n.p., 1900.

Frederick Douglass' Paper. Rochester, NY, 1851–1863.

Friedman, Susan Stanford. "One Hand Clapping: Colonialism, Postcolonialism, and the Spatio/Temporal Boundaries of Modernism." In *Translocal Modernisms: International Perspectives*, edited by Irene Ramalho Santos & António Sousa Ribeiro, 11–40. New York: Peter Lang, 2008.

Gardner, Eric. "Coloring History and Mixing Race in Levina Urbino's *Sunshine in the Palace and Cottage* and Louise Heaven's *In Bonds*." *Legacy* 24, no. 2 (2007): 187–206.

———. *Unexpected Places: Relocating Nineteenth-Century African American Literature*. Jackson: UP of Mississippi, 2009.

Gates, Henry Louis, Jr.. "Foreword: In Her Own Write." *Schomburg Library of Nineteenth-Century Black Women Writers*. New York: Oxford UP, 1988.

———. *The Signifying Monkey: A Theory of Afro-American Literary Criticism*. New York: Oxford UP, 1988.

Gates, Henry Louis, Jr., and Gene Andrew Jarrett, eds. *The New Negro: Readings on Race, Representation, and African American Culture, 1892–1938*. Princeton, NJ: Princeton UP, 2007.

Gates, Henry Louis, Jr., and Nellie Y. McKay. "Introduction: Talking Books." *Norton Anthology of African American Literature*. 2nd ed. New York: Norton, 2004.

Gates, Henry Louis, Jr., and Hollis Robbins, eds. *In Search of Hannah Crafts: Critical Essays on "The Bondwoman's Narrative."* New York: Basic Books, 2004.

Geggus, David. "Haitian Voodoo in the Eighteenth Century: Language, Culture, Resistance." *Jahrbuch für Geschichte von Staat, Wirtschaft und Gesellschaft Lateinamerikas* 28 (1991): 21–51.

Genette, Gérard. *Palimpsests: Literature in the Second Degree*. Trans. by Channa Newman and Claude Doubinsky. Lincoln: U of Nebraska P, 1997.

———. *Paratexts: Thresholds of Interpretation*. Cambridge; New York: Cambridge UP, 1997.

Gikandi, Simon. "The Embarrassment of Victorianism: Colonial Subjects and the Lure of Englishness." In *Victorian Afterlife: Postmodern Culture Rewrites the*

Nineteenth Century, edited by John Kucich and Dianne F. Sadoff, 157–85. Minneapolis: U of Minnesota P, 2000.

Gilbert, Sandra, and Susan Gubar. *The Madwoman in the Attic: The Woman Writer and the Nineteenth-Century Literary Imagination.* New Haven: Yale UP, 1979.

Giles, Paul. *Transatlantic Insurrections: British Culture and the Formation of American Literature, 1730–1860.* Philadelphia: U of Pennsylvania P, 2001.

Gillman, Susan. *Blood Talk: American Race Drama and the Culture of the Occult.* Chicago: U of Chicago P, 2003.

Gilroy, Paul. *The Black Atlantic: Modernity and Double Consciousness.* Cambridge, MA: Harvard UP, 1993.

Gooding-Williams, Robert. *In the Shadow of Du Bois: Afro-Modern Political Thought in America.* Cambridge, MA: Harvard UP, 2009.

Gray, Erik. "FitzGerald and the *Rubáiyát,* in and out of Time." *Victorian Poetry* 46, no. 1 (2008): 1–14.

Gruesser, John Cullen. *Confluences: Postcolonialism, African American Literary Studies, and the Black Atlantic.* Athens: U of Georgia P, 2005.

Hack, Daniel. "Close Reading at a Distance: The African Americanization of *Bleak House.*" *Critical Inquiry* 34, no. 4 (Summer 2008): 729–53.

———. "The Last Victorian Novel: *The Quest of the Silver Fleece,* by W.E.B. Du Bois." In *The Oxford Handbook of the Victorian Novel,* edited by Lisa Rodensky, 755–64. Oxford: Oxford UP, 2013.

———. *The Material Interests of the Victorian Novel.* Charlottesville: U of Virginia P, 2005.

———. "Transatlantic Eliot: African American Connections." In *A Companion to George Eliot,* edited by Amanda Anderson and Harry E. Shaw, 262–76. Blackwell Companions to Literature and Culture. Hoboken, NJ: John Wiley & Sons, 2013.

Hamilton, Walter. *Parodies of the Works of English and American Authors.* 1 vol. London: Reeves & Turner, 1884.

Hardwig, Bill. *Upon Provincialism: Southern Literature and National Periodical Culture.* Charlottesville: U of Virginia P, 2013.

Hardy, Barbara. *Tennyson and the Novelists.* Lincoln: Tennyson Society, 1993.

Hardy, Thomas. *Tess of the d'Urbervilles.* Edited by John Paul Riquelme. Boston: Bedford Books, 1998.

Harper, Frances Ellen Watkins. *A Brighter Coming Day: A Frances Ellen Watkins Harper Reader.* Edited by Frances Smith Foster. New York: Feminist Press at the City University of New York, 1990.

———. *Iola Leroy, or, Shadows Uplifted.* 1892. Edited by Frances Smith Foster. The Schomburg Library of Nineteenth-Century Black Women Writers. Oxford: Oxford UP, 1988.

———. *Minnie's Sacrifice; Sowing and Reaping; Trial and Triumph: Three Rediscovered Novels.* Edited by Frances Smith Foster. Black Women Writers Series. Boston: Beacon Press, 1994.

Harris, Leonard, and Charles Molesworth. *Alain L. Locke: Biography of a Philosopher.* Chicago: U of Chicago P, 2008.

Harrison, Antony H. "Dante Rossetti: Parody and Ideology." *Studies in English Literature, 1500–1900* 29, no. 4 (Autumn 1989): 745–61.

Haven, G. "Modern Literature." *Christian Recorder*, 23 March 1861.

Heilmann, Ann, and Mark Llewellyn. *Neo-Victorianism: The Victorians in the Twenty-First Century, 1999–2009*. New York: Palgrave Macmillan, 2010.

Hopkins, Pauline E. "As the Lord Lives, He Is One of Our Mother's Children." 1903. In *Short Fiction by Black Women, 1900–1920*, edited by Elizabeth Ammons. Oxford: Oxford UP, 1991.

———. *Contending Forces*. New York: Oxford UP, 1988.

———. *The Magazine Novels of Pauline Hopkins*. New York: Oxford UP, 1988.

———. *Of One Blood, or, The Hidden Self*. 1902–03. New York: Washington Square Press, 2004.

Howells, William Dean. *An Imperative Duty*. 1891. Edited by Paul R. Petrie. Peterborough, Ontario: Broadview Press, 2010.

———. "The Spanish Gypsy: A Poem." *Atlantic Monthly* 22 (September 1868): 380–84.

Hughes, Linda K., and Sarah R. Robbins. "Introduction: Tracing Currents and Joining Conversations." In *Teaching Transatlanticism: Resources for Teaching Nineteenth-Century Anglo-American Print Culture*. Edinburgh: Edinburgh UP, 2015.

Hutcheon, Linda. *A Theory of Adaptation*. New York: Routledge, 2006.

Irving, Washington. *A History of the Life and Voyages of Christopher Columbus*. 3 vols. New York: Cargill, 1828.

Jackson, Holly. "Another Long Bridge: Reproduction and Reversion in *Hagar's Daughter*." In *Early African American Print Culture*, edited by Lara Langer Cohen and Jordan Alexander Stein, 192–202. Philadelphia: U of Pennsylvania P, 2012.

James, Henry. "The Spanish Gypsy." *North American Review* 107 (1868): 620–36.

Johnson, James Weldon. *The Autobiography of an Ex-Colored Man*. 1912. Edited by William L. Andrews. New York: Penguin Books, 1990.

Jones, Horace Perry. "Southern Parodies on Tennyson's 'Charge of the Light Brigade.'" *Louisiana Studies* 11 (1972): 315–20.

Kennedy, Arnold. *The Story of the West Indies*. London: H. Marshall and Son, 1899.

Kirkpatrick, David D. "On Long-Lost Pages, a Female Slave's Voice." *New York Times*, 11 November 2001.

Kurnick, David. "Unspeakable George Eliot." *Victorian Literature and Culture* 38, no. 2 (September 2010): 489–509.

Larsen, Nella. *"Quicksand" and "Passing."* Edited by Deborah E. McDowell. New Brunswick, NJ: Rutgers UP, 1986.

Ledbetter, Kathryn. *Tennyson and Victorian Periodicals: Commodities in Context*. Burlington, VT: Ashgate, 2007.

Lee, Julia Sun-Joo. *The American Slave Narrative and the Victorian Novel*. New York: Oxford UP, 2010.

Levine, Robert S. *Martin Delany, Frederick Douglass, and the Politics of Representative Identity*. Chapel Hill: U of North Carolina P, 1997.

———. "Trappe(d): Race and Genealogical Haunting in *The Bondwoman's Narrative*." In *In Search of Hannah Crafts: Critical Essays on The Bondwoman's Narrative*, edited by Henry Louis Gates Jr. and Hollis Robbins, 276–94. New York: Basic Civitas Books, 2004.

———. *"Uncle Tom's Cabin* in *Frederick Douglass' Paper*: An Analysis of Reception." *American Literature* 64, no. 1 (March 1992): 71–93.

Levinson, Marjorie. *Wordsworth's Great Period Poems: Four Essays*. New York: Cambridge UP, 1986.

Lewis, David L. *W.E.B. Du Bois: Biography of a Race, 1868–1919*. New York: H. Holt, 1993.

Lilly, Thomas H. "Contexts of Reception and Interpretation of the United States Serializations of *Uncle Tom's Cabin* (1851–1852) and *Bleak House* (1852–1853)." PhD diss., Emory University, 2003.

Looney, Dennis. *Freedom Readers: The African American Reception of Dante Alighieri and the* Divine Comedy. Notre Dame, IN: U of Notre Dame P, 2011.

Lott, Eric. *Love and Theft: Blackface Minstrelsy and the American Working Class*. New York: Oxford UP, 1993.

Luria, Sarah. "Racial Equality Begins at Home: Frederick Douglass's Challenge to American Domesticity." In *The American Home: Material Culture, Domestic Space, and Family Life*, edited by Eleanor McD. Thompson, 25–43. Winterthur, DE: Henry Francis du Pont Winterthur Museum, 1998.

Manganelli, Kimberly Snyder. *Transatlantic Spectacles of Race: The Tragic Mulatta and the Tragic Muse*. New Brunswick, NJ: Rutgers UP, 2012.

Margolis, Stacey. *The Public Life of Privacy in Nineteenth-Century American Literature*. Durham, NC: Duke UP, 2005.

Marks, Sylvia Kasey. "A Brief Glance at George Eliot's 'The Spanish Gypsy.'" *Victorian Poetry* 21, no. 2 (1983): 184–90.

Marotta, Kenny Ralph. "The Literary Relationship of George Eliot and Harriet Beecher Stowe." PhD diss., Johns Hopkins University, 1974.

McGann, Jerome J. "Tennyson and the Histories of Criticism." In *The Beauty of Inflections: Literary Investigations in Historical Method and Theory*. New York: Oxford UP, 1985.

McGill, Meredith L. *American Literature and the Culture of Reprinting, 1834–1853*. Philadelphia: U of Pennsylvania P, 2003.

———, ed. *The Traffic in Poems: Nineteenth-Century Poetry and Transatlantic Exchange*. New Brunswick, NJ: Rutgers UP, 2008.

McHenry, Elizabeth. *Forgotten Readers: Recovering the Lost History of African American Literary Societies*. Durham, NC: Duke UP, 2002.

McWilliams, Dean. *Charles W. Chesnutt and the Fictions of Race*. Athens: U of Georgia P, 2002.

Meyer, Susan. "Colonialism and the Figurative Strategy of Jane Eyre." *Victorian Studies* 33, no. 2 (1990): 247–68.

Michaels, Walter Benn. *Our America: Nativism, Modernism, and Pluralism*. Durham, NC: Duke UP, 1995.

Miller, Kelly. "The Artistic Gifts of the Negro." *Voice of the Negro* (Atlanta), 1 April 1906: 252–57.

Moretti, Franco. "Conjectures on World Literature," *New Left Review* 1 (January–February 2000).

Morley, John. "The Spanish Gypsy." *Macmillan's Magazine* 18 (July 1868): 281–87.

Morrison, Toni. *Playing in the Dark: Whiteness and the Literary Imagination*. New York: Vintage Books, 1993.

Morton, John. *Tennyson among the Novelists*. London; New York: Continuum, 2010.
Moses, Wilson Jeremiah. *The Golden Age of Black Nationalism, 1850–1925*. New York: Oxford UP, 1978.
Mueller, Monika. *George Eliot U.S.: Transatlantic Literary and Cultural Perspectives*. Madison, NJ: Fairleigh Dickinson UP, 2005.
"Multiple News Items." *Frederick Douglass' Paper*. 28 January 1853.
Nord, Deborah Epstein. *Gypsies and the British Imagination, 1807–1930*. New York: Columbia UP, 2008.
———. "'Marks of Race': Gypsy Figures and Eccentric Femininity in Nineteenth-Century Women's Writing." *Victorian Studies* 41, no. 2 (Winter 1998): 189–210.
"Notes." *The Academy and Literature*. 15 October 1904.
Nwankwo, Ifeoma Kiddoe. *Black Cosmopolitanism: Racial Consciousness and Transnational Identity in the Nineteenth-Century Americas*. Philadelphia: U of Pennsylvania P, 2005.
Oliphant, Margaret. *The Autobiography of Margaret Oliphant*. Edited by Elisabeth Jay. Peterborough, Ontario: Broadview Press, 2002.
Otter, Samuel. *Philadelphia Stories: America's Literature of Race and Freedom*. New York: Oxford UP, 2010.
"Our Literary Cult." *Colored American Magazine*. July 1904.
Paden, W. D. *Tennyson in Egypt: A Study of the Imagery in His Earlier Work*. Lawrence: U of Kansas P, 1942.
Pater, Walter. *The Renaissance: Studies in Art and Poetry*. London; New York: Macmillan, 1888.
Payne, William Morton. "The Poetry of Mr. Moody." *The Dial*. 7 June 1901.
———. "Recent American Poetry." *The Dial*. 16 March 1904.
———. "Recent Poetry." *The Dial*. 16 January 1900.
———. "Recent Poetry." *The Dial*. 1 May 1902.
Perry, Patsy Brewington. "The Literary Content of *Frederick Douglass's Paper* through 1860." *CLA Journal* 17 (1973): 214–29
Peterson, Carla L. *Black Gotham: A Family History of African Americans in Nineteenth-Century New York City*. New Haven: Yale UP, 2011.
———. "Commemorative Ceremonies and Invented Traditions: History, Memory, and Modernity in the 'New Negro' Novel of the Nadir." In *Post-Bellum, Pre-Harlem: African American Literature and Culture, 1877–1919*, edited by Barbara McCaskill and Caroline Gebhard, 34–56. New York: New York UP, 2006.
———. *"Doers of the Word": African-American Women Speakers and Writers in the North (1830–1880)*. New Brunswick, NJ: Rutgers UP, 1995.
Petrie, William L. ed. *Bibliography of the Frederick Douglass Library at Cedar Hill*. Ft. Washington, MD: Silesia, 1995.
Picker, John. "Current Thinking: On Transatlantic Victorianism." *Victorian Literature and Culture* 39 (2011): 595–603.
Posnock, Ross. *Color and Culture: Black Writers and the Making of the Modern Intellectual*. Cambridge, MA: Harvard UP, 1998.
Price, Kenneth M. "Charles Chesnutt, the *Atlantic Monthly*, and the Intersection of African-American Fiction and Elite Culture." In *Periodical Literature in Nineteenth-Century America*, edited by Kenneth M. Price and Susan Belasco Smith, 160–78. Charlottesville: UP of Virginia, 2000.

Price, Leah. *How to Do Things with Books in Victorian Britain*. Princeton: Princeton UP, 2012.

Proceedings of the Pennsylvania Yearly Meeting of Progressive Friends. Kennet Square, Pennsylvania, 1903.

[Quincy, Edmund?]. "The Jerry Rescue Meeting." *Liberator*, 7 October 1853, 158.

Rael, Patrick. *Black Identity and Black Protest in the Antebellum North*. Chapel Hill: U of North Carolina P, 2002.

Raimon, Eve Allegra. *The "Tragic Mulatta" Revisited: Race and Nationalism in Nineteenth-Century Antislavery Fiction*. New Brunswick, NJ: Rutgers UP, 2004.

Redding, Jay Saunders. *To Make a Poet Black*. 1939. Ithaca, NY: Cornell UP 1988.

Rezek, Joseph. "What We Need from Transatlantic Studies." *American Literary History* 26, no. 4 (2014): 791–803.

Rice, Wallace and Frances. *The Humbler Poets (second series): A Collection of Newspaper and Periodical Verse, 1885–1910*. Chicago: A. C. McClurg, 1911.

Riede, David G. "Tennyson's Poetics of Melancholy and the Imperial Imagination." *Studies in English Literature, 1500–1900* 40, no. 4 (2000): 659–78.

Robbins, Bruce. "Telescopic Philanthropy: Professionalism and Responsibility in *Bleak House*." In *Nation and Narration*, edited by Homi K. Bhabha, 213–30. London: Routledge, 1990.

Rossetti, Dante Gabriel. *Letters of Dante Gabriel Rossetti*. Edited by Oswald Doughty and John Robert Wahl. 4 vols. Oxford: Clarendon Press, 1965.

Rubin, Joan Shelley. *Songs of Ourselves: The Uses of Poetry in America*. Cambridge, MA: Belknap Press of Harvard UP, 2007.

Sanborn, Geoffrey. "'People Will Pay to Hear the Drama': Plagiarism in *Clotel*," *African American Review* 45 (2012): 65–82.

———. "The Wind of Words: Plagiarism and Intertextuality in *Of One Blood*." *J19: The Journal of Nineteenth-Century Americanists* 3, no. 1 (2015): 67–87.

Schor, Hilary M. *Dickens and the Daughter of the House*. New York: Cambridge UP, 2000.

Scott, Emmett J. *Tuskegee and Its People: Their Ideals and Achievements*. Edited by Booker T. Washington. New York: D. Appleton, 1905.

Sedgwick, Eve Kosofsky. *Between Men: English Literature and Male Homosocial Desire*. New York: Columbia UP, 1985.

Sedlack, Robert P. "The Evolution of Charles Chesnutt's *The House Behind the Cedars*." *CLA Journal* 19, no. 2 (1975): 125–35.

Semmel, Bernard. *George Eliot and the Politics of National Inheritance*. New York: Oxford UP, 1994.

Shannon, Edgar, and Christopher Ricks. "'The Charge of the Light Brigade': The Creation of a Poem." *Studies in Bibliography* 38 (1985): 1–44.

Sharp, William. *Dante Gabriel Rossetti; a Record and a Study*. London: Macmillan, 1882.

Shaw, Stephanie J. *W.E.B. Du Bois and The Souls of Black Folk*. Chapel Hill: U of North Carolina P, 2013.

Sinfield, Alan. *Alfred Tennyson*. New York: Blackwell, 1986.

Smith, James McCune. *The Works of James McCune Smith, Black Intellectual and Abolitionist*. Ed. John Stauffer. New York: Oxford UP, 2006.

Snead, James A. "Repetition as a Figure of Black Culture." In *Black Literature and Literary Theory*, edited by Henry Louis Gates Jr., 59–79. New York: Methuen, 1984.

Soares, Rebecca. "Literary Graftings: Hannah Crafts's *The Bondwoman's Narrative* and the Nineteenth-Century Transatlantic Reader." *Victorian Periodicals Review* 44, no. 1 (2011): 1–23.

Sollors, Werner. *Neither Black nor White yet Both: Thematic Explorations of Interracial Literature*. New York: Oxford UP, 1997.

———. "Thematics Today." In *Thematics: Interdisciplinary Studies*, edited by Max Louwerse and Willie van Peer, 217–35. Philadelphia: John Benjamins, 2002.

Somerville, Siobhan. "Passing through the Closet in Pauline E. Hopkins's *Contending Forces*." *American Literature* 69, no. 1 (March 1997): 139–66.

Stauffer, John. *The Black Hearts of Men: Radical Abolitionists and the Transformation of Race*. Cambridge, MA: Harvard UP, 2001.

———, ed. "Introduction." *The Works of James McCune Smith, Black Intellectual and Abolitionist*. New York: Oxford UP, 2006.

St. Clair, William. *The Reading Nation in the Romantic Period*. Cambridge: Cambridge UP, 2004.

St. Clair, William, and Annika Bautz. "Imperial Decadence: The Making of the Myths in Edward Bulwer Lytton's *The Last Days of Pompeii*." *Victorian Literature and Culture* 40, no. 2 (2012): 359–96.

"Steadfastness." *Colored American Magazine* (Boston). January 1903.

Stephen, Leslie. *George Eliot*. New York; London: Macmillan, 1902.

Stewart, Garrett. *Novel Violence: A Narratography of Victorian Fiction*. Chicago: U of Chicago P, 2009.

Stone, Harry. "Charles Dickens and Harriet Beecher Stowe." *Nineteenth-Century Fiction* 12, no. 3 (1957): 188–202.

"The Story of a Poem." *Friends' Intelligencer*. 6 June 1903.

Sundquist, Eric J. *To Wake the Nations: Race in the Making of American Literature*. Cambridge, MA: Belknap Press of Harvard UP, 1993.

Symons, Arthur. *Dante Gabriel Rossetti*. Paris: Librairie Artistique et Littéraire, 1909.

"Symposium on the Twenty-Fifth-Anniversary Edition of *The Signifying Monkey: A Theory of African American Literary Criticism*." *Early American Literature* 50, no. 3 (2015).

Syms, M. "Literary Parallels." *Athenaeum*. 1 September 1866.

Tamarkin, Elisa. *Anglophilia: Deference, Devotion, and Antebellum America*. Chicago: U of Chicago P, 2008.

Tate, Trudi. "On Not Knowing Why: Memorializing the Light Brigade." In *Literature, Science, Psychoanalysis, 1830–1870: Essays in Honour of Gillian Beer*, edited by Helen Small and Trudi Tate, 160–80. New York: Oxford UP, 2003.

Taylor, Ina. *George Eliot: Woman of Contradictions*. London: Weidenfeld and Nicolson, 1989.

Tennyson, Alfred Lord. "Author's Prefatory Notes." In *The Works of Tennyson*, edited by Hallam, Lord Tennyson. Vol. 1. London: Macmillan, 1907.

———. *The Letters of Alfred Lord Tennyson*. Edited by Cecil Y. Lang and Edgar F. Shannon Jr. 3 vols. Cambridge, MA: Harvard UP, 1981.

————. *The Poems of Tennyson*. Edited by Christopher Ricks. London: Longmans, 1969.

————. *The Poems of Tennyson*. 2nd ed. Edited by Christopher Ricks. Berkeley: U of California P, 1987.

Tennyson, Hallam. *Alfred Lord Tennyson: A Memoir*. New York: Macmillan, 1897.

"Tennyson in Two of His Poems—'Locksley Hall.'" *Self Culture*. July 1900.

Terrell, Mary Church. *A Colored Woman in a White World*. Washington, DC: Ransdell, 1940.

Terry, Jennifer. "'When Dey 'Listed Colored Soldiers': Paul Laurence Dunbar's Poetic Engagement with the Civil War, Masculinity, and Violence." *African American Review* 41, no. 2 (Summer 2007): 269–75.

Teukolsky, Rachel. "Pictures in Bleak Houses: Slavery and the Aesthetics of Transatlantic Reform." *ELH* 76, no. 2 (2009): 491–522

Thoreau, Henry D. "A Plea for Captain John Brown." 1859. In *Reform Papers*. Edited by Wendell Glick. Princeton: Princeton UP, 1973.

Tucker, Herbert F. *Epic: Britain's Heroic Muse, 1790–1910*. Oxford, UK: Oxford UP, 2008.

Tucker, Irene. *The Moment of Racial Sight: A History*. Chicago: U of Chicago P, 2012.

Turner, Henry McNeal. *Respect Black: The Writings and Speeches of Henry McNeal Turner*. Edited by Edwin S. Redkey. New York: Arno Press, 1971.

Wagner-McCoy, Sarah. "Virgilian Chesnutt: Eclogues of Slavery and Georgics of Reconstruction in the Conjure Tales." *ELH* 80, no. 1 (2013): 199–220.

Wahl, Albert J. "The Progressive Friends of Longwood." *Bulletin of Friends Historical Association* 42, no. 1 (Spring 1953): 13–32.

Walkowitz, Rebecca L. *Born Translated: The Contemporary Novel in an Age of World Literature*. New York: Columbia UP, 2015.

Wallinger, Hanna. *Pauline E. Hopkins: A Literary Biography*. Athens: U of Georgia P, 2005.

Warren, Kenneth. *Black and White Strangers: Race and American Literary Realism*. Chicago: U of Chicago P, 1993.

————. *So Black and Blue: Ralph Ellison and the Occasion of Criticism*. Chicago: U of Chicago P, 2003.

————. *What Was African American Literature?* Cambridge, MA: Harvard UP, 2011.

Washington, Mrs. Booker T. "The New Negro Woman," in *Lend a Hand: A Record of Progress*, edited by Edward E. Hale, vol. 15 (October 1895): 254–60.

Webb, Frank J. *The Garies and Their Friends*. 1857. Baltimore, MD: Johns Hopkins UP, 1997.

Weheliye, Alexander. "In the Mix: Hearing the Souls of Black Folk." *Amerikastudien / American Studies* 45, no. 4 (1 January 2000): 535–54.

Weigall, Constance E. C. *The Temptation of Dulce Carruthers*. London: Cassell's Family Magazine, American edition, 1891.

Weisbuch, Robert. *Atlantic Double-Cross: American Literature and British Influence in the Age of Emerson*. Chicago: U of Chicago P, 1986.

West, Cornel. "Black Strivings in a Twilight Civilization." In *The Future of the Race*, by Henry Louis Gates Jr. and Cornel West. New York: Alfred A. Knopf, 1996.

Whitchurch, Samuel. "Hispaniola." In *Poetry of Slavery: An Anglo-American Anthology, 1764–1865*, edited by Marcus Wood. New York: Oxford UP, 2003.

Williams, Blanche Colton. *George Eliot: A Biography*. New York: Macmillan, 1936.

Williams, Fannie Barrier. "After Many Days: A Christmas Story." 1902. In *Short Fiction by Black Women, 1900–1920*, edited by Elizabeth Ammons, 218–38. The Schomburg Library of Nineteenth-Century Black Women Writers. Oxford: Oxford UP, 1991.

———. "Club Movement among Negro Women." In *Progress of a Race, or, The Remarkable Advancement of the American Negro from the Bondage of Slavery, Ignorance and Poverty to the Freedom of Citizenship, Intelligence, Affluence, Honor and Trust*, by J. W. Gibson and W. H. Crogman, 197–232. Atlanta, Georgia: J. L. Nichols, 1902.

Williams, Wendy S. *George Eliot, Poetess*. Burlington, VT: Ashgate, 2014.

Wilson, Matthew. *Whiteness in the Novels of Charles W. Chesnutt*. Jackson: UP of Mississippi, 2004.

Winter, Kari J. *Subjects of Slavery, Agents of Change: Women and Power in Gothic Novels and Slave Narratives, 1790–1865*. Athens: U of Georgia P, 1992.

Wood, Marcus, ed. *The Poetry of Slavery: An Anglo-American Anthology, 1764–1865*. New York: Oxford UP, 2003.

Worden, Daniel. "Birth in the Briar Patch: Charles W. Chesnutt and the Problem of Racial Identity." *Southern Literary Journal* 41, no. 2 (2009): 1–20.

Wordsworth, William. *Poems of William Wordsworth, Volume 1: Collected Reading Texts from the Cornell Wordsworth*. Penrith, UK: Humanities-Ebooks, 2009.

Wright, John Livingston. "Charles W. Chesnutt. One of the Leading Novelists of the Race." *Colored American Magazine* (Boston). December 1901.

Yellin, Jean Fagan. "*The Bondwoman's Narrative* and *Uncle Tom's Cabin*." In *In Search of Hannah Crafts: Critical Essays on The Bondwoman's Narrative*, edited by Henry Louis Gates Jr. and Hollis Robbins, 106–16. New York: Basic Civitas Books, 2004.

Yohannan, John D. "The Fin de Siècle Cult of FitzGerald's *Rubáiyát of Omar Khayyám*." *Review of National Literatures* 2 (1971): 74–91.

Young, Elizabeth. *Black Frankenstein: The Making of an American Metaphor*. New York: NYU Press, 2008.

Zackodnik, Teresa C. *The Mulatta and the Politics of Race*. Jackson: UP of Mississippi, 2004.

INDEX

abolitionism/antislavery thought, 48, 56; and U. Boston, 56–57; British, 19, 28–29; and E. B. Browning, 181; and Byron, 182; and Dickens, 23, 28–29; and Douglass, 26; and Du Bois, 192; and *Frederick Douglass' Paper*, 49; and Hopkins, 141; and Longfellow, 63; and A. Tennyson, 47, 50, 61; and E. S. Tennyson, 49; and tragic mulatto/a plot, 80

A. C. McClurg (publisher), 192

Adams, James Eli, 64, 230n46

affiliation: and Burgess-Ware, 87–88; and G. Eliot, 17, 75, 78, 80, 83, 88, 90, 93, 96, 100, 101, 236n62, 236n72; and Harper, 81, 83, 84, 98, 101. *See also* identification; identity; loyalty; solidarity

African Methodist Episcopal Church: *The Christian Recorder*, 11, 73, 81, 83

African war chants (Congo chants), 1, 17, 50–51, 54, 64, 160

afterlives: as term, 21–22, 218–19n45

agency, 21, 64; and J. M. Bell, 70; and Boker, 69; and Dickens, 27; and J. M. Smith, 55, 63; and A. Tennyson, 10–11, 62, 63

Aguilar, Grace, *The Vale of Cedars*, 241n37

Albany Atlas, 222n40

allegory: and Beatty, 212; and Du Bois, 198, 199, 201, 203; and A. Tennyson, 66

ancestry: and Burgess-Ware, 87–88; and Chesnutt, 125, 126, 172, 225n59; and Child, 100; in Eliot, 79, 80, 81, 82–83, 84, 89–90, 97, 100; in Harper, 17, 81, 83, 84; and Hopkins, 18, 166, 168, 172; Howells on, 89–90; Stephen on, 89; and tragic mulatto/a plot, 80. *See also* history; identification; identity; past; race

Anderson, Benedict, 24, 31

Andrews, William L., 120

Appiah, Kwame Anthony, 85; *Cosmopolitanism*, 90–91

Arabian Nights, 113, 115, 130

Aristotle, 179–80, 192

Arnold, Matthew, 180, 216n23

Atlantic, 190

"Balaklava" (Crimean War poem), 57

Ballinger, Gill, Tim Lustig, and Dale Townshend, 223n47, 225n63

Balzac, Honoré de, 179

Bancroft, George, 54

Baraka, Amiri, 46

Barthes, Roland, 21

Bautz, Annika, 169–70

Beatty, Paul, 257n17; *The Sellout*, 210–12

Beaumont, Francis, 112

Bell, James Madison, "The Day and the War," 69–71, 72

Bell, Philip A. ("Cosmopolite"; "Fylbel"), 50, 51, 53, 56, 57–58, 61, 66, 70, 71, 228n31, 229n32; "Introductory Note" to "The Day and the War," 70

betrothal plot, 87. *See also* marriage

Bible, 82, 178, 180, 235n48, 246n16

Black Atlantic, 7

blackface performers, 54–55

Blyden, Edward Wilmot, "The Origin and Purpose of African Colonization," 94, 236n74

Boker, George Henry, 118, 232n68; "The Second Louisiana" ("The Black Regiment"), 67–69, 70, 71, 72

Borrioboola-Gha, 26, 28–29, 31, 32, 41

Bosquet, Pierre, 53

Boston, Uriah, 56–57, 58, 65, 66, 69